The Trinity Hurdle

The Trinity Hurdle

Engaging Christadelphians, Arians, and
Unitarians with the Gospel of the Triune God

R. Sutcliffe

WIPF & STOCK · Eugene, Oregon

THE TRINITY HURDLE
Engaging Christadelphians, Arians, and Unitarians with the Gospel of the Triune God

Wipf & Stock
An Imprint of Wipf and Stock Publishers
199 W. 8th Ave., Suite 3
Eugene, OR 97401

www.wipfandstock.com

ISBN 13: 978-1-4982-2398-0

Manufactured in the U.S.A.   12/29/2015

To all my Christadelphian friends, to whom I want to speak the truth in love and give an answer to anyone who asks for a reason for the hope that is in me, with, I pray, gentleness and respect. I promised I'd explain it all one day, and here it is.

And this is life eternal, that they might know thee the only true God, and Jesus Christ, whom thou hast sent.

John 17:3 KJV

Contents

Acknowledgments

To ALL THOSE WHO, knowingly or unknowingly, by direct teaching or example, have supported me on my journey and introduced me to the real Lord Jesus Christ, thank you. In particular I want to acknowledge Rev. Dr. Greg Goswell and the other staff of Presbyterian Theology College, Melbourne, who took me on at the beginning. Also the Rev. David MacDougall for his wise counsel and Godly ministry under the Word. Rev. Dr. John McClean of Christ College, Sydney and Rev. Dr. Gary Millar of Queensland Theology College read the original manuscript and gave me encouragement and invaluable advice. Any errors that remain are mine alone. And of course, my family, who have encouraged and supported my endeavors to write a "God book."

Introduction

The Reasons for this Book

I BELIEVE THERE IS a good deal of misunderstanding on both sides of the discussion between Christadelphians and mainstream evangelical Protestants. I have reached this conclusion as a result of having lived on both sides of the divide. Brought up as a Christadelphian, I spent more than twenty-five years as an active member of this community. At the outset, I want to acknowledge the positives of this heritage; an extended family which instilled in me a love for and solid grounding in the Scriptures and gave me some fine role models. However, growing up in such an insular community gave me a skewed perspective on mainstream Christianity—especially with respect to some fundamental doctrines.

Most Christians know little, if anything, about Christadelphians and when they do meet one, have no idea how to engage with them. I now realize that Christadelphians, for their part, tend to have a somewhat misconstrued view of what mainstream Christians believe and perhaps more significantly, *why* they believe what they do. There is a tendency for Christadelphians to be very defensive about their beliefs, and a strong sense of exclusivity pervades some circles. This is understandable from their point of view; they see themselves as the "remnant," custodians of "The Truth" in these last days, as against the mainstream churches who are viewed as apostate from original New Testament Christianity. This is a view common to many sects and non-mainstream denominations.

From the mainstream perspective, there is a dearth of good quality literature about Christadelphians and their beliefs in theological libraries and religious databases. Compared with the more numerous and higher profile communities such as the Jehovah's Witnesses, Christian Scientists, and Mormons, Christadelphians remain for the most part obscure and neglected. But unless a point of view is clearly understood and articulated, how can there be a fair and critical engagement with it?

Who Are the Christadelphians?

For many Christians, even quite well-informed ones, this is a question to which they can only give the vaguest of answers. Many people haven't even heard of the group, and those who have usually only have a rudimentary awareness of their beliefs. The name "Christadelphian" comes from the Greek words *Christos* (Christ) and *adelphos* (brother) and means "brothers (and sisters) in Christ." It has been used by the community for some one hundred and forty years and its central publication, *The Christadelphian*, has been produced by the Christadelphian Office in Birmingham, UK since 1864. Information on Christadelphian beliefs and practices, as explained by the group itself, may be found on the Christadelphian website http://www.christadelphia.org/ and also that of the Christadelphian Office http://www.thechristadelphian.com/christadelphianoffice.htm, from which official publications of the group may be obtained, although today there are a number of other sites produced by specific Christadelphian subgroups. An introductory pamphlet by Fred Pearce, *Who are the Christadelphians? Introducing a Bible Based Community*, provides a succinct summary of their organization and key beliefs, including a denial of the Trinity. More detail may be found in the book *The Christadelphians: What they Believe and Preach*, by Harry Tennant.

A typical self-description is that Christadelphians are "a Bible-based community," and this is often presented (explicitly or by inference) as a claim to uniqueness. Without doubt Christadelphian personal and corporate devotion is thoroughly centered on the reading of the Bible as inspired and authoritative, but they are by no means unique in this respect. They also regularly claim to be the modern-day manifestation of the original New Testament apostolic faith, which they assert has been corrupted over the years in doctrine and practice by the wider Christian body. A very informative website on the movement has been produced as a resource for current and former Christadelphians and anyone investigating the movement. Although produced by a former Christadelphian, it endeavors to promote a balanced and non-confrontational view: http://www.christadelphianresearch.com/.

With respect to the doctrine of the Godhead, which is the focus of this book, Christadelphians have been self-styled as "Biblical Monotheists," along with other bodies such as the Church of God of the Abrahamic Faith, with which groups Christadelphians have some—but by no means all—beliefs in common. In the context of Biblical Monotheism, Christadelphians ". . . understand there to be one God, the creator and sustainer of all life and the father of Jesus Christ. We understand Jesus to be the Son of God, who came into existence when he was conceived by Mary through the intervention of the Holy Spirit. We understand the Holy Spirit to be the power and presence of God." Worldwide, Christadelphians are estimated to number about sixty thousand adherents.[1]

---

1. Hyndman, "Biblical Monotheism Today," 225–26.

A Personal Journey

When I was a Christadelphian, my growing discomfort with the differences in fundamental doctrines between Christadelphians and other denominations was not alleviated by simplistic comparisons or unfounded assumptions offered up in explanation. I didn't like pat answers that implied Christadelphians had better Bible knowledge, a more objective approach to Scripture, or were truly the only contemporary manifestation of the original apostolic faith. But why did mainstream Christians—particularly scholars whose life work was theology and scriptural engagement—not understand the Bible in the same way "we" did? This was especially pertinent with respect to the fundamental doctrines of the nature of God and of Jesus Christ. I began to wonder, *seriously* wonder, whether we Christadelphians really understood where believers in the Trinity were coming from. It became an imperative for me to investigate what made trinitarian Christians "tick" and to really try to see the Scriptures as they did, in order to form an objective and balanced opinion. And so I went to Bible College. As I studied Scripture, theology, and church history, I began to realize that the wall of ignorance and misconception had two sides. Not only did mainstream Christians know little about Christadelphian beliefs, but Christadelphians just didn't "get" the Trinity, nor a number of other key doctrines, and what they thought they were arguing against was often not what Christians actually believed.

As I began to engage with the breadth and depth of wider biblical scholarship, so much clicked into place. I studied the Bible as I had never studied it before and it was tremendously exciting—but also humbling. It is nothing short of life-changing to realize that what one has held to be truth all one's life is in need of serious correction, as well as to have to part company with the community in which one has been nurtured and been the focus of one's activities and worldview. This was no easy or haphazard decision.

I decided to write this book for two reasons. Firstly, those early decades are not to be wasted. I believe God has given me the benefit of two diverse perspectives and a conviction that there is a need for those holding each perspective to better understand the other. Only then can there be effective engagement with each other's beliefs so that each side may give the other a fair hearing. Christadelphians—and other non-trinitarians—need to understand the doctrines they reject so decisively, and I respectfully submit that the majority of them, in all sincerity, do not. Likewise, there needs to be better understanding of, and engagement with, the beliefs of this not inconsequential community by mainstream Christians. Where is the common ground and where do we differ? What misconceptions must be corrected before we can prayerfully, faithfully, and effectively engage with Christadelphians and similar groups? If any current or former Christadelphians find "the Trinity" a doctrinal stumbling block to exploring mainstream Christianity, then this book may prove helpful.

Secondly, I have written it because I promised some very dear friends who were disappointed and grieved at my leaving the fold, that I would give them a coherent and detailed explanation of the change in my convictions. From the perspective of my Christadelphian friends, I have left "The Truth" for the apostasy of Christendom and surely I must have laid aside my Bible, my conscience and my heritage in so doing! From the opposite perspective I can testify that it has been an enlightenment, a stepping out from a small and introspective world into a large and dynamic one, and a challenging encounter with scriptural truth and with two thousand years of Christian scholarship. Which perspective is correct? I can only assure my readers that I have reached my conclusions by studying the Bible and praying *more*, not less. This was what John Thomas, the pioneer of the Christadelphian position urged people to do, after all.[2] Ultimately, it's not me of course that will convince anyone of the truths of God's word, only his Spirit can convict our hearts and minds, but I owe it to my friends to at least state the case, and invite them to accompany me on the journey I have taken. I pray that they will do so with open hearts and minds, Bible in hand. After all, if anyone's perception of "truth" is in fact true, then it should withstand honest and God-fearing scrutiny.

So then, my objectives are to present the doctrine of the Godhead: Father, Son, and Holy Spirit, as it is understood by most evangelical Christians and as it has been understood during the history of the church. I want to compare, contrast, and evaluate the orthodox and Christadelphian doctrines of the Godhead from a scriptural perspective. I also want to let those who hold particular doctrines speak for themselves rather than second- or thirdhand through the words of those who disagree with them. For this reason there are extensive, referenced quotations from authors of diverse viewpoints throughout this book. Because of the Christadelphian conviction that the church has historically strayed from the pure apostolic faith, an appraisal of some aspects of the history of Christian thought was also warranted. I want to convey what it is about the doctrines of the Trinity, the nature of Christ, and his atoning work that have convinced me, a former stalwart Christadelphian, to change my opinions. It is my hope and prayer that better understanding of different beliefs will produce a deeper and more effective engagement with these differences, that all may come to a knowledge of the truth to the glory of God.

Some Common Ground

The Bible As Foundation

It is essential, right at the outset, to make one thing perfectly clear. The final authority for all discussions in this book will be the Bible, God's inspired word. Although I shall

---

2. Thomas, *Elpis Israel*, 6, 8. This is still encouraged today, apparently, for example, Morgan, *Understand the Bible*, vii.

often be quoting from Christian scholars and from early Christian writers, as well as from Christadelphian literature, I do so to clarify and support assertions about Christians' understanding of different topics, and their opinions are to be taken as subsidiary to Scripture. As Paul wrote to Timothy,

> All Scripture is breathed out by God and profitable for teaching, for reproof, for correction, and for training in righteousness, that the man of God may be complete, equipped for every good work (2 Tim 3:16–17).

I maintain that the Bible is wholly inspired and inerrant, and because these terms have come under some discussion of late, I want to clarify my position by quoting from the *Chicago Statement on Biblical Inerrancy*.[3]

> Holy Scripture, being God's own Word, written by men prepared and superintended by His Spirit, is of infallible divine authority in all matters upon which it touches: it is to be believed, as God's instruction, in all that it affirms: obeyed, as God's command, in all that it requires; embraced, as God's pledge, in all that it promises . . . Being wholly and verbally God-given, Scripture is without error or fault in all its teaching, no less in what it states about God's acts in creation, about the events of world history, and about its own literary origins under God, than in its witness to God's saving grace in individual lives.

The Importance of Correct Doctrine

It *does* matter what we believe, and the Bible singles out certain topics where accurate belief is vital. Absolutely essential is the right knowledge of God as he has revealed himself through his word. God was angry with Job's three companions because they did not speak of God what was right (Job 42:7). Jesus said that to know the only true God is eternal life (John 17:3). The writer to the Hebrews is very clear:

> And without faith it is impossible to please him, for whoever would draw near to God must believe that he exists and that he rewards those who seek him (Heb 11:6).

John adds another dimension: incorrect teaching about Jesus is a very serious matter; to deny that Jesus is the Christ is to be a liar and the antichrist (1 John 2:22). John may be addressing one of the particular heresies that were emerging in the late first century, either Docetism or Gnosticism,[4] but irrespective of whether he has a

3. The *Chicago Statement on Biblical Inerrancy* was formulated in October 1978 by more than 200 evangelical leaders at a conference sponsored by the International Council on Biblical Inerrancy (ICBI), held in Chicago. The statement was designed to defend the position of biblical inerrancy against a perceived trend toward liberal conceptions of Scripture.

4. Docetism, from the Greek verb *dokeō*, "to seem," held that Christ was not truly human, he only seemed to be human. It resulted from the Greek dualistic perspective that matter was evil and incompatible with divinity. Gnosticism was a diverse set of beliefs that infiltrated various religions in the early Christian era. It taught the need for special knowledge to enable the soul to be freed from entrapment in the body and held Christ to be a divine redeemer figure imparting that knowledge, as

specific teaching or generalities in mind, his point is clear. Having the right perspective on the Father and the Son is vital.

Having said that, let's not fall into the trap of assuming we are presently clever enough to understand or explain everything about God to the nth degree. Job thought he had God summed up, but was put in his place simply by considering God in the context of his creation. We can only know God to the extent he has chosen to reveal himself to us. He has given us a lot of detail, but he has not told us everything, not by a long shot. We cannot comprehend, for instance, how God has existed from eternity, how he can be present everywhere, how he can listen to millions of prayers at once, how he controls the future, how he made everything, from atoms to galaxies.

> "For my thoughts are not your thoughts, neither are your ways my ways," declares the LORD (Isa 55:8).

So it will not do to build an argument about the nature of God purely based on what seems comprehensible to us, nor to dismiss something out of hand because it seems illogical—if God says it in his word, then that's the way it is. We will need to be content to wait for the consummation of his kingdom to understand the matter further.

There Is One True God, and One Way of Salvation

We live in a postmodern society. Postmodernism is a pluralistic and relativistic worldview which denies any overarching purpose or "story" behind the way things are, that eschews authority and relativizes truth. In the world today, the only thing not tolerated, it seems, is intolerance. Postmodernist creed says, "What's true for you is true for you, just don't force it on me." Don't be deceived, this is one area where Christians must stand up and be counted. All religions are *not* the same, it *does* matter what you believe and there *are* moral values and absolute truths. There is one God, he made us and he rules. He can, and he has, told us what to do. Humanity is in rebellion against our Creator and were it not for his mercy in sending his own Son, we would be rightly doomed. Jesus Christ has been set forth as the only way of salvation, through faith.

> And there is salvation in no one else, for there is no other name under heaven given among men by which we must be saved (Acts 4:12; from the preaching of Peter concerning Jesus).

> I am the way, and the truth and the life. No one comes to the Father except through me (words of Jesus, John 14:6).

So far I think I will have had no argument from any Christadelphian reader, and rightly so. This is the common ground we hold as Bible believers and people sincerely attempting to follow the Lord. It will pay to keep these things in mind as we

---

against the evil lesser god who created the earth.

explore our differences, to see that the principles on which we must build are sure. But before we start to explore those differences and their import, I want to address a misconception.

Progressive Revelation

In James A. Michener's novel, *The Source*, the author's underlying thesis is that the Judeo-Christian religious tradition evolved. Starting with rudimentary concepts of gods that blessed the crops and could be appeased, onward through the nature and fertility oriented religion of the Canaanites and an evolving concept of "El" as the most powerful God, finally culminating in Jewish monotheism, Michener paints a picture which is altogether at odds with God's own revelation. Some liberal biblical commentaries can sound like this too, asserting that the biblical writers' own increasing sophistication crafted an evolving understanding of God, from "primitive" Old Testament concepts to the lofty heights of the New Testament. Such commentators betray their essential denial of the inspiration and infallibility of Scripture.

Two allegations have been made in confronting the trinitarian concept of God which touch on this issue. One is that trinitarians have been accused of relying on an evolutionary model of Scripture to explain the development of the doctrine of the Trinity. Because this doctrine is not explicitly taught in the Old Testament, it is claimed, its "sudden appearance" in the New Testament, particularly in the later writings, must have been imposed by those writers with a "high Christology" agenda. It is true that such allegations are made by some commentators, particularly those who hold to skeptical, critical schools of thought. The form critical approach attempts to determine the *Sitz im Leben* or setting of life, in which the scriptural passage was written, and then read back into it the agenda of the writer.[5] The second allegation is that as soon as the last sentence of canonical Scripture was penned, a sort of de-volution commenced that saw corruption of the pure teachings of Scripture and that the doctrine of the Trinity is a product of this. To counter these assertions, I hope to show that the roots of the doctrine of the Trinity are indeed to be found in the Old Testament and that the fundamentals of the doctrine were believed consistently from New Testament times until finally enunciated in the creeds of the fourth and fifth centuries.

Nevertheless, it should not surprise us that certain theological concepts are progressively unfolded through Scripture. Just as we catch glimpses of the work of Christ in passages such as Genesis 3:15 and Isaiah 53, but do not see the complete picture of his saving work until the New Testament, so it is with other doctrines concerning God and Christ. They are there in the Old Testament, but only clearly visible through the lens of the New. This is the concept of "progressive revelation" or "salvation history" unfolding through God's dealings with his people through some two thousand

---

5. A brief summary of the pros and cons of form criticism as applied to the gospels may be found in Blomberg, *Jesus and the Gospels*, 92–97.

years of biblical history. There are many aspects of Christ portrayed in the Old Testament, some quite obvious and specific, others a little more obscure, that we might even have missed had not the New Testament writers drawn our attention to them. After all, God's most explicit revelation has been through his Son (Heb 1:1–2). As a general rule, when looking for Christ in the Old Testament, it is an advantage to let the inspired apostles identify and interpret the passages. In doing this systematically, we may encounter a few surprises. As the fifth-century theologian Augustine of Hippo observed, "The New is in the Old concealed, and in the New, the Old revealed."[6]

When Christadelphians think about the Trinity, they tend to start with the fourth- and fifth-century creeds and critique the non-scriptural language. This criticism may have some validity; if those creeds were being formulated from scratch today perhaps the specific words chosen would be different. But to tackle the doctrine of the Trinity this way is to decontextualize it, to ignore the complex thinking upon the Scriptures that resulted in an attempt to define the boundaries of people's understanding of God in terms relevant to the worldview and language of the day. What I propose to do in this book is to start at the other end, with a survey of the scriptural evidence about the unity and plurality of God, about the humanity of Christ, in what sense he is to be considered divine, his relationship to the Father, and the way the Spirit is presented. It is when these doctrines are considered together that the Trinity emerges as the solution to a complex problem.

Where We Differ

I am going to use the term "mainstream Christianity" to refer to the evangelical, Protestant understanding of doctrine, in particular the doctrines of God, Christ, the Holy Spirit, and salvation. In the first centuries of Christianity this position was also understood as "orthodox" or "catholic" in contrast to various heresies, particularly Arianism, which will be discussed in due course. The word orthodox, from the Greek words *orthos*, meaning straight (as opposed to crooked) and *doxa*, glory, originally referred to right belief in contrast to heresy (Greek *hairesis*, a schism or faction) and we will see how "orthodoxy" became an appellation for the doctrine of the Trinity. However, the descriptor "orthodox" later came to be applied to the Eastern, Greek-speaking arm of the old imperial church and has carried into the Greek, Russian, and Coptic Orthodox churches today. Because the term can be rather ambiguous, I will only use it in selective contexts. The word "catholic" comes from the Greek *kata holos*, meaning "according to the whole," or universal. The catholic church is, strictly speaking, the universal church of Christ. It was applied to the early church, and some Protestant denominations still subscribe to the old form of the Apostles' Creed that speaks of the "holy catholic church." However, most people today would associate the

---

6. "Quam quam et in Vetere Novum latet, et in Novo Vetus pateat" (Augustine, *Questiones in Heptateuchum*, 2.73).

word with the Roman Catholic Church, which creates ambiguity, so again this is a word I will only use in specific contexts.

The word "Protestant" derives from the Latin *protestatio*, or protestations of the early reformers against Roman Catholic practices in the sixteenth century. It soon became used as a label for all Christians outside the Roman Catholic and Eastern Orthodox faiths. In this respect, Christadelphians are also Protestants, and many Christadelphians consider their heritage to have some affinity with the sixteenth-century "Radical Reformation" or Anabaptist movement. However, the term in this general sense could also be applied to Jehovah's witnesses, Mormons, and Christian Scientists, among others, whose beliefs do not coincide with either Christadelphians or mainstream Protestant denominations. Hence by itself, the term "Protestant" is not specific enough in the twenty-first century.

A subset of Protestantism is the evangelical movement. It is important for Christadelphians to appreciate that "evangelicalism" does not equate with "Pentecostalism." Pentecostalism is one stream within Christianity which has a distinctive emphasis upon a post-conversion experience of the Holy Spirit's activity. "Evangelicalism" comes from the Greek word for gospel, *euangelion*, the proclamation of good news. *Euangelion*, gospel, and the verb *euanggelizomai*, meaning to evangelize, preach the gospel, announce good news, are found throughout the New Testament. It is interesting that for all the Christadelphian emphasis on the "Gospel," as the good news ("Glad Tidings") of the things concerning the kingdom of God and the name of Jesus Christ, they shun the use of this perfectly acceptable Greek word, presumably because of its association with evangelicalism. Today the appellation is claimed by Protestant churches who are gospel-focused, biblically based and who seek to evangelize, i.e., proclaim the gospel of salvation in Christ. A historical definition of evangelical theology is:

> Its basic substance is drawn from the heritage of orthodox Christian theological formation. Evangelical theology in essence stands in the great Christian theological tradition. (It) goes back to the creeds of the first centuries of the Christian era . . . has strong links with the early medieval church . . . (and) has particular ties with the distinctives of the Protestant Reformation.[7]

However, many of the theological concepts discussed in this book and accepted by evangelical Protestants are also subscribed to by other churches within the broader context of Christianity. Since the majority of churches today, Protestant, orthodox and Roman Catholic hold some key beliefs in common, I will tend to use "mainstream Christianity" rather than the narrower "evangelical Christianity" to generalize about these beliefs, whilst recognizing that differences do exist in doctrine and practice between them.

What this book will seek to demonstrate is the scriptural evidence that:

- God is one, not three Gods

7. Rennie, "Evangelical Theology," 239.

- Jesus is divine and human

- The Holy Spirit is divine and personal

- How this can be understood without falling into some of the traps that have been explored in the history of theology and of which Christadelphians accuse trinitarians today.

- How an understanding of the Godhead underlies the correct understanding of Christ's atoning work and provides the believer with assurance of salvation.

Christadelphian Beliefs Concerning God, Jesus Christ, and the Holy Spirit

These beliefs are summarized from the Christadelphian *Statement of Faith* and accompanying *Doctrines to be Rejected*.

- The only true God is the Father, who manifested himself in his Son, the Lord Jesus Christ and who is everywhere present by the Holy Spirit.

- Jesus Christ is fully human, conceived by the power of the Holy Spirit acting on the virgin Mary. He is not God the Son; although he was sinless he was not intrinsically divine, nor did he exist before his conception.

- The Holy Spirit is not a person of the Godhead, but the power of God.

- Jesus Christ died as a representative of sinful humanity and his death is the basis of forgiveness of sins; salvation is appropriated through belief in the gospel, taking on the name of Christ in baptism and continuing to observe his commandments.

- Christadelphians reject the doctrines that God is three persons, that the Son of God was co-eternal with the Father and that the Holy Spirit is a person distinct from the Father.

- They also reject the principle that the Gospel alone will save, without obedience to Christ's commandments and insist that baptism is necessary to salvation.

Bible Versions

Unless otherwise specified, I will cite Scripture from the English Standard Version This will be, I trust, a suitable compromise. Many, perhaps most, Christadelphians hold that the King James Authorized Version is still the preferred and arguably most reliable translation and many are uncomfortable with modern versions such as the NIV, which is less of a literal translation and is perceived by Christadelphians to have doctrinal biases.[8] Nevertheless, the very intent of the original KJV, translated from

---

8. A reasonably balanced discussion of the Christadelphian perspective on the KJV versus modern

the available manuscripts of the day (without the benefit of older manuscripts now available) was to have a translation in the *common* tongue of English speaking people. The language of the KJV, whilst beautiful and familiar to many (myself included) is nevertheless outdated, and this can be a barrier to those not familiar with it. The English Standard Version, like the KJV, is an "essentially literal" translation that is nevertheless readable and increasingly popular, in both Christadelphian and mainstream circles.

I will also be drawing on the United Bible Societies' Greek New Testament and the Septuagint.[9] The Septuagint, or LXX, is the Greek translation of the Hebrew Scriptures produced from the third to first centuries BC by Jewish scholars in Alexandria, for use by the Jewish diaspora. In the first century, this was the commonly used version of the Old Testament Scriptures and it is the Bible which Jesus and the apostles used and from which the New Testament and early Christian writers quote directly in most instances. Since we will be interpreting the Old Testament with the help of the New, it seems appropriate where we need to refer to original writings, that we read the same Scriptures that Jesus and the Apostles used.

---

translations is found in Purkis et al., *Which Translation?* which is a compilation of articles from the Christadelphian *Testimony* Magazine. The ESV is sold by the Christadelphian Office and is apparently becoming popular in Christadelphian circles (Andrew Bramhill, editor, pers. comm, 2013).

9. To say "*The* Septuagint" is actually inaccurate; rather we should speak of the best oldest available compilations of the Greek Old Testament. However, not having all these manuscripts to hand, a suitable compromise is to use Brenton, *The Septuagint with Apocrypha* in conjunction with *BibleWorks 8* Greek text.

1

God is One

Misconception #1: That trinitarians are not monotheists; that they believe in three Gods.

Corrective: It is fundamental to the doctrine of the Trinity that there is one God.

ONE VERY OBVIOUS THING we learn about God in the Old Testament is his oneness and his exclusive right to be worshiped. Trinitarian Christians do not deny that God is One, no matter how it may be argued otherwise by Christadelphians. The doctrine of the Trinity, correctly understood, upholds the oneness of God, because it is wholly scriptural. So let's start with this common ground and look at the unequivocal biblical evidence.

The Foundational Commandment

> Hear, O Israel: The LORD our God, the LORD is one (Deut 6:4).

This declaration to Israel as they stood poised to enter the promised land stands as the foundation of the law. Jesus affirmed this, when a teacher of the law asked him which is the most important commandment.

Jesus answered, "The most important is, 'Hear, O Israel: the Lord our God, the Lord is one. And you shall love the Lord your God with all your heart and with all your soul and with all your mind and with all your strength'" (Mark 12:29–30). Matthew's version adds that on this and the command to love one's neighbor hang all the law and the prophets (Matt 22:37–40).

The passage is known in Jewish circles as the *Shema*, from the Hebrew for "hear." The Septuagint (Greek Old Testament, or LXX) of Deuteronomy 6:4 reads, *Akoue, Israēl, Kyrios ho Theos hēmōn, Kyrios heis esti.*

Literally, this translates as "Hear, Israel, Lord the God of us, Lord one he is." In Greek, the role of words in a sentence (subject, direct object, etc.) is denoted by their endings, not by word order. The word *heis*, one, could also mean, "only one" or, "one and the same." Hence, this verse could be translated:

- The Lord our God, the Lord is one

- The Lord our God is one Lord

- The Lord is our God, the Lord is one

- The Lord is our God, the Lord alone

The same four translations are possible in the original Hebrew. This verse may rightly be taken as teaching monotheism, that there is a single Being or Entity who is God, and no other Being or Entity can make a similar claim. The context of the passage within Deuteronomy shows that it is this unique God-ness of YHWH, translated "LORD," which is the basis of his claim over Israel as the only God whom they may worship. He is exclusive, he is unique, and he has a unique and exclusive covenant relationship with Israel. This is why "I am YHWH your God, who brought you out of Egypt, out of the land of slavery. You shall have no other gods before me," is the first of the Ten Commandments. God's uniqueness is established on the basis of his being the sole Creator and the sole sovereign Ruler of the universe; this distinguishes him from all other reality. Richard Bauckham[1] describes this as YHWH's "unique divine identity."

> The uniqueness of the divine identity was characterized especially by two features: that the one God is sole Creator of all things and that the one God is sole ruler of all things. To this unique identity corresponds monolatry, the exclusive worship of the one and only God who is so characterized.[2]

> "To whom then will you compare me, that I should be like him?" says the Holy One. Lift up your eyes on high and see: who created these? He who brings out their host by number, calling them all by name, by the greatness of his might, and because he is strong in power not one is missing . . . Have you not known? Have you not heard? The LORD is the everlasting God, the Creator of the ends of the earth. He does not faint or grow weary; his understanding is unsearchable (Isa 40:25–28).

> Thus says God, the LORD, who created the heavens and stretched them out, who spread out the earth and what comes from it, who gives breath to the people on it and spirit to those who walk in it: "I am the LORD; I have called you in righteousness; I will take you by the hand and keep you; I will give you as a covenant for the people, a light for the nations, to open the eyes that are blind, to bring out the prisoners from the dungeon, from the prison those who sit in darkness. I am the LORD; that is my name; my glory I give to no other, nor my praise to carved idols" (Isa 42:5–8).

---

1. Bauckham, *Jesus and the God of Israel*, ix.
2. Ibid., 18.

For thus says the LORD, who created the heavens (he is God!), who formed the earth and made it (he established it; he did not create it empty, he formed it to be inhabited!): "I am the LORD, and there is no other" (Isa 45:18).

The declaration that YHWH is God alone emphasizes the exclusivity of the covenant he made with Israel, the consequences of which form the subject matter of Deuteronomy. It is because of this exclusivity that the *Shema* is followed by "You shall love the LORD your God with all your heart and with all your soul and with all your might" (Deut 6:5). Oneness expresses YHWH's nature; uniqueness, unity, integrity but also carries the necessary conclusion, that therefore worship of YHWH is unique and exclusive; *therefore* Israel was to worship no other gods. The chapter goes on to describe this unique relationship; YHWH alone has the power to deliver Israel, YHWH alone is entitled to their obedience and YHWH alone is able to bless them in the land he will give them. The appropriate outworking is that "It is the LORD your God you shall fear. Him you shall serve and by his name you shall swear" (verse 13, quoted by Jesus in his temptation). This is the essential meaning of the *declaration* of the Oneness, the uniqueness, of the Creator-God in these passages. Of course, this is not the only sense in which God is unique; he alone is Creator and Redeemer, he alone has existed from eternity, as the rest of the Old Testament testifies.

The Old Testament Upholds the Oneness of God

Time and again, the Old Testament states that God is one, there is no other god.

- "See now that I, even I, am he, and there is no god beside me; I kill and I make alive; I wound and I heal; and there is none that can deliver out of my hand" (Deut 32:39).

- ". . .That all the peoples of the earth may know that the LORD is God; there is no other" (1 Kgs 8:60; prayer of Solomon).

- "And the LORD will be king over all the earth. On that day the LORD will be one and his name one" (Zech 14:9).

- "'I, I am the LORD, and besides me there is no savior. I declared and saved and proclaimed, when there was no strange god among you; and you are my witnesses,' declares the LORD, 'and I am God. Also henceforth I am he'" (Isa 43:11–13).

- "Thus says the LORD, the King of Israel and his Redeemer, the LORD of hosts: 'I am the first and the last; besides me there is no god'" (Isa 44:6).

- "I am the LORD, and there is no other, besides me there is no God" (Isa 45:5).

The whole context of this portion of Isaiah is the folly of idolatry, given that YHWH is the only God and Israel's only Savior, despite Israel's unfaithfulness. Israel was chosen and God will keep his unique covenant with them, even though they have broken it. Repeatedly comes the refrain, "I am God, I am the LORD, there is no other."

Because of this exclusivity, this uniqueness of right to be worshiped, God is rightly a jealous God. He will tolerate no competition for his people's affections (Deut 6:15; Exod 20:5; and many others). Because of this exclusive covenant, God is jealous for his people and his land, with the same appropriate jealousy that spouses should have in the exclusivity of their marriage relationship (Ezek 39:25; Joel 2:18; Zech 1:14). The Septuagint word for one who is jealous is zēlōtēs, denoting an intense commitment, interest and enthusiasm. In both the Exodus 20 and Deuteronomy 5 versions of the Ten Commandments, the second commandment, forbidding the making of idols, is supported by the reason that God is a jealous God.

The Christadelphian interpretation is much narrower than this, seeing the oneness of God in a *purely* mathematical sense. Of course, God as One encompasses "one" in a mathematical sense, but there is more to it than that. The most common Hebrew word for God in the Old Testament is the plural elohim, "gods," or "mighty ones." "One," as a whole number, an integer, can be distinguished from "oneness" or "integrity" as a concept as expressed by different Hebrew words, the latter being most commonly applied to God. "The oneness of God is both the most complex, and also the most basic, of all unities" explains Charles Sherlock.[3] There is no other being or entity who can claim to be God, but all those passages are not there in the Old Testament as a refutation of the doctrine of the Trinity, they are there as a refutation of polytheism, denying that any construct of humankind's imagination could be put on a par with YHWH. As Stephen Holmes explains,

> Old Testament monotheism . . . is not a careful claim as to the numbers of deities; rather it is an exclusive devotion that must be learned and won . . . The operative definition of the divine, therefore, is not metaphysical but doxological: God is the one to whom worship may properly be given.[4]

Repeatedly, Christadelphian writers fall into the trap of asserting that trintarianism teaches three gods, not one.[5] It absolutely does not. The Son and Holy Spirit are *never* put up beside the Father as separate Gods, or separate Beings. Within the unique Godhead we have Father, Son, and Holy Spirit; this Godhead alone is God and worthy of worship; no one and nothing else comes close.

Throughout the Old Testament, the Oneness of God is not just a number. It is inextricably tied to the uniqueness of his divinity, his exclusive claim to be Creator God

---

3. Sherlock, *God on the Inside*, 18–19.

4. Holmes, *Quest for the Trinity*, 45–46.

5. Examples can be found throughout Christadelphian writings, from the old (now unavailable) pamphlet *God is One Not Three*, which depicted a three-headed Hindu idol, through to the recently published work *One God, The Father*. This book promises to be a scholarly engagement with Biblical Monotheism versus the Trinity but unfortunately still rests on the standard Christadelphian arguments which often reflect an inaccurate understanding of the doctrines rejected. Adey, "The Shema," 26–30.

and sovereign LORD and his exclusive covenant with Israel. The emphasis on God's Oneness in the Law and the prophets is to stress the evil of idolatry, having anything else before YHWH, that would detract from exclusive devotion to him with the whole heart, soul, mind, and strength. And that still applies today. Jesus countered the temptation to "fall down and worship me [the *diabolos*]" with "Worship the Lord your God, and serve him only" (from Deut 6:13) and reiterated it as the greatest commandment. Yet, as we shall see, everything the *Shema* requires of God's people is now focused on Jesus, not as a second God, but as one who is included in the unique divine identity.

Richard Bauckham has shown how Paul takes the *Shema* of Deuteronomy 6:4 and inserts Christ into it. Since this passage is used as a major proof text by Christadelphians against the Trinity, we will spend some time on it here rather than in our later christological discussions. Paul is at pains to distinguish the uniqueness of Jesus' lordship. In doing so, he introduces a new dimension to the Jewish concept of monotheism.[6] The context concerns food sacrificed to idols. Since there is only one God, idols are nothing, argues Paul, however this is not a license to cause a brother to stumble. There are many "gods" and "lords" in the pagan pantheon, but not so for Christians:

> For although there may be so-called gods in heaven or on earth—as indeed there are many "gods" and many "lords"—yet for us there is one God, the Father, from whom are all things and for whom we exist, and one Lord, Jesus Christ, through whom are all things and through whom we exist (1 Cor 8:5–6).

The parallel with the *Shema* is evident:

Deuteronomy 6:4	1 Corinthians 8:6
Kyrios ho Theos hēmōn,	*hēmin heis theos ho patēr...*
Lord the God of us	to us one God the Father
Kyrios heis esti	*kai heis kyrios Iēsous Christos . . .*
Lord one is	and one Lord Jesus Christ

Paul divides the wording of the *Shema* between God and Jesus and also the description of God as Creator between God and Jesus (compare Rom 11:36). However, the standard Christadelphian interpretation of this verse takes it out of context,[7] forcing a dichotomy or distinction between "Lord" and "God" which is clearly contrary to the intent of Deuteronomy:

---

6. The classic discussion of this is found in Richard Bauckham's work *God Crucified*, now republished in Bauckham, *Jesus and the God of Israel*.

7. For example, Abel, *Wrested Scriptures*, 284; Adey, "The Shema," 32.

| Over here on the one hand we have one God, the Father, who is God, but is not LORD | and over here on the other hand we have Jesus Christ, who is the one LORD, but is not God |

Whereas Paul is saying, in opposition to heathen "gods" and "lords" we have *one* Deity who is God *and* Lord. In the Old Testament, God is LORD and the LORD is God. The New Testament teaches nothing different.

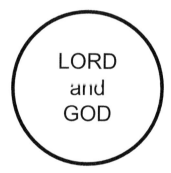

By drawing on the *Shema* in this way, Paul has effectively identified Jesus with the LORD, who is one, redefining monotheism as somehow incorporating Jesus without denying the oneness of the Godhead.[8]

> The only possible way to understand Paul as maintaining monotheism is to understand him to be *including* Jesus in the unique identity of the one God affirmed in the Shema . . . Paul is not adding to the one God of the Shema a "Lord" the Shema does not mention. He is identifying Jesus as the "Lord" whom the Shema affirms to be one . . . (and) he adds the equally unparalleled inclusion of Jesus in the creative activity of God.[9]

8. Baukham, *Jesus and the God of Israel*, 100–104. Adey, "The Shema," 32, attempts to refute Baukham's interpretation, but with little clarity. "There is this replacement of YHWH . . . This Divine Name—absent or alternative ('Lord') mode of presentation of God is a NT theological convention in the light of Jesus' advent. Who Jesus' 'Lord' is he makes clear in citing the Shema . . ." So who then does Adey claim is "Lord"—Jesus Christ, or God the Father? Surely this verse is saying both are Lord, and both are God. If both aren't God, then both aren't Lord, yet Jesus is called Lord extensively in the NT; Lord of Lords, in fact (Rev 19:16).

9. Bauckham, *Jesus and the God of Israel*, 101–2.

We will have a lot more to say about this when we examine the meaning of "Lord," *kyrios*, in the Old and New Testaments and see how the attributes and works of YHWH (LORD) are specifically and deliberately attributed to Christ as the New Testament quotes the Old. Note also, in Isaiah 44:6, we find that Jesus also claims the title of "the first and the last."

The New Testament Affirms the Oneness of God.

> For there is one God, and there is one mediator between God and men, the man Christ Jesus (1 Tim 2:5).

Contrary to what may be implied from some Christadelphian writings, trinitarians affirm the full humanity of Jesus. It is this which qualifies him to be our mediator, as Hebrews 2:14–18 is at pains to explain. Once again, to manipulate this verse to impose a false dichotomy between God and Christ is to take it completely out of context; Paul is emphasizing that there is only one way of salvation, i.e., into relationship with the one God, and that is through Christ. There is one God. There is one mediator, whose humanity qualifies him for that role.

> Since God is one—who will justify the circumcised by faith and the uncircumcised through faith (Rom 3:30).

> You believe that God is one; you do well. Even the demons believe—and shudder! (Jas 2:19).

The Uniqueness of God's Being

Only God is God. The Bible is very clear on this. But what is the nature of this Godhead, this Deity to whom we are to give our allegiance? Richard Bauckham identifies the key features of the identity of God in Jewish monotheistic faith, which unequivocally separate him from all other reality. The contrast with the created order can be represented in a table.

The one God	All other reality
sole Creator of all things	created by God
sole Sovereign Ruler of all things	subject to God's rule
known through his dealings with Israel and the nations; covenant relationship	invited into covenant initiated by God

The one God	All other reality
will achieve his eschatological rule	all creatures will acknowledge YHWH's sovereign deity
YHWH is the name of God in his sovereign identity	whereas "god" (*elohim*) has a less specific range of meanings
God alone may and must be worshiped	no creature may be worshiped
God alone is fully eternal and self-existent	owes existence to God

It is helpful to picture a strict dividing line that separates God from all other reality, everything else in the universe.

God (YHWH)
with his unique identity and attributes

---

everything else in creation

The question is, on which side of the line is Jesus Christ? Which attributes (in which side of the table) does Jesus share?

God As Creator, Distinct from Creation

Firstly, God is separate from his creation. This is an important concept to understand, for a number of reasons. Because we are God's creatures, we owe him love and obedience; he does not owe us. In his grace and condescension he has entered into a covenant relationship with his fallen human creatures through the blood of Christ simply because he loves us and is true to his covenant.

> "To whom then will you compare me, that I should be like him?" says the Holy One. Lift your eyes on high and see: Who created these? . . . Have you not known? Have you not heard? The LORD is the everlasting God, the Creator of the ends of the earth (Isa 40:25, 28).

> Worthy are you, our Lord and God, to receive glory and honor and power, for you created all things, and by your will they existed and were created (Rev 4:11).

Because God is Creator, we must not worship created things. This is the essence of idolatry; everything except God has been created by him; as the Uncreate, he alone is worthy of worship.

> Because they exchanged the truth about God for a lie and worshiped and served the creature rather than the Creator . . . (Rom 1:25).

Therefore, if Christians are to assert that Jesus Christ is somehow God, it must be proven that he is not a creature, but that he is Creator (Col 1:16), and that he is worthy of worship (Matt 28:17; Heb 1:6). We will explore the role of Christ in creation, his preexistence and worthiness to be worshiped in later chapters.

The Holiness and Distinctiveness of God

God is Holy. God is utterly separate from sin and corruption.

> "Holy, holy, holy is the LORD of hosts; the whole earth is full of his glory!" . . .
> And I said: "Woe is me! For I am lost; for I am a man of unclean lips, and I dwell
> in the midst of a people of unclean lips; for my eyes have seen the King, the
> LORD of hosts!" (Isa 6:3, 5).

Interestingly, John says that this incident refers specifically to Isaiah seeing *Jesus'* glory (John 12:41). Jesus is intrinsically holy (Acts 4:27; Heb 7:26), whereas we cannot be intrinsically holy; our holiness comes from him (Col 1:21–22).

God is Spirit. God's essence or being is completely different from ours. Jesus said, "God is spirit, and his worshippers must worship in spirit and in truth" (John 4:24). God is eternal, without beginning or end. In Revelation 1:8 the Lord God proclaims "I am the Alpha and the Omega . . . who is and who was and who is to come, the Almighty." In Revelation 22:13 Jesus makes the same claim, "I am the Alpha and the Omega, the first and the last, the beginning and the end." "Jesus Christ," says the writer to the Hebrews, "is the same yesterday and today and forever" (Heb 13:8). The clear testimony of Scripture is that Jesus shares the unique attributes and identity of God that put him "above the line." Hence the divine uniqueness or oneness is not to be understood as unitarianism and does not preclude distinctions within the divine identity.

The Doctrine of the Trinity Does Not Prescribe Three Gods

The Athanasian creed requires that the substance (or being; Greek *ousia*) of God is not divided and forbids the idea of three Gods, or three Lords. As we shall see in a later chapter, the sense in which God is *one* is quite different from the sense in which he is *three*. This has always been the understanding, even if the precise vocabulary to express it took a bit of working out.

> They are not three eternals, but one eternal. And also there are not three uncreated, nor three incomprehensibles, but one uncreated and one incomprehensible

. . . they are not three Almighties, but one Almighty . . . they are not three Gods, but one God . . . and yet not three Lords, but one Lord.[10]

Theologian Wayne Grudem is at pains to explain that a true understanding of the Trinity requires that the concept of God as one is not sacrificed. To say that the Trinity means there are three Gods is completely erroneous.

> A final possible way to attempt an easy reconciliation of the biblical teaching about the Trinity would be to deny that there is only one God. The result is to say that God is three persons and each person is fully God. Therefore, there are three Gods. Technically this view would be called "tritheism." Few persons have held this view in the history of the church. It has similarities to many ancient pagan religions that held to a multiplicity of gods. . . . this view would destroy any sense of ultimate unity in the universe: even in the very being of God there would be plurality but no unity.[11]

Millard Erickson, one of the most widely respected contemporary theologians, asserts

> The unity of God is basic. Monotheisim is deeply implanted within the Hebrew-Christian tradition. God is one, not several . . . we must keep in mind that we are dealing with one God, not a joining of separate entities.[12]

So it will not do to accuse trinitarians of denying that there is one God, as if that is all that is needed to refute the doctrine. Classical and mainstream Christian discussions of God's nature affirm his full ontological uniqueness.[13] In a later chapter we will explore the apparent contradiction of three Persons in one substance and let the doctrine have a proper hearing. The oneness of God is in no way compromised by embracing Father, Son, and Holy Spirit within the divine identity. The unity of God is not plain and undifferentiated in the sense of the Muslim understanding of Allah. It is a dynamic unity, in which we are invited to participate. Jesus came to bring at-one-ment with God, "that they may all be one, just as you, Father, are in me, and I in you, that they also may be in us, so that the world may believe that you have sent me" (John 17:21).

Summary

- The declaration that God is one is foundational in Scripture, in both the Old and New Testaments.

---

10. https://www.ccel.org/creeds/athanasian.creed.html.

11. Grudem, *Systematic Theology*, 247–48.

12. Erickson, *Christian Theology*, 309.

13. Ontology deals with the nature and essence of things, the principles of being. In theological context it concerns the attributes of God's unique Being. Richard Bauckham suggests that it better to think of God in terms of unique identity rather ontologically; i.e., Who God is is more important than "what" God (or "divinity") is: Bauckham, *Jesus and the God of Israel*, 183.

- The oneness of God is the reason why we are to have no other gods before YHWH. There are no other beings who can be conceived of as "God."

- Thus the oneness of God is inextricably tied to the uniqueness of his divinity, his exclusive claim to be God, and his exclusive covenant with Israel.

- The New Testament effectively identifies Jesus with the LORD, who is one, redefining monotheism as somehow incorporating Jesus without denying the oneness of the Godhead.

- God is uncreate, separate from his creation.

- God is Spirit, eternal, and intrinsically holy; these attributes are his alone.

- The correct understanding of the doctrine of the Trinity requires that the oneness of God be affirmed.

Further Reading

- Wayne Grudem, *Systematic Theology*, chapter 13, "The Character of God: Communicable Attributes."

- Millard Erickson, *Christian Theology*, chapter 14, "God's Three-in-Oneness: The Trinity."

- Richard Bauckham, *Jesus and the God of Israel*. The first chapter comprises his earlier, shorter work, *God Crucified* and contains his main arguments.

2

Jesus Christ Is Fully Human

Misconception #2: That trinitarians deny that Jesus was a man, a real human being.

Corrective: The doctrine of the Trinity and the nature of Christ as understood by mainstream Christians *requires* that Jesus Christ is fully human.

IN THE FOURTH CENTURY AD, in response to the Apollinarians who denied that Christ had a human mind and will as well as a human body, Gregory of Nazianzus penned his famous words, "For that which he has not assumed, he has not healed." His point was that the full humanity of Jesus Christ was essential to his saving work. If Jesus had not been fully human, he could not have accomplished our salvation. Millard Erickson provides a contemporary affirmation of this belief.

> The importance of Jesus' humanity cannot be overestimated, for the issue in the incarnation pertains to our salvation . . . For the validity of the work accomplished in Christ's death, or at least its applicability to us as human beings, depends upon the reality of his humanity . . . Furthermore, Jesus' intercessory ministry depends upon his humanity . . .[1]

A true understanding of the doctrine of Christ must affirm that he was fully human. Mainstream Christians do not deny the humanity of Jesus; to assert that they do is a misrepresentation. To present extensive scriptural arguments (of which there is an abundance) proving Jesus' humanity does not in any way disprove the trinitarian understanding of the nature of Christ, *but only affirms it*. Let's explore this in detail.

The Old Testament Witness to the Humanity of the Christ

When God created humankind, it was in the image of God. While it is not altogether clear exactly what this means, it evidently has something to do with the dominion granted to mankind over the rest of creation (Gen 1:26–27). Adam sinned, and the human race fell. The image of God was not completely lost (Gen 9:6) but was corrupted

---

1. Erickson, *Christian Theology*, 644–45.

by sin. The psalmist observes that mankind was made a little lower than the *elohim* (LXX *aggelois*, angels) and that God gave humans dominion over creation (Ps 8:4–8). The writer to the Hebrews expounds this passage as finding its ultimate fulfilment in Jesus: Jesus is the one made lower than the angels, who suffered death on behalf of everyone. It is he, the representative perfect human being, the second Adam, who will restore the image of God in mankind (Heb 1:5–9; Col 3:10). This was God's plan all along, of course, and no sooner had Adam and Eve received their sentence of death, than God pronounced the solution to the curse.

> I will put enmity between you (the serpent) and the woman, and between your offspring and her offspring; he shall bruise your head and you shall bruise his heel (Gen 3:15).

It would be the offspring (Greek *spermatos*, seed) of the woman who would crush the serpent's head, dealing sin a fatal blow. So the first thing we learn about the coming Savior is that he was to be the offspring of a woman, in other words, a human being. Paul explains, "But when the fullness of time had come, God sent forth his Son, born of woman, born under the law, to redeem those who were under the law, so that we might receive adoption as sons" (Gal 4:4–5). The writer to the Hebrews, continuing his argument that Jesus had to be made a little lower than the angels, explains that,

> Since therefore the children share in flesh and blood, he himself likewise partook of the same things, that through death he might destroy the one who has the power of death, that is, the devil . . . Therefore he had to be made like his brothers in every respect (Heb 2:14–17).

The final outcome of this is described in Revelation, when the "ancient serpent" is cast into the lake of fire and death is no more (Rev 20:2, 10).

The next we hear of this special offspring, or seed, is in the promises to Abraham. Here in Genesis 22:18 God promises "and in your offspring shall all the nations of the earth be blessed." What's rather interesting about this passage, which is ambiguous in English, is that the word offspring is singular (LXX: *en tō spermati*). It refers to a single offspring of Abraham. In fact, when the promises are given to Abraham and his "offspring" (e.g., Gen 12:7; 17:7) it is again the singular word for "seed." Paul picks this up in Galatians.

> Now the promises were made to Abraham and to his offspring [*kai tō spermati autou*]. It does not say "and to offsprings" [*kai tois spermasin*] referring to many, but referring to one, "and to your offspring," [*kai tō spermati sou*], who is Christ (Gal 3:16).

So the Christ was to be Abraham's descendant, through Isaac. This is reiterated over and over again, carrying through in the promises to Isaac, Jacob, and Judah. The next major elaboration on the promise is given to King David, where we learn that the Christ was to be David's descendant:

> When your days are fulfilled and you lie down with your fathers, I will raise up your offspring [*to sperma sou*] after you, who shall come from your body, and I will establish his kingdom (2 Sam 7:12).

The Jews of Jesus' day were in no doubt that the Christ was to be David's descendant. "What do you think about the Christ?" Jesus asked the Pharisees. "Whose son is he?" They said to him, 'The son of David'" (Matt 22:42). Both Matthew and Luke's genealogies make it clear that Jesus Christ was descended from David and from Abraham. The angel Gabriel told Mary explicitly that her son will be given the throne of his father David (Luke 1:32). The human ancestry of Jesus, as a Jewish man and a descendant of a Jewish king, is fundamental to who he is.

The Old Testament prophets give us further insight into the humanity of the coming Messiah. A child would be born, a son given, who would reign on David's throne (Isa 9:6–7). He would be a shoot from the stump of Jesse (father of David; Isa 11:1) and God's suffering servant (Isa 42:1–7) formed in the womb (Isa 49:5), who would grow up before God (Isa 53:2). This servant would be "a man of sorrows, and acquainted with grief" and "cut off out of the land of the living" (Isa 53:3, 8). Daniel writes of "one like a son of man" who comes with the clouds of heaven, approaches the Ancient of Days and is given authority, glory and power and an everlasting kingdom (Dan 7:13–14). Jesus referred to himself frequently as the Son of Man and claimed to be the specific fulfilment of Daniel's prophecy (Matt 26:64).

The New Testament writers acknowledge the descent of Jesus from Abraham and from David:

> Of this man's [David's] offspring God has brought to Israel a Savior, Jesus, as he promised (Acts 13:23).

> . . . concerning his Son, who descended from David according to the flesh . . . (Rom 1:3).

> . . . from their race [Israel] according to the flesh, is the Christ, who is God over all, blessed for ever (Rom 9:5).

The New Testament Witness to the Humanity of Christ

When Jesus walked on earth in the first century, nobody questioned that he was a man. In fact his ordinary background and familiar appearance were a stumbling block to the people who had watched him grow up. Matthew reports an incident in his home town of Nazareth, where his former neighbors were astonished at his teaching and mighty works.

> "Where did this man get this wisdom and these mighty works? Is not this the carpenter's son? Is not his mother called Mary? And are not his brothers James and Joseph and Simon and Judas? And are not all his sisters with us? Where then did this man get all these things?" And they took offense at him (Matt 13:54–57).

Jesus' family background was an established fact: Luke's genealogy of the Lord in 3:23, 38 describes him as "being the son (as was supposed) of Joseph . . . the son of Adam, the son of God." John's gospel reports the violent reaction of the Jews to Jesus' claim to be one with the Father. "It is not for a good work that we are going to stone you," said the Jews, "but for blasphemy, because you, being a man, make yourself God" (John 10:33). There was obviously more to Jesus than simply being the boy next door, or the average man in the street, and it grieved Jesus when people couldn't see it. Nevertheless, his humanity was very real and Jesus never denied it. In fact, even in his resurrection body he made it clear that he was still truly flesh and bone and reinforced the message by eating in front of the disciples (Luke 24:39–43).

John writes in the first verse of his first letter, "That which was from the beginning, which we have heard, which we have seen with our eyes, which we looked upon and have touched with our hands, concerning the Word of life." This complements the statement in the prologue of his gospel that "the Word became flesh and dwelt among us" (John 1:14). John's statement in his first letter may be in response to an emerging heresy among the dualist Greeks: Docetism. The Docetists (from the Greek *dokeō*, to seem) taught that Jesus only appeared to be human but was in fact a divine spirit. This heresy gained momentum in the second century and a number of early church writers refute it by referring to the same verses as we will examine in this chapter, as well as the testimony of those who had encountered Jesus in the previous generation.

Jesus experienced a real birth, in humble circumstances (Luke 2:7) and Mary had to be purified from the birth and its ritual uncleanness, as any other new mother would under the Law (Luke 2:22). He was circumcised (Luke 2:21) and "the child grew and became strong" (Luke 2:40). Jesus experienced the normal weaknesses and physical needs of a human being. He got tired (John 4:6; Luke 8:23) and thirsty (John 19:28) and hungry (Matt 4:2; 21:18). It appears that he was so weakened by his ordeal at the hands of the Roman guards that he could not physically carry his cross (Luke 23:26).

Jesus had a human mind. He learned (Luke 2:52) and submitted obediently to what was required of him (Luke 2:51; Heb 5:8). He had normal human emotions:

- Love (Mark 10:21; John 11:5)
- Compassion (Matt 15:32; Mark 1:41; Luke 7:13)
- Anxiety (John 12:27; 13:21)
- Sorrow (Luke 19:41; John 11:35; Matt 26:38)
- Astonishment (Matt 8:10; Mark 6:6)
- Anger (Matt 21:12; Mark 3:5)
- Exasperation (Mark 8:17)
- Despair (Luke 22:41–46)

Jesus suffered physically and emotionally (Heb 5:7–8; Isa 53:3; Luke 22:44; 24:26) and he was tempted "in every respect, just as we are" and thus can sympathize with our weaknesses (Heb 4:15). In fact, his temptations went way beyond ours, as a consequence of the power and authority that he had—absolute power, which is typically prone to absolute corruption. Immediately after he was filled with the Holy Spirit, Jesus was driven by that Spirit into the wilderness. After forty days of fasting he was hungry (surely an understatement!) and vulnerable to the temptation to use his power to turn stones into bread, to satisfy his personal needs. He was also tempted to bypass the cross and take a short cut to world dominion, and tempted to force the Father's hand to save him in a daring public exhibition (Luke 4:1–13). These were temptations that ordinary people do not face, but they were by no means his only significant temptations. Luke reports that after this particular temptation period, the tempter "departed from him until an opportune time." The temptation to avoid the cross and find an alternate pathway to the promised throne must have been a unique and recurring temptation for Jesus. Two specific recurrences are given in Mark 8:31–33 and Luke 22:40–44.

Jesus' humanity underpins his intercessory ministry, as we have seen in Hebrews 4:15. It is his authentic humanity which equips him to be the sole mediator between God and mankind, our Advocate (1 John 2:1). 1 Timothy 2:5 states there is one God and there is one mediator between God and men, *the man* Christ Jesus. His common experience of temptation not only equips him to be a merciful High Priest and advocate but also qualifies him to be our Judge (John 5:27). Michael Riddell makes this comment on Hebrews 4:15–16:

> This passage is enormously important in understanding the necessity of holding fast to Jesus' humanity. Without it, we have no hope of salvation for our own. The direct link is made here between Jesus' full participation in humanity, and our own hope of mercy and grace.[2]

Apollinarianism Denied the Full Humanity of Jesus

In the fourth century, a theologian of the Alexandrian school named Apollinarius of Laodicea (c. AD 310 to c. 390) promulgated the teaching that Christ did not have a human soul, but rather the eternal *Logos*, the Word of God, took the place of the human soul in the God-Man Jesus. "The divine energy fulfils the role of the animating spirit and of the human mind." He asserted that the Word was the sole life of Christ, infusing him with life even at the physical and biological levels.[3] Apollinarius believed that the elimination of a human psychology from Christ excluded the possibility of him having two contradictory wills and ensured his sinlessness and ability to destroy death. This is referred to in theological discussions as Word-flesh Christology

---

2. Riddell, *Threshold of the Future*, 124.

3. Kelly, *Early Christian Doctrines*, 292.

(the Word being united with flesh, but not with a whole human being, which was the opposing view) and it views Christ as an undivided Person with a single nature; the divine.

I suspect that this is what Christadelphians[4] may be assuming that the doctrine of the Trinity teaches, however this is definitely not the case. Apollinarianism was rejected as heresy at the Council of Constantinople in AD 381 on the grounds that it reduced Christ's humanity to a mere appearance and denied that he was in any sense a man as was clearly depicted in Scripture. This controversy provided the context for Gregory of Nazianzus' famous quote, already referred to, that "What has not been assumed cannot be restored." In other words, it was man's rational soul that was the seat of sin, and it was in this human nature that sin had to be defeated. The Niceno-Constantinopolitan Creed, or Nicene Creed, was an important outcome of the Council which rejected Apollinarianism and reads in part,

> One Lord Jesus Christ . . . Who for us men and for our salvation, came down from heaven and was incarnate by the Holy Spirit and the virgin Mary, and became man and was crucified for us under Pontius Pilate and suffered and was buried . . .

This creedal formulation, which expresses the humanity of Jesus (*incarnate* simply means "in flesh") is accepted by mainstream Christians today.[5]

Son of Man

Jesus often spoke of himself as the Son of Man. To a Jewish audience this phrase would recall the prophets Ezekiel and Daniel. God frequently addressed Ezekiel as "Son of Man." It seemed to emphasize Ezekiel's role as a go-between, delivering the unpalatable message of God's judgments on Israel in very graphic ways, as well as Ezekiel's representative mortality. Ezekiel had to enact the judgments of God on several occasions. In Daniel, the Son of Man is an enigmatic figure, an eschatological figure.[6]

> I saw in the night visions, and behold, with the clouds of heaven there came one like a son of man, and he came to the Ancient of Days and was presented before him. And to him was given dominion and glory and a kingdom, that all peoples, nations, and languages should serve him; his dominion is an everlasting dominion, which shall not pass away, and his kingdom one that shall not be destroyed (Dan 7:13–14).

4. For example, Ashton, *Studies in the Statement of Faith*, 35, incorrectly defines the church's view of the Incarnation as "Jesus as a divine being in an envelope of human flesh."

5. The continuing debates that resulted in the Chalcedonian definition of 451 and the subsequent monothelist schism show how concerned the early church was to maintain the full humanity of Christ. More of this in chapter 6.

6. "Eschatology" is the doctrine of the last things, and the Eschaton is the end time. From the Greek, *eschatos*, last.

When Jesus acknowledged before Caiaphas that he was indeed the Christ, he also claimed to be the Son of Man who would sit at the right hand of Power and be seen coming on the clouds of heaven (Mark 14:61–62). This identified him with the everlasting kingdom promised to David and the genealogical connection detailed in Matthew and Luke also testifies to this. The Jews could readily acknowledge that the Messiah was to be David's son, although they could not see that he would also be much more than this (Matt 22:41–45). It should be noted in that in Daniel 7, the "one like a son of man" is worshiped in the very presence of the Ancient of Days,[7] the first Commandment being still very much applicable. This aspect is downplayed in Christadelphian expositions of the passage. So whilst the title acknowledges Jesus' humanity, it is more enigmatic and far reaching than this aspect alone. Undoubtedly, this connection is what so enraged the High Priest.

Born of a Virgin

Although Jesus was fully human, he was not typical in all respects. The two major differences between Jesus and all other human beings with respect to his humanity are that he was born of a virgin and that he was sinless. Mainstream Christians understand the virgin conception to be the point at which the Word became flesh, the incarnation. Christadelphians attempt to demonstrate from the virgin birth passages that the Son began his existence at his conception and that this is the full extent of meaning of the term "Son of God." So the biblical teaching needs to be carefully explored.

The virgin birth proved to be a stumbling block for Jews and Gentiles. The timing of Jesus' birth, before Joseph and Mary were properly married, was evidently known, and would have been scandalous in first-century Jewish circles. There are possible references to this in some comments by the Jewish leaders, who were evidently keen to find some dirt on Jesus.

"Where is your Father?" they derisively ask (John 8:19) and later make the pointed statement, "We were not born of sexual immorality" (John 8:41). Later, as the gospel spread through the Gentile world and Greek dualist philosophers questioned the true humanity of Jesus, the virgin birth came under fire, not because it was miraculous, but because it was a real, fleshly, physical birth! This is probably why it was important for the compilers of the Apostles' Creed to include the clause, "Who was conceived by the Holy Spirit, born of the virgin Mary." The virgin birth was foretold by Isaiah.

> Therefore the LORD himself will give you a sign. Behold, the virgin shall conceive and bear a son, and shall call his name Immanuel ["God with us"] (Isa 7:14).

---

7. The verb, translated "serve" in the ESV and KJV is *latreuō*, the verb for cultic and sacrificial worship.

The Septuagint word for virgin is *parthenos*. This means a young woman of marriageable age, with an understanding of, or emphasis on, virginity.[8] The original Hebrew word has a broader meaning of young woman, but the choice of the LXX translators is significant. Certainly, the New Testament writers understood Jesus to have been conceived in the womb of a virgin.

> Now the birth of Jesus Christ took place in this way. When his mother Mary had been betrothed to Joseph, before they came together she was found to be with child from the Holy Spirit. And her husband Joseph, being a just man and unwilling to put her to shame, resolved to divorce her quietly. But as he considered these things, behold, an angel of the Lord appeared to him in a dream, saying, "Joseph, son of David, do not fear to take Mary as your wife, for that which is conceived in her is from the Holy Spirit. She will bear a son, and you shall call his name Jesus, for he will save his people from their sins." All this took place to fulfill what the Lord had spoken by the prophet: "Behold, the virgin shall conceive and bear a son, and they shall call his name Immanuel" (which means, God with us) (Matt 1:18–23).

Clearly, this passage is explicitly saying that Mary conceived Jesus without intercourse with a man. This conception was a miraculous work of the Holy Spirit and resulted in the baby being the Son of God; God with us. Matthew tells the story of Jesus' birth from Joseph's perspective, whereas Luke's gospel gives us Mary's.

> In the sixth month the angel Gabriel was sent from God to a city of Galilee named Nazareth, to a virgin betrothed to a man whose name was Joseph, of the house of David. And the virgin's name was Mary. And he came to her and said, "Greetings, O favored one, the Lord is with you!" But she was greatly troubled at the saying, and tried to discern what sort of greeting this might be. And the angel said to her, "Do not be afraid, Mary, for you have found favor with God. And behold, you will conceive in your womb and bear a son, and you shall call his name Jesus. He will be great and will be called the Son of the Most High. And the Lord God will give to him the throne of his father David, and he will reign over the house of Jacob forever, and of his kingdom there will be no end." And Mary said to the angel, "How will this be, since I am a virgin?" And the angel answered her, "The Holy Spirit will come upon you, and the power of the Most High will overshadow you; therefore the child to be born will be called holy—the Son of God" (Luke 1:26–35).

Luke agrees with Matthew that Mary and Joseph had not yet had intercourse and that Mary was a virgin. The conception of Jesus was an act of the Holy Spirit, without human intervention. Luke takes this further to state explicitly that this made Jesus the Son of God. But what does this mean?

One possible (mis)understanding would be that God literally impregnated Mary. This was part of the mythology of pagan religions, including the first-century Greeks, that gods could and did have intercourse with humans and produce offspring who were demi-gods or heroes. But this is not how we are to understand the virgin birth.

---

8. Danker, *Bauer's A Greek-English Lexicon*, 777. Hereafter abbreviated "BDAG."

YHWH is never portrayed in the Old or New Testament as having a consort, and neither Christadelphians nor mainstream Christians understand the conception of Jesus in this way, although precisely how Christadelphians do understand this conception is not clear from their writings.

Another possible understanding of the Matthaean and Lukan accounts is that they are later mythological accretions onto the gospel story, since they are not found in the earliest gospel, Mark. They could therefore be interpreted figuratively. This is the stance held by the Unitarians, a community of very diverse beliefs. The essential Unitarian understanding of Jesus is that he was the natural son of both Joseph and Mary. Hence only the Father is to be addressed as God and worshiped and Jesus is not divine, but fully and solely human.[9] This is not the Christadelphian position either:

> [We] really do believe that Jesus was, and is, literally the Son of God. [We] are not Unitarians, who think of Jesus as just a very superior man; nor are [we] "adoptionists," holding that God "adopted" Jesus as His spiritual Son. [We] believe that Jesus was God's "only begotten Son" in the way the scriptures describe.[10]

A third possibility is the Christadelphian understanding. Christadelphians have been accused of being Unitarians, but this is incorrect.[11] Although Christadelphians deny the trinitarian understanding of the Godhead, they most certainly affirm that Jesus was born of the virgin Mary by the miraculous intervention of the Holy Spirit and that neither Joseph nor any other man was involved in Jesus' conception. Consider the following explanations from three Christadelphian authors.

> How was Jesus Christ both man and the Son of God?
>
> Answer: Because he was begotten of a human virgin-mother by the power of the Spirit of God, and not by a human father. Mary, a damsel descended from David, was his mother; and God was his father. So that on his father's side he was the Son of God, and on his mother's side he was the son of David, and, therefore, a man partaking of David's nature, which was the nature common to all.
>
> Was Jesus both divine and human then?
>
> Answer: He was human as to the substance of which he was made; but divine as to the source from which he came; the Spirit from which he derived his wisdom; and the pattern of the character which he possessed.[12]

> There can be no doubt from these Scriptures (2 Sam 7:14; 1 Chr 17:13; Ps 89:26; Matt 1:20, 23; Luke 1:30–35; John 1:14; 3:16; Heb 1:5; 1 Pet 1:3; Gal 4:4; Isa 7:14) that God was the Father of the Lord Jesus Christ in a unique manner, a way quite different from the Fatherhood of God extended to believers. The expressions, "his only begotten Son," "the Son of the Highest," "the only begotten of

---

9. Breward, "Unitarianism," 700; and http://www.unitarian.org.uk/pages/faith.

10. Pearce, *Jesus*, 2.

11. Although they do not always help their case by quoting from Unitarians to support their thesis that there have always been Bible believers who share their anti-trinitarian stance.

12. Roberts, *Christadelphian Instructor*, articles 43 and 44.

the Father" and "the Son of God" are clear indications of the quite exceptional circumstances attending the conception and birth of the Lord Jesus. To be Bible believers, we must therefore believe that Jesus was truly the Son of God, with no human father whatsoever.[13]

> God sent the angel Gabriel to tell Mary that she would have a child. She became pregnant with Jesus without having had intercourse with a man. The child was conceived in her womb by God's power, the Holy Spirit, and so the child was the son of God and Mary's son . . . He is both the son of God and the son of a human being. He *inherited* many characteristics from his father and he shows us what God is like. He also *inherited* human weaknesses and temptations, but he never sinned.[14]

This interpretation is not without its difficulties either, as it naturally opens up questions about the process involved in Jesus' conception (such as how he "inherited" without the passing on of actual genes) which are not explicitly taught in Scripture and on which Christadelphians do not care to speculate. It's not sufficient to dismiss the mainstream doctrine of the incarnation on the basis of it being too hard to understand or not spelled out mechanistically, when the Christadelphian concept of Jesus' conception is itself rather nebulous.[15] The heartfelt Christadelphian assertion that "Jesus is the Son of God but not God the Son" is usually supported by appeal to passages in an effort to refute the trinity but essentially never by a clear explanation of what being the Son of God actually *means.*

Ron Coleman is one of very few Christadelphian writers to address this void and to do so with an attempt at a fair appraisal of the scriptural and historical foundations of the doctrine of the Trinity. Coleman tackles head-on the problem of how the divine and human could exist side-by-side in Jesus Christ, the very problem the fourth- and fifth-century church tackled and whose deliberations resulted in the doctrine of the Trinity. Coleman's own belief is that half of Jesus' chromosomes came from his mother and half were specially created by God, and combined in a very deliberate fashion to convey divine as well as human qualities. This explains how Jesus could have been sinless without being an automaton, because he inherited from his Father the capacity to know God and to have "a genius for him."[16] Whether many Christadelphians agree with Coleman is difficult to assess, but we will return later to a consideration of his ideas, as at least representing a defense of the Christadelphian position and a serious engagement with issues that most Christadelphian writers avoid.

---

13. Tennant, *The Christadelphians,* 83.

14. Hyndman, *The Way of Life,* 147, 150, my italics.

15. This difficulty is rarely acknowledged by Christadelphians. I did find one honest admission that "these are divine things beyond human experience and they need to be approached humbly and carefully with full consciousness of the limitations of the human mind" (E. J. N., "Jesus The Son of God," 26–27).

16. Coleman, "Jesus, Son of Man, Son of God," part 4.

The mainstream or trinitarian view of the virgin conception is that this is the point at which the eternal Word, intrinsically part of the Godhead, took on flesh and became the man Christ Jesus, maintaining his divine characteristics but also taking on full humanity. This is called the incarnation, from the Latin *carne*, flesh and it was an act of the Holy Spirit. Hebrews 2:17 tells us that Jesus Christ had to be made like his brothers in every way; the Son was not originally like us but had to become human. Further chapters will look in detail at the evidence for the divinity of Christ and his having both divine and human natures. For now, let us look closer at what Scripture teaches about Jesus as God's Son and see that its meaning transcends a single act of conception.

The Old Testament makes reference to the Messiah being the Son of God. Announcing the covenant with David, speaking of the promised offspring, God says "I will be his father, and he will be my son" (2 Sam 7:14). What does God mean by this? The explanation lies in the Old Testament passage quoted most often in the New. David writes in Psalm 110, "The LORD says to my Lord: 'Sit at my right hand until I make your enemies a footstool for your feet.'" This psalm is understood to be speaking of the Messiah, David's seed. Jesus challenged the Pharisees to think carefully about how this passage was to be interpreted. He asked them, "What do you think about the Christ? Whose son is he?" The Pharisees unhesitatingly replied, "The son of David." This of course, was correct. However, this was as far as their shortsighted analysis went. Jesus then asked them, "How is it then that David, in the Spirit, calls him 'Lord,' saying, 'The Lord said to my Lord, sit at my right hand until I put your enemies under your feet?' If then David calls him 'Lord,' how is he his son?" (Matt 22:41–45). The Pharisees had no answer for this. We will explore the significance of the title "Lord" in understanding the passage in a later chapter, but evidently Jesus was making the point that David's son was not going to be *merely* David's son. Something about this descendant would make him worthy of the title, "Lord." The Greek for Lord is *kyrios*, and it is used in the Septuagint to replace the name of God, YHWH, and in the Greek New Testament to translate the passages referring to "The LORD."

This is the crux of what Isaiah means by "God with us." When the angels announced Jesus' birth to the shepherds, they proclaimed him to be "Christ *the Lord*" (*hos estin Xristos kyrios*; dropping the definite article from the word *kyrios*, Lord, equates Lord with Christ). To a first-century Jew whose Bible was the Septuagint, the angel was saying, intriguingly, "This is Christ, THE LORD."

John is even more explicit. Having made clear that the Word was with God in the beginning and was God (John 1:1), he states, "The Word became flesh and dwelt among us, and we have seen his glory, glory as of the only Son from the Father, full of grace and truth" (John 1:14). The word for "dwell" is the Greek *skēnoō*, to take up residence or to tabernacle. It is the word used in the Septuagint of the tabernacle, the dwelling of God among Israel and derives from the Hebrew *shaken*, from which is named the Shekinah glory. The conception of Jesus was the Word becoming flesh—incarnation—the Shekinah glory dwelling in flesh among us: God with us. John says we have seen this Shekinah glory, this dwelling among us or tabernacling glory, the glory of the *monogenēs*, the one-of-a-kind, the only Son, the Unique, or "One and Only" (NIV).

Jesus referred to God as his Father and deferred to the Father in the manner of a Son. We will more closely examine what this means in chapter 5. For now, we will establish that Jesus is referred to both directly and indirectly as the Son of God by the New Testament writers. "Son of God" is a messianic title (2 Sam 7: 14; Ps 2:7; Rom 1:4) that clearly belongs to Jesus, but New Testament usage goes beyond this aspect. Interestingly, it is a title Jesus rarely used of himself in the Biblical record; he more commonly referred to himself as the Son of Man. These are just a sample of the verses to which we could refer:

- Testimony of God the Father: Matt 3:17; 17:5; Mark 1:11; Luke 3:22

- Testimony of Jesus himself: Matt 26:63–64; John 10:36; 17:1

- Testimony of disciples/evangelists: Matt 16:16; John 6:69; Mark 1:1; John 1:34, 49; 3:16–17; 11:27; 20:31

- Testimony of unclean spirits: Mark 3:11; Luke 4:41

- Testimony of the apostles: Acts 9:20; Rom 1:3–4; 8:3, 32; 1 Cor 1:9; Gal 4:4; Heb 1:2, 5; 1 John 1:3; 4:15; 5:5, 20; 2 John 3

Although Jesus did not often speak of himself as Son of God, he frequently referred to God as his Father. Again, the following is only a portion of the passages which could be used.

- Jesus frequently addressed God in familiar terms as Father: Mark 14:36, "Abba, Father!" Luke 10:21; 23:46; John 11:41–42; 12:27–28; 17:11

- He was about his Father's business (Luke 2:49)

- He spoke of God to his disciples as "my Father" e.g., Matt 16:17; 26:29; John 15:1, 10, 23; 20:17

- He spoke to others of God as his Father, e.g., John 2:16; 5:18, 43; 8:19, 54

- He said he was one with his Father (John 10:30; 17:21)

The New Testament writers also speak of God as the Father of Jesus. e.g., Colossians 1:3, "We always thank God, the Father of our Lord Jesus Christ . . ."

So clearly, although Jesus was fully human, he was uniquely the Son of God as well as the Son of Man. These titles convey more than simply parentage. They testify to his being the coming anointed one, and to much more even than that, as we shall see. By virtue of his incarnation and conception in the womb of the virgin Mary, Jesus was certainly different from us. Jesus was fully man, but he was not *merely* man, identical to you or me. The Christadelphian interpretation stops here; for them the virgin conception is the *fundamental* sense in which Jesus' sonship is understood. Yet Son of God means so much more than this in the New Testament and cannot be defined so simplistically. The doctrine of the Trinity describes the relationship of Father and Son as eternal within the Godhead and this we will explore later.

It is important to emphasize that trintarians believe that the *man* Christ Jesus, this unique person, certainly had a beginning at his conception in Mary's womb, at the point of the incarnation of the preexisting Son. It is insufficient to quote verses which speak of this conception as "proof" against the preexistence of the divine Son.[17]

Sinless

The other way in which Jesus the man was different from his fellow human beings is that he was sinless. Christadelphians agree with mainstream Christians on this point, but this raises the complex issue of how a mere man could be sinless. To confirm the uniqueness of Jesus' sinlessness we must first understand that all men and women, since the fall in Eden, have sinned. The most explicit argument for this is found in the early chapters of Paul's letter to the Romans.

> For we have already charged that all, both Jews and Greeks, are under sin, as it is written: "None is righteous, no, not one; no one understands; no one seeks for God. All have turned aside; together they have become worthless; no one does good, not even one" (Rom 3:9–12).

> Therefore, just as sin came into the world through one man, and death through sin, and so death spread to all men, because all sinned (Rom 5:12).

Other scriptural writers bear witness to the universal presence of sin in the human race. Here are some examples:

- Solomon: "There is no one who does not sin" (1 Kgs 8:46).

- James "But each person is tempted when he is lured and enticed by his own desire. Then desire when it has conceived gives birth to sin . . . " (Jas 1:14–15).

- John: "If we say we have no sin, we deceive ourselves . . . If we say we have not sinned, we make him a liar, and his word is not in us" (1 John 1:8–10).

Having established this universal sinful condition, we see the contrast with Jesus. In John 8:29 Jesus stated that he is *always doing* (the Greek is a present continuous verb) what pleases his Father. He challenged the Jews to convict him of sin and received no answer (John 8:46). He kept his Father's commandments and abode in his love (John 15:10).

---

17. This is the argument of Peter Heavyside, that the conception and birth of Jesus was "like any other before it," therefore it was his beginning, therefore it was not an incarnation. But he shoots down his own argument, for if Jesus was conceived in a virgin's womb by the Holy Spirit then it was most definitely *not* a conception *exactly* like any other man's. Heavyside, "Jesus in the Synoptic Gospels," 56.

The declaration of Jesus' sinlessness is more explicit in the New Testament epistles, however. In 2 Corinthians 5:21, speaking of Jesus bearing the sins of others, Paul states "For our sake he made him to be sin who knew no sin," and Hebrews 4:15 declares that Jesus "in every respect has been tempted as we are, yet without sin." He is "holy, innocent, unstained, separated from sinners, and exalted above the heavens" (Heb 7:26). Peter says Jesus was "a lamb without blemish or spot" (1 Pet 1:19) and that "He committed no sin, neither was deceit found in his mouth" (1 Pet 2:22, quoting Isa 53:9). John says "in him there is no sin" (1 John 3:5). Jesus is regularly referred to as righteous (Acts 3:14; 7:52; 1 Pet 3:18; 1 John 2:1).

That Jesus was fully human and yet without sin is the essential prerequisite of both his atoning and his mediating work. Jesus came to do what no other man had ever done: to obey God perfectly, and to do so as a man. By condemning sin in the very flesh in which it normally held sway, he completely destroyed its power.

> For God has done what the law, weakened by the flesh could not do. By sending his own Son in the likeness of sinful flesh and for sin, he condemned sin in the flesh [NIV: "in sinful nature"] (Rom 8:3).

> Since therefore the children share in flesh and blood, he himself likewise partook of the same things, that through death he might destroy the one who has the power of death, that is, the devil, and deliver all those who through fear of death were subject to lifelong slavery (Heb 2:14–15).

By leading a sinless life in obedience to his Father, Jesus was able to offer himself as the perfect, spotless sacrifice, to which the Old Testament sacrifices pointed and of which they were but a feeble shadow. Jesus was able to bear the sins of the world on the cross, the punishment humanity deserved.

> Surely he has borne our griefs and carried our sorrows; yet we esteemed him stricken, smitten by God, and afflicted. But he was wounded for our transgressions; he was crushed for our iniquities; upon him was the chastisement that brought us peace, and with his stripes we are healed. All we like sheep have gone astray; we have turned—every one—to his own way; and the LORD has laid on him the iniquity of us all (Isa 53:4–6).

Finally, Jesus' sinlessness in the face of normal human temptation makes him both a sympathetic advocate and a righteous judge (Heb 4:14–16).

The importance of the humanity of Christ cannot be overplayed. Throughout history, an acknowledgement that Jesus Christ was a real man who was born, lived, suffered, and died, and was tempted in every way yet without sin, has been fundamental to the true understanding of who Jesus is and what he has done. In the fourth century, a young man named Athanasius, living in Alexandria, wrote a treatise on why the Word of God became flesh, and the consequences and implications of this. He later went on to become one of the great Christian theologians and we will hear about him again in the discussion of how the early church came to understand the nature of the Godhead. He wrote,

It was our sorry case that caused the Word to come down, our transgression that called out His love for us, so that He made haste to help us and to appear among us. It is we who were the cause of His taking human form, and for our salvation that in His great love He was both born and manifested in a human body.[18]

Summary

- The humanity of Jesus is essential for his atoning work and his work as mediator.

- Christadelphians and mainstream Christians acknowledge the full humanity of Jesus Christ.

- The Old Testament prophesied that the seed of the woman would crush the power of sin and further that this Savior would be a descendant of Abraham and of David.

- The Gospels present Jesus as a real man.

- The New Testament writers emphasize the humanity of Jesus.

- A correct understanding of the gospel has always necessitated an acknowledgement that Jesus was fully human.

- Jesus Christ was conceived of a virgin by the power of the Holy Spirit without the intervention of a human father. God was his Father; he was the Son of God in a unique way; the Word made flesh.

- Jesus was tempted in every way yet was without sin.

Further Reading

- Wayne Grudem, *Systematic Theology*, chapter 26, "The Person of Christ."

- Millard Erickson *Christian Theology*, chapter 32, "The Humanity of Christ."

- I. Breward, "Unitarianism."

---

18. Athanasius, *Incarnation of the Word*, 1.4.

3

The Divinity of Jesus in the Old Testament

JESUS IS THE ONLY way to God; he reveals God to us. Who then is Jesus? Our answer to this question is critical.

> I am the way, and the truth, and the life. No one comes to the Father except through me . . . Whoever has seen me has seen the Father (John 14:6, 9).

> And this is eternal life: that they know you the only true God, and Jesus Christ whom you have sent (John 17:3).

Knowledge of God and Jesus Christ is eternal life. This is not an academic sort of head-knowledge, simply knowing *about* God, but having a personal relationship with him. But without a basis in truth, how can this knowledge be attained? We need to get it right, because it's life and death. Christadelphians are, rightly, very interested in the Old Testament. They put much store on the alleged absence of any trinitarian concepts or evidence for the divinity of Christ in its pages. This chapter addresses this misconception.

Misconception #3: That the Old Testament teaches nothing about the doctrine of the triune God, and in fact contradicts it.

Corrective: Whilst not overtly taught so early in salvation history, God's triune nature, in particular the divinity of the coming Christ, is evident in the Old Testament writings, especially as interpreted by the inspired New Testament writers.

The literary and theological turning point of Mark's gospel is Peter's confession of Christ, given in response to Jesus' challenging question, "But who do you say I am?" Peter answered, "You are the Christ" (Mark 8:27–29). As John's gospel approaches its climax, which is the revelation that Jesus is the Christ, the Son of God, belief in whom bestows life, Thomas cries, "My Lord and my God!" (John 20:28, 31). How did these Jewish men come to make these declarations? In order to answer this, we need to begin, once again, at the beginning.

The Old Testament is all about Jesus; this is abundantly clear from the perspective of the New Testament. He is there from beginning to end, as the seed of the woman, the seed of Abraham, the promised son, the Passover lamb, the whole burnt offering, the High Priest, the mercy seat, the savior who leads the people over Jordan into the promised land, the righteous Judge, the kinsman-redeemer, the King who will sit on David's throne, the greater than Solomon, the one to come "whose right it is" to have the kingdom, the suffering servant, the anointed one, the Prophet, the Son of Man, the Messenger of the Covenant. Every book presents a different facet of the Prophet, Priest, and King. Even though he is not identified by name, it is clear in retrospect that these various pictures are all portraits of the same magnificent person, the Messiah, God's Anointed.

Furthermore, the Old Testament is full of descriptors of what constitutes the uniqueness of God, what separates God from all creation. These attributes, God as sole Creator, Sovereign Lord over all things, Savior, King, Judge, and the only Being worthy of worship are later attributed to Jesus and place him squarely "above the line" that separates God from all other reality.

Christ and Creation

The New Testament makes some astonishing statements about Christ and creation.

> He [the Son] is the image of the invisible God, the firstborn of all creation. For by him all things were created, in heaven and on earth, visible and invisible, whether thrones or dominions or rulers or authorities—all things were created through him and for him. And he is before all things, and in him all things hold together (Col 1:15–17).

> There is but one Lord, Jesus Christ, through whom are all things and through whom we exist (1 Cor 8:6).

> [His Son] is the radiance of the glory of God and the exact imprint of his nature, and he upholds the universe by the word of his power . . . But of the Son he says, "Your throne, O God, is forever and ever . . ." And, "you, Lord, laid the foundation of the earth in the beginning, and the heavens are the work of your hands" (Heb 1:3, 8, 10).

> In the beginning was the Word, and the Word was with God and the Word was God. He was in the beginning with God. All things were made through him, and without him was not anything made that was made . . . And the Word became flesh and dwelt among us (John 1:1–3, 14).

The words describing the Son's involvement in creation, in the original Greek, are

- *eis auton:* into/toward/with respect to him

- *di' autou:* through/via/by him

- *en autō*: in him or by his agency

This collection of prepositions is informed by each of three cases, accusative, genitive, and dative, which together encompass every sense of association between Jesus and creation; it was created in him, by his agency, through him and focuses towards him. In effect, we see Jesus associated with creation from every direction or perspective;[1] he is its originator and reason for coming into being, and he is the end or purpose for which all was created, and he is the means whereby creation occurred, is sustained, and by which it will be renewed. As Athanasius said, "the renewal of creation has been wrought by the Self-same Word who made it in the beginning."[2] If *every* created thing owes its existence to the Son, then the Son himself cannot be a created being.

So, do we find any hint of Christ in the Genesis creation account? It is possible that the use of the plural, "Let us make man in *our* image, after *our* likeness" (Gen 1:26) reflects deliberation within the Godhead, *elohim*, but this interpretation is controversial. The other plausible alternative is that it reflects God's imperative to the angelic court. Although other proposals have been put forward,[3] these have been rejected by most commentators, and for good reason. The Hebrew word *elohim* can mean "mighty ones," which is the favored Christadelphian interpretation, but it is typically used in an unambiguous way to refer to God or gods. Any interpretation of *elohim* and the plural imperative "let us" in verse 26 must grapple with verse 27, which uses the singular: "So God created man in *his* own image, in the image of God he created him." Elsewhere in Scripture, man is described as being in the image of God, but not in the image of the angels, however this could be an argument from silence, and in some places angels are described as appearing like men. The Septuagint, however, is unambiguous:

kai eipen ho Theos poiēsōmen anthrōpon	*kat' eikona hēmeteran kai kath' homoiōsin.*
And God said, "Let us make man	according to our image and [according to] likeness"

"God" here is the standard singular word for the only God, *Theos*, whereas the verb "let us make" is in the first person plural. Image and likeness are singular. The plural verb stands out incongruously in a language that is typically pedantic about agreement

---

1. For further detail on the roles of Father and Son in creation as depicted through various Greek cases, see Bowman and Komoszewski, *Putting Jesus in His Place*, 188–91.

2. Athanasius, *Incarnation of the Word*, 2.

3. Suggestions include, the equivalent of the "royal We," or plural of majesty; an anthropomorphic self-deliberation and a polytheistic remnant or throwback. Discussion of these may be found in commentaries such as Mathews, *Genesis 1–11*, 161; Wenham, *Genesis 1–15*, 27.

of verbs with their subject in number and person. If the unambiguous Septuagint is permitted to have the last word over the ambiguous Hebrew, there is scope for either of the two main interpretations, except for the difficulty of precisely in whose image man was made. Ultimately, whilst this verse may be supportive of a dialogue within the Godhead, it is not a definitive proof. One thing is certain, however, and that is that God created without the assistance of another. The angels did not create; they are created beings and are not to be worshiped (Isa 40:12–14; Heb 1:6–14; Rev 22:8–9).

To determine the involvement of Christ in creation, we must rely on the New Testament's witness, and put these passages together with the opening verses of Genesis to perceive that the Father-God, the Word/Christ, and the Holy Spirit were each active in creation. Genesis 1:1 tells us that the Spirit of God was hovering over the waters. The context is "in the beginning" which is a little difficult to translate from the Hebrew; it may mean "In the beginning God created . . ." or "When God began to create." This has implications for the arguments about pre-Adamic creation which are off our present topic, but it is important to note that the Septuagint simply says *en archē*, "in beginning," without the use of the definite article. So when John's gospel commences with the same phrase *en archē*, he places the Word in the context of creation—the Word who was somehow both God and with God, and who later became flesh and dwelt among us. This is the plain reading of the text.

Another verse in which God speaks in the plural is Genesis 3:22: "Then the Lord God said, 'Behold, the man has become like one of us in knowing good and evil.'" Again, it is not clear whether the "us" (Greek *hēmōn*, first person plural pronoun) refers to a plurality within the Godhead or encompasses God and the angels. The interpretation hinges on what "knowing good and evil" means, for this is the distinguishing character of "us" that man has now acquired. The most likely meaning is that man has usurped for himself God's prerogative of moral autonomy.[4] In an allusion to this passage in Ezekiel 28:1–19, the king of Tyre is metaphorically expelled from Eden for wickedness, violence, pride, corruption of his wisdom because of his splendor, sins, and dishonest trade. This was despite his initial perfection, wisdom, and blamelessness. If the "knowledge of good and evil" equates to claiming moral autonomy, the right to define good and evil, then only God has this prerogative, not even the angels. This interpretation would give indirect support to the "us" referring to God alone.

---

4. Wenham, *Gen 1–15*, 63–64 lists the alternative interpretations, which are (i) man has known good as a result of obedience and evil as a result of disobedience, but this would not make him like God or, arguably, like the angels; (ii) man acquired moral discernment, but if he did not already have this, why was he held accountable for his transgression? (iii) man acquired sexual knowledge; but this knowledge is not reserved for God or for the angels, who "do not marry" and it is not intrinsically evil (iv) man acquired omniscience—obviously not (v) man acquired wisdom, but how could this occur by disobedience and why would it be a cause for punishment? Another possibility is presented by the doctor-patient analogy: both "know" cancer but in different ways. Likewise God "knows" all about evil but man "knows" it from direct experience.

The Old Testament Veil

What eighth-century-BC Jew, hearing the prophet Hosea's message, would have thought that the statement, "When Israel was a child, I loved him, and out of Egypt I called my son" (Hos 11:1) referred to anyone or anything other than the nation of Israel? And yet Matthew calmly comments in passing, that the flight of Joseph, Mary, and baby Jesus into Egypt to escape Herod was a direct fulfilment of this verse! Sometimes the New Testament surprises us in the interpretations it puts on the Old. Hidden in verses such as these, which would have had a plain contemporary meaning, are profound and explicit statements about Christ.

> The Old Testament may be likened to a chamber richly furnished but dimly lighted: the introduction of light brings into it nothing which was not in it before; but it brings out into clearer view much of what was in it but was only dimly or not at all perceived before. The mystery of the Trinity is not revealed in the Old Testament; but the mystery of the Trinity underlies the Old Testament revelation, and here and there almost comes into view. Thus the Old Testament revelation of God is not corrected by the fuller revelation which follows it, but is only perfected, extended and enlarged."[5]

Christ is only gradually revealed in the Old Testament, as we discussed in the introduction. So-called "progressive revelation" should not frighten us. David and the prophets were privileged to know a lot more about the coming Messiah than the patriarchs did. Nevertheless, even the explicit prophecies of the suffering servant and the coming King seem blurred and indistinct without the New Testament's commentary. We are told that the Old Testament (which the New Testament refers to as "The Scriptures") gives us glimpses of Christ and that these often require elucidation.

> You search the Scriptures because you think that in them you have eternal life; and it is they that bear witness about me (John 5:39; Jesus to the Jews).

> And beginning with Moses and all the Prophets, he interpreted to them in all the Scriptures the things concerning himself (Luke 24:27; Jesus on the road to Emmaus).

Yet without the guiding light of apostolic commentary, even Jews and God-fearing Gentiles who were well educated in the Scriptures, missed the christological interpretations of many passages. For example, the Ethiopian eunuch did not know to whom Isaiah's suffering servant prophecy referred (Acts 8:30–35). Paul explains that the Jews, in their unbelief, effectively had a veil over their faces when reading the Scriptures (2 Cor 3:14–16). On several occasions, Jesus chided the Jewish leaders for not "knowing" the Scriptures and how they applied to the Messiah, e.g., Matt 21:42; 22:29.

So, to examine what the Old Testament says about Christ's divine attributes, *we need to read it through the lens of New Testament interpretation*. This is a different way

---

5. Warfield, *Biblical Doctrines*, 141–42.

of thinking for many Christadelphians,[6] but allows us to avoid the speculation and misinterpretation which can arise by putting the hermeneutical cart before the horse.

The Great *I AM*

The God of Abraham, Isaac, and Jacob heard the cry of their descendants in Egypt and commissioned Moses to show the Egyptians God's wonders and lead them out with a mighty arm. Awestruck, Moses stood before the burning bush and dared to ask God his name.

> God said to Moses, "I AM WHO I AM." And he said, "Say this to the people of Israel, 'I AM has sent me to you.'" God also said to Moses, "Say this to the people of Israel, 'The LORD, the God of your fathers, the God of Abraham, the God of Isaac, and the God of Jacob, has sent me to you.' This is my name forever, and thus I am to be remembered throughout all generations" (Exod 3:14–15).

In these two verses we have several names and titles for God. In the Hebrew, the word translated "God" is *elohim*, which we discussed in the context of creation. The words "I am" here are spelt in Hebrew *aleph-he-yodh-he* ('HYH), which is usually interpreted to be a future tense, "I will be."[7] In verse 15, we have the LORD, which is the more familiar form *yodh-he-waw-he*, YHWH. The original Hebrew had only consonants, but from the seventh to tenth centuries the Masoretes produced a Hebrew text of the Old Testament in pointed script, meaning they inserted vowel points to aid pronunciation. The *Interlinear Hebrew-English Old Testament*[8] reproduces these such as to render the pronunciation YeHWoH where the e is a very short sound, virtually silent, and the o is a long o as in roll. Thus we have, "Elohim said to Moses, 'HYH who HYH'... HYH sent me to you ... YHWH, elohim of your fathers ... has sent me to you."

The Jews, out of reverence, did not like to pronounce the name YHWH, instead they would substitute *Adonai*, Lord, when reading the text. This has carried over into English translations, where we see LORD substituted for the divine "tetragrammaton" (four letters) of YHWH. When the Jews of the Diaspora translated their Hebrew Scriptures into Greek, they rendered the name of God in Exodus 3 as *ego eimi ho ōn*; "I am the being-one" and "Lord" as the regular word for Lord or master, *kyrios*. The

---

6. The hermeneutical basis of theology is very important. Mainstream Christians give hermeneutical priority to the New Testament, i.e., the Old Testament is interpreted in light of the New, an approach which has scriptural warrant. Christadelphians tend to interpret the New Testament in light of the Old rather than interpreting the Old in light of the New. For example, the description of the temple in Ezekiel 40–48 is determined to be a *literal* future temple and therefore dictates what the New Jerusalem will be like, and that animal sacrifices will be resumed after Christ's return to earth. This interpretation would contradict Rev 21:22 and Heb 10:1–14.

7. The Christadelphian understanding of Jesus' derived divinity, which they term "God manifestation," begins with this verse and the emphasis on the future tense 'HYH. This will be discussed in detail in chapter 6.

8. Kohlenberger, *Hebrew-English Old Testament*, 151.

word *kyrios* means one who is in a position of authority, such as a master over a slave, a father over a son, a husband over a wife, or an official in high position. It is a term of respect toward one's superior and denotes a rightful, legitimate authority.[9] In the Septuagint, the Scriptures of Jesus, Paul, and the early church, *theos* (God/god) translates *elohim* (God) and *kyrios* stands in for YHWH, following the Jewish tradition of reading *Adonai*. We will have more to say about the New Testament's use of *kyrios* as a title for Jesus later. Returning to the rendering of God's name YHWH as *ego eimi ho ōn*, "I am the being-one" in the Septuagint of Exodus 3:14, we do not find the early church using this as an appellation for God. Instead, God and Jesus are both referred to as "Lord," *kyrios*.[10]

Interestingly, where we do find the Greek equivalent of YHWH, "I am the being-one," it is on the lips of Jesus in reference to himself, not to God his Father. Typically, Greek verbs do not require a pronoun, because the ending of the verb specifies the number and person. Hence, it would be perfectly acceptable to render "I am" simply as *eimi*, the first person singular of the verb "to be" in its present tense. Adding the pronoun *ego*, which is the first person singular pronoun "I," is quite superfluous, although grammatically sound. It just makes the expression stand out somewhat; it adds emphasis. It is insufficient to brush it off as "Jesus simply uses the present tense of the verb 'to be,'"[11] because it has an unusual emphasis that is prominent in John's gospel, the gospel that particularly aims to set out who Jesus is.

Seven of these occurrences of *ego eimi* are with a predicate ("I am something")

- I am the bread of life (John 6:35 and variants in verses 41, 48, 51).
- I am the light of the world (John 8:12).
- I am the door of the sheep (John 10:7, 9).
- I am the good shepherd (John 10:11, 14; see later discussion of the shepherd motif of the God of Israel applied to Jesus).
- I am the resurrection and the life (John 11:25).
- I am the way, and the truth, and the life (John 14:6).
- I am the true vine (John 15:1, 5).

Two occurrences are associated with a participle that describes what Jesus is doing:

- I am the-one-speaking to you (John 4:26).

9. BDAG, 576–78.

10. It is intriguing as to why some within the Christadelphian tradition cling to the use of YHWH as a direct address or descriptor for God, given that this was not the way the Jews of either Old and New Testament times dealt with Scripture. Furthermore, it would seem to be inappropriate given the example and directive of Jesus for his followers to call God "Father." See Nicholls, *Remember the Days of Old*, 52–54.

11. which is the rather inadequate explanation offered in Abel, *Wrested Scriptures*, 293.

- I am the-one-testifying concerning myself (John 8:18).

And six are used in an absolute sense, without any sort of predicate i.e., without the "he" that appears in some translations such as the ESV.

- I am / it is I; do not be afraid (John 6:20).

- If you do not believe that I am [he], you will die in your sins (John 8:24).

- Then you will know that I am [he] (John 8:28).

- Before Abraham was [became], I am (John 8:58).

- So that when it occurs, you may believe that I am [he] (John 13:19).

- Jesus said to them, "I am [he]" (John 18:5, 6, 8).

Where *ego eimi* is used without a predicate, in the absolute sense, the most likely referent is Isaiah chapters 40 to 55 where God discloses himself repeatedly as "I am he" which the Septuagint consistently renders *ego eimi*.

- Who has performed and done this, calling the generations from the beginning? I, the LORD, the first, and with the last, I am he [*ego eimi*] (Isa 41:4).

- I, I, am he [*ego eimi, ego eimi*] who blots out your transgressions, for my own sake, and I will not remember your sins (Isa 43:25).

- Thus says the LORD, the King of Israel and his Redeemer, the Lord of hosts: "I am the first and I am the last; besides me there is no god (Isa 44:6; compare Rev 1:17; 2:8; 21:6; 22:13).

- I [*ego eimi, ego eimi*] the LORD speak the truth; I declare what is right (Isa 45:19).

- Even to your old age I am he, [*ego eimi, ego eimi*] and to grey hairs I will carry you (Isa 46:4).

- Listen to me O Jacob, and Israel, whom I called! I am he; I am [*ego eimi*] the first and I am [*ego eimi*] the last (Isa 48:12; again the "first and last," as applied to Jesus in the book of Revelation).

- Thus says the LORD, your Redeemer, the Holy One of Israel: "I am [*ego eimi*] the LORD your God, who teaches you to profit, who leads you in the way you should go (Isa 48:17).

- I, I, am he [*ego eimi, ego eimi*] who comforts[12] you (Isa 51:12).

- Therefore my people shall know my name. Therefore in that day they shall know that it is I [*ego eimi*] who speak; here I am [literally, "I am present"] (Isa 52:6).

12. An interesting side point: the verb here for "comforts" is a participle; God is the One-who-comforts. In John 14:16 where Jesus has been explicitly speaking of his relationship with the Father, he tells the disciples that he will ask the Father to send them *another* comforter; *parakletos*, the noun corresponding to *parakaleō*, to comfort or counsel.

D. A. Carson, one of the foremost New Testament scholars today, commenting on John 8:24, explains the significance of the allusion to these passages in Isaiah.

> In Isaiah, the contexts demand that "I am he" means "I am the same", "I am forever the same" and perhaps even "I am Yahweh," with a direct allusion to Exodus 3:14 (cf. Isa 43:11–13). For others to apply this title to themselves was blasphemous, an invitation to face the wrath of God (Isa 47:8; Zeph 2:15). For Jesus to apply such words to himself is tantamount to a claim to deity, once it is clear that the other potential meanings of *ego eimi* are contextually impossible.[13]

In Isaiah 47:8 the daughter of Babylon attempts to usurp the claim, "I am [*ego eimi*] and there is no one besides me." In Zephaniah 2:15, Nineveh makes a similar claim. This is blasphemy.

In Revelation, we see several references to the eternal being-ness of God.

- Grace to you and peace from him who is and who was and who is to come (Rev 1:4).

- "I am the Alpha and the Omega," says the Lord God, who is and who was and who is to come, the Almighty (Rev 1:8).

- Holy, holy, holy is the Lord God Almighty, who was and is and is to come (Rev 4:8).

- We give thanks to you, Lord God Almighty, who is and who was, for you have taken your great power and begun to reign (Rev 11:17).

- Just are you, O Holy One, who is and who was, for you brought these judgments (Rev 16:5).

- I am the Alpha and the Omega, the first and the Last, the beginning and the end (Rev 22:13).

In this final passage, it is *Jesus* who is picking up the theme and claiming the title of Alpha and Omega, which has been ascribed previously, in Isaiah and Revelation, to the Lord God.

When we put ourselves in the position of first-century readers of John's gospel and Revelation, readers steeped in the Greek Scriptures, to hear Jesus speaking of himself as *ego eimi*, beginning and end, Alpha and Omega, there could be only one conclusion; these divine titles and ascriptions are his. No wonder that, on hearing his claim, the unbelieving Jews, mistakenly fired with the indignation of Isaiah 47:8 and Zephaniah 2:15, took up stones to stone him.

13. Carson, *John*, 344.

Lord of Lords

We have seen that the Septuagint uses *kyrios*, Lord, in place of the tetragrammaton, YHWH. The inspired New Testament writers see fit to cite from the Greek Scriptures, including this use of *kyrios*. In doing so, a number of attributes and works attributable to the Lord YHWH in the Old Testament are attributed to the Lord Jesus in the New.

The title *kyrios*, "Lord," was a favorite descriptor of Jesus Christ used by the Apostle Paul. It is central to Paul's theology of Christ and expressive of Jesus' relationship to his church and to all creation. The lordship of Jesus is to pervade every aspect of the believer's life. It shall be demonstrated that by calling Jesus "Lord," in common with other New Testament writers, Paul is signifying that Jesus shares in the divinity of YHWH, Lord God of Israel and that he—not Caesar or other worldly power—has supreme authority over all things. Paul's use of the title *kyrios* for Jesus Christ is ubiquitous in his writings. Christadelphian John Thorpe[14] has argued that because the word *kyrios* does not refer exclusively to God in the New Testament and because Paul distinguishes Jesus from God, Paul cannot be ascribing a title of God to Jesus. This is overly simplistic, however, because of the sheer volume and particular ways in which Paul uses the title, including applying Old Testament passages referring to Lord God to Lord Christ. The following is a selection.[15]

1 Cor 1:31; 2 Cor 10:17 "boast in the Lord"	Jer 9:24
1 Cor 2:16 "mind of the Lord"	Isa 40:13
Rom 14:11; Phil 2:10–11 "every knee shall bow"	Isa 45:23
Rom 9:33 "a stone of stumbling"	Isa 8:13–14
1 Cor 8:6 "one Lord"	Deut 6:4
1 Cor 10:21 "table of the Lord"	Mal 1:7–12
1 Cor 10:22 "provoke the Lord to jealousy"	Deut 32:21
1 Thess 3:13 "the coming of the Lord with all his holy ones [saints]"	Zech 14:5

14. Thorpe, "Jesus and Paul," 100.

15. Adapted from Bauckham, *Jesus and the God of Israel*, 187–88.

2 Thess 1:7–8 "The Lord revealed in fire"	Isa 66:15
2 Thess 3:5 "The Lord direct your hearts"	1 Chr 29:18
2 Thess 3:16 "The Lord of peace"	Num 6:26
Acts 2:21; 1 Cor 1:2; Rom 10:13 "Call on the name of the Lord"	Joel 2:32; Zeph 3:9; Zech 13:9; Jer 10:25 and elsewhere
1 Cor 1:10; 5:4; 6:11; 2 Thess 1:12; 3:6; Col 3:17 "the name of the Lord"	Gen 12:8; Mic 4:5 and elsewhere
1 Cor 1:8; 5:5; 2 Cor 1:14; 1 Thess 5:2; 2 Thess 2:2 "the day of the Lord"	Joel 1:15; 2:1, 11, 31; Amos 5:18; Isa 13:6, 9 and elsewhere
Rom 12:11; 16:18; Col 3:24 "serve the Lord" (Gk *douleuō*)	Ps 2:11 (LXX *douleuō*)
1 Thess 1:8; 2 Thess 3:1 "the word of the Lord"	Isa 2:3 and elsewhere
2 Cor 5:11; Col 3:22 "the fear of the Lord"	Prov 1:7; Isa 2:10, 19, 21 and elsewhere
2 Cor 3:18; 2 Thess 2:14 "the glory of the Lord"	Exod 24:16, 17; 40:34, 35; Ezek 1:28 and elsewhere
Phil 4:5 "the Lord is near/at hand"	Pss 34:18; 145:18

As to the distinction between Jesus and the Father, that will be discussed in chapter 5.

The lordship of Jesus was a significant concept for Paul and his theology but did not originate with him. On the day of Pentecost, at the birth of the church, Peter had stood and proclaimed "God has made him both Lord and Christ, this Jesus whom you crucified" (Acts 2:36). Paul was later to write the astounding promise, "If you confess with your mouth that Jesus is Lord and believe in your heart that God raised him from the dead, you will be saved" (Rom 10:9). That this confession was no mere throwaway line but a central tenet of the early church's faith can be gleaned from his writings to the Corinthians: "to . . . all those who in every place call upon the name of the Lord Jesus Christ, both their Lord and ours" (1 Cor 1:2) and "For what we proclaim is not ourselves, but Jesus Christ as Lord" (2 Cor 4:5). He concludes his letter with an Aramaic phrase which he evidently expects his Greek readers to understand: *Marana tha*; "Our Lord, come!" (1 Cor 16:22). *Mar* was the Aramaic word for "lord," equivalent to the Greek *kyrios*. Genuine confession of Jesus' lordship could only be accomplished by the working of the Spirit (1 Cor 12:3) and the confession probably occurred formally at baptism.[16] Paul uses *kyrios* well over 200 times in his writings. The most common usage is as a title (73 times) for Jesus/Jesus Christ, especially in the introductions and conclusions to his letters. Paul also makes extensive and almost unique use of the phrase "in the Lord," *en tō kyriō*, to express the state of unity with Christ and thus each other that underpins Christian greeting, service, love, joy, submission, and steadfastness.

Whilst *kyrios* was used as a designation for some pagan gods, more so in the Eastern mystery religions than the Greek pantheon, Paul is at pains to distinguish the uniqueness of Jesus' lordship. In so doing he introduces a new dimension to the Jewish concept of monotheism, as we saw earlier.

> For although there may be so-called gods in heaven or on earth—as indeed there are many "gods" and many "lords"—yet for us there is one God, the Father, from whom are all things and for whom we exist, and one Lord, Jesus Christ, through whom are all things and through whom we exist (1 Cor 8:5–6).

Not only is Jesus' lordship here associated with creation, Paul has effectively inserted this statement into the *Shema*, the declaration in Deuteronomy 6:4, "The Lord our God, the Lord is one," as we discussed in chapter 1, and connects him with God's creating work, as Lord. Paul identifies Jesus with the Lord, who is one, "redefining monotheism as somehow incorporating Jesus without denying the oneness of the Godhead."[17] We cannot impose a dichotomy here between God and Lord, or "God" is not "Lord" any more than the "Lord" is "God."

Another remarkable passage, which may be a pre-Pauline hymn,[18] but nevertheless has been appropriated, if not written by Paul, relates Christ's empting himself,[19] in taking the nature of a servant and in the humiliation of the cross:

> Therefore God has highly exalted him and bestowed on him the name that is above every name, so that at the name of Jesus every knee should bow, in heaven and on earth and under the earth, and every tongue confess that Jesus Christ is Lord, to the glory of God the Father (Phil 2:9–11).

---

16. Dunn, *Theology of Paul*, 245, 247.

17. Wright, *Mission of God*, 111; Bird, *Bird's-Eye View of Paul*, 125; Gorman, *Reading Paul*, 104.

18. Nicholls, *The Name*, 65, attributes this insight to another Christadelphian, T. J. Barling, however it must be respectfully pointed out that rather than being an original insight, Barling has evidently obtained this view from mainstream NT scholarship, in which it is widespread. See Witherington, *Many Faces*, 73–81; Hurtado, *Lord Jesus Christ*, 112.

19. This passage, which speaks of Christ's taking on of humiliation and servanthood, will be discussed in detail later.

This is a clear reference to Isaiah 45:22–23, "I am God, and there is no other . . . To me every knee shall bow, every tongue shall swear allegiance" and prior to this, "I am the Lord, and there is no other" (v. 18). This universal acclamation which God the Lord has reserved for himself alone is specifically granted to the Lord Jesus, and this glorifies God the Father. It is important to understand that "the name that is above every name," is now the given name *of* Jesus (the Greek has the genitive case), not the name "Jesus."[20] The *name* of Jesus is "Lord," the name of YHWH God of Israel. Paul affirms that Jesus shares the identity and uniqueness of YHWH by inserting his name into this text.[21]

This leads us to explore further the identification of Jesus with God through the use of *kyrios* in the Greek Bible. First-century Jewish and Christian readers of the Septuagint would have understood *kyrios* as the name of the God of Israel,[22] just as with the Aramaic equivalent *mar*. Paul the ex-Pharisee would doubtless have been familiar with the Hebrew Scriptures, and potentially with other Greek versions which used the Hebrew YHWH,[23] but he chose to cite the Septuagint with its use of *kyrios* for the Lord God. Paul not only applies *kyrios* specifically to Jesus, there are also many passages where it is unclear whether God or Jesus is meant, and passages where Paul is alluding to or quoting Septuagint references to *kyrios*-God, some of which he applies to Jesus. Some examples will illustrate this.

In Romans 4:8, "blessed is the man against whom the Lord will not count his sin," Paul cites Psalm 32:2, where the referent is God. Similarly, Romans 9:28–29, "For the Lord will carry out his sentence upon the earth fully and without delay. And as Isaiah predicted, 'If the Lord of hosts had not left us offspring, we would have been like Sodom, and become like Gomorrah'" is a quotation from Isaiah 10:22–23 and an allusion to Isaiah 1:9. Romans 12:19, "It is written, 'Vengeance is mine, I will repay, says the Lord'" quotes Deuteronomy 32:35. Romans 14:11 "As I live, says the Lord, every knee shall bow to me, and every tongue shall confess to God" quotes Isaiah 45:23 which Paul in Philippians refers to Jesus. These and many other examples illustrate Paul's deliberate use of the Septuagint and carry over its use of *kyrios* to translate YHWH.

Romans 10:13 provides a clear application of *kyrios* from the Old Testament to Jesus. The whole context of this passage is clearly talking about the Lord Jesus:

20. Christophe, *Jesus is Lord*, 29, observes that it is "at the name *of* Jesus," i.e., the name Jesus has been given, not at the name "Jesus," that every knee will bow.

21. Wright, *Mission of God*, 109.

22. Rosel, "Reading and Translation," 414; Wright, *Mission of God*, 108.

23. Howard, "The Tetragram and the New Testament," 63, asserts on the basis of some pre-Christian Greek manuscript fragments that the Divine name was initially transliterated or written in Hebrew letters but later replaced with *kyrios* by Christian copyists, generating ambiguity between Christ and God in later texts. Rosel, "Reading and Translation" disputes this thesis, arguing from internal evidence that *kyrios* was the original representation of the first translators. Regardless of sequence, Paul has chosen to use the LXX with *kyrios*. Dunn, *Theology of Paul*, 249, acknowledges Howard but asserts that *kyrios* would have been spoken when the texts were read, as confirmed by Paul's usage in OT quotations as well as by Philo and Josephus.

"Everyone who calls on the name of the Lord will be saved." This is a quotation from Joel 2:32 which was similarly cited by Peter at Pentecost with reference to Jesus (Acts 2:16, 21, 36). Here an Old Testament text referring to Lord God is applied to Lord Jesus. "Calling on the name of the Lord" is associated with salvation in Christ and baptism into his name in the New Testament (Acts 9:14, 21; 22:16; 1 Cor 1:2), but has its roots in calling on the name of YHWH in the Old (Gen 12:8; 26:25; Pss 99:6; 105:1). In the Old Testament, salvation belongs to God alone (Exod 15:2; Ps 68:20; Isa 43:3). His Son takes the role of Savior, as Christ the Lord (Luke 2:11) in bringing justification (1 Cor 6:11) reconciliation (Rom 5:1, 11) eternal life (Rom 6:23) in short, salvation (1 Thess 5:9). The New Testament presents both "God" (1 Tim 1:1; 2:3; 4:10; Titus 1:3; 2:10; 3:4; Jude 1:25) and Jesus (Luke 2:11; John 4:42; Acts 5:31; 13:23; Eph 5:23; Phil 3:20; 2 Tim 1:10; Titus 1:4; 3:6; 2 Pet 1:11; 2:20; 3:2; 1 John 4:14) as "our Savior." Is this apparent ambiguity a contradiction? Hardly; Jesus shares in God's unique identity as the one Savior (Titus 2:13; 2 Pet 1:1).

Another group of references concerns the "Day of the Lord," which has been transformed from the Day of YHWH (Isa 13:6–9; Ezek 30:3; Joel 1:15; 2:31; 3:14; Amos 5:18–20; Zech 14:1; Mal 4:5) to the Day of the Lord Jesus. "For you yourselves are fully aware that the day of the Lord will come like a thief in the night," warns Paul in 1 Thessalonians 5:2 and similarly 1 Corinthians 1:8; 5:5; 2 Corinthians 1:14; and 2 Thessalonians 2:2. This Day is associated with judgment, a prerogative of God that has been given to Jesus. In Psalm 96:13 "the Lord . . . comes to judge the earth. He will judge the world in righteousness and the peoples in his faithfulness." In Romans 2:16 Paul states that God will judge through Jesus Christ. Paul interchanges the judgment seat of God (Rom 14:10) and of Christ (2 Cor 5:10). Thus we see that the lordship of Jesus is associated with functions and attributes ascribed to YHWH.[24] The inescapable conclusion from Paul's application of the designation *kyrios* to Jesus is that he somehow shares in the identity of YHWH.

Deuteronomy 10:17 informs Israel "For the Lord your God is God of gods and Lord of lords [*kyrios tōn kyriōn*] the great, the mighty, and the awesome God, who is not partial and takes no bribe." Psalm 136:3 further exhorts us to "Give thanks to the Lord of lords, for his steadfast love endures forever." Paul in 1 Timothy 6:15 speaks of "God . . . he who is the blessed and only Sovereign, the King of kings and Lord of lords."

It is quite remarkable then, when the angel explains to John that "the Lamb will conquer them, for he is Lord of lords and King of kings" (Rev 17:14). Furthermore, the Word of God, the rider on the white horse, whose robe is dipped in blood and who will rule the nations with an iron scepter, bears the name "King of kings and Lord of lords" (Rev 19:13–16).

---

24. Ladd, *New Testament*, 457; Wright, *Mission of God*, 110.

Worthy of Worship

Nothing is more adamantly proclaimed in association with the oneness of God in the Old Testament as YHWH's exclusive right to worship. Worship is the absolute right of YHWH and of him alone, as we have seen in our discussion of what it means that God is One. Exodus 34:14 makes this clear: "For you shall worship no other god, for the LORD, whose name is Jealous, is a jealous God." In response to temptation, Jesus defers to Deuteronomy 6:16 (LXX): "Worship the Lord your God, and serve him only."

> You are the LORD, you alone. You have made heaven, the heaven of heavens, with all their host, the earth and all that is on it, the seas and all that is in them; and you preserve all of them; and the host of heaven worships you (Neh 9:6).

This contrasts with the Hellenistic view that divinity was a matter of degree and therefore worship was a matter of degree. Lesser divinities could be accorded lesser degrees of worship, hence emperor worship could be simply grafted on to other religious convictions. Not so to the Jews and Christians; the exclusive worship of YHWH was a recognition and response to his uniqueness.[25] In Revelation 19:10 John mistakenly falls down to worship the angel, who reprimands him, "Do not do it! . . . Worship God!" Yet in this great vision, John has heard the Lamb described as worthy to receive power, wealth, wisdom, strength, honor, glory and praise (Rev 5:12–13).

One Septuagint rendering of Deuteronomy 32:43 commands "worship him, all you sons of God," and this specific version has been chosen by the writer to the Hebrews to show Christ's superiority to the angels; they are to worship him (Heb 1:6). The "one like the son of man" in Daniel 7:13–14 is worshiped. Jesus was worshiped during his life on earth by the magi (Matt 2:2, 11) the disciples (Matt 14:33; 28:9; Luke 24:52) and the man born blind (John 9:38). The specific vocabulary of worship will be discussed in the following chapter. Worthiness to be worshiped is essential to God's uniqueness and inclusion in this puts Jesus clearly on the God side of the dividing line.

Judge of All the Earth

In the Old Testament, God is consistently portrayed as Judge of the earth. A number of passages speak of the Lord coming in judgment, judging in righteousness (eg 1 Chr 16:33; Pss 50:6; 96:12–13; 98:9; Mic 4:3) and Isaiah 33:22 associates the roles of judge, lawgiver, king and savior with the Lord. This judgment will be with fire (Isa 66:15–16 and see 2 Thess 1:8 below).

The context of the judgment verses of Joel, such as 3:2, 12, is "the Day of the Lord" (2:28–32) which we know from the Apostle Peter refers directly to the work of the Lord Jesus Christ, on whose name one must call to be saved (Acts 2:16–21).

25. For a thorough discussion of monolatry as the corollary of monotheism, in contrast to polytheism and the concept of "intermediary" or semi-divine figures, see Bauckham, *Jesus and the God of Israel*, 11–17 and throughout.

There are clear hints in the Old Testament that the Messiah will actually be the one to administer divine judgment.

- There shall come forth a shoot from the stump of Jesse . . . with righteousness he will judge the poor, and decide with equity for the meek of the earth (Isa 11:1–4).

- But, O Lord of hosts, who judges righteously, who tests the heart and the mind, let me see your vengeance upon them, for to you have I committed my cause (Jer 11:20).

- I the Lord search the heart and test the mind, to give every man according to his ways, according to the fruit of his deeds (Jer 17:10).

In the New Testament, whom do we consistently find portrayed as the coming judge?

- The Father judges no one, but has given all judgment to the Son, that all may honor the Son, just as they honor the Father . . . And he has given him authority to execute judgment, because he is the Son of Man (John 5:22–23, 27).

- . . .when the Lord Jesus is revealed from heaven with his mighty angels in flaming fire, inflicting vengeance on those who do not know God and on those who do not obey the gospel of our Lord Jesus (2 Thess 1:7–8).

- I am he who searches mind and heart, and I will give to each of you according to your works (Rev 2:23; compare Jer 17:10).

- Then I saw heaven standing opened, and behold, a white horse! The one sitting on it is called Faithful and True, and in righteousness he judges and makes war (Rev 19:11).

The Lord Who Forgives

In the Old Testament, the LORD is the one who forgives sin.

- The LORD, the LORD, a God merciful and gracious, slow to anger, and abounding in steadfast love and faithfulness, keeping steadfast love for thousands, forgiving iniquity and transgression and sin . . . (Exod 34:6–7).

- [The LORD] who forgives all your iniquity, who heals all your diseases (Ps 103:3).

- I, I am he who blots out your transgressions for my own sake, and I will not remember your sins (Isa 43:25).

When Jesus healed the paralytic in Mark 2:5–12, he claimed the authority for forgiveness of sins, correctly assumed to be the prerogative of God alone. This forgiveness is the key to salvation, the work of the Lord for whom John was to prepare the way (see below) as foretold in Zechariah's song (Luke 1:76–77). Jesus forgave the sins of the penitent woman in Simon the leper's house and linked this with the declaration of her salvation (Luke 7:47–50).

In Acts 10:43 Peter goes so far as to say, "To him all the prophets bear witness that everyone who believes in him receives forgiveness of sins through his name." Peter is speaking of Jesus, whom God appointed as judge of the living and the dead. If we ask, where did "all" the prophets testify that forgiveness of sins comes through belief in Jesus?—we must conclude that where the prophets speak of the Lord's forgiveness, the referent is Jesus.

Christ As Lord at God's Right Hand

The resurrection began Christ's actual reign as Lord, seated at the right hand of God, the ultimate position of power and authority (Rom 8:34; Col 3:1; Eph 1:20–23).

> For to this end [context: belonging to the Lord] Christ died and lived again, that
> he might be Lord both of the dead and of the living (Rom 14:9).

Psalm 68 alternates between addressing or describing "God" and "the Lord." David makes it clear that the two are the same, in verse 4: "Sing to God, sing praises to his name; lift up a song to him who rides through the deserts; his name is the LORD; exult before him!" Also, verse 16 uses Hebrew poetic parallelism "the mount that God desired for his abode, yes, where the Lord himself will dwell forever." When we come to verses 17 and 18 the identity of God and Lord is still evident: "The chariots of God are twice ten thousand, thousands upon thousands; the Lord is among them . . . You ascended on high, leading a host of captives in your train and receiving gifts among men, even among the rebellious, that the Lord God may dwell there." This passage is quoted in Ephesians 4:8, speaking of the grace which Christ has apportioned to his people as a result of his death, resurrection and exaltation. Paul has specifically identified Christ with God the Lord.

This concept of the Christ as Lord at the right hand of God is the fulfilment of the most oft-quoted Old Testament text[26] in the New Testament—Psalm 110:1, which in the Septuagint reads

---

26. Bauckham sees Ps 110:1 as a key text for early Christology, cited across a wide range of NT and patristic literature and frequently linked with other texts such as Ps 8:6 and Dan 7:13–14 and in contexts which describe Christ's participation in God's sovereign rule over all things. See *Jesus and the God of Israel*, particularly 173–76.

ho kyrios	tō kyriō mou	kathou ek dexiōn mou
the lord	to the lord of me	sit at the right of me

In the Hebrew text, the first *kyrios* equates to YHWH, the second to *Adonay*, the Hebrew for "Lord." Accordingly, the Septuagint translates these instances as "Lord." In taking his place at the right hand of God, Jesus was exalted as Lord. Whilst he had been "Lord" to his disciples on earth (John 13:13 and elsewhere), his lordship entered a new universal phase, "in power" subsequent to his resurrection. Hence, Paul often refers to Jesus simply as "the Lord."

All three synoptic gospels (Matt 22:41–45; Mark 12:35–37; Luke 20:41–44) relate Jesus' challenge to the Pharisees regarding the interpretation of this passage. They had rightly identified that the Christ was the son of David, but they could see no further than this. David called Messiah *Kyrios*—Lord, which meant he was more than David's physical descendant. All three gospels go on to record Jesus' prediction before the Sanhedrin, that they would see the Son of Man sitting at the right hand of the Mighty One and coming on the clouds of heaven. This clear allusion to both Daniel 7:13 and Psalm 110:1 in Jesus' response to Caiaphas' question is a claim that he belongs right alongside God, worthy to judge and worthy to be worshiped.[27]

There are numerous references in the New Testament to Jesus sitting at the right hand of the Father; Acts 2:34; 5:31; Rom 8:34; Eph 1:20; Col 3:1; Heb 1:3; Heb 8:1; 10:12; 1 Pet 3:22. This is his exalted place, the position of ultimate and absolute power, and from which he makes intercession for his saints. What must be understood is that this is not a secondary position, as if there were one large throne for the Father and a separate, smaller throne off to the (right) side for the Son. On the contrary, there is but one throne in heaven. The divine throne in the highest heaven is a word-picture of the sovereignty of God over all things. The imagery of height (highest heaven, on high, Most High God, mountain of the Lord, etc.) reinforces this absolute sovereignty, as does the fact that in heaven God is the only one who sits. The angels and other creatures who attend him stand, as befits the posture of servants (1 Kgs 22:19).[28] This imagery of height is applied to Jesus in the New Testament (Eph 1:21; 4:10; Phil 2:9; Heb 1:3–4).

Psalm 45:6 addresses God thus: "Your throne, O God, is for ever and ever. The scepter of your kingdom is a scepter of righteousness . . ." The writer to the Hebrews specifically and unambiguously applies this to the Son (Heb 1:8) and goes on to address him with "You, Lord, laid the foundation of the earth in the beginning, and the heavens are the work of your hands" (Heb 1:10) and finishes with another strong

27. Jesus' claim to these two passages, Ps 110:1 and Dan 7:13 as a claim to divinity is discussed in detail in Bowman and Komoszewski, *Putting Jesus in His Place*, 243–49.

28. More detailed discussion of this imagery, including that found in Second Temple Jewish literature, may be found in Bauckham, *Jesus and the God of Israel*, 161–64.

allusion to the throne of God/the Lord with a citation of Psalm 110:1 in reference to sitting at the right hand of God (Heb 1:13).

Hebrews continues, demonstrating the Son's superiority to angels and Moses and the Levitical priesthood. In 4:16, speaking of Christ's priestly mediation, which is so strongly associated with Jesus' position at God's right hand, he exhorts us to approach the throne of grace with confidence. When Hebrews 12:2 speaks of Jesus *sitting down* at the right hand of God, the Greek expression is *en dexia*, with the dative case; literally "in the right hand," denoting togetherness rather than separation.

Likewise, in Revelation 3:21, Jesus speaks of sitting down with his Father on his throne (*en tō thronō autou*) again using *en* and the dative. It is a shared throne. In Revelation 7:15–17, those who have come out of the great tribulation serve God before his throne and he who sits on the throne spreads his tent over them, with the conclusion, "For the Lamb at the center of the throne will be their shepherd." (For discussion of the important shepherd motif, see below). In Revelation 20 through 22 the throne imagery recurs, but this time with some ambiguity as to who is on the throne.

- The one on the great white throne is evidently the judge (20:12–15), which we know from extensive evidence elsewhere is the Son, to whom judgment has been committed (20:11; also 21:27 specifies that it is the Lamb's book of life).

- A loud voice (whose?) announces from the throne that the dwelling of God is with men (21:3).

- He who is seated on the throne says, "I am making all things new" (21:5).

- This same Person says, "It is done! I am the Alpha and the Omega . . ." and invites all who thirst to come to him (21:6; 22:13 specifies that the Alpha and Omega is the one coming soon—Jesus).

- This same Person promises to be the God of any who overcome (21:7).

- The function of the temple, as God's dwelling amongst his people, has been taken up by "its temple [singular] is the Lord God almighty and the Lamb" (21:22).

- The throne [singular] of God and of the Lamb (22:1, 3).

With respect to Jesus sitting at God's right hand, far from showing that there is a separation of roles, the argument is clearly that their roles are merged and that Jesus occupies the same position of absolute sovereignty as God. With this in mind, we may look at another important Old Testament passage about God's throne which the New Testament interprets for us.

> In the year that King Uzziah died I saw the Lord sitting upon a throne, high and lifted up; and the train of his robe filled the temple. Above him stood the seraphim. Each had six wings: with two he covered his face, and with two he covered his feet, and with two he flew. And one called to another and said: "Holy, holy, holy is the LORD of hosts; the whole earth is full of his glory!" (Isa 6:1–3).

Isaiah was distressed because he, a man of unclean lips, had seen the King, the Lord Almighty. His sin was atoned for symbolically and the vision continues:

> And I heard the voice of the Lord saying, "Whom shall I send, and who will go for us?" Then I said, "Here am I! Send me." And he said, "Go, and say to this people: 'Keep on hearing, but do not understand; keep on seeing, but do not perceive.' Make the heart of this people dull, and their ears heavy, and blind their eyes; lest they see with their eyes, and hear with their ears, and understand with their hearts, and turn and be healed" (Isa 6:8–10).

The Apostle John quotes this passage in the context of the unbelief of the Jews in the face of Jesus' miraculous signs. Matthew 13:14–15 and Mark 4:12 also cite Isaiah 6:9–10 as being specifically fulfilled in the parabolic teaching of Jesus and the Jewish response of unbelief.

> Therefore they could not believe. For again Isaiah said, "He has blinded their eyes and hardened their heart, lest they see with their eyes, and understand with their heart, and turn, and I would heal them." Isaiah said these things because he saw his glory and spoke of him (John 12:39–41).

John is explicitly stating that the vision of the Lord which Isaiah saw, was of the Lord Jesus. Jesus, seated on the throne, the King, the Lord Almighty, attended by seraphs, his glory filling the earth. The theme is reiterated in Revelation 4:11. The scene is the throne in heaven, surrounded by living creatures, which proclaim day and night, "Holy, holy, holy, is the Lord God Almighty, who was and is and is to come . . . Worthy are you, our Lord and God, to receive glory and honor and power, for you created all things, and by your will they existed and were created." The theme repeats again in 5:12 where thousands of angels encircle the throne and sing, "Worthy is the Lamb who was slain, to receive power and wealth and wisdom and might and honor and glory and blessing . . . To him who sits on the throne and to the Lamb be blessing and honor and glory and might for ever and ever!" This is the glory of the Lord Jesus Christ, at the right hand of the Father, upon his throne.

Preparing the Way of the Lord

As we have seen, the coming judgment of God upon Israel and the nations was frequently spoken of in the prophets as "the Day of the Lord." It will be a day of destruction of the ungodly (Isa 13:6, 9; Joel 1:15) especially of the nations (Ezek 30:3; Obad :15) but also of vindication for the righteous and to uphold the cause of his people (Isa 34:8). It will be characterized by wrath, clouds, doom (Isa 13:9; Ezek 30:3) and darkness (Amos 5:18, 20). There is an urgency in the prophets' message—the day of the Lord is near and inevitable (Ezek 39:8; Zeph 1:14). The coming of the Day of the Lord will be preceded by the sending of the prophet Elijah (Mal 4:5).

In the New Testament, the same themes emerge, but it is clear that the Day of the Lord has become the Day of the Lord Jesus, which of course is what it was always intended to be in its ultimate fulfilment. It will be great and glorious and will be marked by darkness and fiery destruction. It will come like a thief and on this day those who are blameless in Christ will be saved. Whilst there were days of God's judgment on Israel in the past, Paul assures the Thessalonians that *the* Day of the Lord is yet to come (2 Thess 2:2). Added to these passages are those which speak of the day of the coming of the Son of Man, the return of the master, "that day," the last day, the day of our Lord Jesus Christ, and so forth, and we have a clear picture that the Lord who is associated with this "Day" in the Old Testament is the Lord Jesus Christ.

Malachi gives us some intriguing additional information. On the eve of about four hundred years of silence before the voice of a prophet was to be heard again in Israel, Malachi provided the bridge to the events immediately preceding the coming of Christ. Having berated the Jews who had returned from exile for their apathetic and God-dishonoring pseudo-worship, Malachi announces the coming of the day of the Lord.

> Behold, I send my messenger, and he will prepare the way before me. And the Lord whom you seek will suddenly come to his temple; and the messenger of the covenant in whom you delight, behold, he is coming, says the LORD of hosts. But who can endure the day of his coming, and who can stand when he appears? For he is like a refiner's fire and like fullers' soap (Mal 3:1–2).

There are two messengers in this passage; the first is "my messenger" who prepares the way before "me"—the "me" being the Lord Almighty, who is speaking here. The second is the "messenger of the covenant," whose coming will be difficult to endure and who will be a refiner and purifier (verses 2–3). In verse 5 this second messenger is further clarified: "Then I will draw near to you for judgment" says the Lord Almighty.

Then in chapter 4:5–6, in the closing verses of the Old Testament, The LORD Almighty speaks again of this day of judgment which will burn up the wicked and release those who fear his name. "Behold, I will send you Elijah the prophet before the great and awesome day of the LORD comes. And he will turn the hearts of fathers to their children and the hearts of children to their fathers; lest I come and strike the land with a decree of utter destruction."

In a strikingly similar passage in Isaiah 40 we learn more about the first messenger, the one who prepares: "A voice cries: in the wilderness prepare the way of the LORD; make straight in the desert a highway for our God . . . And the glory of the LORD shall be revealed" (Isa 40:3, 5). "Go on up to a high mountain, O Zion, herald of good news; lift up your voice with strength, O Jerusalem, herald of good news, lift it up, fear not; say to the cities of Judah, 'Behold your God!' Behold, the LORD God comes with might . . ." (Isa 40:9–10). In the Septuagint, the Greek word for the good news which is brought to Jerusalem; is *euaggelizō*, exactly the same word for preaching the gospel, or good news, in the New Testament. Just looking at these Old Testament passages in their own right we can see that a messenger will be sent to proclaim the imminent arrival of the Lord God himself, as judge and refiner. But when the expected Lord shows up, just as was predicted, it's *Jesus*.

There's no doubt that the voice calling in the wilderness, "Prepare the way of the Lord," is John the Baptist (Matt 3:3; Mark 1:3; Luke 3:4–6; John 1:23) and that John spoke of the one who would follow, who would winnow, gathering his wheat and burning the chaff, a metaphor for judgment (Matt 3:11–12; Luke 3:17). John is also specifically identified as Malachi's "my messenger" (Mark 1:2). The angel told Zechariah that John "will go before him [the Lord] in the spirit and power of Elijah, to turn the hearts of the fathers to the children, and the disobedient to the wisdom of the just, to make ready for the Lord a people prepared" (Luke 1:17). After John's birth, Zechariah foretold, "And you, child, will be called the prophet of the Most High; for you will go before the Lord to prepare his ways" (Luke 1:76). John is specifically said to have preached the good news—*euaggelizō*, (Luke 3:18). In John 1:30–31 John the Baptist testifies that the one coming after him surpasses him because he was before him, and that the reason he came baptizing was to reveal that one to Israel.

Just in case people missed it, John even dressed like Elijah (Matt 3:4; Mark 1:6; cf. 2 Kings 1:8)! And so there can be absolutely no room for doubt, Jesus identifies John as "Elijah who is to come" (Matt 11:14; 17:10–13; Mark 9:11–13). So if John the Baptist was the preparer/"my messenger"/voice/Elijah, then the One whose coming he announced must be the Messenger of the Covenant/the Lord Almighty/"Your God."

So, we can summarize as follows:

the preparer = John the Baptist	the Lord = Jesus
"my messenger" (Mal 3:1)	"Messenger of the covenant" (Mal 3:1)
will prepare the way before ME (Mal 3:1)	the Lord whom you seek [ME = Lord Almighty] in whom you delight (Mal 3:1)
	who can endure/ stand when he appears? He will purify/ refine (Mal 3:2–3)
	So I will come near to you for judgment says the Lord Almighty (Mal 3:5)

the preparer = John the Baptist	the Lord = Jesus
I will send you the prophet Elijah (Mal 4:5)	... before the day of the Lord (Mal 4:5)
the voice of one calling in the desert, "prepare the way of the Lord" (Isa 40:3)	The Lord (his way prepared by the one calling in the desert) (Isa 40:3)
the bringer of good tidings (Isa 40:9)	Here is your God! The Sovereign Lord comes with power (Isa 40:9, 10)

The faithful Jews of Jesus' day, discerning the meaning of these passages, would have immediately recognized John as the one preparing the way of "the Lord," the Lord God himself. And who shows up in fulfilment of this? Jesus of Nazareth! He was to be Immanuel—God with us (Matt 1:22–23 fulfilling Isa 7:14). Elizabeth recognized the significance of her relative Mary's baby; "And why is this granted to me that the mother of my *Lord* (*kyrios*) should come to me?" (Luke 1:43). The angels, announcing Jesus' birth to the shepherds, said, "For unto you is born this day in the city of David a Savior, who is Christ *the Lord*" (Luke 2:11, *kyrios*). To a first-century Jew, steeped in the ancient prophecies and familiar with them in the words of the Greek Scriptures, there was only one "Lord" that this could be.

The Lord Is My Shepherd

The shepherd motif is an important Old Testament descriptor of God. The most well known ascription of this role to God is found in Psalm 23:1, "The Lord is my shepherd, I shall not want." There are a number of other passages where God is described as shepherd of his people, for example Psalm 28:9; Psalm 80:1; Jeremiah 31:10. God also requires the human leaders of his people to play a shepherding role; the prototype of such a shepherd-king was of course David. Examples include 2 Samuel 7:7; 1 Kings 22:17; 1 Chronicles 11:2 and Psalm 78:71.

However, those in authority in Israel often failed to be good shepherds. Rather than tending the flock and servicing the needs of God's people as a priority, they served their own needs and desires. For example, Jeremiah 23:1–2; Zechariah 11:15–17. Ezekiel 34 is a particularly stinging indictment of the evil shepherds of Israel, who exploited the flock for their own gain and treated them brutally (Ezek 34:1–6). Because of this, God set himself against these shepherds (verses 7–10). Instead of relying on these shepherds, God himself declared he would be the shepherd of his people.

> For thus says the Lord GOD: "Behold, I, I myself will search for my sheep and will seek them out. As a shepherd seeks out his flock when he is among his sheep

that have been scattered, so will I seek out my sheep . . . I myself will be the shepherd of my sheep, and I myself will make them lie down," declares the Lord GOD. "I will seek the lost, and I will bring back the strayed, and I will bind up the injured, and I will strengthen the weak, and the fat and the strong I will destroy. I will feed them in justice" (Ezek 34:11–16).

But then a little later in verses 23 and 24, God seems to delegate this job to his servant David. "And I, the LORD, will be their God, and my servant David shall be prince among them." In verse 31 he concludes, "And you are my sheep, human sheep of my pasture, and I am your God, declares the LORD God." In Isaiah 40:10–11 "the LORD God comes with might . . . He will tend his flock like a shepherd: he will gather the lambs in his arms; he will carry them in his bosom, and gently lead those that are with young." In Micah 5:1–4 we read of the one who will come out of Bethlehem Ephrathah to be ruler over Israel. This ruler's origins (literally, out-goings) are from the beginning and from days of eternity. This ruler will stand and shepherd his flock in the strength of the Lord, in the majesty (glory) of the name of the Lord his (LXX lit. *their*) God.

So it should come as no surprise that the Shepherd who can so take this role of God is the Lord Jesus. In John 10, hard on the heels of his denunciation of the Pharisees for their spiritual blindness and callous treatment of the man born blind, he essentially accuses them of being thieves and robbers breaking into the sheepfold. Then he announces (one of the *ego eimi* sayings) "I am the good shepherd." The contrast would have drawn his audience's minds to passages such as Ezekiel 34. Hebrews 13:20 describes the Lord Jesus as "the great shepherd of the sheep." Peter describes Jesus as "the Shepherd and Overseer of your souls" (1 Pet 2:25) and "the chief Shepherd" (1 Pet 5:4). In Revelation 7:17, it is declared that "For the Lamb in the midst of the throne will be their shepherd, and he will guide them to springs of living water, and God will wipe away every tear from their eyes." Once again we see Jesus assuming a role and title ascribed in the Old Testament to God himself and, furthermore, as the fulfilment of the prophecies whereby the LORD God shepherds his people.

Summary

The New Testament sheds unexpected light upon many Old Testament themes and passages, directly and indirectly attributing to Jesus a number of titles, prerogatives, deeds, and attributes of God. These include:

- Presence and active involvement in creation
- The title "I am"
- The title "Lord" and Lordship over all
- Worthy of worship

- Judge of all the earth

- Forgiveness of sins

- Seated at the right hand of the Father, with him on his throne

- The coming of God in the foretold "Day of the Lord"

- Shepherd of his people

Further Reading

- T. Alan Christophe, *Jesus is Lord.*

- Larry W. Hurtado, *One God, One Lord: Early Christian Devotion and Ancient Jewish Monotheism* and *Lord Jesus Christ: Devotion to Jesus in Earliest Christianity.*

- Christopher Wright, *The Mission of God.*

- Richard Bauckham, *Jesus and the God of Israel.* Includes the previously published *God Crucified.*

4

The Divinity of Jesus in the New Testament

The New Testament gives us the most detailed revelation of who Jesus is. There are some explicit statements and a large body of descriptive evidence that attest to the divinity of the Lord Jesus Christ. Bowman and Komoszewski have usefully organized this evidence within a systematic structure.[1]

- Jesus shares the honors due to God

- Jesus shares the attributes of God

- Jesus shares the names of God

- Jesus shares in the deeds that God does

- Jesus shares God's throne

Christadelphians tackle this evidence in various ways and some writers go further than others in the extent to which they regard Jesus as "divine." However, all Christadelphians assert that Jesus' divinity was not *intrinsically* his as the preexistent Son, but rather was bestowed on him because he was a man who perfectly manifested his Father's attributes. This chapter presents the New Testament case for the intrinsic, preexistent divinity of Christ.

Misconception #4: That Jesus's divinity is an appellation bestowed on him at his exaltation; he is not intrinsically divine and his "preexistence" is to be understood metaphorically.

Corrective: Scripture teaches that Jesus shares the attributes, names and works of God and is due the honor accorded to God. The literal preexistence of the Son is clear from Scripture.

---

1. This excellent, detailed but readable book on the deity of Christ is Bowman and Komoszewski, *Putting Jesus in His Place*. These authors systematically discuss Jesus's deity using the anacronym HANDS: Jesus possesses the Honour, Attributes, Names of God, does the Deeds and shares the Seat (throne) of God. They also address a number of Jehovahs Witnesses's arguments against Christ's deity, some of which are aligned with Christadelphian thinking and some of which are not.

Misconception #5: That Christadelphians are Unitarians who deny any attribution of divinity to Jesus

Corrective: Christadelphians acknowledge that Christ was in a sense divine, but see it as a derived rather than an intrinsic divinity, a reward for what he accomplished, which was bestowed at his exaltation.

God With Us

Matthew, having explained that Mary would conceive her son by the Holy Spirit, states that this is a direct fulfilment of Isaiah 7:14: "Behold, the virgin shall conceive and will give birth to a son, and shall call his name Immanuel"—which means, "God with us." "God" here takes the article, *ho Theos*, literally "the God," which Scripture uses for God himself rather than a god generally. So this child would be God, with us. John takes a somewhat different but equally explicit tack. The prologue of his gospel account[2] declares,

> In the beginning was the Word, and the Word was with God, and the Word was God. He was in the beginning with God. All things were made through him, and without him was not anything made that was made . . . And the Word became flesh and dwelt among us, and we have seen his glory, glory as of the only Son from the Father, full of grace and truth. (1:1–3, 14)

"In the beginning" reminds the reader immediately of the very beginning, in Genesis 1.[3] Verse 2 reinforces that the Word was there at the beginning and verse 3 continues the connection with creation. There can be no doubt what John's context is.

But who or what is the Word? Evidently it is that which became flesh and dwelt among us, the one and only who came from the Father. Although the Greek word *logos* had a wide meaning in first-century Greek, including a rational principle, inner thought, reason, outward expression, speech, or message, we do not need to examine secular Greek usage, because there is plenty of foundation in the Old Testament. The Hebrew word for "word," *dabar*, is connected with God's powerful creating, revelatory and saving activity. We read that "the word of the Lord came to . . ." or "by the word of the Lord," or "God sent forth his word" (Gen 1:3 and following; Ps 33:6; Jer 1:4; Isa 9:8; Ezek 33:7; Ps 107:20; Isa 55:11). In the Jewish inter-testamental literature the "word" is often personified, as is the wisdom of God. Jewish and Gentile readers alike would relate to the richness of meaning in John's use of the word *logos*.

> In short, God's "Word" in the Old Testament is his powerful self-expression in creation, revelation and salvation, and the personification of the "Word" makes

2. I am indebted to the work of Carson, *John* for the underlying scholarship of this section.

3. Christadelphians deny that John 1 teaches the literal preexistence of the Son, but rather expresses Christ's preexistence in the mind of God. Paul Wyns interprets the "beginning" in John 1:1 to signify the beginning of the new creation in Jesus' ministry and resurrection: Wyns, "Jesus in John's Writings," 76–77.

THE DIVINITY OF JESUS IN THE NEW TESTAMENT

it suitable for John to apply it as a title to God's ultimate self-disclosure, the person of his own Son.[4]

This is essentially what the writer to the Hebrews also says in Hebrews 1:1–2. Christadelphian commentators such as Ron Abel,[5] arguing against the preexistence and deity of the Word, tend to place their emphasis on the impersonal uses of *dabar* and *logos* in Scripture, as if that proved that this must be John's intention too. This is equivalent to arguing that Jesus can't really be "the light of the world" because everywhere else the word *phos*, "light," simply means electromagnetic radiation in the visible spectrum. Because the semantic range and literary usage of the word *logos* are so broad, these uses cannot themselves determine precisely what John meant by *logos*. For that, we must listen to what John himself says. John insists that the Word, this preexistent self-expression of God was both with God, and nothing less than God himself. This is the plain meaning of the passage:

ho logos ēn	*pros ton theov*	*kai theos*	*ēn ho logos*
the word was	with (the) God	and God	the-word-was

Pros is a preposition which attends the accusative case, and may mean "to" or "toward," but can mean "with" when its object is a person, usually expressing an intimate relationship (compare its use in Mark 6:3; 2 Cor 5:8; Phlm 1:13; 1 John 1:2). The implication is that the Word was in personal relationship with God.

Furthermore, John says the Word was God. At this point, Christadelphian and Jehovah's Witness commentators will usually appeal to the Watchtower Society's translation of this passage; "The Word was a god."[6] This translation is virtually unique and runs counter to accepted understanding of Greek grammar. "Word" and "God" here both take the nominative case. One is the subject and the other is the complement (predicative nominative): the thing that the subject *is*. In English, the subject and predicate are distinguished by word order; not so in Greek. In Greek, word order is used for emphasis. The grammatical function is determined by which noun takes the article, that being the subject. Hence *ho logos*, "the Word," is the subject. The complement or predicate, with which the Word is equated, *necessarily* drops the article, and is typically placed before the verb. Far from excluding the equation of the Word with God, it emphasizes it, particularly since *Theos* ("God") has been brought to

4. Carson, *John*, 116.

5. Abel, *Wrested Scriptures*, 285–86.

6. The *Emphatic Diaglott*, or New World Translation is cited, for example, in Abel, *Wrested Scriptures*, 286. Interestingly, "God" appears without the article in verses 6, 12, 13, and 18 of John 1, but is comfortably translated "God" and Christadelphian commentators are strangely silent on this point of inconsistency.

the beginning of the clause. Thus the meaning is effectively, "*GOD* is what the Word was."[7] It must be understood at this point that the passage is *not* saying "The Word was the Father" or that the Word is all that there is to God (more of that later). It is wise to not rest one's theology on nuances of grammar, however it is Christadelphians and Jehovah's Witnesses who have mounted the challenge here, and the weight of grammatical evidence supports the orthodox understanding of the passage.

Jesus Christ, the Word made flesh, is elsewhere addressed or described as God. John's opening words make this identification, and so too does the climax of the book. In John 20:28, Thomas addresses Christ as "My Lord and my God!" Now, if ever there was an opportunity for Jesus to correct a most fundamental theological error, it was now. But we don't hear Jesus saying, "Why do you call me God, there is no God but the Father," or some similar contradiction. Instead, this affirmation by Thomas leads into Jesus' positive appraisal of his declaration: "Have you believed because you have seen me? Blessed are those who have not seen and yet have believed." Furthermore, John takes this opportunity to attach his purpose statement for the whole gospel to this exchange between Thomas and Jesus; ". . . that you may believe that Jesus is the Christ, the Son of God, and that by believing you may have life in his name" (John 20:30–31).[8]

Returning to John's prologue, having established that the Word was involved in creation, that "in him was life," and that the world which he made did not recognize or receive him, verse 14 states expressly that "The Word became flesh and dwelt among us, and we have seen his glory, glory as of the only Son from the Father, full of grace and truth." There is a tremendous amount of impact in this passage. First, the Word became flesh. That is simply what the word incarnation means; from the Latin *carne*, flesh; the in-fleshing of the Word. God's very self-expression became humanity; "in these last days he has spoken to us by his Son . . . through whom also he created the world" (Heb 1:1–2). The juxtaposition of the verb *skenoō* (to tabernacle, spread a tent, dwell) and the noun *doxa*, glory, is significant. The related noun to *skenoō* is *skēnē*, used for the tabernacle, and for the tent David pitched for the ark in Jerusalem, and for tents generally. There is an association between God's dwelling and his glory, as can be seen in these passages:

- Then the cloud covered the tent of meeting, and the glory of the LORD filled the tabernacle (Exod 40:34).

- Then all the congregation said to stone them with stones. But the glory of the LORD appeared at the tent of meeting to all the people of Israel (Num 14:10).

---

7. Mounce, *Basics of Biblical Greek*, 28; Wenham, *Elements of New Testament Greek*, 35. Another example of this structure would be *ho Theos agapē estin*, "God is love" in 1 John 4:16. As an abstract noun, *agapē*, love, would normally have a definite article, but it drops it here as the complement.

8. Two other passages referring to Christ as God are of interest at this point. Rom 9:5, "Christ, who is God over all," and Heb 1:8; "Your throne, O God."

- O LORD, I love the habitation of your house and the place where your glory dwells (Ps 26:8).

This is the idea of the Shekinah glory, the dwelling-glory of God in the tabernacle and in the temple; the visible manifestation of God (eg., 1 Kgs 8:10–11; Ezek 10). The incarnate Word is the true *shekinah*, the ultimate manifestation of the presence of God among men.

> He is the radiance of the glory of God and the exact imprint of his nature, and he upholds the universe by the word of his power (Heb 1:3).

> And I heard a loud voice from the throne saying, "Behold, the dwelling place of God is with man. He will dwell with them, and they will be his people, and God himself will be with them as their God" (Rev 21:3).

John and his fellow witnesses saw the glory of the Word made flesh; Jesus' glory was displayed in his signs (John 2:11; 11:4, 40) and he was supremely glorified in his death, resurrection and exaltation (John 7:39; 12:16, 23; 13:31–32). This glory is God's merciful, just and gracious character (Exod 33:18–19; 34:6–7), most fully displayed in the cross of Christ. "No one has ever seen God," says John, then concludes his prologue with the corrective, "the only God, who is at the Father's side, he has made him known" (John 1:18). This revelation supersedes the revelation of God to Moses; compare John 1:14, 17.

> And now, Father, glorify me in your own presence with the glory that I had with you before the world existed (John 17:5).

This glory of the Word made flesh is the glory of the only Son (ESV) or One and Only (NIV). This is a more accurate rendering than "only begotten" (KJV). The phrase is

doxan hos monogenous para patros

glory as/that one-of-a-kind from father

Monogenēs is used to translate "only" in the sense of an only or dearest son, as in Hebrews 11:17. The root word is *genea*, meaning a race, kind or generation. *Monogenēs* then means the only one of its kind within a specific relationship, one of a kind, unique.[9] It does not mean begettal or birth. Later in verse 18, John uses this expression again: "the only God," (ESV) or "God the One and Only," (NIV) who is at the Father's side, has made him known.

---

monogenēs Theos ho ōn   *eis ton kolpon tou patros*   *ekeinos exēgēsato*

---

9. BDAG, 658. Wayne Grudem explains that the words "only begotten" which have generated much controversy are in fact an inappropriate translation; modern translations read "one and only." This is confirmed by use of the same expression in Heb 11:17, describing Isaac not as Abraham's only begotten son, but his unique son; the son of the promise. Grudem, *Systematic Theology*, 1233–34.

one-of-a-kind God the one-being	in the bosom of the father	that one he made known

"The one-being one-of-a-kind God" is all in the nominative case, and together forms the subject of the clause. The one who is the one-of-a-kind, God, is the one who came from the Father, full of grace and truth, whose glory John saw.

Some Other Interesting Verses

A number of other passages are used to support the divinity of Christ. Some do not have clear-cut or unanimously agreed translations. Nevertheless, we need to tackle them, as they are recognized bones of contention between Christadelphian and mainstream interpreters.

> Pay careful attention to yourselves and to all the flock, of which the Holy Spirit has made you overseers, to care for the church of God, which he obtained with his own blood (Acts 20:28).

The Greek reads

poimainein tēn ekklēsian tou Theou,	*hēn periepoiēsato*	*dia tou haimatos tou idiou,*
to shepherd the church of God,	which he obtained	through the blood of his own

Most English translations take "of his own" to refer back to God, because there is no other referent in the context of the verse. An alternate rendering by the NRS adds the word *hiou*, Son, to render it "which he obtained by the blood of his own Son." Although there are a few textual variants of this passage in the extant manuscripts, none inserts the word "Son." Either rendering is theologically and grammatically appropriate, but it is interesting that the text says what it says in the way that it does. Whilst it may not be specifying God's own blood, it certainly can't be argued that the word Son is grammatically essential or original to the passage.

> To them (the Jews) belong the patriarchs, and from their race, according to the flesh, is the Christ, who is God over all, blessed for ever. Amen (Rom 9:5).

kai ex hōn ho Christos	to kata sarka,	ho hōn epi pantōn Theos	eulogētos eis tous aiōnas
and from whom the Christ	according to the flesh	the one being over all God	blessed into the age

Eulogētos (blessed) is an adjective descriptive of *Theos* (God), and has dropped the article ("the") which is consistent with "blessed God" being the complement of "the Christ."

Two different translations have been offered[10] for this final line:

1. "and from whom is the Christ, according to the flesh, the one who is God over all, blessed forever"

2. "and from whom is the Christ, according to the flesh. God who is over all be blessed forever."

The second translation would suit the Christadelphian position, and is supported by many scholars. However, it has some weaknesses: the word order is awkward and inconsistent with comparable passages. The natural antecedent of *ho ōn*, the one being or one-who-is, is the immediately preceding noun, "the Christ."

The majority of mainstream scholars prefer the first option; it makes better sense grammatically and also within the context of Paul's argument in this part of Romans. "According to the flesh" carries negative connotations; that is the way Israel was thinking—they had a "fleshly" view of Christ and were seeking justification by their own works. The antithesis of this is provided by the doxology to Christ and correlates with Romans 1:3–4 "who was descended from David according to the flesh and was declared to be the Son of God in power according to the Spirit of holiness."

> On the one hand, there is no denying the roots of the messianic expectation and the cultural origins of Jesus; but, on the other hand, resistance to recognizing Jesus as the Christ involved the question of his divinity, which Paul boldly claims at the end of this introduction . . . This sets the stage for arguing in 10:9 that confessing Jesus as "Lord" leads to salvation, and in 10:12 that Jesus is Lord of all. If salvation results from calling on the "name of the Lord" (10:13), then the salvation of "all Israel" in 11:26 would entail their recognition that Jesus is "really God over all things" (9:5).[11]

> Waiting for our blessed hope, the appearing of the glory of our great God and Savior Jesus Christ, who gave himself for us to redeem us from all lawlessness

---

10. I am indebted here to the exegesis and commentary of Jewett, *Romans*, 567–68.

11. Jewett, *Romans*, 568.

and to purify for himself a people for his own possession who are zealous for good works (Titus 2:13–14).

There is only one subject in this passage, not two. "Our great God and savior" is Jesus Christ, the one whose appearing we await, who gave himself for us and purified for himself a people. Great, God, savior and Jesus Christ are all in the genitive singular, appearance is singular and there is only one "and"—Jesus Christ is God and savior. It twists the plain meaning of the Greek to translate this as "the glorious appearing of our great God *and of* our savior Jesus Christ," as if there were two separate subjects. There are no textual variants for this passage which would support such a rendering.[12]

The Lord Our Savior

We are very familiar with the appellation of "savior" to Jesus. His very name means "YHWH saves;" He was given the name Jesus because he would save his people from their sins (Matt 1:21). Jesus is frequently referred to as our savior, often in conjunction with the divine title "Lord." The following passages specifically refer to Jesus as savior: Luke 2:11; John 4:42; Acts 5:31; 13:23; Eph 5:23; Phil 3:20; 2 Tim 1:10; Titus 1:4; 3:6; 2 Pet 1:11; 2:20; 3:2, 18; 1 John 4:14.

To a first-century Jew steeped in the Old Testament however, there would be only one person who had the right to the title "savior," and that of course is Israel's God. There are over thirty occasions in the Old Testament where the Lord God is described as Savior, both personally and corporately. In fact, the teaching of the law and prophets was clear that there is no savior besides God.

- I, I am the LORD, and besides me there is no savior (Isa 43:11).

- Declare and present your case; let them take counsel together! Who told this long ago? Who declared it of old? Was it not I, the LORD? And there is no other god besides me, a righteous God and a Savior; there is none besides me (Isa 45:21).

- But I am the LORD your God from the land of Egypt; you know no God but me, and besides me there is no savior (Hos 13:4).

This teaching is reiterated in the New Testament, which refers to God as savior, interspersed with references to Jesus Christ as savior: 1 Timothy 1:1; 2:3, 4:10; Titus 1:3; 2:10; 3:4; Jude 1:25. So who is the only Savior? The answer is obvious; God *and* Jesus, without contradiction, for as we saw in Titus 2:13–14, Jesus Christ is "our God and savior." A similar conjunction is found in 2 Peter, in fact 2 Peter and the pastoral

12. Bowman and Komoszewski make reference to the work of grammarian Granville Sharp who established that this construction of singular personal nouns refer in this way to a single person, for example Mark 6:3; John 20:17; Col 4:7; Heb 12:2; Gal 1:4; Jude 4 among many others. Bowman and Komoszewski, *Putting Jesus in His Place*, 151–52.

epistles (1 and 2 Timothy and Titus) are rich in passages about God *and* Jesus being our savior, effectively alternating between the two without distinction.

> Simeon Peter, a servant and apostle of Jesus Christ, To those who have obtained a faith of equal standing with ours by the righteousness of our God and Savior Jesus Christ (2 Pet 1:1).

Consider these closely approximated passages in Titus:

1:3 God our Savior	1:4 Christ Jesus our Savior
2:10 God our Savior	2:13 our great God and Savior, Jesus Christ
3:4 God our Savior	3:6 Jesus Christ our Savior

Bowman and Komoszewski note three things about the title "Savior" as applied to Jesus. First, the New Testament calls Jesus Savior in an ultimate, cosmic sense; he is "the Savior of the world" (John 4:42). Second, the New Testament calls Jesus Savior in conjunction with the divine titles "Lord" and "God." Third, the New Testament calls Jesus our Savior in the same breath that it calls God our Savior, as we see in Titus and elsewhere.[13] They also make the important point that when the Bible uses names and titles of God for Jesus, such as Lord, Savior, Shepherd, Rock, Bridegroom, it does so in contexts that also establish or proclaim his divinity.

> These three contextual factors—that Jesus receives an array of divine names, often in the same passage; that Jesus often receives these divine names in allusions to, or quotations from, Old Testament texts speaking about God; that Jesus receives these designations in reference to his divine honors, attributes, works and position, in relation to all creation—are closely related. They converge in such a way as to prove that when the Bible calls Jesus by such names as Lord and God, it is applying those names to him in the highest possible sense.[14]

The Image and Form of God

Jesus as the Image of God

There is a variety of Hebrew words for "image" or idol in the Old Testament, translated by various Greek words. When Scripture speaks of the image of God, however, the word is *eikōn*, in the Septuagint and New Testament. The actual formula *eikōn tou*

---

13. Bowman and Komoszewski, *Putting Jesus in His Place*, 174–76. See also p. 171–73 for a discussion of God and Jesus as the bridegroom/husband.

14. Ibid., 128–29.

Theou, "image of God," occurs in very few texts, and the three Old Testament references are all variations on the first.[15]

- Then God said, "Let us make man[kind] in our image [Heb *tselem*; LXX *eikōn*], after our likeness [Heb *demuth*; LXX *homoiosis*]. And let them have dominion over the fish of the sea and over the birds of the heavens and over the livestock and over all the earth and over every creeping thing that creeps on the earth" (Gen 1:26).

- So God created man in his own image [*tselem/eikōn*], in the image of God he created him; male and female he created them (Gen 1:27).

- Whoever sheds the blood of man, by man shall his blood be shed, for God made man in his own image [*tselem/eikōn*] (Gen 9:6).

A related passage is Genesis 5:1–3 which speaks of humanity being made in the likeness [*demuth*/ LXX *idea*] of God, and Seth in the image [*tselem/eikōn*] of Adam. The New Testament uses this concept with reference to Christ and those in Christ, in which the image marred by sin is being renewed.

Here are some further verses containing *eikōn*.

- For those whom he foreknew he also predestined to be conformed to the image [*eikōn*] of his Son, in order that he might be the firstborn among many brothers (Rom 8:29).

- For a man ought not to cover his head, since he is the image [*eikōn*] and glory of God (1 Cor 11:7).

- Just as we have borne the image [*eikōn*] of the man of dust, we shall also bear the image [*eikōn*] of the man of heaven (1 Cor 15:49).

- The light of the gospel of the glory of Christ, who is the image [*eikōn*] of God (2 Cor 4:4).

- He [the Son] is the image [*eikōn*] of the invisible God, the firstborn of all creation (Col 1:15).

- And have put on the new self, which is being renewed in knowledge after the image [*eikōn*] of its creator (Col 3:10).

- With [the tongue] we curse people who are made in the likeness [*homoiosin*] of God (Jas 3:9).

Interestingly, Hebrews 1:3 does not use either *eikōn* or *homoiosin* to describe how Christ "images" (KJV) God. Instead, the words are:

---

15. I am indebted to the scholarship of Sherlock, "Human Wholeness," 41–60 for some of this discussion on the image of God.

hos ōn apaugasma tēs doxēs	*kai charaktēr tēs hupostaseōs autou*
who being radiance/reflection of the glory	and exact likeness/imprint of the substance of him

None of these passages tell us what precisely the image of God is. There are various interpretations, but whether "the image" relates to a physical, intellectual, spiritual, relational, or occupational property (such as dominion over the earth) remains open to discussion.

> There is a great danger in trying to locate the image of God in some aspect of humanity. To imagine we can *define* the image of God is to break the commandment. It leads to a wrong understanding of God and of ourselves. If we could define the image, we would be defining God, making him in our image . . . We should cease trying to locate the image in some aspect or other—or even any combination of aspects. We are not told what the image of God is, and should not expect to know![16]

Although Scripture does not tell us *what* the image of God is, it does tell us *who* the image is; Christ, the firstborn over all creation (Col 1:15; Heb 1:3). So Jesus claims, "Have I been with you so long, and you still do not know me, Philip? Whoever has seen me has seen the Father. How can you say, 'Show us the Father?'" (John 14:9). When speaking of Jesus as the image of God, we must not think of "image" as a lifeless or inanimate copy of the original, but something which partakes of the reality and nature of the original. For example, the law was a *shadow(skia)*, not the *true form* (*eikōn*) of the good things to come (Heb 10:1).

Jesus As the Firstborn

What does it mean that Christ is the firstborn? It could be implied that this means first-made, that Christ is a creature of the Father. This was the position taken by the Arians (and modern day Jehovah's Witnesses), but it is incorrect. We have seen that creation is attributed to Christ, which is a strong argument against him being himself created; more about this shortly. The word for firstborn is *prōtotokos*, and it is used throughout the Old Testament to refer to the eldest son who held the family birthright (eg., Esau, Manasseh, Reuben), those who were slain by the destroying angel in Egypt and those who were consecrated to God (Exod 13:2). In contrast to a large number of Old Testament references, there are only eight in the New Testament, one of which refers back to the slaying of the Egyptian firstborn (Heb 11:28), one is plural in reference to the members of the church (Heb 12:23), while all the rest refer to Jesus.

16. Sherlock, "Human Wholeness," 47.

- Jesus was the firstborn son of Mary (Luke 2:7).

- Jesus is the firstborn from the dead (Col 1:18; Rev 1:5).

- He is the "firstborn," brought into the world, whom the angels are summoned to worship (Heb 1:6).

- He is the firstborn of all creation (Col 1:15).

- He is the firstborn of many brothers, by virtue of our conforming to his image (Rom 8:29).

Because these New Testament references are few and diverse we need to look at the Old Testament context to derive the meaning of the expression and how it would have been understood as applying to Jesus, when the New Testament texts were written. In its most literal sense it pertains to birth order, but it also carries the meaning of the special status associated with a firstborn.[17] The firstborn received a double portion of the father's goods (Deut 21:17). David is appointed "firstborn" in Ps 89:27, i.e., "the highest of the kings of the earth," even though he was neither the eldest of Jesse's sons nor the first legitimate king of Israel. This is why God claims that Israel (Exod 4:22) the Levites (Num 8:18) and Ephraim (Jer 31:9) are his firstborn sons, without contradiction. Thus to call Jesus the firstborn is a comment on his status, not his origin. This is abundantly clear in Colossians 1:15–20, which explains the supremacy of Jesus in detail through the following attributes:

- He is the image [eikōn] of the invisible God.

- He is the firstborn of all creation—because by him and for him all things were created, in heaven and on earth.

- He is before all things.

- In him all things hold together.

- He is the head of the church.

- He is the beginning and the firstborn from the dead—so that in all things he might be preeminent.

- All God's fullness dwells in him.

- Through him all things are reconciled to God.

So, far from implying that Jesus Christ is a created being, this passage reinforces his supremacy over and separateness from creation. This participation in God's rule is further highlighted by the reference to "all things" or "heaven and earth." God is

17. There is a fascinating theme running through the OT narratives of the failure of the natural firstborn and the elevation of younger sons to the status of firstborn; the only "firstborn" who truly deserved the rights of firstborn was Jesus—all the others were a disappointment. Consider Cain, Ishmael, Esau, Reuben, Manasseh, David's elder brothers, David's sons, etc.

distinguished from "all things" and rules over "all things" because he created them (Isa 44:24; 66:2; Rom 11:36). Creation and sovereign rule over "all things" (including angels) are also attributed to Christ (Matt 11:27; John 1:3; 3:35; 13:3; Eph 1:10, 22; 4:10; Col 1:16–20; Heb 1:2–14).

Fullness and Emptying

All of God's fullness dwells in Christ (Col 1:19; 2:9). The Greek word is *plērōma*, which carries the idea of filling to completion. What, then, would we consider to be lacking? In Christ, as part of his body, Christians partake of this fullness (Eph 1:22–23; 3:19; 4:13; Col 2:10).

> What Paul says about Christ . . . is that all the fullness of what constitutes God dwells bodily in Christ. The presence and nature of God is totally or wholly ("all" or "whole") found in Christ; it is fully ("fullness") found in Christ; it is found in him personally ("in him"); and it is found in him bodily. It is difficult to imagine a more forceful, emphatic affirmation that Jesus Christ literally embodies God's very being . . . in the case of Christ it resides in him personally and bodily, whereas in our case that fullness is mediated to us through our relationship with Christ.[18]

Another important passage which describes the relationship of Jesus to Deity warrants detailed discussion.

> Have this mind among yourselves, which is yours in Christ Jesus, who, though he was in the form of God, did not count equality with God a thing to be grasped, but made himself nothing, taking the form of a servant, being born in the likeness of men. And being found in human form, he humbled himself by becoming obedient to the point of death, even death on a cross. Therefore God has highly exalted him and bestowed on him the name that is above every name, so that at the name of Jesus every knee should bow, in heaven and on earth and under the earth, and every tongue confess that Jesus Christ is Lord, to the glory of God the Father (Phil 2:5–11).

The context of this passage is an exhortation to humility in imitation of Christ. It is regarded as being an early Christian hymn, either written by Paul or appropriated by him to illustrate his point.[19] Ron Abel, in his ironically titled work *Wrested Scriptures*, argues against a trinitarian interpretation of this passage by misinterpreting the trinitarian position and the correct theological understanding of the *kenosis* or emptying which the Son underwent. Arguing against an erroneous interpretation of a theological position does not prove that the position is false, and this is a consistent problem with many Christadelphian attacks on orthodox theology.

---

18. Bowman and Komoszewski, *Putting Jesus in His Place*, 77.

19. Schreiner, *Paul*, 168–73 provides a readable and sensible exegesis of this passage.

If "in the form of God" means the very nature of God, then Christ could not have been "Very God" while on earth, as trinitarians assert, since this is what he is said to have sacrificed and left behind in coming to the earth. [20]

Abel also asserts "The NIV translation is inexcusable and betrays the theological position of the translators. The Greek word *morphē* (translated "form" in the AV) does not refer to "essential nature" as the trinitarian cause requires . . . *Eidos*, not *morphē* is the Greek word which conveys the idea of essential nature." Abel goes on to select two lexicons which allegedly provide support for his theological position, as against "The majority of lexicographers (who) blatantly import into their explanation of this word their belief in the trinity. Trinitarians will be able to muster far more lexicon articles in support of their views."

Now, this simply will not do. Abel is saying in effect, "I will select the lexico-graphical evidence (albeit in the minority) which supports my theological position, and that's fine, and I will set it against all the other lexicographical evidence which is invalid because it supports the trinitarian position." This is quite unacceptable scholarship, especially given the unfortunate Christadelphian propensity to prefer obscure, biased and often incorrect translations and interpretations (eg., the New World Translation) over established works of scholarship. His is a circular argument; "This interpretation is biased and wrong because it supports the Trinity; the Trinity cannot be proven from these passages because they are biased and wrong." So let's meet his two assertions head-on; that trinitarians believe that Christ left his essential nature behind when he came to earth, and that *morphē* does not mean "nature."

Firstly, the meaning of *morphē*. The essential meaning is form, outward appearance or shape,[21] which is evident in passages such as Daniel 3:19 where the form of Nebuchadnezzar's face alters toward the three Jews, and in Mark 16:12 where Jesus appears in "another form" to two disciples after his resurrection. However, as with many words in the rich Greek vocabulary, there are other layers and perspectives depending on the context. Romans 2:20 attacks the Jewish false security in their possession of the law which has the embodiment (*morphē*; "form" in the KJV) of knowledge and truth. The law did not just have the outward appearance of knowledge and truth; Psalm 119 has some 176 verses which argue to the contrary; indeed the Law of God *embodies* knowledge and truth as the ESV and NIV translate here. In Galatians 4:19 we have the related verb *morphoō*, to form or shape; Paul says he is in the pains of childbirth until Christ is formed in his readers. Doubtless Paul would not be satisfied with the mere outward appearance of Christ-likeness in the Galatians.

In Philippians 2, *morphē* is used twice; once for Christ being in the form of God, secondly for Christ taking the form of a servant. It is unreasonable to think that Paul has used the same word completely differently in such closely related verses. So if Christ only had the outward, superficial appearance of God, then he also had only

20. Abel, *Wrested Scriptures*, 304–5.
21. BDAG, 659.

the outward, superficial appearance of a servant. If he really took on the nature of a servant, then he also had the nature of God. Millard Erickson[22] claims that *morphē* denotes "the set of characteristics which constitutes a thing what it is . . . the genuine nature of a thing." Erickson contrasts this with the word *schēma*, which can also be translated "form," but in the sense of superficial appearance rather than substance. It is this word which is used in Philippians 2:8 "and being found in appearance (*schēma*) as a man . . ."

Abel asserts that the Greek word *eidos*, rather than *morphē*, is the appropriate term for essential nature and argues (from a vacuum) that if this is what Paul meant by Christ being in nature God, then this is the word he would have used. We must disagree, and draw our understanding from the Apostle's actual choice of vocabulary, rather than the other way around. *Eidos* definitely means the outward appearance, the shape and structure as it appears to someone, or even the act of seeing, and is related to the verb *eidenai* (to perceive by sight) and the *eidōl-* word group (from which we get the term idol) which describe various cultic images.[23]

Schreiner is therefore wise in his proposal that, "The safest way to resolve this debate is to confine ourselves to the existing context instead of attempting to import the meaning of *form* from other passages."[24] So, the best course of action would seem to be to cease arraying one set of lexicographical definitions (that suit a particular position) against another array (that suit the opposing position) and accept that the few uses of the word *morphē* in Scripture suggest a rather more diverse and deeper spectrum of meaning than simply "outward appearance." Instead, we shall determine our theological position by the overall exegetical context of the passage.

Before we do this, though, we need to correct Abel's assertion that the trinitarian position requires Christ to have abandoned his essential divine nature when he came to earth. Whilst it is true that a nineteenth-century school of thought, called Kenoticism, advocated this interpretation of Philippians 2, this is not the position of mainstream trinitarian theology. As Erickson points out, Kenoticism, or the view that Jesus emptied himself of the actual *morphē Theou* (form of God), is really another iteration of the early heresy of modalistic monarchianism whereby Jesus is not seen as God and man simultaneously, but successively.[25] The word kenosis comes from the verb *kenoō*, in Philippians 2:7, to empty or make void. The key issue in understanding this passage is to determine in what way, or of what, Jesus emptied himself.

> . . . what Jesus emptied himself of was not the divine *morphē*, the nature of God. At no point does this passage (Phil 2:6–7) say that he ceased to possess the divine nature. This becomes clearer when we take Colossians 2:9 into account: "For in Christ all the fullness of the Deity lives in bodily form." The kenosis of

22. Erickson, *Christian Theology*, 295.

23. BDAG, 280.

24. Schreiner, *Paul*, 171.

25. Erickson, *Christian Theology*, 668. Modalism is discussed in chapter 5 of the present work.

Philippians 2:7 must be understood in the light of the *plērōma* of Colossians 2:9. What does it mean then, to say that Jesus "made himself nothing"? Some have suggested that he emptied himself by pouring his divinity into his humanity as one pours the contents of one cup into another. This, however, fails to identify the vessel from which Jesus poured out his divine nature when he emptied it into his humanity. A better approach to Philippians 2:6–7 is to think of the phrase "taking the very nature of a servant" as a circumstantial explanation of the kenosis. Since *labōn* (taking) is an aorist participle adverbial in function, we would render the first part of verse 7, "he made himself nothing by taking the very form of a servant." The participle phrase is an explanation of how Jesus emptied himself, or what he did that constituted kenosis. While the text does not specify of what he emptied himself, it is noteworthy that "the very nature of a servant" contrasts sharply with "equality with God" (v 6). We conclude that it is equality with God, not the form of God, of which Jesus emptied himself.[26]

Wayne Grudem, in his *Systematic Theology*, agrees:

> We must first realize that no recognized teacher in the first 1800 years of church history, including those who were native speakers of Greek, thought that "emptied himself" in Philippians 2:7 meant that the Son of God gave up some of his divine attributes . . . the text does describe what Jesus did in this "emptying:" he did not do it by giving up any of his attributes but rather by "taking the form of a servant," that is, by coming to live as a man, and "being found in human form he humbled himself and became obedient to death, even death on a cross" (Phil 2:8). Thus, the context itself interprets this "emptying" as equivalent to "humbling himself" and taking on a lowly status and position . . . The emptying includes change of role and status, not essential attributes or nature.[27]

We will have more to say about Christ's subordination to the Father during his earthly ministry, in chapter 5. For now, let us be clear that the Christadelphian position as advanced by Ron Abel has misrepresented mainstream trinitarian understanding of this passage. John Thorpe[28] makes the same mistake, explicitly defining the trinitarian understanding of Philippians 2 in kenotic terms and confusing the definitions of *morphē* and *schēma*.

Hence this passage in Philippians, by way of encouraging the readers to humbly put aside their own interests in order to prioritize the interests of others, teaches that the Son gave up the status and privilege that was his in heaven. Although he was in the *morphē Theou*, he did not see equality with God a thing to be grasped, or clung to. The word is *harpagmos*, which has a breadth of meaning encompassing a violent seizure of property i.e., robbery; something to which one can claim or assert title by gripping or grasping, something claimed; a windfall, prize, or gain.[29] It is most probable that

---

26. Erickson, *Christian Theology*, 670.

27. Grudem, *Systematic Theology*, 550.

28. Thorpe, "Jesus and Paul," 100–102.

29. BDAG, 133–34.

harpagmos in the context of Philippians 2 is to be best understood as exploiting or taking advantage of.

> Christ Jesus, before his incarnation, was equal to God and displayed the splendor of God's glory. When he came into the world, however, he did not take advantage of these privileges. He subjected himself to humiliation for the sake of human beings (compare 2 Cor 8:9) . . . . The emptying of Christ, then, consisted of an adding. He emptied himself by becoming fully human. The text does not say that he emptied himself by surrendering his deity; it says that he humbled himself by adding humanity. We have already seen in Philippians 2:6 that he did not exploit or take advantage of his deity in becoming human, and thus the privileges of his divinity were not exercised on earth. But the text nowhere says that he surrendered his divinity or left it behind in the incarnation. The idea is that he did not exploit the advantages of deity, which were his by nature. As a man he lived in dependence on the Holy Spirit, in the same way other human beings do.[30]

Christadelphian writers such as Abel and Thorpe are therefore attacking a straw man, an incorrect interpretation of the trinitarian position. Instead of Jesus discarding his divinity, he emptied himself by humbly assuming the form or nature of a servant, being made in human likeness. This humbling extended to obedience to death on a cross. As a result, God the Father exalted him once more.

Jesus anticipated this exaltation in John 17:5: "And now, Father, glorify me in your own presence with the glory that I had with you before the world existed." Similarly, Paul speaks of the process in 2 Corinthians 8:9 "For you know the grace of our Lord Jesus Christ, that though he was rich, yet for your sake he became poor, so that you by his poverty might become rich." In what sense was Jesus "rich" and then became "poor" in coming into the world? What riches did he give up? It will not do to explain away the plain meaning of these verses as God's foreknowledge of the glorification of Christ. There is no hint of foreknowledge or predestination, preparation or choosing in these passages.[31] To attempt to so flavor them is to read into the passages a preconceived theological interpretation—the very thing of which Christadelphians accuse trinitarians.

The Philippians hymn concludes with the exaltation of Christ to the highest place, which we have seen is the throne of God, and he has been given the name above every name: *kyrios*, Lord, YHWH, that at this name—the name possessed by Jesus—every knee should bow.

> Great indeed, we confess, is the mystery of godliness: He was manifested in the flesh, vindicated by the Spirit, seen by angels, proclaimed among the nations, believed on in the world, taken up in glory (1 Tim 3:16).

The NIV renders the passage, "he appeared in a body" and the KJV, similarly to the ESV, as "God was manifest in the flesh" and this translation of this verse has

---

30. Schreiner, *Paul*, 172.

31. Tennant, *The Christadelphians*, 102–3; Abel, *Wrested Scriptures*, 297.

become the foundation stone of the Christadelphian understanding of "God manifestation" as the explanation for the attribution of divinity to Christ. This will be explored in chapter 6. The mainstream Christian understanding is that in the incarnation, God was revealed, disclosed, made known, in the flesh of humanity. The Word was made flesh and dwelt among us. This same God was seen, preached and believed on and taken up in glory. "We have seen his glory, glory as of the only Son from the Father, full of grace and truth" (John 1:14).

Jesus Shares the Attributes of God

In support of Jesus' bearing the divine nature whilst he was on earth, we can consider how he shared the exclusive attributes of God. It is important to acknowledge that these attributes were exercised *during his earthly ministry*, the period of his "emptying" or humbling, not confined to the time after his exaltation to the Father's right hand.

Worthy of Worship

The English word "worship" means "to attribute worth," but this doesn't do justice to the scriptural vocabulary of worship, which is fundamentally linked to how we can be in right relationship with God, encompassing the whole orientation of our lives. It is certainly not confined to ritual activities, but expresses the covenant relationship established first with Israel and later with the people of the new covenant. As David Peterson explains, "Acceptable worship under both covenants is a matter of responding to God's initiative in salvation and revelation, and doing so in the way that he requires."[32]

Under the old covenant, the prescribed approach to God was through the rituals and moral imperatives of the Law. With the new covenant came the shift; Jesus as High Priest, believers as priests; Jesus' body the temple, believers as the temple in whom God dwells by his Spirit. The worship language of the Old Testament was reapplied to the worship in Spirit and in truth. We worship God now by means of Christ and this side of his supreme sacrifice we no longer need to participate in the ritual forms of worship that pointed toward it.

The Bible uses several different words which could be translated "worship," and worship involves more than is encapsulated by any one word. It is important to capture the sense of what activities are involved in worship; when we include these, the instances of "worship" of Jesus and the imperatives to worship him, increase. The Greek and Hebrew words which can be translated "worship" have different meanings in context and worship can be described without using specific "worship" vocabulary.

32. Peterson, *Engaging with God*, 19. Peterson's book is a readable and thorough exploration of Bible teaching on worship.

It is therefore simplistic to assert that because a given word is not applied to Christ, that this means he was not worshiped or is not to be worshiped.

Ritual worship or service according to the prescriptions of the law, expressed in the LXX and New Testament by the *latreuō* word group, is rarely applied to Christ (See Acts 13:2 and Dan 7:14), and this is presented by some as an argument against the worship of Christ.[33] However, the ritual or cultic worship of the Levitical priesthood and tabernacle/temple was abolished with the sacrifice of Christ, so it is not surprising that it is not applied directly to him. However, the types expressed in this cultic worship, such as sacrifice, Passover lamb, washing and priesthood find their fulfilment in him. Also, the "one like a son of man," a descriptor Jesus applies to himself (Mark 14:62) *does* receive *latreuō* worship (Dan 7:14).

The word typically translated "worship" as applied to Christ is *proskuneō*, meaning to bow down or do obeisance. Israel was specifically commanded not to do this to any other god (Exod 34:14) and it is this word which Jesus cites when combating his own temptation in the wilderness: "You shall worship [*proskuneō*] the Lord your God and him only shall you serve [*latreuō*]" (Matt 4:10; Luke 4:8). In Revelation 22:8–9 the angel forbad John to worship [*proskuneō*] him; he is to worship [*proskuneō*] only God. Another word for serve is *douleuō* (to serve as a slave) and this is applied to serving God in the Old and New Testaments as well as Christ in the New (e.g. Rom 14:18; Col 3:24).

Phobeō means to fear, *sebazomai* means reverential worship and *thrēskeia* means cultic rites.[34] The Old Testament clearly establishes the principle that no God other than the Lord, YHWH, is to be worshiped (Exod 34:14—*proskuneō*; Deut 6:13; 8:19—*latreuō*; 2 Kings 17:35—*proskuneō, phobeō, latreuō*; Ps 29:2; Ps 99:5, 9—*proskuneō* are a few examples). Angels, *even though they can represent God*, and even speak as God, are not to be worshiped (Col 2:18—*thrēskeia*; Rev 22:8–9—*proskuneō*). No created being is worthy of the worship reserved for the Creator alone (Rom 1:25—*sebazomai, latreuō*). To worship and serve a created being or thing is idolatry. The following verses must be read in this context; they testify to Jesus Christ being worthy of worship, and the appropriateness of worshiping him, not only in his current exalted state, but during his earthly ministry, and even before that, as a newborn.

> [The Magi] asked, "Where is the one who has been born king of the Jews? We saw his star in the east and have come to worship him . . ." On coming to the house, they saw the child with his mother Mary, and they bowed down and worshiped him (Matt 2:2, 11—*proskuneō*).

During his ministry, Jesus was worshiped by a leper (Matt 8:2), Jairus (Matt 9:18), a Syro-Phoenician woman (Matt 15:25), Legion (Mark 5:6), the man born blind (John 9:38), and the disciples (Matt 14:33). These are also verses where the word "worship"

33. This is Andrew Perry's argument, citing J. D. G.Dunn; Perry, "Jewish Monotheism," 52–53. He states that the *latreuō* word group is *never* applied to Christ, but Acts 13:2 arguably does and in Dan 7:14 the word describes the worship offered to the Son of Man.

34. BDAG, 459, 587, 882, 917, 1060.

(*proskuneō*) is specifically used, the same word Jesus quotes from Deuteronomy in Matthew 4:10 so there is no mistaking the intent. Matthew, writing within a clearly Jewish framework, uses *proskuneō* of Jesus frequently, culminating in chapter 28 where it is linked with Jesus' subsequent claim to absolute authority and the instruction to baptize in the threefold name. Jesus was worshiped following his resurrection, prior to and at the time of his ascension (Matt 28:9, 17; Luke 24:52). There are a number of other instances where the word "worship" is not specifically used but the action and/ or speech is characteristic of worship (e.g., the woman with the alabaster jar in Matt 26:6–13 or Thomas' declaration in John 20:28). The angels of God were commanded to worship the firstborn (Jesus) at the time he was brought into the world (Heb 1:6, probably alluding to Ps 97:7, a command to the *elohim* to worship YHWH). The exalted Jesus is also worthy of worship (Phil 2:10; Rev 5:12). Christians are those who "call on the name of the Lord"—used of God in the Old Testament and Jesus Christ in the New. If all this isn't worship, what is?

In contrast, the Christadelphian position is that the Father bestowed on Christ his name and worthiness to be worshiped *after* his resurrection and exaltation:

> So the risen Lord has "a new name," which is "the name of my God, and the name of the city of my God" . . . Thus the title of *Kyrios*, applied by the disciples to their Master after his resurrection, the title attributed to him at the very end of the Book—"Amen, Even so, come, *Lord Jesus*"—implies much more than the English translation "Lord" suggests . . . In short, the Lord Jesus, "the coming one," is Lord, and bears the excellent Name which by inheritance he hath obtained as the Beloved, the Only Begotten Son of the Living God.[35]

We would certainly agree that the designation "Lord" for Jesus is much more than a respectful title, but is truly the Name of God, as has been demonstrated earlier. However two points of disagreement must be discussed. Firstly, the title *Kyrios* was not just applied to Jesus after the resurrection; the title is used by the disciples throughout the gospels (a few examples of many: Matt 20:30; 21:3; Luke 1:43; 2:11; 6:46; 10:40; John 6:68; 11:3; 13:13–14). Secondly, we would disagree that the title "Lord" was something obtained by inheritance, rather than being intrinsically his; see the previous discussion.

The respected Christadelphian writer Harry Tennant puts their position explicitly:

> The doctrine of the Son of God as believed by Christadelphians greatly exalts the Lord Jesus Christ, without diminishing his glory as the Son of God. How great is his work! From the lowly beginnings when he shared our nature, he overcame the temptations of sin, entered and conquered death, and has ascended in immortality and abounding glory to the right hand of God in heaven. This is Bible teaching. We honor and praise the Son of God, believing that he was truly born, was truly tempted, truly died, truly rose and was truly exalted to the right hand of the Father. His honor and authority and power have been given to him by the

---

35. Nicholls, *The Name*, 73.

Father: (Matt 28:18; Eph 1:20–22; Phil 2:9). The power and glory and authority of Christ have been bestowed upon him by the Father. They are derived and none of them would be his if they had not been given to him by God the Father: (John 3:34; 14:10, 24; 7:16; 10:32; Acts 10:38; 2:22).[36]

Trinitarians have no argument with any of these Bible passages, which show that the authority of Jesus came from God the Father. This was the role which the Son took upon himself, and will be discussed in detail in chapter 5. The point of difference is this; mainstream Christian scholarship views that the divine power and authority of the Lord Jesus Christ are *intrinsically his* as God the Son, even though he did not grasp at them in taking the form of a servant. In contrast, Christadelphians teach that these attributes are wholly derived and were bestowed at his post-resurrection exaltation.

Supremacy

There are many passages in Scripture where the superiority of Jesus is noted, in comparison to men and to angels. The gospels testify that this superiority was evident during Jesus' earthly ministry, prior to his resurrection and exaltation. Jesus is said to be greater than John the Baptist (Matt 3:11; Mark 1:7–8; John 1:15, 30), Jonah (Matt 12:41; Luke 11:32), David (Matt 22:43–45), Solomon (Matt 12:42), the disciples (John 13:13–16), Adam (1 Cor 15:45–47), Moses (John 1:17; Heb 3:3), Melchizedek and the Levitical priesthood (Heb 7), and angels (Heb 1:5, 13; 2:5–8).

> He who comes from above is above all. He who is of the earth belongs to the earth and speaks in an earthly way. He who comes from heaven is above all. He bears witness to what he has seen and heard, yet no one receives his testimony (John 3:31–32).

This passage, which follows John the Baptist's testimony, is probably a reflective explanation by the apostle John and draws together themes from the wider passage. Jesus must become greater as John the Baptist diminishes (verse 30), because Jesus alone is from above and is therefore above all. The new birth "from above" (verse 3) can be experienced only by faith in the One who is from above. All others, in contrast, are from the earth, even John although he was sent from God (1:6). Only Jesus can speak with supreme authority of heavenly things, because he speaks from direct experience.

Colossians 1:15–20 is a passage which exalts Christ and emphasizes his supremacy. We have already looked at this passage in connection with Christ as the image of God and the firstborn, but it's worth revisiting it in the context of Christ's supremacy. It is probably a poem with the twofold theme of Christ's lordship over creation and over the church.[37] The middle part of the poem provides the central theme; "And he

---

36. Tennant, *The Christadelphians*, 100–101.

37. See a full discussion of this passage in Schreiner, *Paul*, 173–78.

is before all things, and in him all things hold together." Christ is the image of the invisible God, and by him and for him all things were created. He is the beginning and the firstborn so that in everything he might have the supremacy, for all God's fullness dwells in him (also Col 2:9). "Having the supremacy" translates *prōteuō*, to be first or have first place.

Jesus' Self-consciousness and the Claims He Made

One of the more basic arguments of Christadelphians and of those who would strip Christianity of its supernatural aspects is that Jesus did not explicitly and overtly claim to be God—in so many words, as in "I am God." However, if we take into account the claims he *did* make we find them to be totally inappropriate for anyone who was less than God. We have already looked at passages which ascribe God's lordship to Jesus, as well as the "I am" statements in John, and Jesus' affirmation of Thomas' declaration, "My Lord and my God." For what it's worth, Jesus' enemies certainly chose to believe that he was claiming to be God and Jesus didn't correct them (John 10:33). Let's look at some of these claims.

- Jesus referred to the angels and to the kingdom of God as his (Matt 13:41; cf. Luke 12:8–9; 15:10).

- Jesus claimed, and exercised, the prerogative to forgive sins (Mark 2:5–12) without correcting the rhetorical question, "Who can forgive sins but God alone?"

- Jesus claimed the prerogative of judging the world (Matt 25:31–46).

- He directed people to believe in himself in order to be saved (John 14:1).

- Jesus claimed to be Lord of the Sabbath, in other words he had the right to determine what was appropriate to do on the Sabbath and had jurisdiction over this God-appointed institution which was established at the time of creation (Matt 12:8; Mark 2:28; Luke 6:5; John 5:2–18).

- Jesus claimed a unique relationship with the Father; to be one with the Father (John 10:30) and that to see and know him is to see and know the Father (John 14:7–9).

- Jesus juxtaposed his own words with Scripture, placing his own authority on a par with God's word. Instead of saying, like the Old Testament prophets, "Thus says the Lord," or "The word of the Lord came to me," he says simply, "But I tell you . . ." (Matt 5:21–22, 27–28). He spoke with a final, overriding authority and claimed that his words, unlike heaven and earth, would never pass away (Matthew 24:35; cf. Isaiah 40:8).

- Jesus summoned men to faith in himself, against an Old Testament background that emphasized that only God was to be trusted as Lord, redeemer and savior.

In John 14:1 he exhorted the disciples to believe in him as they believe in God.

- Jesus claimed to be the Way, the Truth and the Life. He claimed to be the only way to God (John 14:6) and the only one who could reveal God (Matt 11:27). His truth would set people free (John 8:32).

- He not only claimed the power of life and death but claimed to *be* the resurrection and the life (John 11:25. See also John 20:31; 3:15–16; Acts 3:15).

So these are Jesus' own claims, which demonstrate his self-understanding. When we read them today we can gloss over them, because the claims are so familiar—of course Jesus can forgive sins and raise the dead and speak with divine authority! But if we put ourselves in the perspective of the first-century Jews who first heard these claims, they are *astounding*. Unedited and unqualified as they are, from the lips of Jesus, they are no less than the exercise of the unique prerogatives of God. C. S. Lewis puts it delightfully:

> Then comes the real shock. Among these Jews there suddenly turns up a man who goes about talking as if He was God. He claims to forgive sins. He says He has always existed. He says He is coming to judge the world at the end of time . . . God, in their language, meant the Being outside the world, who had made it and was infinitely different from anything else. And when you have grasped that, you will see that what this man said was, quite simply, the most shocking thing that has ever been uttered by human lips.
>
> One part of the claim tends to slip past us unnoticed because we have heard it so often that we no longer see what it amounts to. I mean the claim to forgive sins: any sins. Now unless the speaker is God, this is really so preposterous as to be comic. We can all understand how a man forgives offences against himself. You tread on my toes and I forgive you, you steal my money and I forgive you. But what should we make of a man, himself unrobbed and untrodden on, who announced that he forgave you for treading on other men's toes and stealing other men's money? Asinine fatuity is the kindest description we should give of his conduct. Yet this is what Jesus did. He told people that their sins were forgiven, and never waited to consult all the other people whom their sins had undoubtedly injured. He unhesitatingly behaved as if He was the party chiefly concerned, the person chiefly offended in all offences. This makes sense only if He really was the God whose laws are broken and whose love is wounded in every sin. In the mouth of any speaker who is not God, these words imply what I can only regard as a silliness and conceit unrivalled by any other character in history. Yet (and this is the strange, significant thing) even His enemies, when they read the Gospels, do not usually get the impression of silliness and conceit. Still less do unprejudiced readers. Christ says that He is "humble and meek" and we believe Him; not noticing that, if He were merely a man, humility and meekness are the very last characteristics we could attribute to some of his sayings."[38]

So let's explore in more depth some of these claims made by and about Jesus.

---

38. Lewis, *Mere Christianity*, 352–53.

Jesus' Healing Power, Power over Demons

In ancient times, there was very little sound medical knowledge, and it was tainted by unscientific supposition and superstition. No wonder the woman with the flow of blood suffered a lot under the physicians who attended her. Many diseases, even simple infections, which we take for granted as curable today, were life-threatening and feared, right up until the nineteenth or twentieth centuries. Any hope of healing for the majority of illnesses lay with the miraculous power of God. Sickness, and its consequence, death, entered the world as a result of sin and so they persist. Even with the God-given blessings of modern medicine, there are still diseases which cannot be cured, and it is still inevitable that in Adam all die. In Exodus 15:26 God claims jurisdiction over sickness and health; "I will put none of the diseases on you that I put on the Egyptians, for I am the Lord, your healer." There are numerous examples of divine healing in the Old Testament, either directly by God, often in response to prayer, e.g. Miriam, Hezekiah, or through the agency of his prophets, e.g., Naaman. Although the book of Job demonstrates that specific illnesses are not necessarily the result of specific sins, nevertheless the overall connection between illness, death and sin generally is evident. Thus there is a general connection between forgiveness and healing.

> Bless the LORD, O my soul, and forget not all his benefits, who forgives all your iniquity, who heals all your diseases (Ps 103:2–3).

> "For I will not contend forever, nor will I always be angry; for the spirit would grow faint before me, and the breath of life that I made . . . I have seen his ways, but I will heal him; I will lead him and restore comfort to him and his mourners, creating the fruit of the lips. Peace, peace, to the far and to the near," says the LORD, "and I will heal him" (Isa 57:16–19).

It is no wonder then, that healing and forgiveness were regularly linked in Jesus' ministry. Jesus sought faith in those he healed. He claimed the commission of Isaiah 61:1–2 (Luke 4:18–19) and his works of healing established his claim to be Christ (Matt 11:4–6). Specific acts of healing had occurred in Old Testament times, but Jesus' work was on a whole different level. He healed "every disease and every affliction among the people," including conditions that are still incurable today, such as severe pain, demon possession,[39] seizures and paralysis (Matt 4:23–24) and congenital blindness (John 9:32). Moreover, he healed with a word or a touch (Matt 8:3, 8, 16; 9:21; 14:36; 17:18) and often healed multitudes at a time (Matt 19:2; Mark 1:32–34; Luke 6:19). As a result, the people could exclaim, "Never was anything like this seen

---

39. I risk opening a jumbo, catering-size can of worms here, but it would be a digression to explore the nature of demons and evil spirits and their association with disease and what precisely Jesus did in his interaction with them. Suffice it to say that the Christadelphian view is significantly different from that of mainstream Christianity and also Pentecostalism, and to acknowledge this and move on. For information on the Christadelphian position, see Tennant, *The Christadelphians*, 162–71 or Roberts, *Christendom Astray*, 203–8.

I am simply going to refer to demons and evil spirits in the face-value way that Scripture does.

in Israel!" (Matt 9:33). In fact, Jesus' casting out of demons was nothing less than an indication that the kingdom of God had been inaugurated (Matt 12:28; Luke 11:20).

Apart from the sheer scale (quantity and quality) of Jesus' healing ministry, the aspects that stand out are the *authority* with which he healed and cast out demons, and the association of his healing work with forgiveness. The centurion knew, from his own experience as a man of authority, that Jesus had only to speak a word and his servant would be healed (Matt 8:8–9). The people were amazed at the realization that Jesus had authority over evil spirits (Mark 1:27) which Mark's gospel attributes to the spirits' recognition of Jesus (Mark 1:34; 3:10–12; 5:13).

> And they were all amazed and said to one another, "What is this word? For with authority and power he commands the unclean spirits, and they come out!" (Luke 4:36).

Jesus was also able to delegate or impart power to his disciples to heal and to cast out evil spirits (Matt 10:1; Mark 3:14–15; 16:17–18; Luke 10:17–20). These miraculous works were done in Jesus' name, both before and after his resurrection (Acts 3:6; 4:9–10; 9:34; 16:18; 19:11–17). Those who believe in Jesus receive what they ask for in prayer, asking in *his name* (John 14:12–14).

The synoptic gospels refer to these healing events and other supernatural demonstrations as miracles (*dynamis*) or works (*ergon*) whereas John selects only a few to discuss in detail and calls them signs (*sēmeion*). He explains that Jesus did many other miraculous signs, which he did not record, but he chose those he did record specifically as evidence that the readers might believe that Jesus is the Christ, the Son of God, and by believing, have life in his name (John 20:30–31).

Jesus' miraculous works were attributed on some occasions to God working in him through the Holy Spirit (Matt 9:8; 12:28; Luke 4:18; John 9:33; Acts 2:22; 10:38) but on other occasions directly to Jesus (Matt 8:2–3; Mark 16:17–18; Acts 3:6, 16; 4:10; 9:34; 16:18). We will discuss the relationship between Jesus and the Father and the power of the Holy Spirit in chapters 5 and 7, but suffice it to say that these passages are not contradictory, nor do they undermine the essential authority of Jesus, if we correctly understand the relationships and roles of Father, Son, and Holy Spirit, and the submission and dependence of the earthly Jesus.

Power over Death

God is the source and giver of life; he created Adam and breathed into him the breath of life (Gen 2:7) and "In him we live and move and have our being" (Acts 17:28). God gives and preserves life, and God takes life away (Job 1:21).

> You are the LORD, you alone. You have made heaven, the heaven of heavens, with all their host, the earth and all that is on it, the seas and all that is in them; and you preserve all of them; and the host of heaven worships you (Neh 9:6).

> Who among all these does not know that the hand of the LORD has done this? In his hand is the life of every living thing and the breath of all mankind (Job 12:9–10).

In Jesus' ministry we see him wield the power of life. He raised several people that we know of: Jairus' daughter, the widow of Nain's son, Lazarus, and still more through his apostles. Many others who were as good as dead he healed and there was no doubt in people's minds that he could prevent the terminally ill from dying (Matt 9:18; John 11:21–22, 37). Jesus certainly has the power of life, and he has the power of death also (Rev 1:18). But there is more to it than delegated authority to heal and raise the dead. Jesus intrinsically has the power of life, just as his Father does. In Acts 3:15 Jesus is called the author of life.

In John 1:4 we read of the Word that "in him was life." John 5:21 says, "For as the Father raises the dead and gives them life, so also the Son gives life to whom he will." This is because "as the Father has life in himself, so he has granted the Son also to have life in himself" (John 5:26).

> Truly, truly, I say to you, whoever hears my word and believes him who sent me has eternal life. He does not come into judgment, but has passed from death to life (John 5:24).

> Truly, truly, I say to you, if anyone keeps my word, he will never see death (John 8:51).

In John 11:25–26, Jesus told Martha, "I am the resurrection and the life. Whoever believes in me, though he die, yet shall he live, and everyone who lives and believes in me shall never die." He said this in response to her faithful confidence that her brother Lazarus would rise again at the last day, and that even then, when he was dead, she knew that Jesus could raise him if he chose to (verse 22). Jesus took this a step further; he was not only able to raise the dead, he *is* the resurrection and the life (one of the "I am" sayings). Jesus grants eternal life to those who believe in him; it is his prerogative (John 5:21, 25; 6:39–40, 47; 8:51; 10:28; 17:2; Phil 3:21). Furthermore, Jesus had the authority to lay down his own life, and to take it again (John 10:18).

Power over Nature

Job was thoroughly humbled when he contemplated the absolute power which God has over his creation (Job 38:1—42:6). Many verses in the Psalms speak of the power of God in his creation. In the Old Testament we read of God bringing the flood upon the earth, of bringing famine and drought, earthquakes, plagues of "natural" events in supernatural proportions, dividing the Red Sea and the Jordan, creating and stilling storms, multiplying food, stalling a sunset, and moving shadows backwards.

Jesus had power over nature during his earthly ministry; he fed multitudes with a small amount of food, turned water into wine, walked on water,[40] drew a huge catch of fish into the disciples' nets and produced tax money from a fish's mouth. He caused a fig tree to wither and calmed storms at sea. John says that the turning of water to wine manifested Jesus' glory and prompted the disciples' belief in him (John 2:11).

> He said to them, "Where is your faith?" And they were afraid, and they marveled, saying to one another, "Who then is this, that he commands even winds and water, and they obey him?" (Luke 8:25).

In these two examples we see that it is Jesus specifically (not the Father or Holy Spirit) who is glorified and who is obeyed.

We saw in the previous chapter that creation is ascribed to Christ. Another aspect of the work of God which Jesus does is the sustaining of that creation. God gives life and breath and food to his creatures (Acts 17:25–28; Ps 104:24–30). The New Testament also ascribes this work to Jesus.

> For by him all things were created, in heaven and on earth, visible and invisible, whether thrones or dominions or rulers or authorities—all things were created through him and for him. And he is before all things, and in him all things hold together (Col 1:16–17).

> . . . one Lord, Jesus Christ, through whom are all things and through whom we exist (1 Cor 8:6).

> He is the radiance of the glory of God and the exact imprint of his nature, and he upholds the universe by the word of his power (Heb 1:3).

Just as the Father continues to sustain the universe and give life to his creatures, so also the Son continues to work (John 5:17).

Authoritative Teaching

People were regularly astonished at the authority with which Jesus spoke. The Old Testament prophets spoke with authority too, but always made it clear that they were speaking the words given to them by God; "Thus says the Lord," or, "The word of the Lord came to . . ." Jesus did not prefix his words this way. He spoke with a direct authority (Matt 7:28–29; Mark 1:22; Luke 4:32). This was in contrast to the scribes, whose authority derived from God through Moses and the mass of oral tradition and reasoning of previous rabbis. "No one ever spoke like this man," declared the guards (John 7: 46). The chief priests and elders questioned his authority (Matt 21:23–27;

---

40. A convincing case for Jesus' walking on water as being a direct fulfilment of and allusion to God's work in bringing the Israelites through the Red Sea is found in Bowman and Komoszewski, *Putting Jesus in His Place*, 204–6.

Luke 20:2) and wondered where he got his understanding, having had (apparently) no formal scholarly training (John 7:15–16). Hebrews 1:1–2 supports the superiority of the Son's revelation over that of the prophets.

Jesus even saw fit to elaborate on, or move beyond what was written in the Old Testament Scriptures, or at least the way they were commonly interpreted. He gave an authoritative interpretation of the Sabbath (Mark 2:23–28; Luke 13:13–16), which had been divinely ordained even before the Ten Commandments which made it explicit. The Ten Commandments (Exod 20:13) directed, "You shall not murder," but Jesus elaborated; "But I say to you that everyone who is angry with his brother will be liable to judgment" (Matt 5:21–22). Likewise, the Law said, you shall not commit adultery, but Jesus went further; "But I say to you that everyone who looks at a woman with lustful intent has already committed adultery with her in his heart" (Matt 5:28). Where the law permitted divorce (Jesus made it clear elsewhere that this was a reluctant concession to hardheartedness), "But I say to you that everyone who divorces his wife, except on the ground of sexual immorality, makes her commit adultery, and whoever marries a divorced woman commits adultery" (Matt 5:32). He told them not to swear but simply tell the truth (Matt 5:34) and overrode the "eye for an eye" provision with the command to not resist an evil person (Matt 5:39). In each of these the phrase used is *ego de legō*; the word *legō* alone is the first person singular of the verb "say" and implies the pronoun; the *ego* is grammatically redundant but adds emphasis; "But *I* say . . ." In speaking this way, Jesus gave his words the authority equivalent to Scripture; quite appropriate for the Word made flesh to do. He even overrode the Mosaic law when he declared all foods clean (Mark 7:19).

Jesus also made the astonishing claim in Matt 24:35 that "Heaven and earth will pass away, but my words will not pass away;" a greater permanence than he gave to the Law and Prophets, which would last "until all is accomplished" (Matt 5:18). No wonder it was said that no one ever spoke like this! Where did Jesus claim his authority came from? He made it clear that his teaching was God's teaching. He was the fulfilment of Isaiah 54:13, the means by which "they will all be taught by God" (John 6:45). The context of this claim is Jesus' statement that he is the living bread which came down from heaven. To come to Jesus, a person must be drawn by the Father and everyone who listens to and learns from the Father comes to Jesus. Jesus is the only one who has seen the Father; he came from the Father and that is where his teaching originates; the Godhead (John 6:44–46). A little later, when some of his disciples deserted him, Jesus said, "The words that I have spoken to you are spirit and life" (verse 63) and Simon Peter made the encouraging confession, "Lord, to whom (else) shall we go? You have the words of eternal life" (verse 68). Elsewhere in John, Jesus affirmed the divine origin of his words:

- If anyone's will is to do God's will, he will know whether the teaching is from God or whether I am speaking on my own authority (John 7:17).

- I have much to say about you and much to judge, but he who sent me is true, and I declare to the world what I have heard from him (John 8:26).

- So Jesus said to them, "When you have lifted up the Son of Man, then you will know that I am he [*ego eimi*] and that I do nothing on my own authority, but speak just as the Father taught me" (John 8:28).

- I speak of what I have seen with my Father, and you do what you have heard from your father (John 8:38).

- For I have not spoken on my own authority, but the Father who sent me has himself given me a commandment—what to say and what to speak. And I know that his commandment is eternal life. What I say, therefore, I say as the Father has told me (John 12:49–50).

- Do you not believe that I am in the Father and the Father is in me? The words that I say to you I do not speak on my own authority, but the Father who dwells in me does his works (John 14:10).

- Whoever does not love me does not keep my words. And the word that you hear is not mine but the Father's who sent me (John 14:24).

Coupling these verses with those that demonstrate Jesus' personal authority ("But I say to you . . .") we can see that there is no separation between the words of Jesus and those of the Father. Jesus exhibited divine authority, but it was not autonomous. The message originates within the Godhead and Jesus, the Word Made flesh, spoke what he had seen and heard.

Authority to Forgive Sins, to Judge

Sin is the transgression of God's commandments, rebellion against his authority. All sin is against God; David realized this in his confessional Psalm; "Against you, you only, have I sinned and done what is evil in your sight" (Ps 51:4). As C. S. Lewis so eloquently expressed it, God is the one offended by every sin, and he is the only one whose right it is to forgive in the ultimate sense. Likewise, God is the final arbiter of what constitutes sin, and the judge of all the earth. The Old Testament contains a number of prophecies about God himself coming to rule in might and to judge (for example, Ps 96:12–13). Yet in the New Testament, we find Jesus claiming the divine prerogatives of forgiveness and of judgment.

When Jesus confronted the paralytic (Mark 2:3–12) he perceived a greater need than physical healing. Instead of initially curing the man's paralysis, in response to the faith displayed he said, "Son, your sins are forgiven." This caused a stir; on face value this was blasphemy; "Who can forgive sins but God alone?" reasoned the teachers of the law. Jesus challenged them; which was easier to say; "Your sins are forgiven?" or

"Rise, take up your bed and walk?" Of course, both were just as easy to *say*, as mere words, but for anyone but God they would be hollow and meaningless. Only God could heal a paralytic, and only God could forgive sins. Nevertheless, the former was readily demonstrated, and would prove the credibility of the latter: "But that you may know that the Son of Man has authority on earth to forgive sins . . ." A similar challenge was thrown down in Luke 7:36–50. The promiscuous woman had been forgiven, and showed her love in response by anointing Jesus' feet in an act of worship. When challenged by his Pharisee host, he explained that her many sins had been forgiven, as demonstrated by her love. He made it clear to all present; "Your sins are forgiven," to which those present responded, "Who is this, who even forgives sins?"

Jesus also has the prerogative of divine judgment. There are many references in the gospels to his coming in judgment at the end of the age (eg., Matt 13:41–42; 16:27; 25:31–46). As with the authority of his teaching, Jesus' authority to judge comes from God the Father:

- The Father judges no one, but has given all judgment to the Son (John 5:22).

- And he [the Father] has given him authority to execute judgment, because he is the Son of Man (John 5:27).

The context of John 5:16–30 is Jesus' explanation of the parallel working relationship between himself and the Father; they are not operating separately or in conflict in any way, although there is a separation of roles. Jesus and his Father work together (verse 17) a concept which enraged the Jews when they recognized in this a claim to equality with God (verse 18). Jesus explained that the Son does nothing of himself, but does only what his Father does (verse 19). Mainstream trinitarians have always held that the Father and Son have distinct but complementary roles; the Father initiates, sends, commands, grants; the Son responds, obeys, performs his Father's will and receives his authority.[41] To use such passages to argue against the concept of the triune Godhead is to misrepresent the doctrine. But more of that later.

> It is impossible for the Son to take independent, self-determined action that would set him over against the Father as another God, for all that the Son does is both coincident with and coextensive with all that the Father does . . . It follows that separate, self-determined action would be a denial of his sonship. But if this last clause of v 19 takes the impossibility of the Son acting independently and grounds it in the perfection of Jesus' sonship, it also constitutes another oblique claim to deity; for the only one who could conceivably do *whatever the Father does* must be as great as the Father, as divine as the Father.[42]

The statement that the Son does nothing by himself but only what he sees his Father doing (verse 19) is supported in the Greek by four for/because (*gar*) statements:

41. A comprehensive exegesis of John 5:16–30, which carefully elaborates on this Father–Son relationship may be found in Carson, *John*, 246–59.

42. Carson, *John*, 251.

- *Because* whatever the Father does the Son also does (verse 19).

- *For* the Father loves the Son and shows him all that he does (verse 19).

- *For* as the Father raises the dead and gives them life, even so the Son gives life to whom he is pleased to give it (verse 21).

- [*For*] the Father judges no one, but has entrusted all judgment to the Son (verse 22).

The reason the Father has entrusted all judgment to the Son is given in verse 23: "that all may honor the Son, just as they honor the Father."

> This goes far beyond making Jesus a mere ambassador who acts in the name of the monarch who sent him, an envoy plenipotentiary whose derived authority is the equivalent of his master's. That analogue breaks down precisely here, for the honor given to an envoy is never that given to a head of state. The Jews were right in detecting that Jesus was "making himself equal with God" (verses 17–18). But this does not diminish God. Indeed, the glorification of the Son is precisely what glorifies the Father . . . just as in Philippians 2:9–11.[43]

There is another reason why the Father has delegated the authority to judge to the Son, as stated in verse 27; because he is the Son of Man. Jesus is one of us, he has shared our experiences, he can sympathize (Heb 4:15–16)—but this is insufficient reason of itself. Jesus is the Apocalyptic Son of Man of Daniel 7:13–14 (see Matt 26:64–65) who receives from the Ancient of Days the prerogatives of Deity. The combination of these features, human and divine, makes him uniquely qualified to judge.

> He commanded us to preach to the people and to testify that he is the one appointed by God to be judge of the living and the dead (Acts 10:42; see also Acts 17:31).

> On that day when, according to my gospel, God judges the secrets of men by Christ Jesus (Rom 2:16).

> Why do you pass judgment on your brother? Or you, why do you despise your brother? For we will all stand before the judgment seat of God; for it is written, "As I live, says the Lord, every knee shall bow to me, and every tongue shall confess to God." So then each of us will give an account of himself to God (Rom 14:10–12).

The preaching of the apostles confirmed the appointment of Jesus Christ as judge of the world. God appointed him to judge, it is God who judges through him and the judgment seat of Christ is no less than the judgment seat of God, in fulfilment of Isaiah 45:23.

---

43. Ibid., 254–55.

Knowledge of People

God is omniscient; "God is greater than our heart, and he knows everything" (1 John 3:20). "And no creature is hidden from his sight, but all are naked and exposed to the eyes of him to whom we must give account" (Heb 4:13). He both knows and determines the future (Isa 46:9–10; Ps 139:4; Matt 6:8).

Jesus demonstrated a knowledge of people's thoughts and intentions (Matt 12:25; Mark 2:8; Luke 5:22; John 1:48; 4:17–18) and knew what would happen in the future (John 6:64; 13:11, 26, 38; 18:4; Matt 24). Of course, God gave specific insights to prophets in the Old Testament as well (eg., 1 Kgs 13:1–3; 14:5–12; 2 Kgs 5:26 and throughout the writings of the prophets), but Jesus' knowledge went beyond that. He knew what was inside people's hearts (John 2:25; 16:30; 21:17). This knowledge of the secrets of our hearts is the basis for his judgment (Rom 2:16; 1 Cor 4:5). Jesus knows us in the way God knows us (Acts 1:24; Rev 2:2, 9, 13, 19; 3:1, 8, 15). Interestingly, whereas Jesus specifies that his authority to judge and forgive sins, and his teaching came from the Father, each of these ascriptions of divine knowledge to Jesus come without the specification or implication that these insights were given him. Jesus simply knows.

Can Jesus Function as God without Being God?

Charles Sherlock[44] makes a powerful point when he says that in most situations, a person can "function" in a role that is not intrinsically theirs. For example a person might function quite adequately as a teacher without being a teacher, or be as a parent to a child without being the child's biological mother or father. However, this does not hold true when talking about God. The early Christians worshiped Jesus Christ and ascribed to him the honor due to God and the names, attributes, and deeds of God. For them, as for Christians through the ages, Jesus functions as God. To treat someone other than God as our God is idolatry; we cannot separate Jesus' functioning as God from his being God. Taken together, the New Testament titles, claims and ascriptions of deity to Jesus Christ are overwhelming. He is no less than God with us.

Summary

- The eternal Word became incarnate in the womb of the Virgin Mary by the power of the Holy Spirit; her child was the Word made flesh; God with us.

- Jesus Christ is addressed or referred to as God in several key passages.

- Jesus Christ is the image of God and in him all the fullness of Deity dwells.

- Jesus Christ has the status of firstborn over all creation and is preeminent, yet he

44. Sherlock, *God on the Inside*, 58.

took the form of a servant and a subordinate position; he has now been exalted once more.

- Jesus Christ shares the attributes of God; his supremacy, his worthiness to be worshiped, the authority to forgive sins, to judge and to speak as God; he has the power to heal and cast out demons, power over the forces of nature and of life and death and knows the hearts and minds of people.

Further Reading

- C. S. Lewis, *Mere Christianity*.

- Millard Erickson, *Christian Theology*, chapter 31, "The Deity of Christ."

- D. A. Carson, *The Gospel According to John*.

- Robert M. Bowman Jr. and J. Ed. Komoszewski, *Putting Jesus in His Place: The Case for the Deity of Christ*.

5

Father and Son

CHRISTADELPHIANS BELIEVE THAT JESUS' relationship with his Father as portrayed in Scripture is incompatible with the doctrine of the Trinity. Their arguments against the Trinity are often based on demonstrating Jesus' distinctiveness from and subordination to, his Father. Sometimes mainstream Christians shy away from these passages because they are not sure what to make of them, in their desire to exalt the Lord Jesus. This chapter examines the relationship between Jesus and his Father in order to address these misconceptions.

Misconception #6: That calling Jesus God makes him the same person as the Father.

Corrective: Whilst Jesus shares the divine essence or nature, he is a person distinct from the Father.

Misconception #7: That Jesus' subordinate role to the Father precludes him being part of the Godhead.

Corrective: Jesus is one with the Father in divine nature, but subordinate in role.

Misconception #8: That Jesus' conception by the Holy Spirit is the entire focus of what it means for him to be the Son of God.

Corrective: Jesus' sonship expresses an eternal relationship within the Godhead.

The Father Is God, but God Is not Limited to the Father

We have spent two chapters arguing that in some way (yet to be fully explored) Jesus Christ is God; that he shares the divine identity and attributes, is the exact image of God and in him dwells all God's fullness, and he is specifically referred to as God. We are to respond to Jesus as we would to God; we are to honor, glorify, worship, pray to, sing to and about, believe in, fear or reverence, religiously serve, love, and obey Jesus as we would God.[1] However, if we left it at that there could be the mistaken impression

---

1. Bowman and Komoszewski, *Putting Jesus in His Place*, 73.

that somehow the Father and the Son are the same. We would also have left hanging the multitude of verses that speak of the Son's subordination to, and dependence on the Father. In exploring the relationship between the Father and the Son, we first need to clarify that when Scripture talks about "God," many times this means specifically the Father, but at other times it does not. Paradoxically, but inescapably, the New Testament both distinguishes Jesus from God and identifies him as God, sometimes in juxtaposition (John 1:1; 20:28–31; Heb 1:8–9; 2 Pet 1:1–2). We should not shy away from this, nor dismiss it, nor play one aspect off against the other or favor one over against the other. Rather, we must seek to understand it and accept it as God's intended teaching regarding the nature of his Son.

God the Father

It should be obvious to anyone who reads the New Testament that the Being referred to as the Father is none other than the God of Israel, YHWH.

- Jesus speaks of him as "your Father" or "your Father in heaven" and instructs us to address him as "our Father" in prayer. See especially the sermon on the mount in Matthew 5 to 7 for examples of this teaching.

- Jesus refers to God as his Father and addresses him as "Father" or uses the more familiar and intimate Aramaic word *Abba* (Mark 14:36).[2]

- The Father is Lord of heaven and earth (Luke 10:21).

- The Father is to be worshiped; in spirit and in truth (John 4:23) and honored (John 5:23) and glorified (John 12:28; 14:13; Phil 2:11).

- The Father has life in himself; he raises the dead and delegates judgment (John 5:21–27).

"Father" language is never used in the Bible in an abstract, impersonal way to name God; God as "father" in the Bible always involves God being the Father *of someone*. Calling the creator God "Father" is primarily a New Testament perspective, but has some precedent in the Old Testament:

> Do you thus repay the LORD, you foolish and senseless people? Is he not your father, who created you, who made you and established you? (Deut 32:6).

God is not depicted as the "father of creation," analogous to heathen gods siring progeny, nor as the literal father of Israel; the Israelites were God's children by

---

2. Paul refers to an early Christian practice of believers crying "Abba, Father" in Rom 8:15, Gal 4:6 by the prompting of the Holy Spirit. This may have been an ecstatic utterance, especially since Paul's Gentile readers probably didn't know any Aramaic, or perhaps Jesus' practice and example was widely known as part of very early preaching about him. Either way, just as "Abba" was the cry of the Son and heir, it is appropriately the cry of God's children who are joint heirs with Christ. See Witherington, *Many Faces*, 73–74.

election—God's sovereign choice. The references to God as "father" are few in the Old Testament and always relational. In the New Testament, the Father is explicitly equated with God, but always as the Father of Jesus and, by adoption, the Father of those in Christ. "Father" is a relational word describing the distinctive relationship of God the Lord to the children of God.[3] Here are some examples:

- Jesus answered, "If I glorify myself, my glory is nothing. It is my Father who glorifies me, of whom you say, 'He is our God'" (John 8:54).

- Jesus said to her [Mary], "Do not cling to me, for I have not yet ascended to the Father; but go to my brothers and say to them, 'I am ascending to my Father and your Father, to my God and your God'" (John 20:17).

- And call no man your father on earth, for you have one Father, who is in heaven (Matt 23:9).

- Yet for us there is one God, the Father, from whom are all things and for whom we exist, and one Lord,[4] Jesus Christ, through whom are all things and through whom we exist (1 Cor 8:6).

- One God and Father of all, who is over all and through all and in all (Eph 4:6).

- And made us a kingdom, priests to serve his God and Father, to him be glory and dominion for ever and ever. Amen (Rev 1:6).

Paul refers to God as:

- "Our Father" (Rom 1:7; 1 Cor 1:3; 2 Cor 1:2; Gal 1:3, 4; Eph 1:2; Phil 1:2; 4:20; Col 1:2; 1 Thess 1:3; 3:11, 13; 2 Thess 1:1; 2:16; Phlm 1:3);

- "The God and Father of our Lord Jesus Christ" (Rom 15:6; 2 Cor 1:3; 11:31; Eph 1:3, 17; Col 1:3);

- "God the Father" (Gal 1:1; Eph 5:20; 6:23; Phil 2:11; Col 3:17; 1 Thess 1:1; 1 Tim 1:2; 2 Tim 1:2; Titus 1:4).

Often, Paul will use two of the terms, one after the other in subsequent verses, in interchangeable combinations. The other New Testament letters show a similar pattern.

God Encompasses More Than the Father

The Father of Jesus Christ is clearly God, but "God" is not just the Father. We have seen in the last two chapters that Jesus Christ, Son of God, has the attributes of God; in him

---

3. Charles Sherlock has an excellent discussion of the fatherhood of God, which has informed my argument here. Sherlock, *God on the Inside*, 141–50.

4. See extensive discussion on this passage in chapter 1.

dwells all God's fullness (Col 1:19; 2:9). The relationship between Father and Son needs further unpacking, so the reader will please bear with me and leave all the "Yes, but —!" questions for the moment. We are also going to comprehensively address the deity of the Holy Spirit in chapter 7; for now let's just mention a few points to set the scene.

Father, Son, and Holy Spirit are so often linked together in the New Testament as to raise the question, Why? What is the association between these names?

> The grace of the Lord Jesus Christ and the love of God and the fellowship of the Holy Spirit be with you all (2 Cor 13:14).

Christadelphians are very uncomfortable with doxologies and greetings such as these, and rarely if ever express them. Amongst some Christadelphian communities, the baptismal formula which is employed conveys baptism into the name of Jesus Christ (alone).[5] Other groups will use the threefold formula, acknowledging that it is commanded in Scripture.

> Go therefore and make disciples of all nations, baptizing them in the name of the Father and of the Son and of the Holy Spirit (Matt 28:19).

Notice that it is the *name* (*onoma*; singular) not names; the one name of God encompasses Father, Son, and Spirit. Furthermore, we don't read, "in the name of the Father and of the Son and of the angels," or "and of the apostles," or the patriarchs, or Moses or the virgin Mary, and rightly so. The angels, patriarchs, apostles, Mary, and every other human being, no matter how commendable they may be for their faith, cannot be put in the same category as Father, Son, or Holy Spirit. Angels and humans are created beings and they are not God. They are not to be worshiped (Rom 1:25) and it would be blasphemous to baptize in their name (see also 1 Cor 1:13). Other examples of triadic formulae include 1 Corinthians 12:4–6 and Ephesians 4:4–6.

> When Christadelphians admit that they would not naturally speak in the same terms as, for example, Paul's threefold blessing for the Corinthian church (2 Cor 13:14), or that they would never think of using the threefold baptismal formula of Matt 28:19, had it not been provided in that one verse, they show that they are not really living in the same three-fold experience that the first believers knew.[6]

The other question posed by this verse and the myriad others that group Father, Son, and Holy Spirit together in various ways is, why is the Holy Spirit included with Father and Son? The Christadelphian view is that the Spirit is an impersonal power or energy breathed forth from God, and while God and his Spirit are one, in the sense of light emanating from the sun, the Holy Spirit is not a person.[7] If this is the correct

5. The present author speaks from personal experience of this; a typical formula would be, "Upon this confession of your faith (in the things concerning the kingdom of God and the Name of Jesus Christ) I baptize you into the saving name of the Lord Jesus Christ, for the remission of sins, now past."

6. Clementson, "Christadelphians and the Trinity," 175.

7. Roberts, *Christadelphian Instructor*, 10; Tennant, *The Christadelphians*, 115.

way to view the Spirit, it seems a strange combination, effectively "In the name of the Father and of the Son and of the power of God." In chapter 7 we will discuss the personal nature of the Holy Spirit and the way Scripture often speaks of "God" and "Holy Spirit" (or spirit or spirit of God) interchangeably (eg., Gen 1:1–2; Acts 5:3–4; 1 Cor 12:6, 11) and groups Father, Son, and Holy Spirit together in intriguing ways (e.g. 1 Pet 1:2). For now, let's touch on some aspects of the relationships between the three.

- Jesus does the work of his Father (John 5:36) by virtue of he and the Father mutually indwelling; the Father, living in Jesus, was doing his work (John 14:10).

- God works in his people, imparting various gifts; this is the work of the Spirit (1 Cor 12:6, 11).

- Sometimes the Spirit is called the Spirit of God, at other times the Spirit of Christ (e.g., Rom 8:9–11; Phil 1:19; 1 Pet 1:11; 1 John 4:2).

- The Holy Spirit was sent from the Father and from the Son and in this way Jesus was said to be with them (John 14:16–18, 26; 15:26; 16:7–8, 13–15; 20:22; Acts 1:4–5; 2:38; 5:32).

So as not to preempt the later discussion, it will be left here for now, with the following interim conclusion. There is an intimate working relationship between Father, Son, and Holy Spirit and what one does, the others are also involved with and said to also be doing. Therefore, it is important to realize that while unqualified use of the name "God" in the New Testament generally means the Father (being addressed or spoken of by his children), this is not always the case, and "God" in both Testaments encompasses more than the Father. The Son and the Holy Spirit, *in some way*, must also be taken into account when coming to terms with who and what God is, what he does and how he works. This must be done whilst simultaneously acknowledging two essential concepts:

1. God is one; there are not three Gods.

2. Father, Son, and Holy Spirit are distinct; they are not the same "person" and they have different but complementary roles.

> The early Christian community worshiped Jesus, and was committed by those writings which it read in worship and regarded as Scripture to the belief that God could not be named adequately without speaking of Jesus (and the Holy Spirit). A doctrine of God that made sense of these practices and commitments would take centuries to work out, but that should not blind us to the reality and seriousness of the doxological practices and the exegetical commitments that shaped the community far more than its formulated doctrine.[8]

The unity of the Godhead has been explored in chapter 1 and defines the uniqueness of Deity and the separateness of God from creation such that God alone is to

8. Holmes, *Quest for the Trinity*, 55.

be worshiped. We have seen that Jesus Christ belongs on the "God" side of the line that divides God from all other reality. The distinctiveness and relationship between Father and Son will be the subject of the remainder of this chapter and that of the Holy Spirit in chapter 7. We will also look at different "models" for understanding what, on the surface, seems to be a contradictory set of assertions. We must find a way of speaking about God that does justice to all of the biblical elements and that includes speech about Jesus and the Spirit. When the evidence is assembled we will be in a position to compare the orthodox doctrine of the Trinity with the Christadelphian doctrine of God manifestation.

Blurring the Distinctions

One of the early heresies of the Christian church, as it struggled to understand the divinity of Jesus and his relationship to the Father, was *modalism*.[9] This term was coined by Adolf von Harnack to describe the common element of some second- and third-century schools of thought associated with the teachings of Noetus, Praxeas, and Sabellius. Modalism treats the Father, Son, and Spirit as different "modes" of the Godhead, in an attempt to safeguard against tritheism, the false doctrine that there are three Gods, and to uphold the unity of the Godhead. These writers concluded that there was one God, and that his self-revelation took place in different ways (modes) at different times.

There are variations on the idea of modalism, but all regard the Father as the aspect or mode of God revealed as creator and lawgiver, the Son as savior, and the Spirit as the sanctifier and giver of eternal life. Chronological modalism, also called Sabellianism, holds that these roles were successive; God was the Father at one point in history, the Son at a subsequent point and finally God appears as Spirit. Functional modalism teaches that God operates in different modes simultaneously. The danger in this view, and the reason it was rejected as an appropriate explanation of the relationship between Father, Son, and Spirit by the mainstream church, is that it blurs or eliminates the distinctions between the three. As we will see shortly, this is indefensible in terms of the scriptural evidence. It also underpins the erroneous idea of *patripassianism*, which teaches that the Father suffered as the Son on the cross. The Christadelphian doctrine of God manifestation verges on modalism, as can be seen from this explanation by an early Christadelphian.

> To speak of the Deity apart from "the Spirit of the Deity" in such a matter as this, is a mistake. The Deity and His Spirit are *one* . . . What one does, the other cannot be said not to do. The difference between the Father and the Spirit, is only a difference from our point of view . . . The spirit is but the infinite extension, so

---

9. For a good summary of modalism and other historical variations on and departures from accepted Trinitarian doctrine, see McGrath, *Christian Theology*, 254–68.

to speak, of Himself; and when the spirit does anything, it is the Father doing it, because the spirit is not separate from the Father.

Now on the question of God's manifestation in the flesh, the language is derived from God's point of view, because God is the actor. To ask then, whether it was the Father or the Spirit of the Father, that was veiled in the flesh, is to go off the track. The Father (by the Spirit) veiled himself in the flesh, and the result was Jesus of Nazareth, the Son of God and King of the Jews.

So Christ being the Father veiled in our flesh is styled the Deity, but this does not exclude the fact that literally, he is but the manifestation of him, viz., the Son of God, the man Christ Jesus. The two aspects co-exist.

Indeed, there is *a* trinity in the case, though not *the* Trinity. Jesus is "the Father, (manifested in (a) Son (by the) Holy Spirit," and in combination "these three are one."[10]

It was to combat the error of modalism that the Athanasian Creed included the prohibition against "confounding the Persons . . . for there is one Person of the Father, another of the Son and another of the Holy Spirit." When Scripture speaks of Father, Son, and Holy Spirit they are distinctive identities, interacting concurrently, not merely modes of being. This was particularly evident at Jesus' baptism.

And when Jesus was baptized, immediately he went up from the water, and behold, the heavens were opened to him, and he saw the Spirit of God descending like a dove and coming to rest on him; and behold, a voice from heaven said, "This is my beloved Son, with whom I am well pleased" (Matt 3:16–17).

The Son Is Not the Father

We have seen that the first-century Jew, Jesus of Nazareth, was uniquely the Son of God by virtue of his incarnation and conception in the womb of the Virgin Mary and that he is frequently referred to as Son of God and repeatedly spoke of God as his Father. Trinitarian Christians understand that the Son has always been "the Son" in eternal relationship to "the Father," and that these terms of themselves do not originate *solely* with the virginal conception. Jesus came to reveal the Fatherhood of God, something intrinsic to God himself, and something that had always been part of the relationships within the Godhead (John 5:37, 43; 6:46; 7:29; 8:19, 42; 17:5; Matt 11:27).

The angel declared to Mary that her child would be the Son of God (Luke 1:32). God the Father declared that Jesus is his beloved Son, in whom he is pleased (Matt 3:17; 17:5; Mark 1:11; 9:7; Luke 3:22; Acts 13:33). Jesus was acknowledged as the Son of God by Peter (Matt 16:16; John 6:69), John the Baptist (John 1:34), the disciples (Matt 14:33), Nathanael (John 1:49), and Martha (John 11:27). Demons/unclean spirits acknowledged him as the Son of God (Matt 8:29; Mark 1:24; 3:11; 5:7; Luke 4:41; 8:28). His enemies knew that he was called the Son of God, and Jesus did not refute this claim (Matt 26:63–64; 27:40, 43; Mark 14:61–62; Luke 4:3, 9; 22:70). Mark

10. Robert Roberts, cited in Nicholls, *Remember the Days of Old*, 42–44.

declares his gospel to be of Jesus Christ, the Son of God (Mark 1:1) and John stated that the purpose of his writing was to promote belief in Jesus as Son of God (John 20:31). Paul preached Jesus as the Son of God (Acts 9:20; Rom 1:3–4; 2 Cor 1:19).

Jesus Christ the Son of God and God the Father can be clearly demonstrated to be distinct from each other. They interact in an extraordinarily and uniquely close relationship, but they have different roles and they are different persons. It is important to understand that the doctrine of the Trinity does not deny this, and that proving a distinction between the Father and his Son does not refute the doctrine of the Trinity. In fact, orthodox trinitarianism is equally concerned to avoid modalism as it is to avoid subordinationism (see later) and tritheism.

God Sent His Son into the World.

The scriptural testimony is clear and explicit that the Father sent the Son into the world. The language of this sending does not imply that the Son's existence began at the point of his conception, but if anything that the Father–Son relationship was already established at the point when, "in the fullness of time," the sending occurred in the birth from a woman. Consider the following passages.

- For God so loved the world, that he gave his only Son, that whoever believes in him should not perish but have eternal life. For God did not send his Son into the world to condemn the world, but in order that the world might be saved through him (John 3:16–17).

- And the Father who sent me has himself borne witness about me. His voice you have never heard, his form you have never seen, and you do not have his word abiding in you, for you do not believe the one whom he has sent (John 5:37–38).

- Jesus said to them, "If God were your Father, you would love me, for I came from God and I am here. I came not of my own accord, but he sent me" (John 8:42).

- Do you say of him whom the Father consecrated and sent into the world, "You are blaspheming," because I said, "I am the Son of God?" (John 10:36).

- And this is eternal life, that they know you the only true God, and Jesus Christ whom you have sent (John 17:3).

- For I have given them the words that you gave me, and they have received them and have come to know in truth that I came from you; and they have believed that you sent me (John 17:8).

- For God has done what the law, weakened by the flesh, could not do. By sending his own Son in the likeness of sinful flesh and for sin, he condemned sin in the flesh (Rom 8:3).

- But when the fullness of time had come, God sent forth his Son, born of woman, born under the law (Gal 4:4).

- In this is love, not that we have loved God but that he loved us and sent his Son to be the propitiation for our sins . . . And we have seen and testify that the Father has sent his Son to be the Savior of the world (1 John 4:10, 14).

This was not a unilateral decision on the Father's part, however, because there is no conflict or coercion within the Godhead. The Son willingly accepted this role. Nevertheless, it was the role of the Father to send the Son, and the role of the Son to go.

> Then I said, "Behold, I have come to do your will, O God, as it is written of me in the scroll of the book" (Heb 10:7).

> Jesus said to them, "My food is to do the will of him who sent me and to accomplish his work" (John 4:34).

In John 5:17–20 we have seen that the Son does nothing of himself, but does what the Father does; he seeks the will of his Father (John 5:30). He came in his Father's name (John 5:43) and the Father set his seal on him (John 6:27). Because he came from God, Jesus knows the Father in a unique way.

> All things have been handed over to me by my Father, and no one knows the Son except the Father, and no one knows the Father except the Son and anyone to whom the Son chooses to reveal him (Matt 11:27).

> You know me, and you know where I come from. But I have not come of my own accord. He who sent me is true, and him you do not know. I know him, for I come from him, and he sent me (John 7:28–29).

The Father responded to the Son whom he sent, by always hearing him.

> I knew that you always hear me, but I said this on account of the people standing around, that they may believe that you sent me (John 11:42).

> Do you think that I cannot appeal to my Father, and he will at once send me more than twelve legions of angels? (Matt 26:53).

In summary, the trinitarian view sees the relationship between Father and Son as being established prior to the incarnation and "sending." The Christadelphian view sees the Son's existence beginning at conception and a subsequent commissioning or "sending."

The Son's Submission to the Father

Jesus prayed to his Father (Mark 1:35; 6:46; Luke 6:12; 11:1) and subjected his will to the Father's (Luke 22:42). He obeyed his Father, as the following passages affirm.

- And he said to them, "Why were you looking for me? Did you not know that I must be in my Father's house?" (Luke 2:49). (The word "house" is not in the original Greek, which reads literally "in the (things) of my Father it is necessary me to be." Hence some translations read, "about my Father's business.")

- And going a little farther, he fell on his face and prayed, saying, "My Father, if it be possible, let this cup pass from me; nevertheless, not as I will, but as you will" (Matt 26:39; Mark 14:35–36 is similar).

- I can do nothing on my own. As I hear, I judge, and my judgment is just, because I seek not my own will but the will of him who sent me (John 5:30).

- But I do as the Father has commanded me, so that the world may know that I love the Father (John 14:31).

- If you keep my commandments, you will abide in my love, just as I have kept my Father's commandments and abide in his love (John 15:10).

- For Christ did not please himself, but as it is written, "The reproaches of those who reproached you fell on me" (Rom 15:3).

- Then he added, "Behold, I have come to do your will" (Heb 10:9).

This submission to the Father's will was intrinsic to the emptying that Jesus underwent, as explained in the christological hymn:

> Who, though he was in the form of God, did not count equality with God a thing to be grasped, but made himself nothing, taking the form of a servant, being born in the likeness of men. And being found in human form, he humbled himself by becoming obedient to the point of death, even death on a cross (Phil 2:6–8).

> In the days of his flesh, Jesus offered up prayers and supplications, with loud cries and tears, to him who was able to save him from death, and he was heard because of his reverence. Although he was a son, he learned obedience through what he suffered (Heb 5:7–8).

Jesus is also spoken of as God's servant and is the fulfilment of the servant prophecies in Isaiah. See Acts 3:13, 26; 4:27, 30; Philippians 2:7–8; Hebrews 3:2; 5:8.

Jesus experienced a number of limitations to his authority in his earthy life:

- He said to them, "You will drink my cup, but to sit at my right hand and at my left is not mine to grant, but it is for those for whom it has been prepared by my Father" (Matt 20:23).

- But concerning that day and that hour, no one knows, not even the angels in heaven, nor the Son, but only the Father (Mark 13:32; also, Matt 24:36).

- So Jesus answered them, "My teaching is not mine, but his who sent me. If anyone's will is to do God's will, he will know whether the teaching is from God or whether I am speaking on my own authority" (John 7:16–17).

In addition, Scripture specifies that there were a number of things which it was *necessary* for Jesus to do, in order to fulfil Scripture and complete the work which the Father had given him. These included submitting to baptism (Matt 3:15) preaching (Mark 1:38; Luke 4:43) surrendering to suffering and death (Matt 26:54; Luke 24:26, 46; John 18:11; Heb 2:9) and being raised (John 20:9; Acts 17:3).

Christadelphians, Jehovah's Witnesses, and Unitarians see these limitations as "proof" that the Son was not intrinsically divine, but a human being who had to be exalted to "divinity" as a reward for his obedience and for the completion of the work of manifesting the Father. Trinitarians see these limitations as proof of his willing submission in taking the form of a servant, emptying himself as described in Philippians 2.

The Distinctiveness of Father and Son

There are numerous other passages which show that Jesus Christ and the Father are distinct persons. These are popular proof texts with Christadelphians, who believe that by demonstrating that the Son and the Father are distinct they have disproved the Trinity. However, the doctrine of the Trinity fully acknowledges that the Father and Son are distinct and does not blur their identities.

- And about the ninth hour Jesus cried out with a loud voice, saying, "Eli, Eli, lama sabachthani?" that is, "My God, my God, why have you forsaken me?" (Matt 27:46).

- You heard me say to you, "I am going away and I will come to you." If you loved me, you would have rejoiced, because I am going to the Father, for the Father is greater than I (John 14:28).

- I am the true vine, and my Father is the vine dresser (John 15:1). (This is obviously a metaphor, but as with many of Jesus' illustrations and parables, he and the Father play different roles.)

- This Jesus God raised up, and of that we all are witnesses (Acts 2:32).

- But I want you to understand that the head of every man is Christ, the head of a wife is her husband, and the head of Christ is God (1 Cor 11:3).

- Then comes the end, when he delivers the kingdom to God the Father after destroying every rule and every authority and power. For he must reign until he has put all his enemies under his feet. The last enemy to be destroyed is death. For "God has put all things in subjection under his feet." But when it says, "all things are put in subjection," it is plain that he is excepted who put all things in subjection under him. When all things are subjected to him, then the Son himself will also be subjected to him who put all things in subjection under him, that God may be all in all (1 Cor 15:24–28).

- Blessed be the God and Father of our Lord Jesus Christ, who has blessed us in Christ with every spiritual blessing in the heavenly places (Eph 1:3).

- For to which of the angels did God ever say, "You are my Son, today I have begotten you"? Or again, "I will be to him a father, and he shall be to me a son"? (Heb 1:5).

- You have loved righteousness and hated wickedness; therefore God, your God, has anointed you with the oil of gladness beyond your companions (Heb 1:9).

These passages from Hebrews 1 must be read in the context of the description of the supremacy of Christ, in which he is addressed as "God" and Creator and is worthy of worship.

There are also many passages which speak of Jesus being given things by his Father. These things are all-encompassing; *all* authority, *all* things (Matt 11:27; 28:18; Luke 10:22; John 3:35; 13:3; 17:2, 7; Eph 1:22; Heb 1:2; 2:8). Nothing is left out when we understand that Jesus has been given "all things" but Scripture also singles some things out as having been specifically given to Jesus by his Father:

- His testimony/words/teaching (John 3:11, 32, 34; 7:16; 8:26, 28, 38, 40; 12:49–50; 14:10, 24; 17:8)

- Judgment (John 5:22, 27; Acts 10:42)

- Life in himself (John 5:26; 10:17–18)

- Works (John 5:36; 14:10; 17:4)

- People (John 6:37, 39; 10:29; 17:6, 9, 11, 12; Heb 2:13)

- Glory (John 17:22, 24; 1 Pet 1:21; 2 Pet 1:17)

- "The cup" (John 18:11)

- The Name above every name (Phil 2:9; Heb 1:4)

- The Spirit (John 3:34–35)

Scripture is also clear that "God" (sometimes specifically the Father) raised Jesus Christ from the dead (Acts 2:24; 3:26; 4:10; 5:30–31; 10:40; 13:30, 33, 37; Rom 10:9; 1 Cor 6:14; 15:15; 2 Cor 4:14; 13:4; Gal 1:1; Eph 1:19–20; Col 2:12; 1 Thess 1:10; Heb 13:20; 1 Pet 1:21).

The Unity of Father and Son

Although it is clear that the Father and Son are distinct, with different roles, there is also an undeniable unity to their relationship, a unique association that transcends a normal father–son relationship.

But Jesus answered them, "My Father is working until now, and I am working." This was why the Jews were seeking all the more to kill him, because not only was he breaking the Sabbath, but he was even calling God his own Father, making himself equal with God. So Jesus said to them, "Truly, truly, I say to you, the Son can do nothing of his own accord, but only what he sees the Father doing. For whatever the Father does, that the Son does likewise" (John 5:17–19).

For the Son to be able to do *whatever* the Father does, he must be divine. Father and Son work together, not separately or at crossed purposes, as can be seen from these passages.

- "That all may honor the Son, just as they honor the Father. Whoever does not honor the Son does not honor the Father who sent him" (John 5:23).

- "And he who sent me is with me. He has not left me alone, for I always do the things that are pleasing to him" (John 8:29).

- "I and the Father are one" (John 10:30).

- When he had gone out, Jesus said, "Now is the Son of Man glorified, and God is glorified in him. If God is glorified in him, God will also glorify him in himself, and glorify him at once" (John 13:31–32).

- "Do you not believe that I am in the Father and the Father is in me? The words that I say to you I do not speak on my own authority, but the Father who dwells in me does his works" (John 14:10).

- "That they may all be one, just as you, Father, are in me, and I am in you, that they also may be in us, so that the world may believe that you have sent me. The glory that you have given me I have given to them, that they may be one even as we are one" (John 17:21–22).

The Father and Son glorify each other; the glorification of one glorifies the other. It is a shared glory. Take particular note, in each of the following verses, *who* is to receive glory, and from *whom*.

- Jesus answered, "If I glorify myself, my glory is nothing. It is my Father who glorifies me, of whom you say, 'He is our God'" (John 8:54).

- But when Jesus heard it he said, "This illness does not lead to death. It is for the glory of God, so that the Son of God may be glorified through it" (John 11:4).

- When he had gone out, Jesus said, "Now is the Son of Man glorified and God is glorified in him. If God is glorified in him, God will also glorify him in himself, and glorify him at once" (John 13:31–32).

- "Whatever you ask in my name, this I will do, that the Father may be glorified in the Son" (John 14:13).

- When Jesus had spoken these words, he lifted up his eyes to heaven, and said,

"Father, the hour has come; glorify your Son, that the Son may glorify you" (John 17:1).

- "And now, Father, glorify me in your own presence with the glory that I had with you before the world existed" (John 17:5).

- "Father, I desire that they also, whom you have given me, may be with me where I am, and to see my glory that you have given me because you loved me before the foundation of the world" (John 17:24).

- To the only wise God be glory for evermore through Jesus Christ! Amen (Rom 16:27).

- The light of the gospel of the glory of Christ, who is the image of God . . . For God, who said, "Let light shine out of darkness," has shone in our hearts to give the light of the knowledge of the glory of God in the face of Jesus Christ (2 Cor 4:4–6).

- He [the Son] is the radiance of the glory of God and the exact imprint of his nature (Heb 1:3).

- [God] equip you with everything good that you may do his will, working in us that which is pleasing in his sight, through Jesus Christ, to whom be glory for ever and ever. Amen (Heb 13:21).

- In order that in everything God may be glorified through Jesus Christ. To him belong glory and dominion for ever and ever. Amen (1 Pet 4:11).

- But grow in the grace and knowledge of our Lord and Savior Jesus Christ. To him be the glory both now and to the day of eternity. Amen (2 Pet 3:18).

- To the only God, our Savior, through Jesus Christ our Lord, be glory, majesty, dominion and authority, before all time and now and for ever. Amen (Jude 1:25).

- And I heard every creature in heaven and on earth and under the earth and in the sea, and all that is in them, saying: "To him who sits on the throne and to the Lamb be blessing and honor and glory and might for ever and ever!" (Rev 5:13).

The above include just a selection of verses which ascribe glory to God the Father, or to Jesus, or both, or in some cases it is unclear which of the two is being glorified. This sharing of glory is all the more remarkable in the light of God's adamant declarations in Isaiah of the exclusivity of his glory; he will not give his glory to another (Isa 42:8; 48:11). Correctly understood, these Isaiah passages do not contradict the passages which speak of God sharing his glory with his Son, whom we understand to also be the Lord, YHWH.

The Subordination of the Son

We now appear to have a dilemma. There are passages which ascribe divinity to Jesus, including his lordship and participation in the name YHWH, his activity in creation and his being the image of God, sharing God's glory and encompassing all God's fullness. Yet we see that he, as the Son of God, is distinct from the Father, both in personhood and in role. In fact while on earth he was clearly in a position of dependence on the Father, a position which theologians refer to as subordination.[11] How are these features to be reconciled?

Christadelphians and other non-trinitarians see the subordination of the Son to the Father as clear evidence that Jesus Christ is inferior *in being* to the Father and therefore not God.[12] This would contradict the evidence we have explored to this point. The doctrine of the Trinity fully embraces the distinctiveness of the Persons of Father and Son, and also the willing subordination of the Son to the Father in his role as Savior and Redeemer of humanity.

Different Roles

The Father, the Son and the Holy Spirit relate to the created world in different ways; they have different functions or roles. Trinitarian theologians speak of the "economy of the Trinity" or the "economic Trinity," using a now rather obsolete sense of the word "economic," meaning the ordering of activities, similar to the ordering of a household ("home economics").[13]

In creation, God the Father spoke the words which brought the universe into being, but the Son, the Word of God, carried out these creative decrees (John 1:3; Col 1:16; Ps 33:6; 1 Cor 8:6; Heb 1:2) and the Holy Spirit was also active as an agent (Gen 1:2; Ps 104:30). In redemption, God the Father planned redemption and sent his Son into the world (see the numerous passages about the sending of the Son in the previous section). The Son obeyed the Father and accomplished this redemption. After Jesus rose and ascended into heaven, the Father and the Son sent the Holy Spirit (John 14:26; compare John 15:26 and 16:7), to regenerate (John 3:5–8), sanctify (Rom 8:13–17;

---

11. The doctrine of the subordination of the Son, which mainstream trinitarians accept, must be distinguished from the doctrine of subordination*ism*, which orthodox Christianity has regarded as heresy. Subordination*ism* holds that the Son is inferior in *being* to the Father, not just subordinate in role. A form of subordinationism was promulgated by Origen c. AD 185–254, so care must be taken in citing Origen's views as representative of mainstream Trinitarian thought. See Grudem, *Systematic Theology*, 245.

12. For example, "Jesus . . . did not claim to be equal with his Father . . . Jesus regularly explained the superiority of his Father in every respect" (Morgan, *Understand the Bible*, 107).

13. However, "economic trinitarianism" can be a synonym for dispensational trinitarianism which teaches that the three Persons with their distinctive roles only appeared at creation and will merge back together at the consummation, so we need to watch the terminology and context of the discussion carefully. See Bray, *Doctrine of God*, 128.

15:16; 1 Pet 1:2) and empower (Acts 1:8; 1 Cor 12:7–11) believers. We will have more to say about the work of the Holy Spirit and his relationship to the Father and to the Son in chapter 7. The sixteenth-century reformer, John Calvin, put it this way:

> Nevertheless, it is not fitting to suppress the distinction that we observe to be expressed in Scripture. It is this: to the Father is attributed the beginning of activity, and the fountain and wellspring of all things; to the Son, wisdom, counsel and the ordered disposition of all things; but to the Spirit is assigned the power and efficacy of that activity.[14]

In carrying out these roles, the Father and Son relate to each other exactly the way in which we would expect a father and son to do, in an ideal family. Of course, the human experience is modelled in the image of God, not vice versa. The Father directs the Son and has authority over him; the Son responds to and obeys the Father. The Father and Son love each other in a sharing relationship. In a human family, a son's submission to his father does not make the son any less a person, an inferior being. It is his *role* which is one of submission, out of respect for the father's position in the family. Likewise, in the antitype of the human family, the Son's submission to the Father does not make him a lesser being in the ultimate sense, even though as Father he is "greater" (John 14:28). In contrast, as Lord (*Adonai*/YHWH) the Christ is greater than his human father David (Ps 110:1; Matt 22:41–45).[15] As a child, Jesus submitted to his human parents, even though he was their Lord (Luke 2:51). The fifth-century theologian Augustine of Hippo has an excellent and detailed explanation of the subordination of the Son, but we can only touch on a couple of his summary statements here.

> Christ with respect to himself is called God; with respect to the Father, Son. Again, the Father with respect to himself is called God; with respect to the Son, Father. Insofar as he is called Father with respect to the Son, he is not the Son; in so far as he is called the Son with respect to the Father, he is not the Father; in so far as he is called both Father with respect to himself, and Son with respect to himself, he is the same God.[16]

> Provided then that we know this rule for understanding the scriptures about God's Son and can thus distinguish the two resonances in them, one tuned to the form of God in which he is, and is equal to the Father, the other tuned to the form of a servant which he took and is less than the Father, we will not be upset by statements in the holy books that appear to be in flat contradiction with each other. In the form of God the Son is equal to the Father, and so is the Holy Spirit, since neither of them is a creature . . . In the form of a servant, however, he is less than the Father, because he himself said, "The Father is greater than I" (John

---

14. Calvin, *Institutes* I.13.18.

15. In the Hebrew, "the Lord" is YHWH, "my Lord" is *Adonai*. In the LXX, which Jesus quotes, both are *Kyrios*, Lord.

16. Augustine, *Psalms*, cited in Calvin, *Institutes*, I.13.19.

14:28); he is also less than himself, because it is said of him that "he emptied himself" (Phil 2:7).[17]

Augustine contrasts a number of statements about the Son and explains them in terms of these two "forms." This is only a selection from a long and comprehensive list:[18]

in the form of God	taking the form of a servant
all things were made by him (John 1:3)	he was made of a woman, made under the law (Gal 4:4)
I and the Father are one (John 10:30)	he did not come to do his own will but the will of him who sent him (John 6:38)
so also the Son has life in himself (John 5:26)	if it can be, let this cup pass from me (Matt 26:39)
he is true God and life eternal (1 John 5:20)	he became obedient unto death (Phil 2:8)
everything that the Father has is his (John 16:15; 17:10)	his doctrine is not his own (John 7:16)

In John's gospel, Jesus seems to take great pains to explain in detail this Father–Son relationship of which he is a part. Given that the Jews to whom he presented his case viewed him as a mere regular human being, the natural son of Joseph and Mary (Mark 6:3), why would they react so vehemently against Jesus' claims about this Father–Son relationship, reading into it a clear claim on Jesus' part to be divine, if the thrust of his argument were to prove his *inferiority* of being? In reality, what the continual reiteration of the Father–Son relationship does, is prove Jesus' unique relationship with his Father, a relationship which blueprints but transcends that of a human family. In reading these passages in John, far from getting the impression that Jesus is downgrading his role, we begin to see how closely associated he is with the God of the universe. They are inseparable. Read again John 10:24–39 and see to what it was that Jews were taking exception, and how Jesus described his relationship with the Father.

So, once again, in quoting verses which speak of Jesus' submission to his Father, doing his Father's will, receiving his authority from the Father, etc., Christadelphians

17. Augustine, *De Trinitate*, 86 (book 1, 22).

18. Ibid., 86–96 (book 1, 22–30).

are attacking a straw man if they believe this disproves the deity of the Son or the doctrine of the Trinity. The full doctrine of the Trinity *includes* the concept of equality of being and subordination in role; it is an integral part of how the Trinity is understood. The doctrine is not only big and sophisticated enough to encompass the subordination of the Son to the Father, the idea is *essential* and *intrinsic* to a correct articulation of the doctrine. To argue otherwise and say, for example,

> There probably is no greater refutation of the doctrine of the Trinity than the repeated declarations by Jesus of His subserviency to the Father: and not only His subserviency, be it particularly remarked, but His very nature's antagonism to His Father's will.[19]

is to simply misrepresent the trinitarian understanding of the Godhead.[20] It's just plain *wrong*, and it betrays either misunderstanding or deception on the part of those who seek to refute the trinitarian position in this way. It's just as fruitless and erroneous as arguing that proving the full humanity of Jesus disproves the doctrine of the Trinity.

Eternal Subordination?

It is clear that the Son was subordinate to the Father during his incarnation; at the very least until his exaltation. It is also evident that the Father, Son, and Holy Spirit continue to interact with creation in distinct roles now. But this begs the question as to whether the roles of Father, Son, and Holy Spirit were so defined prior to the incarnation, indeed prior to creation—and whether they will continue in these relational roles for eternity. Ultimately, there is very little that can be discerned from Scripture as to what God was "doing" before creation and precisely what will happen through all future eternity. God has chosen to reveal very little of this to us. But we can look at what evidence there is and reverently surmise within these limitations.

First and foremost, God is absolutely self-sufficient and independent. He does not *need* his creation, even though he created it for his glory.

> Nor is he served by human hands, as though he needed anything, since he himself gives to all mankind life and breath and everything (Acts 17:25).

Many verses in the Psalms, in God's self revelation to Job and elsewhere indicate that God is above his creation and has no reliance upon it. But what about companionship, relationship? Was God "lonely" for eternity prior to making man in his image? That is clearly not the case. In an earlier chapter we discussed the possible implications

19. White, *Doctrine of the Trinity*, 105. This author quotes extensively from contemporary "eminent Trinitarians" of non-specific background—and evidently quite out of context. He cites several succinct descriptions of the Son's subordinate role, which on the surface appear to support his contentions, but when correctly understood in the context of the full doctrine of the Trinity, are quite irrelevant to his argument.

20. For example, Roberts, *Christendom Astray*, 159–61; Tennant, *The Christadelphians*, 88–90; Roberts, *Bible*, 55–56.

of the plural of *elohim* in Genesis 1:26; "Let us make man in our image . . ." Whether this is interpreted as a communication within the Godhead or between God and the angels, evidently there was some sort of plurality and interaction before humans were made relationally as male and female. We are not told when God created the angels, but the implication would appear to be that it was prior to the creation of the earth in its present form (Job 38:4–7). Nevertheless, the angels are created beings (Psalm 148:2–5) because only God intrinsically has immortality (1 Tim 6:16) even though the angels have evidently been granted immortality now (Luke 20:36).

But what about the eternity before the creation of the angels? Was God alone then? Were there prior creations? We have no way of knowing in this life, because God has not chosen to reveal this detail, however he has told us that he had *relationship* before the present creation.

> And now, Father, glorify me in your own presence with the glory that I had with you before the world existed (John 17:5).

The Greek here for "with you," as the ESV and KJV translate it, is the preposition *para* with the dative:[21] *para seautō*, meaning with, or in the presence of. Christadelphians endeavor to explain away this passage by attributing it to God's foreknowledge of the glory the Father would share with his Son after his exaltation. But this will not do, it is not what the passage is saying; the context of Jesus' prayer in John 17 is all about having been sent into the world and subsequently leaving the world, there is nothing to hint of foreknowledge. Later in the chapter, Jesus again refers to his relationship with the Father prior to creation.

> Father, I desire that they also, whom you have given me, may be with me where I am, to see my glory that you have given me because you loved me before the foundation of the world (John 17:24).

Again, Christadelphians will argue that God looked forward to the day of Christ and loved him in anticipation. Verses typically cited are Rev 13:8 "the book of life belonging to the Lamb that was slain from the creation of the world," and 1 Pet 1:20 "He was chosen before the creation of the world, but was revealed in these times for your sake." The accompanying argument is that Jesus did not die before the first century AD, so this must be speaking of foreknowledge and predestination, therefore the same applies to Christ having glory with the Father before creation. Similarly, they argue that because Jesus' birth was foretold in the Old Testament as a future event that the Son could not have preexisted[22] (which fails to distinguish between the preexistent Son and the beginning of the man Jesus at the incarnation). This sort of logic is flawed.

---

21. Abel, *Wrested Scriptures*, 296–97, tries to argue from other uses of *para* that *para* means from, not with or alongside, however he completely ignores the basic grammatical principle that in Greek the case determines the meaning of the preposition, not vice versa. The dative in John 17:5 indicates the sense of with, not from (genitive) or to (accusative).

22. Heavyside, "Jesus in the Synoptic Gospels," 60–61.

Certainly the Son's role as Lamb of God was foreordained before the incarnation, but this does not preclude his preexistence, especially in view of verses which clearly speak of sharing God's glory in his presence. If anything, the *certainty*[23] of the Son's destiny in his work on earth would seem to go hand in hand with his literal existence, rather than disproving it.

The Christadelphian position relies upon a metaphorical interpretation of all passages which speak of or allude to Christ's preexistence.[24] Appeal is sometimes also made to the foreordaining of God's kingdom (Matt 25:34), of the election of believers (Rom 8:29; 9:23; Eph 1:4; 2 Tim 1:9), and the commissioning of specific people for a particular task before birth (e.g., Jer 1:5). If God foreordained these things, then surely that is what is meant in the passages which appear to suggest Christ preexisted, so the argument goes. The problem is, these latter passages about the kingdom, elect believers, Jeremiah etc., *specify* that they are talking about God's foreordaining; no one reading these passages would dream of interpreting them as Jeremiah or others literally existing before creation. However the context and terminology of these passages is different from the context and terminology about Christ. There is no direct comparison. The plain meaning of texts such as John 17:5 and 24, as well as John 6:62 and verses which teach the Son's involvement in creation is that *he was there*, not just that he was anticipated. Whilst the Son's redeeming *work* and its consequences were foreordained and not actuated until his presence on earth, the argument for his preexistence as a being stands.

Having digressed somewhat, we return to the discussion of what we know of God prior to creation. In summary, we have established that the Son was loved by the Father and shared his glory. Another aspect to consider is that God is, in a fundamental sense, unchangeable. Without entering into the discussion about God's responsiveness to people, whereby he makes conditional covenants, appears to change his mind or "repent,"[25] we can affirm that in terms of his being and essential character, God does not change.

23. In order to sustain their interpretation of the atonement, Christadelphians tend to emphasize that the success of Christ's mission was not a certainty, because he was merely human but not God incarnate, so there was every possibility he could have failed to be sinless. This is a complex subject, but the following explanation is typical. "If Jesus was part of an eternal Godhead, his mission to earth was really bound to succeed—it couldn't be otherwise. But if he first came into existence on earth, there was no certainty about the success of his mission. It depended upon him and his willingness to do his Father's will" (Morgan, *Understand the Bible*, 109). This seems to require an annulment of the sovereignty of God and the certainty of his promises in order to refute the divinity of the Son. See also Alfred Norris's struggle with the logic of this position in the booklet *The Person of the Lord Jesus Christ*, 23–24.

24. Coleman, "Jesus, Son of Man, Son of God," part 1, is one Christadelphian author who bravely acknowledges this and shows that denial of the literal preexistence of the Son is what makes Christadelphians look like adoptionists.

25. This is an enormous subject in itself, and reinvigorated in the debate concerning Open Theism and the views of limited divine foreknowledge put forward by Clark Pinnock and others. The various perspectives on the subject are presented in Beilby and Eddy, *Divine Foreknowledge*. A comprehensive

But you are the same, and your years have no end (Ps 102:27).

In this psalm, God's unchangeableness is contrasted with the transience of what humans would perceive to be most permanent; the heavens and earth.

For I the LORD do not change; therefore you, O children of Jacob, are not consumed (Mal 3:6).

This verse speaks of the unchanging nature of God's covenant faithfulness; a consistent aspect of his perfect character.

Every good gift and every perfect gift is from above, coming down from the Father of lights with whom there is no variation or shadow due to change (Jas 1:17).

Again, God's loving character and faithfulness to his people do not change. God's counsel, or plans for his creation, the "big picture" of his plan of redemption and the consummation of his kingdom, are also unchanging (Isa 46:9–11; Ps 33:11; Matt 25:34; Eph 1:4, 11; 3:11) and are *guaranteed* of fulfilment.

This makes it difficult to rest the success of God's plan on any uncertainty with respect to the obedience of Christ, as if his human will were stronger than the divine influence, which has to be the Christadelphian position in order to defend their doctrine of Christ's person. But without this restrictive view, rather than the success of God's eternal plan being left to chance in order to make Jesus' temptations "real," the problem is solved by Jesus being fully man (and hence really tempted) and yet fully God (hence able to overcome temptation).[26]

Interestingly, Hebrews 13:8 tells us that "Jesus Christ is the same yesterday and today and forever." At first glance this verse seems a bit awkward and out of context. It isn't, if we take the whole context of Hebrews, including 1:10–12, which quotes Psalm 102:25–27 verbatim as a statement about the Son, who endures and whose years have no end. But what does 13:8 actually mean? The word for yesterday, *echthes*, is used only eight times in Scripture and in the other seven verses it means, literally, the day before today. The word "today," *sēmeron*, is used extensively and sometimes means literally the current twenty-four hour period but can also carry the sense of the present time, as in "currently," or "now" (eg., Matt 6:30; Luke 13:33; Acts 22:3). The word "forever" is *aiōnas*, and may mean an age, such as the age to come, or eternity. So overall this verse is rather vague in what it suggests; does "yesterday" link with

survey of the Open Theism view is presented in Pinnock et al., *The Openness of God*. There is very little written specifically on the subject of God's foreknowledge and immutability in Christadelphian literature. Robert Roberts in *The Ways of Providence*, argues via extensive biblical examples that God works through and with human agency and that chance does occur. Generally, the Christadelphian position on human free will and predestination versus foreknowledge tends to be Arminian rather than Calvinist, although they would eschew both labels.

26. Contra Alfred Norris, who must allow enough divine influence on the human Jesus to permit his sinlessness, yet deny its inevitability, and all without any divine coercion or interference with Jesus' human nature! Norris, *The Person of the Lord Jesus Christ*, 23–24.

eternity and imply the infinite past, or simply a short, recent period? How far ahead does *aiōnas* stretch? In what way is Jesus Christ "the same" during this period past, present and future? It cannot mean the same in a physical sense, for Jesus' existence on earth as a human being had a defined beginning with his conception. As usual, we must turn to the context for assistance.

Hebrews 13 is a chapter of encouragement and refers to the past experiences of God's people (verse 2), some of God's unchanging laws and principles (verses 4–5), the completeness and efficacy of Christ's redeeming work (verses 10–12) and God's steadfast faithfulness (vv. 5–6) and eternal covenant (verse 20). In the midst of this, verse 8 would seem to suggest that what remains the same is Christ's integral and eternal role in the interaction of God with his people, embedded in his love and covenant faithfulness; like Father, like Son.

There are clues that the roles and relationships of Father, Son, and Spirit have applied prior to creation. It seems reasonable that, what God is now, is what he has always been. Human fatherhood and family derive from the Fatherhood of God (Eph 3:14–15). If the work of commanding and sending is the work of the Father, then election was a work of the Father in eternal past (Eph 1:3–4; Rom 8:29). When the Father predestined, it was a predestination to be conformed to the image of his Son (Rom 8:29). God sent his Son into the world when the time was right (John 3:16–17; Gal 4:4; Luke 20:13) indicating a Father–Son relationship before the incarnation. Likewise, Scripture speaks of the Father creating through the Son (John 1:3; 1 Cor 8:6; Heb 1:2) rather than the Son or Holy Spirit creating through the Father. The limited evidence we have from Scripture concerning the time before creation indicates an eternal relationship whose out-workings are seen in the different roles of Father, Son, and Holy Spirit.

There is nothing to suggest that these roles involved the sort of submission or subordination that the Son undertook in his incarnation, however. Philippians 2:6–8, which we have already discussed in some detail, tells us that Jesus was in the form of God and had equality with God, something he refused to exploit in humbling himself to take the form of a servant. Hebrews 5:8 tells us that the Son, although he was a son, learned obedience by the things which he suffered. The fact that obedience was something he *learned* means that the original nature of his sonship excluded the necessity of obedience (the Godhead being all of one mind and purpose); it was a new experience and was associated with his suffering as God's servant.

We have seen that the role of the Son involved a willing subordination or submission to the Father who sent him. There is abundant detail in the New Testament concerning this subordination during Jesus' time on earth, as we have seen. The question remains, to what extent does this subordination or humbling (as we discussed in the context of Phil 2) continue now that the Son has been raised and exalted to the Father's right hand? This question needs to be addressed in terms of two phases; first, Jesus' status and work now, and second his status following his return and the final consummation of the kingdom.

Jesus' Current Status and Role

After his resurrection and prior to his ascension, Jesus told his disciples that "All authority in heaven and on earth has been given to me. Go therefore and make disciples of all nations, baptizing them in the name of the Father and of the Son and of the Holy Spirit" (Matt 28:18–19). Jesus already had extensive authority during his earthly ministry, as we have seen, but now he has *all* authority, and this is linked with the commission to use the three-fold name in baptizing. He was worshiped during this post-resurrection period (e.g., Matt 28:9; Luke 24:52) but we have also seen that he was worshiped before his death as well (e.g., Matt 14:33). He told Mary Magdalene "I am ascending[27] to my Father and your Father, to my God and your God" (John 20:17), and a week later Thomas addressed him as "My Lord and my God" (John 20:28). Jesus still regarded God as his Father and obviously as God, even though he himself accepted being addressed as God.

Following the period of forty days with his disciples after his resurrection, Jesus ascended to heaven as he had told Mary he would (Luke 24:51; Acts 1:9–11). He took his place at the right hand of God the Father (Acts 2:33; 7:56; Eph 1:19–20; Col 3:1; Heb 1:3, 13; 8:1; 10:12; 12:2; 1 Pet 3:22) sharing his throne (Rev 3:21). God has exalted him to the highest place and given him the name above all names, YHWH, that at this name *of his*, every knee should bow and every tongue confess that Jesus Christ is Lord, to the glory of God the Father (Phil 2:9–11). There is no inconsistency in the lordship of Jesus being to the glory of the Father. As we have seen, to glorify the one is to bring glory to the other. To honor the one is to honor the other. We thus see a symmetry in this passage which comes full circle; God the Father exalts—gives Jesus the Name—Jesus is Lord—God the Father is glorified. There is a strong allusion to Isaiah 45, which declares that there is no God and savior other than YHWH and before him every knee will bow and every tongue swear (Isa 45:21–23).

We read of several appellations of Jesus which apply to the exalted Christ.

- He is Lord of all; he is King of Kings and Lord of Lords (Acts 10:36; Rev 19:16—compare 1 Tim 6:15).

- He is the Alpha and Omega, beginning and end (Rev 2:8, 22:13, and compare 1:8; 21:6).

- He is the head of the church (Eph 1:22; Col 1:18).

- All things are in subjection under him (Eph 1:22; Heb 2:5, 8; 1 Pet 3:22).

- Has become higher than the heavens, perfected forever (Heb 7:26).

- He is Prince and Savior (Acts 5:31).

27. The ESV and KJV translate the word as "ascending," but the NIV's "returning" is not a good translation, even though the idea is elsewhere supported; the word is *anabainō*, ascend.

Jesus is not passively waiting for his time to return to earth; he is active in the ongoing processes of salvation and sanctification.

- He is our mediator (1 Tim 2:5; Heb 2:18; 4:15; 7:24–25; 8:6; 9:15; 12:24) and advocate (1 John 2:1).

- He sends the Spirit (Acts 2:33).

- He walks among the lampstands; he knows his church (Rev 1–3) and works in it (e.g., Acts 1:24).

- He provides access to the Father; prayer is made in his name (John 14:13–14; 15:16; Rom 7:25; Eph 2:18; Col 3:17) although there are some examples of prayer directly to Jesus (Acts 1:24; 7:59–60).[28]

Is the Son still submissive or subordinate to the Father in his exalted state? A couple of verses in 1 Corinthians need to be addressed in order to answer this question.

> But I want you to understand that the head of every man is Christ, the head of a wife[29] is her husband, and the head of Christ is God (1 Cor 11:3).

The word "head" here is *kephalē*, which means, primarily, the part of the body containing the brain. It also has the secondary connotation, as in English, of headship, superior rank or high status as well as meaning "source" or origin.[30] Christ is not only head of the church (Eph 4:15–16; Col 1:18), but is head over everything (Eph 1:10, 22; Col 2:10). The context of 1 Corinthians 11:3–16 is propriety in worship for both genders and the word *kephalē* appears thirteen times in these few verses. Apart from verse 3, every other usage implies the physical head:

- Every man who prays or prophesies with his head covered dishonors his head.

- Every woman who prays or prophesies with her head uncovered dishonors her head, as if her head were shaved.

- If a woman does not cover her head she should have her hair cut off; if this would be a disgrace she should cover her head.

- A man ought not to cover his head since he is the image and glory of God.

- Because woman came from man and was created for man, and is the glory (note, not the image) of man, and because of the angels, the woman ought to have authority on her head. (The Greek simply reads, "authority on her head," not "a sign or symbol" of authority).

---

28. A chapter on prayer to Jesus in Scripture may be found in Bowman and Komoszewski, *Putting Jesus in His Place*, 47–53.

29. The ESV has a footnote explaining that the Greek *gynē* may be translated as woman or wife, and *anēr* as man or husband, depending on context. The context of the chapter appears to be wives and husbands because of the reference to the veil that married women wore.

30. BDAG, 541–42.

If we connect these rather obscure verses back to verse 3, it makes sense if the man covering his head was seen to be covering Christ, his head. Man was created in the image of God (so, actually, was woman—Gen 1:27) although only Christ fulfils this image and truly glorifies God. Conversely, it is appropriate for the woman/wife to cover her head, which is, or represents, the man/husband. This covering equates in some way to authority.[31] The difference between men and women here is not the image of God, for they both bear that, but something to do with glory and authority. Thiselton, in his thorough exegesis of this passage, concludes that in drawing on the relationship between God and Christ, Paul is emphasizing both order and differentiation on one side and mutuality and reciprocity on the other.[32] There are many interpretations of this passage, but it seems that the argument Paul is using in verses 4–10, which presumably made perfect sense to his first-century readers, is somewhat obscure today and it is difficult to say whether verse 3 is meant to explain verses 4–10 or vice versa. Ultimately though, verse 3 would seem to indicate that God—either the Father or the Godhead overall—is the seat of authority and/or glory with respect to Christ.

> Paul stresses first of all the pattern of relationships which God has written into the Christian community . . . In other words, the divine order is: God . . . Christ . . . husband . . . wife. The husband is no more superior to his wife than God is superior to Christ. But as Christ chose to submit himself to his Father, so the wife should choose to submit herself to her husband . . . So God is the source of Christ, Christ (as creator) is the source of man, and man ("out of his side"—Gen 2:21) is the source of woman (so 11:8).[33]

Gordon Fee argues that the passage is about appropriate relationships and distinctions between men and women, for which the relationship between God and Christ is the theological point of reference.[34] As God is the source of Christ in incarnational terms, so too is Christ the source of man as both original Creator and as source of the new creation, in which he is head of the church (1 Cor 11:12).

Jesus' Future Status and Role

Several major events occur around the time of the *parousia*, or coming of Christ. Without getting side-tracked into discussion concerning the meaning and timing of the thousand year period or the exact sequence of these events, in summary:

---

31. There is undoubtedly tremendous cultural significance in these verses, which we probably fail to appreciate. First-century Greek women wore a veil (*kalumma*) on their hair; the exceptions were mistresses, prostitutes, and pagan priestesses; slaves and adulteresses had shaved heads. In contrast to what Paul advocates here, Jewish synagogue tradition was, and still is, that men worship with covered heads. Prior, *1 Corinthians*, 180.

32. Thiselton, *First Corinthians*, 803–4.

33. Prior, *1 Corinthians*, 183.

34. Fee, *First Corinthians*, 504–5.

- There will be a general resurrection (1 Cor 15; 1 Thess 4:13–17; Rev 20:4–6, 11–13).

- There will be a gathering of the elect (Matt 24:30–31).

- The Day of the Lord will come as a thief and be a time of dreadful judgment in which the enemies of God will be destroyed (Matt 13:24–30; 24:30–31, 36–44; 25:31–46; Acts 17:31; Rom 2:5, 16; 2 Cor 5:10; 2 Tim 4:1, 8; 2 Pet 3:7; Rev 20:11–15; 21:8).

- The earth will be purged and renewed (Matt 5:5; 2 Pet 3:7, 10, 13; Rev 5:10; 21:1).

- There will be no more sin or sorrow or death (1 Cor 15:25–26, 51–56; Rev 21:4, 27; 22:1–2, 15).

- God will dwell with humankind (Rev 21:3, 22–24; 22:5).

Apart from announcing the continuation of God dwelling with humankind in the new heavens and new earth, the abolition of sin and death and this glorious existence into eternity, the revelation essentially stops here. As with the infinite period of time before creation, there is little revealed in Scripture concerning the details and events of the infinite period of time beyond the second coming of Christ and the consummation of the kingdom. There are two key passages: 1 Corinthians 15 and Revelation 21–22.

> For as in Adam all die, so also in Christ shall all be made alive. But each in his own order: Christ the firstfruits, then at his coming those who belong to Christ. Then comes the end, when he delivers the kingdom to God the Father after destroying every rule and every authority and power. For he must reign until he has put all his enemies under his feet. The last enemy to be destroyed is death. For "God has put all things in subjection under his feet." But when it says, "all things are put in subjection," it is plain that he is excepted who put all things in subjection under him. When all things are subjected to him, then the Son himself will also be subjected to him who put all things in subjection under him, that God may be all in all (1 Cor 15:22–28).

When Christ completes the work of consummating the kingdom, bringing everything into subjection and abolishing death, he will hand over the kingdom to God the Father. This will be the culmination of Christ putting everything (except God) under his feet and God putting everything under Christ. This seems at first contradictory; who is actually doing the putting-under? The difficulty disappears if we understand there is no dichotomy between God and Christ. It is not as if God was not reigning up to this point, or that there was nothing subject to him until this time, but it is a change in the character of God's reign in that everything that opposes him has been put down and the work of Christ as mediator is at an end. Nevertheless, at the very end, the Son himself, in his completed role as servant, mediator and priest is made subject[35] to "him who put all things in subjection under him;" which must be God the Father (verse 24). The purpose and outcome of this willing subjection is "that God may be all in all."

The passage does not explain what God being "all in all" means, but we can form a picture of sorts from the final chapters of Revelation.

- The New Jerusalem, the bride of the Lamb, symbolizing the sanctified elect, will be joined in marriage with the Lamb (21:2, 9–10).

- The dwelling of God will be with men (21:3) and his servants will serve him and see his face (22:3–4).

- Everything will be made new (21:5).

- God and the Lamb are the Temple and the source of light for the city (21:22–23; 22:5).

- The throne of God and of the Lamb is in the city (22:3).

Overall then, Scripture speaks of the Father glorifying the Son and the Son glorifying the Father, and the Holy Spirit glorifying both. The Father gives everything he has to the Son, the Son gives everything to the Father and the Spirit serves both. The Father gives all authority in heaven and earth to the Son; the Son then delivers the kingdom to the Father and subjects himself to the Father, who put all things under the Son, with the result that God is all in all.

The Father was at the forefront of the work of creation, but both the Word and the Spirit were present and involved, as agents. The Son was at the forefront of the work of redemption, but both the Father and the Spirit were present and involved (2 Cor 5:19; Heb 9:14); the Father in giving the Son and the Son's work accomplished through the Spirit. The Spirit is at the forefront of the work of sanctification, but both Father and Son are present and involved; they both send the Spirit of Christ/Spirit of God. The Son and Spirit always work with the Father and will do so throughout eternity, God all in all.

Does this mean that the eternal subordination of the Son contradicts or repudiates the doctrine of the Trinity, as Christadelphians claim? The answer is no; it is completely compatible with the Trinity, as correctly understood. To support this assertion, let's hear a trinitarian, evangelical perspective.[36]

> A brief account of the early Church councils and the Church fathers shows that
> they adopted the doctrine of the eternal subordination[37] of the Son, and that

---

35. Augustine has an interesting and detailed discussion of this in *De Trinitate*, 83–85 (book 1, 20–21).

36. Kovach and Schemm, "Eternal Subordination of the Son," 461–76.

37. Kovach and Schemm note the important distinction of subordination from subordination-*ism*, the view that the Son and the Spirit are inferior to the Father in essence and status, endangering the Son's essential divinity (ibid., 463).

this doctrine continues in the Church as orthodoxy to this day. The biblical record also confirms the eternal subordination of the Son. There are at least two main categories that affirm eternal subordination: the Son's relation to the Father and the Son's role on behalf of the Father. Economic subordination, adopted by the Council of Nicea, means that while all three divine Persons are identical in essence, the Son is economically subordinate to the Father with respect to his eternal mission and function. The Son is no less than the Father, but has voluntarily submitted himself to the will of the Father.

The idea of subordination does not necessarily entail inferiority . . . Subordination is *not* inferiority and it *is* God-like. The principle is embedded in the very cohesion of the eternal Trinity . . . it is not a mark of inferiority to be subordinate, to have an authority, to obey. It is divine. Voluntary subordination is always necessary to the establishment of genuine community. This is true for the Godhead as well as for people.

From the second century onward a concept of the Son's subordination to the Father has been combined with a concept of the full equality among the Three. Each is seen to be fully, equally and eternally divine, although in their relationship to one another, the Father assumes supremacy and the others a subordinate role.

Summary

- The Father is God, but God is not limited to the Father.

- Father, Son, and Holy Spirit work as a functional unity and are commonly described in association with each other.

- Modalism, with which Christadelphian beliefs have some kinship, is an inadequate expression of the relationship between Father, Son, and Holy Spirit.

- The Son of God is distinct from the Father. The Father sent the Son into the world. The Son's role was one of submission to the Father and he did the Father's will. The Father gave authority and teaching to the Son. The Father raised the Son from the dead.

- Nevertheless, there is a special unity between Father and Son; they work together and glorify each other.

- Father, Son, and Holy Spirit have different roles in respect to how they relate to creation and to humanity in particular.

- Intrinsic to these different roles is the functional subordination of the Son to the Father; this is necessary to a full understanding of the doctrine of the Trinity.

- There are few direct clues in Scripture as to the eternal roles within the Godhead, but the evidence strongly indicates that the subordination of the Son is not limited to his time on earth.[38]

38. There is currently some debate about the doctrine of eternal subordination of the Son amongst evangelical theologians. The contrasting position, that the subordination of the Son to the

- God is unchangeable in his nature, being and character and the indications are that the relationships of Father, Son, and Holy Spirit are eternal.

Further Reading

- Wayne Grudem, *Systematic Theology*, chapter 14, "The Trinity," especially section D, 284–52.

- Stephen D. Kovach and Peter R. Schemm, "A Defense of the Doctrine of the Eternal Subordination of the Son."

- Augustine, *De Trinitate* [*The Trinity*]. Also available at http://www.ccel.org/ccel/schaff/npnf103.iv.i.iii.html but this older translation is much less readable than Edmund Hill's book.

Father applied to his incarnation and "humbling" only, and is not an eternal status, is presented by Bilezikian, "Subordination in the Godhead," 57–68.

6

Reconciling the Divine and Human in Christ

Misconception #9: That it defies logic for Jesus to be fully God and fully man.

Corrective: Truth is not constrained by what we find easy to comprehend; God determines what is true.

Misconception #10: That Christadelphians deny any attribution of divinity to Jesus.

Corrective: Christadelphians teach that Christ has a derived or bestowed divinity.

Misconception #11: That the Christadelphian doctrine of God manifestation adequately accounts for the attribution of divinity to Jesus.

Corrective: The manifestation of God in Jesus Christ is an important aspect of Christ as "God with us," but the Son's identity goes beyond the pattern established by angelic representation.

SO FAR, WE HAVE argued from Scripture that Jesus Christ is the Word made flesh; God incarnate, and that he is both divine and human. We have seen that the Son is distinct from the Father, and although he is God, he has willingly taken a subordinate role to the Father with respect to God's dealings with his creation and the salvation of humankind. In this chapter we need to explore further how it can be that Jesus is both God and man, divine and human, Son of God and Son of Man and what the implications of this are. We will compare and contrast the mainstream and orthodox Christian view (the Trinity) with the Christadelphian view (God manifestation). Then, in subsequent chapters, having explored the doctrine of the Holy Spirit, we will bring the various threads together to present the full doctrine of the Trinity.

The incarnation of the Son, the coming together of the divine and human in the man Jesus Christ, is a concept with which Christadelphians have tremendous difficulty. Unfortunately, their writings tend to misrepresent trinitarian understanding of the subject and present scriptures to "disprove" what trinitarians don't actually believe. Here are a few examples.

> Robert Roberts (1884): Trinitarianism propounds—not a mystery, but a contradiction—a stultification—an impossibility. It professes to convey an idea, and no sooner expresses it than it withdraws it, and contradicts it. It says there is one God, yet not one but three, and that the three are not three but one. It is a mere juggle of words, a bewilderment and confusion to the mind . . .[1]

> Christendom believes Christ to be the incarnation of one of three distinct essences, or personalities, which are supposed to constitute the God-head; and that though clothed in human form, he was God in the absolute sense of being the Creator . . . The supremacy and unity of the Father would not be affirmable if there were three co-equal personalities in His One personality—a doctrine which presents us with a contradiction in terms as well as in sense. Jesus emphasizes the distinction between himself and the Father.[2]

> Percy E White (1913): . . . how that Jesus had pre-existed as the Second Person of the Trinity—"the Word"—and how that this "Word" was clothed with human flesh to effect the means of salvation for man. Jesus, therefore, when on earth, would be a person of ordinary outward appearance, and dominated within by His perfect self, His real being, the soul —which in this particular case would be "the Word"—such as is commonly urged is resident in every man to will: the body alone being purely the medium of the soul's deliberations . . . given that the soul of Jesus was the "Word" which became resident in flesh to work the joint determination of the Father, the Son and the Holy Ghost, it is immediately obvious that but one will could have dominated Jesus . . .[3]

> Michael Ashton (1991): Jesus was a whole and complete character. He brought his closeness to God to bear upon the problems all human beings receive as sons of Adam, and overcame them. He could only do this if he truly shared these same characteristics. The established church's view of Jesus as a divine being in an envelope of human flesh (what they define as the Incarnation) utterly fails to provide an answer to this need.[4]

---

1. Roberts, *Christendom Astray*, 135. Roberts goes on to argue for the oneness of God and the distinctions between Father, Son, and Holy Spirit, as if these contradict the Trinity. He has also misrepresented the trinitarian position in asserting that God is held to be one *in the same sense* as he is held to be three; see chapter 8.

2. Ibid., 155. Roberts here makes the contradiction in terms. Trinitarian theology teaches that there are three persons within the essence or being of the Godhead, not three persons in one person, and that the Son is the incarnation of one person, not one of three essences. This betrays a lack of understanding of the doctrine or its scriptural basis. And again, to prove that the Son is distinct from the Father is no argument against the Trinity, which affirms this truth.

3. White, *The Doctrine of the Trinity*, 108–11. White is here attacking, not the mainstream trinitarian position, but the heresy of Apollinariansim, the extreme form of Word-flesh Christology, which was rejected at the Council of Constantinople in AD 381, and which denied that Christ had a human soul. See chapters 2 and 9. He hasn't done his homework.

4. Ashton, *Studies in the Statement of Faith*, 35. Ashton has made the same error as White; he assumes, incorrectly, that trinitarians teach that the divine Word was simply encapsulated in a body, without a human soul.

Julian Clementson, in a clear and balanced discussion of the differences between Christadelphian and evangelical beliefs concerning the Godhead, makes the helpful observation that much of the misunderstanding comes down to differences of language.

> Much popular language used for the Trinity is not helpful for those from a Christadelphian background. The simple statement, "Jesus is God," can be misleading and is certainly incomplete . . . the statement without qualification seems to be, at best, a contradiction or, at worst, a denial of Jesus' humanity . . . The statement, "The Holy Spirit is a person," is similarly open to the misunderstanding that it refers to a separate being . . . Nor is the "three persons" language of the patristic era particularly helpful . . . to the modern mind a person is a distinct individual being, and on these terms, God is clearly one person, not three.[5]

As a former Christadelphian who has come to terms with what trinitarianism really means, I concur with Clementson's appraisal, with the following rider. Whilst it is understandable that the average "Christadelphian in the street" would be confused by unqualified trinitarian language, I don't think it's excusable for Christadelphian apologists, who commit their polemics against the Trinity to writing, to so misrepresent the doctrine as some of those quoted in the present work do. One notable exception is Thomas Gaston, in his commendable endeavor to engage in a scholarly manner with the doctrines of the Trinity and "Biblical Monotheism." In his introduction he carefully defines the doctrine of the Trinity as three Persons in one substance and points out some common misunderstandings of it.[6] Unfortunately, some of the contributing authors in his book are not so careful and fall into some of the misinterpretations we have been discussing.

Once again, Ron Coleman presents the Christadelphian position with refreshing honesty.

> We often describe our belief by saying that Jesus was the Son of God, not God the Son . . . However if someone were to ask us, "What is the difference between God the Son and the Son of God?" we might find it rather a difficult question to answer. If the questioner were to prompt us by saying "Do you think Jesus is divine, then?" we would probably reply "Yes." But the next question might well be—"If Jesus is divine, don't you believe in two Gods—God the Father and Jesus?" "No," we would say, "Jesus is not divine in the same way God is. He said his Father was greater than he. So he cannot be co-equal and co-eternal with God, as the doctrine of the Trinity maintains." "What then," our questioner might persist, "is Jesus a demi-God, half man and half God?" I imagine that most of us would find it difficult to answer that question. So what at first seems to be a very satisfactory belief leads us quickly to something we would have considerable doubt about. If a lion is mated with a tiger, the offspring is a creature which has some features of a lion and some features of a tiger, but is neither a lion nor a tiger. Christians have always refused to believe that Jesus was a hybrid of this kind and I imagine that

---

5. Clementson, "Christadelphians and the Trinity," 174–75.

6. Gaston, *One God the Father*, 12.

we would be of their number. Our belief amounts in effect to a refusal to pronounce on how Jesus can be both son of man and Son of God at the same time.[7]

Christians wrestled with the reconciliation of the divine and human in Christ for several centuries and came up with a number of alternatives. Christadelphians are not alone in finding it a difficult doctrine to articulate, although few Christadelphian authors really acknowledge this, preferring to play down the complexity of their own view.

The Word Made Flesh: The Unity of the Person of Christ

It is clear from the scriptural evidence that Christ has a human nature and a divine nature, but this raises some important questions. Does Christ have two natures, or one? If two, then how are they combined? How can God become man? Did he have two wills, or one? How can he be both fully God and fully man? Before we address these issues, we need to first understand the significance and necessity of Christ being *both* divine and human.

In order for Jesus Christ to bridge the spiritual gap between God and humanity, Jesus needed to unite both. In order to atone for sin, he needed to partake fully of sinful flesh and experience the temptations and frailties that are common to humanity; he needed to be one of Adam's race. But in order to save us and become our righteousness, fully satisfying the righteousness of an infinite and holy God, he needed to be God. Yet it is not a case of God and man side by side as it were, within a single body. That would not be true unity and it would not bridge the gap. We will discuss the implications of the trinitarian and non-trinitarian understandings of the person of Christ for the atonement in the final chapter. For now, let's reinforce the fact that Jesus Christ is one person, with all his attributes perfectly united.[8]

Jesus Christ Is a Unified Person

There are no references in Scripture to a duality in Jesus' being. There are references to both his divine and human origin and attributes, which are clearly united in a single person. John 1:14 tells us that the Word became flesh and dwelt among us and we have seen *his* glory, glory as of the only Son from the Father. Galatians 4:4 states that God sent forth his Son, born of woman. He made his dwelling, we saw his glory; he is God's Son, but born of a woman—one person.

> Great indeed, we confess, is the mystery of godliness: He was manifested in the flesh, vindicated by the Spirit, seen by angels, proclaimed among   the nations, believed on in the world, taken up in glory (1 Tim 3:16).

---

7. Coleman, "Jesus, Son of Man, Son of God," part 1. Note that this magazine *Endeavour* is not regarded as an officially sanctioned Christadelphian publication.

8. I draw upon the work of Millard J. Erickson for this section; *Christian Theology*, 660–73.

The same "he" appeared incarnate, was present and active in the world and ascended to heaven. This verse is interesting because it is the basis for the Christadelphian doctrine of God manifestation, based on the KJV translation; "God was manifest in the flesh." The Greek is *hos ephanerōthē en sarki*, where the verb *phaneroō* means to make manifest or to reveal (more of that later). The verse does not actually specify "God," it says "*who* was manifest in the flesh," but the context of the preceding verse makes it clear we are talking about "the living God," who is described in the context of "his church," a descriptor which usually relates to Jesus.

Ephesians 2:14–18 summarizes the work of Christ in reconciling both Jew and Gentile to God and providing access to the Father by the Spirit; the emphasis is on unification and it was accomplished in himself, in one body. 1 John 4 speaks of God sending his Son as a propitiation or atoning sacrifice (4:10, 14), who came in the flesh (verse 2) and is the Son of God (verse 15). Passages such as 1 Corinthians 2:8, John 3:13, and John 6:62 describe his work, juxtaposing his divine and human attributes but in all respects speaking of the single person Jesus Christ.

At no point do we get the impression from Scripture that Jesus was in any way a dual or "split" personality, or a divine mind in a fleshly shell. However, in a sense there *is* a duality in Jesus; God and man, powerful yet weak, all-knowing (John 1:47; 4:29; 16:30) and yet limited in knowledge (Mark 13:32). B. B. Warfield explains that "a duplex life is attributed to him as his constant possession . . . The glory of the Incarnation is that it presents to our adoring gaze, not a humanized God or a deified man, but a true God-man—one who is all that God is and at the same time all that man is."[9] Bowman and Komoszewski elaborate further, in defense of the complexity of Christ's person and our need to not shy away from this.

> One of the attributes of God is that he is *incomprehensible*. This does not mean that we cannot know anything about God or that we cannot know him in the sense of having a personal relationship with him. What it does mean is that a full, complete, definitive understanding of God is beyond our capacity . . . Likewise, although we may know something about Jesus Christ, he remains to some extent inscrutable and incomprehensible (Matt 11:27) . . . Would we expect to understand how he could experience our humanity to the full and still be God? We would *expect* paradoxes or mysteries, all down the line, with respect to his attributes. And that is exactly what we find.
>
> On the other hand, if Jesus were merely a great human being or even an angel who somehow became a human being, we would not expect him to have been a fundamentally incomprehensible individual. Precisely because Jesus is both God and man, he is the preeminent, paradoxical person.[10]

This duality is seen clearly in respect to his will, or wills, especially in the incident in the garden of Gethsemane. Jesus prayed, "My Father, if it be possible, let this cup pass from me; nevertheless, not as I will, but as you will" (Matt 26:39, see also Mark

9. Warfield, "The Human Development of Jesus," 163, 166.

10. Bowman and Komoszewski, *Putting Jesus in His Place*, 122–23.

14:36 and Luke 22:42). Given that Jesus's will is elsewhere described as completely in line with his Father's (John 4:34; 5:30; 6:38) we have an apparent contradiction. This seems to be a tension of wills in which we see two tendencies within Jesus, that of the flesh versus that of the divine, in which the flesh submits to the divine. *Overall*, Jesus always did what pleased his Father; *overall*, the divine will prevailed within the person of Jesus, which was part of the process of experiencing—yet overcoming—temptation (Heb 4:15) and condemning sin within the very flesh in which it normally reigns (Rom 8:3). Indeed, if there had not been such a tension, there would have been no real temptation and no real victory over sin.

Getting the Right Balance

We have seen in previous chapters that Jesus demonstrated both human and divine attributes. In terms of his humanity, he truly shared our nature. He lived amongst the people of Galilee and Judea like any other man and experienced hunger, fatigue, suffering, temptation, and the full range of human emotions. His humanity was essential to his work of overcoming sin in "the flesh" and being a truly representative sacrifice, as well as a compassionate and understanding mediator. Yet he also demonstrated divine authority and powers, he spoke the words of God and claimed a unique relationship with the Father which surpassed that of other men. The titles by which he is described portray his humanity (Messiah/Christ, servant, son of David, Son of Man) and his divinity (Lord, God, Son of God, Holy One of God, Alpha and Omega, King of Kings).

The thinkers and writers of the early church mulled over this combination of human and divine and sometimes came up with erroneous ideas that were biased toward one aspect or the other. Each of these ideas was rejected by orthodox Christianity as it moved toward the current understanding of the unity of natures in Christ. As in most situations where it is necessary to carefully balance two diverse concepts, it is very easy to swing too far one way or the other; extremes beget extremes and divergent opinions misrepresent each other. Consequently many of these heresies sprang up in a misplaced endeavor to combat an opposing heresy.

Some ideas over-emphasized Jesus' humanity and downplayed his divinity:

- *Adoptionism* (Ebionism)—In this second-century Jewish-Christian school of thought, Jesus was merely a man, albeit a great prophet. He was the natural son of Joseph and Mary but did not become anything special until the Holy Spirit descended on him at his baptism. By fulfilling the law he earned the title Christ, but was in no way divine.

- *Arianism*—Fourth-century teachings of Arius, who agreed that the Son was pre-existent and divine, but his divinity was only derived and he was in fact a creature; "there was a time when he was not." Arianism persisted for some centuries and prompted the major theological discussions which resulted in the elucidation of the orthodox doctrine of the Trinity. The Jehovah's Witnesses today are successors of the Arians in their understanding of Jesus Christ.

- *Nestorianism*—A fifth-century school of thought that, in opposition to Apollinarianism, and in an attempt to emphasize the humanity of Jesus, stressed the two natures in Christ to the point where Christ was effectively seen as two persons in one body. It may not actually have been quite as extreme as this, however, since much of what we know of this teaching was written by its opponents.

Other ideas over-stressed Jesus' divinity and downplayed his humanity:

- *Docetism*—A second-century heresy hinted at as early as the New Testament, which taught that Jesus only *seemed* human, his humanity and suffering were not real but merely an appearance.

- *Gnosticism*—In some versions of this widespread second- to fourth-century cult, Jesus takes the role of the heavenly redeemer figure who imparts the secret knowledge that frees souls from their captivity to matter.

- *Apollinarianism*—Fourth-century Alexandrian doctrine which overplayed the divinity of Christ at the expense of his humanity, teaching that the divine *Logos* took the place of the human soul in the man Jesus, making him a divine being clothed in a shell of flesh, with a single, divine will. This doctrine was repeatedly condemned by the fourth-century church councils, which recognized the importance of the doctrine of Christ's humanity. Christadelphians are prone to confusing mainstream trinitarianism with Apollinarianism.

- *Eutychianism*—An ill-defined, fifth-century spin-off from Alexandrian theology that taught Christ had only one nature, the divine.

It was in the context of these opposing and unbalanced views that the final position of the church was established. This context provides the background to the creeds of the ancient church and the key to interpreting them.[11] In particular, the Chalcedonian Definition of AD 451 was a response to the conflict between Apollinarianism/Eutychanism and Nestorianism. It is not so much a trinitarian definition of who Jesus *is*, but sets the boundaries concerning who and what he is *not*. This explains why it reads the way it does. We'll return to the full definition in chapter 9, but for now note the main points.

---

11. Christadelphians are very critical of these creeds and argue that they demonstrate a gradual and consistent movement away from biblical truth. But an understanding of the historical and theological context of the creeds shows they were written to combat specific heresies, rather than to replace scriptural teaching, as will be shown in chapter 9. The Christadelphians use their *Statement of Faith* and *Doctrines to be Rejected* in a similar way to how the mainstream churches use the creeds, but would vehemently deny that they "replace" Scripture—it would be good to show trinitarians the same courtesy.

1. To combat reductions of the divinity of Christ

    *   "Perfect in Godhead . . . truly God . . . consubstantial with the Father according to the Godhead"

    *   "Christ, Son, Lord, Only-begotten . . . God the Word"

2. To combat reductions of the humanity of Christ

    *   "Perfect in manhood . . . truly man . . . of a reasonable soul and body"

    *   "Consubstantial with us according to the Manhood"

    *   "In all things like unto us, without sin"

    *   "In these latter days, for us and for our salvation, born of the Virgin Mary"

3. To combat division of Christ into two persons

    *   "One and the same Son, our Lord Jesus Christ"

    *   "Of a reasonable soul and body"

    *   "One and the same Christ, Son, Lord, Only-begotten"

    *   "To be acknowledged in two natures, inconfusedly, unchangeably, indivisibly, inseparably; the distinction of natures being by no means taken away by the union, but rather the property of each nature being preserved, and occurring in one Person and one Subsistence"

    *   "Not parted or divided into two persons, but one and the same Son, and only begotten, God the Word, the Lord Jesus Christ"

The Doctrine of Two Natures in One Person

Whilst the Chalcedonian definition helps set the boundaries of the envelope, beyond which a teaching reflects an imbalance between the divine and human aspects of Christ, it essentially works from the outside in, countering extreme and incorrect views, rather than from the inside out, starting from a scriptural perspective and developing it. That's not so much a criticism—it served a historical-theological purpose—but it is a limitation. So let's get back into Scripture.

Returning to Philippians 2:6–8 and recapping, we saw that the "emptying" that Jesus underwent was not an emptying of his divine attributes, but a relinquishing of the rights of equality with God. He submitted or subordinated himself to the Father, taking on the form of a servant, and being found as a man. In doing this, he accepted certain limitations on the functioning of his divine attributes. The essential point is that these voluntary limitations were not the result of a *loss* of divine attributes, but of the *addition* of human attributes.

We also see in countless examples of Jesus' words and deeds that his divine and human natures did not function independently, as if the left hand and the right hand were autonomous. He did not exercise his deity at some times and his humanity at others. They always worked in concert in a unified and whole individual. Perhaps the best illustration of this is during Jesus' childhood and adolescence, of which Scripture gives us only the briefest glimpse.

- And the child grew and became strong, filled with wisdom. And the favor of God was upon him (Luke 2:40).

- And all who heard him were amazed at his understanding and his answers (Luke 2:47).

- And he said to them, "Why were you looking for me? Did you not know that I must be in my Father's house?" (Luke 2:49).

- And Jesus increased in wisdom and in stature and in favor with God and man (Luke 2:52).

Hebrews 4:15 states that we do not have a high priest who is unable to sympathize with our weaknesses, but one who in every respect has been tempted as we are, yet without sin. Luke tells us that as a child, Jesus *grew* in strength and wisdom, from a helpless babe to a twelve-year-old who could converse with the scholars in the temple and give them a run for their money, and then on to become a mature man. He *grew* in favor with God, God's grace was upon him and at least by twelve years of age he knew who he was and the course his life would take. We are not privy to any more details than that, but throughout this process of growth—a very human experience and quite a limitation for one being "in the form of God"—he *never sinned*. What two year old *never* threw a tantrum in selfish indignation? What child *never* disobeyed his parents, taking another child's toys, or bopping them on the head, or refusing to come when called? What child *never* pushed the limits of the parental admonition, "Don't!"? What adolescent was *never* defiant or selfish or insolent?

Only one child, one adolescent, one man, in the entire history of humanity: Jesus. We know he was *tempted* to do all of these things, otherwise Hebrews 4:15 is meaningless, but he never carried those temptations over the boundary line where they gave birth to actual sins (Jas 1:15). God in his divine perfection cannot be tempted, and certainly cannot sin, but Jesus in his humanity could be, and was, tempted yet did not yield to that temptation. Here is the essence of what it means for Christ to be both divine and human. If he was merely human, he could not have overcome temptation, he couldn't have been sinless. If he were lacking in humanity,[12] he could not have been truly tempted.

12. The counterpoint to "if Christ was merely human" could be phrased as "if Christ were merely God," but that seems a completely inappropriate way to express the idea of divinity without humanity, but I expect my meaning is evident.

It is virtually impossible to find anything in older Christadelphian writings which tackles *how* Jesus could have been sinless, without being God. The issue is approached, but sidestepped, and usually attributed to a special awareness of God, or reliance on Scripture or sheer force of will in dedication to his calling.[13] Alfred Nicholls says that Jesus inherited Adam's nature from his mother, and from God his Father he inherited a perfect character able to withstand temptation, and a keen spiritual insight.[14] Harry Tennant merely says "The obedience of the Lord Jesus Christ grew and was tested under the stress of chastisement and the allurement of temptation," without discussing how this might happen in a boy whose character was "developing."[15] Tecwyn Morgan introduces the element of uncertainty with his claim that "there was no certainty about the success of [Jesus'] mission. It depended upon him and his willingness to do the Father's will . . . God caused a Son to be born and asked him to surrender his life in total obedience. This Jesus did, He did not have to do it; he chose to do it, and that is an important difference."[16]

Of the "classical" Christadelphian writers, Alfred Norris probably tackles the issue in most detail. He argues that it was not inevitable that Jesus was sinless, by virtue of being the Son of God, or his temptations would have been ineffectual (which, he claims, is the case with the doctrine of the Trinity). Jesus' reward "was the fruit of high achievement, which in fact meant total self-abasement." However, being the Son of God must have had some effect on Jesus' sinlessness, otherwise any man could have done it.

> Without divine begettal we can safely suppose that the Lord could not have been a sinless man, and could not, if for that reason alone, have been our Savior . . . If, in achieving that end, it was needful that he be endowed with help which the rest of us have not, should we be envious on that account?

Norris goes on to suggest that because Jesus had been perfectly enlightened by God, he could not possibly have sinned through ignorance (which still doesn't explain how the child Jesus was sinless whilst still growing in wisdom).[17] It would seem that far from "depriving Him of any real victory," an appropriate balance of divine strength and human weakness is equally applicable to the concept of the incarnate Son, whose natures were perfectly unified.

Erickson explains succinctly that "By taking on human nature, [Jesus] accepted certain limitations upon the functioning of his divine attributes. These limitations were

---

13. To a large extent this evasiveness is attributable to a series of significant schisms within Christadelphia over the nature of Christ, such that anyone venturing to speculate on the extent of divine influence on the human Jesus is likely to be misunderstood or even condemned by some elements of the group. With a new generation of writers the topic is receiving renewed attention.

14. Nicholls, *Remember the Days of Old*, 60, 63.

15. Tennant, *The Christadelphians*, 98.

16. Morgan, *Understand the Bible*, 109–11.

17. Norris, *The Person of the Lord Jesus Christ*, 23–25.

not the result of a *loss* of divine attributes but of the *addition* of human attributes."[18] He adds the helpful analogy of the world's fastest sprinter voluntarily entering a three-legged race, or the world's greatest boxer fighting with one hand tied behind his back. "Ability is not in essence diminished, but the conditions imposed on its exercise limit actual performance." This is why we have the apparent paradox of Jesus knowing so much about people and about events still future, yet not knowing the day of his return at the time of the Olivet prophecy (Matt 24:36). Part of this voluntary self-limitation seems to be so that he could learn and experience dependency upon the Father; perhaps that is why he saw the temptation to turn stones into bread as an unacceptable solution to his hunger, even though he was quite willing to provide bread miraculously for four or five thousand at a time, or why he chose to walk and become weary, when he could conceivably have travelled like Elijah (1 Kgs 18:46) or Philip (Acts 8:39–40).

In contrast, the Christadelphian understanding of what it meant to be the Son of God is focused entirely on his conception.

> It may be asked, How then was Christ different from any other child? The answer is positive and simple: God was his Father. The marks of the Fatherhood of God were to be seen in Jesus. Jesus knew that God was his Father, and by this means he had an affinity with God which no other person had even known, even though he bore this affinity in the frailty of human flesh. His mind was wonderfully alert and active.[19]

> Jesus inherited from his Father the capacity to know Him, to be open to Him, to have a genius for Him . . . In the world of Jesus there was no secular education. Sons learned their trade as apprentices from their fathers. How successfully they did so would depend upon the aptitude and disposition of the son to learn, and also of the readiness of the father to teach. With this Father and Son both conditions were perfectly fulfilled . . . Because of (his) human inheritance Jesus could have thwarted or suppressed his divine genius, or allowed it to wither. Supremely gifted men often carry, together with the precious gift of genius, failings which blemish that gift. This was possible for Jesus. But he took this human nature and hardened and tempered it in the fires of temptation until it became a new nature, complete, sinless, filled with the spirit and utterly tendered in loving obedience to God.[20]

This is somewhat helpful, but doesn't really explain how the two-year-old, ten-year-old or fifteen-year-old Jesus (still in the process of tempering his nature) could have been sinless, without requiring the direct, coercive influence of God to override his natural (and immature) human tendencies. Granted that Jesus *grew* in his understanding of who he was, there would have been a time when his understanding was limited and how then was temptation to be overcome? Clementson observes:

---

18. Erickson, *Christian Theology*, 670. The italics in the quotation are mine. Augustine's arguments in *De Trinitate*, book 1 are essentially the same.

19. Tennant, *The Christadelphians*, 97.

20. Coleman, "Jesus, Son of Man, Son of God," part 4.

> We must exercise caution when Jesus is made to seem "superhuman" by virtue of a special nature brought about by his virginal conception. There is a weakness in Christadelphian doctrine precisely at the point where it understands the "divinity" of Jesus in terms of special qualities present in his unique human nature, because it makes him too different from the rest of us to be a viable example for living.[21]

In other words, the more divine influence we must impose upon Jesus for him to be sinless, the less his humanity remains isolated. The more humanity we demand, undiluted from divinity, the less likely he could have overcome sin. This issue is resolved by recognizing the *full* humanity and *full* divinity of Christ, but is never truly resolved by Christadelphians.

Is the Incarnation a Logical Impossibility?

Christadelphians criticize the creeds, and any attempts to explain the doctrine of the Trinity or the incarnation, as being illogical, confusing, contradictory, and downright impossible; they allege them to be against reason.[22]

> It is no small matter either that those who most diligently support this doctrine [the Trinity] candidly admit that it involves them in the meshes of contradiction and absurdity. While many continue to illogically hide behind the cry that the whole doctrine is a mystery, there are those who admit the inconsistency of grafting this incomprehensible doctrine on to the simple and reasonable system of religion—pre-eminent among religions for its clarity—originally revealed by God himself and in latter times effectually confirmed in Jesus Christ.[23]

Let's address this charge. First, we do well to exercise a little humility here. Just because I find something difficult to understand, even incomprehensible, does not mean it is wrong. Human reason can only go so far when talking about God. This does *not* mean that we should leave our reason behind when we do theology, but sometimes we need to acknowledge that the limitation may be with us. Job had to learn that lesson when he questioned God's justice and was firmly put in his place. I don't understand how God can listen to millions of prayers at once, determine the future, and preside over an incomprehensibly large universe, nor how he has always existed without beginning. I cannot comprehend his absolute knowledge and power. Nor do I have the foggiest idea how he will resurrect people long turned to dust or scattered ashes and renew our natures to be incorruptible and immortal. But I don't reject these

21. Clementson, "Christadelphians and the Trinity," 168.

22. The most vehement accusations tend to be made in the writings of the "Pioneers" of the Christadelphian faith, and the early to mid-twentieth-century writers, as well as more recently those of Logos Publications, South Australia. Apart from the latter, since the 1980s the tone has tended to be rather more respectful of others' beliefs.

23. White, *The Doctrine of the Trinity*, 79. The author goes on to very briefly cite, without any context whatsoever, "four writers upon theological matters" who admit to the doctrine of the Trinity as being confounding, incompatible with human ideas and unintelligible.

doctrines on the grounds of my own feeble reason. Occasionally a Christadelphian writer is generous enough to recognize our human limitations:

> The divine sonship and the humanity of Jesus are therefore essential to preserve the full truths of the revelation and redemption. But these are divine things beyond human experience and they need to be approached humbly and carefully and with full consciousness of the limitations of the human mind. From early in the Christian era to our own day history abounds with examples of the difficulty of comprehending with finite minds and expressing through the inadequate medium of human language the merging of the divine and human in the person of our Lord.[24]

Ultimately, whether one accepts the mainstream trinitarian view of Scripture that asserts God took on humanity in the person of Jesus Christ at the time of his conception, or the Christadelphian view that the Holy Spirit acted in some way within Mary, to produce a human being who was in some sense the image and fullness of Deity without actually being God—ultimately no one is going to be able to explain *either* of these doctrines experientially or through "reason." For example, "The Eternal Christ-power, veiled in and manifested through the flesh,"[25] is not immediately comprehensible either. This issue is not, "Which one makes more sense to me," but, "What is scriptural teaching?" We need to be aware that our own presuppositions and prior teaching can be very entrenched. If "We don't really know the answer to that" is acceptable to one party, that party should be gracious in allowing the other party to hold that position. Conversely, if one party disparages another for an incomplete or obscure explanation, their own argument must be presented for equivalent scrutiny. As Coleman puts it, "The passion with which we deny the doctrine of the Trinity is as great as that of those who accept it . . . Is it appropriate to feel so strongly as this about an answer which seems to amount to a 'don't know'?"[26]

Having said that, we can address the issue of whether the incarnation is as irrational and unreasonable as Christadelphians assert. One of the most helpful perspectives on this is that of Millard Erickson,[27] and I draw on some of his thoughts in what follows. The important issue with respect to what is "possible" or "makes sense," is that we are talking about Almighty God here. He made mankind in his image in the first place, so why should it be thought incredible that he could enter into humanity in the way the incarnation portrays? The idea that the divine nature could not assimilate with human nature comes from Greek philosophy, not from the Bible. The Greeks saw a stark dichotomy between divinity and humanity, between spirit and matter. This is why Docetism arose, the idea that Christ only seemed human, an error that John was probably addressing already toward the end of the first century (1 John 4:2). Likewise,

---

24. E. J. N., *Jesus, the Son of God*, 26–27.

25. John Thomas, cited in Nicholls, *Remember the Days of Old*, 41.

26. Coleman, "Jesus, Son of Man, Son of God," part 1.

27. Erickson, *Christian Theology*, 671–73.

Gnostics could not cope with the idea that the ultimate Deity, the Father of the Christ, could have sullied his hands with the creation of matter, so they attributed creation to a lower demi-god and taught that man's highest aspiration was to have his soul liberated from the body. But from the biblical perspective, could not the creature closest to God, made in his image and ultimately to be transformed into a sinless, immortal being, be assimilated by his Maker into the Word made flesh? Erickson suggests that perhaps not only our concept of God's capabilities is too limited, but our respect for God's own design of a creature in his image is too limited as well.

Erickson makes the insightful point that we should not begin with traditional conceptions of humanity and deity but recognize that both are most fully known in Jesus Christ. We look around at humanity and we see it in its fallen state, not as God intended it to be. The divine image is marred, distorted, corrupted by sin. This is not the picture we see of Jesus; he had our nature, as a son of Adam, but he was without sin. "The question," observes Erickson, "is not whether Jesus was fully human, but whether we are." Everyone else we have ever met, or heard about or read about has sinned and thus fallen short of the glory of God (Rom 3:23). Jesus' humanity, on the other hand, was evidently quite compatible with deity.

Jesus also provides us with knowledge of deity. "No one has ever seen God; the only God, who is at the Father's side, he has made him known" (John 1:18). Jesus is Immanuel, God with us. It is also important to acknowledge that the initiative for the incarnation came from God, not from us. When man tries to become God, in his own strength and for his own glory, as attempted by the Babel tower builders and as Nebuchadnezzar boasted, it is a terrible sin. How could a human ever aspire to be God, somehow adding deity to one's humanity? It could not happen that way, and that's not what the incarnation is about. But for God to add humanity to his deity is not impossible; who are we to tell God that he couldn't do this because it doesn't tally with our experience or comprehension? Why should we be embarrassed by a paradox impenetrable to human understanding? He is God, and if he says the Word became flesh and dwelt among us, then it happened.

God Was in Christ

Our discussion so far has demonstrated that divinity and humanity were combined in the Lord Jesus Christ. Before moving on to the doctrine of the Holy Spirit and a consideration of the Trinity, we need to explore the Christadelphian concept of the divine and human in Christ. They call this doctrine *God manifestation*.

The Christadelphian Understanding of Jesus' Divinity; Derived and Bestowed

It is doubtful whether most Christadelphians today could enunciate the doctrine of God manifestation, any more than most mainstream Christians could really explain the doctrine of the Trinity. The Christadelphian understanding of the nature of Jesus Christ, in most of their general literature, tends to be confined to either a positive or a negative expression in fairly simple terms. An example of a positive expression is, "How then was Christ different from any other child? The answer is positive and simple: God was his Father."[28]

An example of a negative expression is:

> We reject that God is three persons. The doctrine of the trinity being false, it remains that God is a Being of Spirit; the Lord Jesus Christ is His Son, born of the Virgin Mary; the Holy Spirit is His power. We reject that the Son of God was co-eternal with the Father. Jesus was begotten of the virgin Mary; he was only "known" beforehand in the mind and purpose of Yahweh from the beginning.[29]

Alfred Nicholls, editor of *The Christadelphian Magazine* in 1977, set out to restore some perspective which he felt was lacking, in terms of what the "Pioneers" of the Christadelphian faith had actually expressed on certain topics. One of these topics is the deity and humanity of Christ.

> Trinitarianism teaches the incarnation of "the Son;" the truth recognizes the incarnation of the Father, resulting in a Son, which is a very different thing. "Jesus Christ, in the days of his weakness, had two sides, the one Deity and the other man . . ." Dr. Thomas[30] does not say that the two sides of the Christ were: 1st, the divine Son; 2nd, man. He affirms that which the scriptures declare—that his two sides were: 1st, the Father who was manifested in him, and 2nd, the medium of manifestation—the man who was of the seed of David according to the flesh, begotten by the Spirit. This manifestation of the divine and human was Jesus Christ. Jesus Christ was not the human or the divine separately, but both in combination, constituting the Son.
>
> Now on the question of God's manifestation in the flesh, the language is derived from God's point of view, because God is the actor . . . The Father (by the Spirit) veiled himself in the flesh, and the result was Jesus of Nazareth, the Son of God and King of the Jews. If it be asked, "was not the Father as much dwelling in light, in the heavens, after Jesus was born, as before?" the answer is, Certainly; and it was to this glorious and everlasting Father that Jesus prayed and taught his disciples to pray; but who nevertheless dwelt in Jesus.
>
> Indeed, there is *a* trinity in the case, though not *the* Trinity. Jesus is "the Father, (manifested in a) Son (by the) Holy Spirit." and in combination "these three are one."

So the first major point of difference between Christadelphian and mainstream beliefs is that Christadelphians believe that the deity manifested in Christ is that of the Father, not of a separate divine person called the Son. The second major point of

---

28. Tennant, *The Christadelphians*, 97.

29. *Doctrines to be Rejected*: http://www.christadelphia.org/reject.htm.

30. John Thomas was the founder of the Christadelphian faith. He is being quoted here by Robert Roberts, his successor in the promulgation of Christadelphian beliefs. The entire quotation in turn, with accompanying discussion, is to be found in Nicholls, *Remember the Days of Old*, 41–44.

difference is that Christadelphians believe that the Son only began his existence when the man Jesus was conceived; he did not in any way preexist.

> Jesus was the Word become flesh. This process began in begettal and conception, and resulted in the birth of the Son of God. It was then that he personally existed for the first time.[31]

> It requires stressing that the description of the birth of Christ precludes the possibility of his having a prior existence . . . The divine action involved in the coming of God's Son into the world is not kept secret or made mysterious. Instead, it is plainly explained in Luke 1:34–35; Matt 1:18, 20. The description of these passages indicate the creation of a new person by means of God's power acting on Mary, and thereby rules out any possibility that Christ personally existed in some manner prior to his birth.[32]

> God always had Jesus in mind, but Jesus did not exist until he was conceived . . . Jesus, as the central figure in God's purpose, is spoken of as existing from the beginning in God's mind and plan, although physically he did not do so.[33]

Trinitarians would agree that "the man Christ Jesus" did not exist prior to the action of the Holy Spirit upon Mary. Trinitarians also agree that the Father continued to dwell in light, in the heavens after Jesus was born, just as before. The point of difference is, who was made flesh—the Father, or the Son?

The third point of difference is that Jesus' lordship and worthiness to be worshiped were not, according to Christadelphians, intrinsically his, but bestowed on him by the Father as a reward when he was exalted to the Father's right hand.[34]

> Christ, therefore, though now possessed of inherent life, had been invested with it; it is not in this case underived. It is only the Great Uncreate, the Father, that can say, "I am, and there is no one else beside me." He was the Son of God, the manifestation of God by spirit-power, but not God himself. The spirit descended upon him in bodily shape at his baptism in the Jordan, and took possession of him. This was the anointing which constituted him *Christ* (or the anointed), and which gave him the superhuman powers of which he showed himself possessed.
>
> Before his anointing, he was simply the "body prepared" for the divine manifestation that was to take place through him . . . When raised from the dead and glorified, he was exalted to "all power in heaven and earth:" his human nature was swallowed up in the divine; the flesh changed to spirit. Hence, as he

---

31. Tennant, *The Christadelphians*, 100. Trinitarians would not disagree that the *man* Jesus Christ existed for the first time at conception, as he was the product of the Word taking on flesh. Erickson, *Christian Theology*, 672, reminds us that "the heavenly Second Person of the Trinity antedated the earthly Jesus of Nazareth. In fact, there was no such being as the earthly Jesus of Nazareth prior to the moment he was conceived in the womb of the Virgin Mary."

32. Abel, *Wrested Scriptures*, 276–77. Abel, like Tennant, does not understand that the doctrine of the incarnation fully agrees that someone new began existence at the conception of Jesus Christ. See Grudem, *Systematic Theology*, 530.

33. Hyndman, *The Way of Life*, 149.

34. Nicholls, *The Name*, 73. We have already demonstrated, contra Nicholls' assertion, that Jesus was called Lord well before his resurrection.

now exists, "In him dwelleth all the fullness of the God-head bodily" (Col ii.9). He is now the corporealisation of life-spirit as it exists in the Deity.[35]

> There can be no clearer indication (Philippians 2) that the Divine Name and title have been bestowed upon the Lord Jesus, and that the disciples were quite right in changing their usual form of address to him during the days of his flesh . . . to *Kyrios*, Lord . . . [The] fact that the Father is ever exalted above the Son, reveals the total inadequacy of the doctrine of the Trinity, which makes the Father and Son co-equal and co-eternal. Those who think they thus glorify the Lord Jesus in truth diminish the glory of God.[36]

> The power and glory and authority of Christ have been bestowed upon him by the Father. They are derived and none of them would be his if they had not been given to him by God the Father.[37]

Apart from the verses which speak of God's foreknowledge of Jesus' role in his eternal plan, which are used to attempt to metaphorically explain references to Christ's preexistence, the lynchpin of the Christadelphian case for the derivative nature of Christ's divinity is:

> After making purification for sins, he sat down at the right hand of the Majesty on high, having become as much superior to angels as the name he has inherited is more excellent than theirs (Heb 1:3–4).

The argument is that the Son *inherited* his superiority to the angels and his superior name; it was not eternally and intrinsically his. The fact that this passage is lifted out of the context wherein God commands his angels to worship the Son, the Son is addressed explicitly as "God" and creation is attributed to him seems to escape attention. Also off the radar are the ascriptions of lordship and the attributes of divinity to Christ "in the days of his flesh," *prior* to his resurrection and (re)exaltation.

Christadelphians believe that the ascriptions of divinity to Christ, and the appellation of the divine Name are his "by Divine gift;" Alfred Nicholls says, "We must never lose sight of the fact that this power was his because of his obedience unto death: it was 'when he had by himself purged our sins' that he 'sat down on the right hand of the majesty on high,' until the time appointed of the Father to take his great power and to reign."[38]

The word "inherit," *klēronomeō*, is the regular word for inheriting an estate, and in the New Testament for inheriting eternal life, the kingdom and the promises of God. In this verse it is in the perfect tense, meaning an action completed in the past with ongoing effect. The superior name he inherited was given him at his exaltation, when

---

35. Roberts, *Christendom Astray*, 159–60. This passage is virtually adoptionist (see below) and, to be fair, it may not be representative of the beliefs of most contemporary Christadelphians, despite the high regard in which Roberts' writings are still held.

36. Nicholls, *The Name*, 69–70. Nicholls seems to overlook the fact that Jesus was called Master and Lord and worshiped "during the days of his flesh," not just following his resurrection.

37. Tennant, *The Christadelphians*, 101.

38. Nicholls, *The Name*, 67, 70.

he sat down at the right hand of the majesty. His exaltation followed his humbling, his emptying, as we have seen, and he became the "firstborn," with all the rights of the eldest Son. We have seen that this concept relates to status and to privilege rather than necessarily implying literal birth order. In Hebrews 1:2 the Son is spoken of as being appointed heir (*klēronomos*) of all things and the one through whom God made the universe and in verse 3, the one who sustains all things by his powerful word. In verse 6 the worship of the Son by angels is commanded at the moment of his being brought into the world. Contra the Christadelphian position, it is clear that the concept of "inheritance" here is meant to exalt the Lord Jesus, to speak of his rights as the heir of the Father, not to in any way downplay his status or imply that his divinity is derived.

To summarize, the trinitarian and Christadelphian positions are in once sense close, in that they both acknowledge the lordship and divinity of Christ, but in another sense far apart, in that the former assert that these attributes *always* belonged to the preexistent Christ, whereas the latter claim that they were merely *bestowed* on Jesus Christ at his exaltation, in response to his obedient completion of his mission of salvation. In very simplistic terms, the difference between the two positions can be represented with the following diagram:

All the features of Christ's divinity are interpreted by Christadelphians in terms of delegation, except for creation and preexistence, which are interpreted metaphorically. The Christadelphian position does not ignore the arguments for the preexistence of the Son, his involvement in creation, nor the nature of the incarnation, but rather explains these in terms of preexisting in the foreknowledge and purpose of God and through the concept of God being manifest in the flesh in the person of Jesus Christ.[39] Christadelphians also understand that the Old Testament prophecies concerning Jesus

---

39. The most detailed statement of the Christadelphian position and an attempt to engage with the "problem" verses which speak of Christ's preexistence is the pamphlet (no author specified) *Did Jesus Exist in Heaven Before His Birth?* The arguments presented in that pamphlet have been addressed in detail in the course of the present work.

had a future fulfilment and claim that this proves the Son did not already exist. Clearly though, they refer to the incarnation and subsequent work of Jesus Christ, which was future, and do not contradict the evidence for the preexistence of the Son, which has been presented in detail in the present work. An analogy would be that astronomers might predict a meteorite will strike the earth at a given place and time. The effects of the meteorite are not apparent to the inhabitants of earth until it strikes, but this doesn't mean that the meteorite did not exist until its time of impact with the earth.

The following table compares the two positions:

concept	Trinitarian	Christadelphian
humanity of Christ	Christ was fully human from the point of conception; the God-man "Jesus Christ" began existence then	Christ was fully human from the point of conception; the man "Jesus Christ" began existence then
divinity of Christ	The Son took on flesh in the womb of Mary; Christ was also fully divine	The Father became manifested in flesh in the womb of Mary; Jesus' divine characteristics were inherited (in an unspecified way) from his Father
preexistence	The Son existed with the Father for all eternity and will exist for all eternity	The Son was foreseen by the Father from all eternity but only began to exist at conception in the womb of Mary
Christ as Lord and God	Christ was and always will be Lord and God	The Father bestowed on Christ the titles Lord and God at his exaltation

concept	Trinitarian	Christadelphian
the emptying and the exaltation	When the Son took on humanity, he humbled himself, taking the form of a servant and temporarily and voluntarily relinquishing status and privilege; these he regained at his exaltation	The Son was born into lowly estate at the beginning of his existence and did not seek equality with God. God exalted him as a result of his obedience to death
co-equality	The Son is co-equal with the Father and Holy Spirit	The Son is inferior to the Father and the Holy Spirit is God's power

In terms of comparison with beliefs held by other groups in the history of Christian thought, the Christadelphian position appears to be unique. Erickson proposes that there are six basic heresies concerning the person of Christ and all departures from orthodox doctrine are variations of one of these.[40]

- Denial of the genuineness of Jesus' deity (eg., Ebionism)
- Denial of the completeness of Jesus' deity (eg., Arianism)
- Denial of the genuineness of Jesus' humanity (eg., Docetism)
- Denial of the completeness of Jesus' humanity (eg., Apollinarianism)
- Division of Jesus' person into two (eg., Nestorianism)
- Confusion of the two natures of Jesus (eg., Eutychianism)

Christadelphianism is clearly a denial of the completeness of Jesus' deity, which they say is acquired and derived, not intrinsically his and Jesus remains inferior to the Father in being as well as in role. Superficially, Christadelphians appear to also deny the genuineness of Christ's deity, but a careful reading of the more detailed works on the subject reveals it is not so much that they believe he is not divine, at least in an appointed sense, but rather the manifestation of the *Father* in a human being, rather than the incarnation (dwelling in flesh) of the *Son*. They certainly uphold the genuineness and completeness of Jesus' humanity and, contrary to some erroneous assertions,

40. Erickson, *Christian Theology*, 673.

are most definitely not Unitarians,[41] although they will quote freely from Unitarian writings and refer to common predecessors to support their anti-trinitarian stance.[42]

There is some difficulty in discerning what Christadelphians understand in terms of whether Christ is thought to have one nature or two, which is sometimes compounded by imprecise terminology.

> The child thus born according to the Word of God, the very embodiment of it in all its purposefulness, was one whole being. He was not part Word and part flesh. He was the Word made flesh. His was one nature, not two. There was not a God and a man separate and distinct within the one being. The Son of God was the Son of man, and the Son of man was the Son of God.[43]

> That being so begotten of God, and inhabited and used by God through the indwelling of the Holy Spirit, Jesus was Emmanuel, God with us, God manifest in the flesh—yet was, during his natural life, of like nature with mortal man, being made of a woman, of the house and lineage of David, and therefore a sufferer, in the days of his flesh, from all the effects that came by Adam's transgression, including the death that passed upon all men, which he shared by partaking of their physical nature.[44]

Commenting on the preceding statement, Michael Ashton explains, "He was therefore both Son of God and Son of Man at one and the same time in the unity of his nature . . . It is not helpful when attempting to understand Jesus' nature to separate these two aspects of his being. Jesus was a whole and complete character."[45]

> Jesus Christ, in the days of his weakness, had two sides, the one Deity and the other man . . . This manifestation of the divine in the human was Jesus Christ. Jesus Christ was not the human or the divine separately, but both in combination, constituting the Son.[46]

On balance, most Christadelphians would consider Christ to have a single nature, his human nature, in which God was manifested, such that he was the image of God. They would also consider him to have a single will, distinct from the Father's, even though he brought that will into subjection to the Father's.

Christadelphianism has some similarity to Arianism, in that they consider Christ's divinity to be derived, and yet they part company with Arius (and the Jehovah's

41. Christadelphians definitely reject the idea that Jesus was merely a regular man, the natural son of Joseph and Mary. For example see Roberts, *Christendom Astray*, 155–58; *Christadelphian Statement of the Faith*, article II (also called the Birmingham Amended Statement of the Faith or BASF. This is the confession of the worldwide Christadelphian community and contains both positive statements of belief as well as doctrines to be rejected); Ashton, *Studies in the Statement of Faith*, 136; Tennant, *The Christadelphians*, 91.

42. For example, Snobelen, "Antitrinitarian Textual Criticism," 186–96.

43 Tennant, *The Christadelphians*, 97.

44. Article X of the *Christadelphian Statement of the Faith*; Ashton, *Studies in the Statement of Faith*, 137.

45. Ashton, *Studies in the Statement of Faith*, 35.

46. Nicholls, *Remember the Days of Old*, 41, citing Robert Roberts who cites John Thomas.

Witnesses) in not discerning Christ's presence at creation. Arius taught that the Son was a creature and not self-existent, that he had a beginning ("There was when he was not") and was not of the same essence or being as the Father, and was God in name only; nevertheless he was the creator and "born outside time."[47] Christadelphians would disagree with this position; they assert that the Son had a beginning at his conception and did not literally participate in creation and was not God in name only, but the manifestation of the Father in the flesh.

Are Christadelphians Adoptionists?

Christadelphians have been accused of being adoptionists, a position they deny, although they believe Jesus' *lordship* began at his post-resurrection exaltation. The Christadelphian position is in a sense a form of adoptionism, but not quite, because they anchor Jesus' sonship in his conception, not a later point. The original adoptionism (also called dynamic monarchialism) of the late second century as taught by Theodotus, held that Jesus was an ordinary albeit virtuous man until his baptism, when the Spirit/Christ descended upon him, although this did not make him divine.[48] Again, this is at odds with the Christadelphian view, for they hold that Jesus was the Son of God from conception, even though he only became anointed ("Christ") with the Holy Spirit at his baptism. Robert Roberts' description of the "anointing" of "the body prepared" comes perilously close to adoptionism, but the majority of Christadelphian writers emphasize Jesus' sonship beginning at conception, which makes them not adoptionists by the commonly accepted definition.[49] Adoptionists referred to essentially the same texts as do Christadelphians, in support of their position.

- Jesus of Nazareth [was] a man attested [KJV approved] to you by God with mighty works and wonders and signs that God did through him in your midst (Acts 2:22).

- God has made him both Lord and Christ, this Jesus whom you crucified (Acts 2:36).

- [God] will judge the world in righteousness by a man whom he has appointed (Acts 17:31).

- [Jesus] was declared to be the Son of God in power according to the Spirit of holiness by his resurrection from the dead (Rom 1:4).

If these passages are taken literally, and the claims of Jesus and others in support of his divinity interpreted only in a bestowed sense, and those speaking of preexistence taken metaphorically, it could be said there is a tentative case for Jesus being

47. Kelly, *Early Christian Doctrines*, 227–30.
48. Ibid., 116.
49. Ibid., 116; McGrath, *Christian Theology*, 486.

merely human. However, if the preexistence passages and claims to divinity are taken literally, then these "adoptionist" passages could be interpreted in the context of Jesus' humbling prior to his subsequent exaltation. The Christadelphian position could be seen as part way between preexistent divinity and pure adoptionism. Seen from the preexistence perspective, which Christadelphians clearly reject, their position could be construed as adoptionist, although they deny it. Conversely, in rejecting adoptionism or unitarianism, they must forge an alliance with those who recognize Christ's divinity and his sonship from conception and thus move closer to the preexistence camp. It essentially comes down to which passages are read literally and which metaphorically, when a "verse against verse" approach is used. Adoptionists must "explain" the preexistence passages metaphorically, and trinitarians must "explain" the "adoption" passages. Christadelphians seem to get tangled between the two.

Are Christadelphians Socinians?

In the last few decades, Christadelphians have become interested in tracing the development of anti-trinitarian thought and in identifying groups who held similar beliefs. One Christadelphian survey[50] of denominations with beliefs identifiable as "Biblical Monotheism" (anti-trinitarian) lists Christadelphians, the Church of God of the Abrahamic Faith, Church of God (General Conference), The Way International, Spirit and Truth Fellowship International, Living Hope International Ministries and Christian Disciples Church, but it should be noted that these groups hold to quite a diversity of doctrinal beliefs in other areas. Some Christadelphian writers[51] and others have identified the Socinians as the movement's predecessors. Earliest Socinianism was not the same as unitarianism, even though it was a forerunner of it. Interestingly, John Thomas the founder of the Christadelphians, denied that the group is Socinian.[52]

The Socinians, or as they preferred to be called, the Polish Brethren, were a community of antitrinitarian churches in Poland and Lithuania in the seventeenth century, which spread extensively through Europe. The name derives from Faustus Socinus (or Fausto Sozzini) (1539 to 1604) who had been based at Racow in Poland. Unitarians such as John Locke and John Biddle were strongly influenced by Socinianism. Socinians rejected the doctrine of the Trinity as being unscriptural and against reason and defined God as an immutable being located in heaven but who acts in time. Christ was merely human, born without sin of the Virgin Mary through the power of the Holy Spirit, but did not preexist (although Socinus taught that Jesus visited heaven before his ministry and was taught by God). After Jesus' death, he was raised and exalted to the right hand of God. They believed that the Holy Spirit has no

---

50. Hyndman, "Biblical Monotheism Today," 225–40.

51. For example, John Adey describes the Socinians as "our 17th century Bible-based unitarian predecessors" (Adey, "The *Shema*," 27).

52. John Thomas, *Eureka* vol. 2, cited in Carr, *Handbook of Bible Principles*, 56.

personal identity but is merely the power of God. They also rejected the expiation of human sin on the cross, teaching that Christ's significance was in showing the way to salvation, which is achieved by correct belief in Christ and obedience to his commandments. If this description[53] is accurate, then their position is very close to that of the Christadelphians.

However, the Socinians denied that humans are intrinsically corrupted by sin and rejected divine foreknowledge, as well as the death of Christ being an atonement for sin, a satisfaction of God's justice or an appeasement of his wrath. The doctrinal scheme of the Socinian Minor Reformed Church was the Racovian Catechism, first published in 1605.[54] An important distinction between Socinianism and Arianism is that Socinians, like Christadelphians, denied the preexistence of Christ as well as the Trinity, whereas Arians (and Jehovah's Witnesses) denied the Trinity but accepted the preexistence of Christ.

Despite the similarities with Socinianism, ultimately it seems fruitless to label the Christadelphian position on the Godhead with any other historical, divergent teaching. It is much more appropriate to call it what they themselves call it; the doctrine of "God manifestation," and seek to understand what *they* actually mean by this.

God Manifested in the Flesh

The expression "God manifestation" takes its name from the keynote verse 1 Tim 3:16 in the King James Version (KJV). The word "manifest" only appears once in the NIV but it appears extensively in both testaments in the KJV, which has traditionally been the Christadelphians' preferred scriptural version, and less so in the ESV which is gaining popularity within the group. In nearly all cases it is a translation of the Greek word *phaneroō*, to manifest, make manifest or reveal. The NIV and other modern translations tend to translate *phaneroō* as "reveal" or "make known." Two related words are *epiphanaiō* (to appear) and *epiphaneia* (the appearance, particularly of a deity), which Paul uses to refer to the appearing of Christ.[55]

> And without controversy great is the mystery of godliness: God *was manifest* in the flesh, justified in the Spirit, seen of angels, preached unto the Gentiles, believed on in the world, received up into glory (1 Tim 3:16, KJV; the ESV is essentially the same).

> Beyond all question, the mystery of godliness is great: He *appeared* in a body, was vindicated by the Spirit, was seen by angels, was preached among the nations, was believed on in the world, was taken up in glory (1 Tim 3:16, NIV).

53. Szczucki, "Socinianism," 85–86; Smith, "Truth in a Heresy?," 221–24.

54. The text may be found at: http://webuus.com/timeline/Socinus.html.

55. This is particularly evident in the pastoral epistles, 1 and 2 Timothy and Titus, where Christ's appearance is portrayed as the visible revelation of God. See Andrew Y Lau, *Manifest in the Flesh: The Epiphany Christology of the Pastoral Epistles* referenced in Bowman and Komoszewski, *Putting Jesus in His Place*, 226. Quite a different take on this "key" verse.

Another key verse is John 17:6, where Jesus says to God, "I have *manifested* thy name unto the men which thou gavest me out of the world" (KJV; again, the ESV is very similar) or, "I have *revealed* you to those whom you gave me out of the world" (NIV).

Christadelphians believe that the attribution of deity to Christ is to be understood as God the Father's manifestation in the person of Jesus, and that Christ, although foreordained and hence preexistent in the mind and purpose of God, began his existence at his conception by the Holy Spirit and his deity was his by bestowal from the Father, not intrinsic to his being.

> The Lord Jesus . . . is the manifestation of the Father by the Spirit . . . The Father is eternal and underived; the Son is the manifestation of the Father in a man begotten by the Spirit; the Holy Spirit is the focalization of the Father's power, by means of His "free spirit," which fills heaven and earth. There is, therefore, a trinity of existences to contemplate, and a certain unity subsisting in the trinity, inasmuch as both Son and Spirit are manifestations of the one Father; but the trinitarian conception of the subject is excluded.[56]

The doctrine of God manifestation is expressed with different vigor by different writers. It was very much the cornerstone of understanding of the person and work of Christ by the "pioneers" of the Christadelphian tradition, such as John Thomas and Robert Roberts and finds enthusiastic support today amongst those who particularly revere and promote these pioneers and their writings. Apart from these, the seminal work on the topic was C. C. Walker's *Theophany: A Study in God-Manifestation*, currently out of print. However, it is not so much written about in other circles. Harry Tennant, for example, in what is otherwise a careful and detailed dissertation on the breadth of Christadelphian belief, doesn't mention it at all, or even cite 1 Timothy 3:16. The closest he comes is to talk about the Word becoming flesh and Christ being the image of the Father. However, there seems to be a renewed interest in presenting the doctrine. As recently as 2010 a compendium of "pithy summaries" of "the clear and simple teachings of the Bible," previously published in the *Testimony* magazine includes a chapter on God manifestation.[57] Because it is a succinct and readable summary, in contrast to the older works, I will draw on it extensively.

> God-manifestation is the display of the glory of God. It is God's fundamental purpose with His creation (Num 14:21), and is associated particularly with the revelation of His character and attributes . . . When Adam fell because of his sin, he no longer displayed the image of his Creator as he had previously done; and so he became estranged from God (Gen 1:27; 3:24). God's ultimate purpose is that this estrangement of mankind from Him should be reversed, and that, in bringing about human salvation, He should make "a new creation" of men and

---

56. Roberts, *Christendom Astray*, 154–55.
57. Green, "God Manifestation," 53–56.

women in whom His glory will be finally and fully displayed in all its moral and physical perfection.[58]

So far so good; this introductory explanation has scriptural warrant and would attract little argument from mainstream evangelical Christians. The explanation continues; because God dwells in unapproachable light and no one can see God and live (1 Tim 6:16; Exod 33:20), God has revealed himself since the fall by means of intermediaries, "God manifest in others." Notably, God revealed himself to Moses by means of an angel in the burning bush, who spoke as God, calling himself "I AM," the divine name YHWH. The angel explained the importance of the meaning of this name, better translated as "I will be Who I will be." *Who* God will be is the multitude of the redeemed, immortalized people whom he is preparing as manifestations of his name. It was an angel who declared the character of God to Moses in Exodus 34:6–7 and it was as "the Angel of His Presence" that God (probably the Holy Spirit; Isa 63:9–12) travelled with and watched over the Israelites in the wilderness. Although the role of angels as representatives of God who can bear the name YHWH is by no means foreign to mainstream theology, there is a wide range of scholarly opinion on the meaning of the name YHWH; this will be discussed a little later. But it is in the next stage in the elucidation of the doctrine of God manifestation that Christadelphians part company with mainstream Christians.

Jesus is regarded by Christadelphians as the ultimate manifestation of God, in that he is a man in whom the fullness of God dwelt, but he is still a human intermediary, the culmination of a long succession of men and angels who "manifested" God's glory by speaking God's words and displaying aspects of his character (glory). As the Word made flesh, Jesus was the thought, mind and purpose (*logos*) of God expressed in speech and personally in real human flesh. He had no authority or intrinsic divinity, no light of his own but manifested the character and words of God the Father.

> By service and suffering he was made perfect, a full manifestation of his Father (Phil 2:7–8; Heb 2:10; 5:8–9). He has therefore been raised to the manifestation of God in Divine nature, inheriting a name greater than angels, and glorifying God in the process (Heb 5:5; 1:4; Phil 2:9–11). Jesus is now the anointed Son of the Father in a greater sense (Acts 13:33; Heb 1:9). He carried the name "THE LORD (Yahweh) OUR RIGHTEOUSNESS" (Jer 23:5–6) and, particularly when he returns, men will bow to the Father through him, and his glory will be revealed (Isa 45:23).[59]

This is, as we have seen, the Christadelphian position that Christ is divine only in a derived sense and that his exaltation is a reward for his obedience, not a return to a former status. Salvation for human beings then involves their manifestation as sons of God, of whom Jesus Christ is the firstborn. This requires people to receive the Word of God and believe and obey a body of truth. Then with baptism they become children of

58. Ibid., 53.
59. Ibid., 54.

God. By abiding in the doctrine of Christ, believers manifest the Father and the Son, being sons of God now whilst being conformed to the image of his Son. The future manifestation of these sons of God will allow them to partake of incorruptible divine nature (at the resurrection) and reign in glory with Christ upon the earth.[60]

On the surface, this idea of God being manifest in a multitude of saints who are made co-heirs with the firstborn Son, Jesus, the full manifestation of the Father, might seem a reasonable and interesting perspective and like most heresies, God manifestation has enough scriptural "support" and is close enough to the truth to sound acceptable. However, there are two major problems with this doctrine as an explanation of the person and work of Christ. Firstly, Jesus Christ is merely the ultimate human manifestation of God in a line of men and angels; he is not intrinsically divine. A parallel would be the Islamic concept of Muhammad as the last and greatest of the prophets, now in an exalted position in heaven with Allah. Secondly, apprehension of Christ's saving work is by imitation, effectively by works, for which believers are rewarded. The Christadelphian view of the atonement will be examined in more detail in chapter 10, so for now we will concentrate on what their doctrine of God manifestation says about the Lord Jesus Christ.

In the more detailed expositions of the doctrine of God manifestation in the writings of Thomas, Roberts, and Walker, it can be seen to encompass not only their doctrine of the nature of Jesus Christ. It is viewed as the *whole point* of God's interaction with humankind, even the focus of the gospel, and has its foundation in the Christadelphian understanding of the meaning and significance of the name of God, YHWH. John Thomas wrote extensively on the meaning, pronunciation and significance of the name Yahweh, in his works *Eureka* and *Phanerosis*. He is credited by later Christadelphian writers with being virtually unique in grasping the true significance of the name as prophetic. He, and later writers, claim that the correct translation and meaning of the tetragrammaton is "I will be who I will be."[61] Christadelphian writers make a great deal about the correct pronunciation and interpretation of YHWH and are adamant that it should be Yahweh, never Jehovah, and that the future tense is the correct translation. The point, they allege, is that,

> God will be revealed upon earth, first IN a Son of David and Son of God who shall be *Immanuel*, God with us (*asher Ehyeh*, Who I will be), and lastly IN a multitude like him who shall be "gods". . . But this future purpose of God declared to Moses at the Bush (Exod. 3) in the revelation of the Memorial Name of God, is not likely to be understood by Trinitarian theologians who suppose that God was already revealed IN a "co-equal" and "co-eternal" Son in heaven, when by the angel at the Bush he spoke these words to Moses.[62]

---

60. Ibid., 55–56.

61. Walker, *Theophany*, 9.

62. Ibid., 16.

In his book *Theophany*, C. C. Walker asserts that the Name of God is borne by the angels; they are the *elohim*, or mighty ones, and they speak as if they are God himself rather than with the prophetic rider, "Thus says the Lord" (Exod 23:20–21; Judg 2:1–4). This accounts for the occasional plural connected with *elohim*, such as "Let us make man in our image" (Gen 1:26). This direct divine authority vested in the angels who bear the Name is equivalent to the way Jesus speaks with direct authority, because he came in the Father's name, spoke God's words, but was not actually God, any more than the angels are.[63] Unfortunately, this comparison ignores the fact that no angel has ever sat on God's throne or received worship there, which is the prerogative of the Lord Jesus, so the comparison is actually invalid as an explanation of Christ's status.

"Angelic theophany" is held to be an important pillar of the doctrine of God manifestation. This was the way God often appeared to men in Old Testament times, in the form of angels which bore his name. For example, in Genesis 32:1–2 where Jacob wrestles with an angel; "God in these verses is *Elohim*, the mighty ones or angels."[64] The classic text cited is the appearance of the "three men" to Abraham in Genesis 18. Verse 1 says the LORD (YHWH) appeared to Abraham, but Abraham sees three *men* (verse 2). He addresses one as "Lord," (*Adonai*; verse 3) and persuades them to stay for a meal. They ask him where his wife Sarah is (verse 9) and then "the LORD" says, "I will surely return to you about this time next year, and Sarah your wife shall have a son" (verse 10). Sarah laughs at this, and the LORD (YHWH) asks why Sarah questions the LORD's ability to do this (verses 13–14). When the "men" get up to leave, the LORD explains to Abraham that he is about to destroy Sodom and Gomorrah and Abraham subsequently pleads with the LORD in order to save Lot.

It is clear from the text that one of the "men" is speaking as YHWH, in the first person, and described by the narrator as YHWH, in the third person. The word "angel" does not appear in this chapter, in either the visit of the three men, nor the subsequent dialogue with the LORD. However, chapter 19 follows straight on; the LORD having finished speaking with Abraham and left (18:33) "the two angels" arrive at Sodom, and in the subsequent narrative of the threatened assault and Lot's deliverance, the words "angels" and "men" are used interchangeably. One of them announces that he will overthrow the cities (19:21–22) and the narrative subsequently says the LORD overthrew them (19:24–25). Walker's interpretation is that the three men were angels and one of these, presumably an archangel, had the delegated power and authority of YHWH; God himself did not physically descend from heaven.[65] Jesus, likewise, bore the name of the Father and had the delegated authority of YHWH.

Walker argues that the theophany experienced by Moses at the burning bush revealed God's purpose to resurrect the dead, making Abraham, Isaac, and Jacob sons of God and thus the future manifestation of God. This connection is made via several

63. Ibid., 27.

64. Ibid., 34.

65. Ibid., 28–29.

verses. First, God reveals himself to be the God of Abraham, Isaac and Jacob (Exod 3:6). Jesus quoted this verse to the Sadducees in Mark 12:25–27 and Luke 20:35–38 as proof that God is God of the living, not the dead and therefore intended to raise the Patriarchs from the dead. When the dead rise, says Jesus, they will be like the angels in heaven (Mark 12:25). Furthermore, they are God's children, since they are children of the resurrection (Luke 20:36). Next, Romans 8:19 says, "For the creation waits with eager longing for the revealing of the sons of God." This relates in verse 23 to "the redemption of our bodies," viz., the resurrection. Likewise, Jesus himself was declared to be the Son of God . . . by his resurrection from the dead (Rom 1:3–4). This is the covenant with Abraham, Isaac and Jacob which God remembered at Horeb (Exod 2:24).[66] Walker's point is, that the "I will be" of YHWH's proclamation is his intention to be manifest in a multitude of resurrected sons of God, of which Jesus Christ is the first fruits.

So, who spoke to Moses from the bush? Exodus 3:2 says it was the angel of the LORD (YHWH), but in verse 4 the LORD (YHWH) sees that Moses comes over to look at the bush and God (*Elohim*) speaks to him from within the bush. And so the narrative continues, sometimes attributing the speech to God, at other times to the LORD. Finally, Moses asks the name of "The God of your fathers," and God says to Moses I AM WHO I AM, or, I WILL BE WHAT I WILL BE (Exod 3:14). This was the angel speaking in the name of YHWH.[67] The idea that the angel of the Lord can be closely identified or equated with YHWH is not exclusive to Christadelphian expositors, however. Referring to the same passages as Walker expounds (Gen 16:7, 9,11; 22:15; 31:11, 13; Num 22:22–35; Judg 2:1–5; 6:11–23; Zech 3:1–6; 12:8), Peter Enns[68] expresses it this way:

> The precise identity of the angel of the Lord has always been a matter of debate. The Hebrew can also be translated "messenger[69] of the LORD," which is precisely the role this angel plays . . . Nevertheless, it is best not to think of the two figures as simply equated. We should see this in the context of the ancient Near East, where messengers normally spoke for the sender . . . Simply equating the angel of the Lord with Yahweh tends to obliterate the clear fact that they are presented as two distinct figures in the Old Testament.
>
> These two then, are to be identified in some sense, yet they are distinct from each other. This close relationship has led many to suggest that the angel of the Lord is an Old Testament manifestation of the incarnate Christ . . . The notion of the close relationship in the Old Testament between the messenger/angel of the Lord and Yahweh himself is something that is fully manifested in the person of Christ, who is both one with the Father yet distinct from him as the second Person of the Trinity. This is not to say, however, that the angel of the Lord *is* a

---

66. Ibid., 45–46.

67. Ibid., 48.

68. Enns, *Exodus*, 96.

69. The Hebrew word is *malak*, as in Malachi, "my messenger." We have seen that in Mal 3:1 the "messenger of the covenant" is Jesus Christ, "the Lord whom you seek."

preincarnate manifestation of Christ. Rather, the angel of the Lord foreshadows
Christ in the same way that Moses, the priesthood, or the sacrificial system do.

Another major angelic theophany in the record is discussed in relation to Exodus
33 and 34, where YHWH promises Moses that "My presence will go with you," (33:14)
and Moses asks to see God's glory (33:18). YHWH says he will cause all his goodness
to pass before Moses and "I will proclaim before you my name, the LORD" (33:19).
YHWH descends in a cloud and proclaims his name and allows Moses to see his
back (33:22–23; 34:5–7). This, Walker claims, was the angel of the Presence, bearing
and proclaiming the name YHWH, and foreshadowing Jesus Christ, who specially
revealed the characteristics of the name of YHWH—without actually being YHWH.[70]

There are three main theories among Old Testament scholars regarding the identity of the angel (messenger) of the LORD, the *malak YHWH*. One is the representation theory, that the angel represents YHWH and speaks as YHWH but is distinct
from him. Another is the angel-Christ or logos theory, that the angel is the pre-incar-
nate Christ. The third is the identity theory, which equates the angel/messenger with
YHWH himself. The representation theory is widely held and there is little difficulty
demonstrating that the angel/messenger speaks as YHWH. What is actually much
harder to demonstrate throughout the various Old Testament examples, is that the
angel/messenger is separate and distinct from YHWH.[71] Even if the representation
theory is accepted, the terminology may not be all that relevant. Whether the term
to use is "God manifestation" or "God representation" or "God's messenger" or some
other expression, this is as far as the doctrine goes; the angel represents God in a
very close association, speaking as YHWH, but not being fully equated with YHWH.
Nor will there be much argument that this foreshadows a greater fulfilment in Christ.
What we *cannot* assume that these passages teach is that this means that the way Christ
manifests YHWH is *exactly* the same as the way the angel manifests YHWH. After
all, Christ is not an angel; he far surpasses them (Heb 1:4–8). Angels are not to be
worshiped (Rev 19:10; 22:8–9) but Christ is worthy of worship (Heb 1:6; Rev 5:8–14).
Even in Malachi 3 where the coming of Christ as "the messenger of the covenant" is
prophesied, that messenger is "the Lord whom you seek" who comes to *his* temple.

Theophany continues with further examples of the angel of the Lord, and connects various events and themes with the manifestation of the Name of YHWH to
Israel, such as the Passover and God's triumph over the Egyptians. There follows a
systematic survey of prophecies which point forward to Christ and those he redeems.
There is little to argue with in terms of the richness of detail with which the Old
Testament points forward to Christ, as we have discussed in an earlier chapter. Some
of Walker's allegories are a little tenuous, others have clear support from the context

---

70. Walker, *Theophany*, 31–32, 100.

71. For a detailed discussion of the strengths and weaknesses of the representation theory, see
Malone, "Distinguishing the Angel of the Lord," 297–314. Malone argues that a distinction between
the angel and YHWH is permitted by many texts but rarely substantiated.

in which the passages are quoted in the New Testament. However, throughout, it is difficult to see how any of the passages, individually or en mass testify to Christ as anything contrary to what orthodox doctrine understands—the coming LORD.

A chapter of *Theophany* is devoted to seraphim and cherubim, in which they are presented as immortal sons of God, either angels or immortal saints; "the Eternal Spirit post resurrectionally manifested in Jesus and his brethren."[72] This may be pushing the interpretation; Scripture is enigmatically brief in its depiction of cherubim, and the descriptions are not uniform. They are present at the east of the garden of Eden, they were on the lid of the ark of the covenant, above which God was enthroned, and depicted on the curtains of the tabernacle and temple, at the entrance to the Most Holy Place. They appear to accompany the presence of God as King on his throne or in his chariot. In Exodus they are described as having faces and wings and in Ezekiel they are depicted as composite creatures with multiple faces and wings, but that is not to say they are identical in the two settings.[73] In Isaiah 6 creatures called seraphim attend the throne of God. They have hands, feet, faces and wings and the term may be connected to the fiery serpents of Numbers 21:6, Isaiah 14:29, and 30:6. They are associated with God's holiness and as creatures they cover themselves before their Creator and praise him. In Revelation 4 at least, they are probably only a symbolic description, since they differ in detail from the Old Testament depictions and can be convincingly identified as representing creation in general, fulfilling its destiny to worship God. They can also be seen as agents of God and servants of the Lamb.[74] They seem to embody aspects of the highest forms of life on earth, which accords with Ezekiel's description of "living creatures." They exhibit life in a state of power and activity as well as intelligence. This kind of life "was life most nearly and essentially connected with God—life as it is, or shall be, held by those who dwell in His immediate presence, and form . . . spiritual and holy life."[75] In Revelation 4 we may be seeing the real possessors of the life of God, members of the redeemed and glorified community giving honor, glory and thanks to God and the Lamb, although it is interesting that they do not appear in association with the new heavens and new earth, suggesting that they speak more of a promise of the restored condition than the restored themselves.[76]

So Walker's equation of the cherubim with the saints may not be too far off the mark, but to include Christ in the symbolism is inappropriate, as they are clearly distinguished from the Lamb and from the LORD, whose glory they accompany (Isa 6, cf. John 12:41; Exod 25:20; Ezek 1). Not only that, but the cherubim are around or under the throne of God/mercy seat/entrance to his presence, never *on* the throne, whereas the Lamb is on the throne (Gen 3:24; Exod 25:20–21; 1 Sam 4:4; 2 Kgs 19:15;

---

72. Walker, *Theophany*, 104–5.

73. Steinmann, "Cherubim," 112–13.

74. Beale, *Revelation*, 328–33.

75. Fairbairn, *Typology*, 227.

76. Ibid., 230–33.

Ps 99:1; Ezek 10; Rev 4). Furthermore, those on the temple veil yield to the One whose blood was shed as the way to the presence of God is opened (Matt 27:51).

When he comes to the New Testament, Walker clearly expresses his belief that Jesus is merely the first of many "sons of God," setting the pattern of "probation before exaltation," in a very works-based exposition of the Christian's relationship to the saving work of Christ. For Walker, Christ is an example to follow in the struggle for glory, rather than the One whose sacrifice is all-sufficient. For Christadelphians, as we shall see later, Christ died as a representative of the human race, not as a substitute; the sin-bearing, Lamb of God.

> In the four gospels we have the Lord's own doctrine of Theophany—his relation to the Father who begat him, and to those "many sons" whom he is "bringing unto glory" (Heb 2:10) . . . It would seem indeed that this is the Father's purpose with all His "sons," for even the *elohim* admitted knowledge of good and evil when sentence was pronounced upon our first parents . . . Probation before exaltation would appear to be the law of God's universe . . . for it is revealed and practically manifested that the Father's name has been and is to be manifested upon earth in sons who have "known good and evil," both in the sense of perceiving good and evil and choosing the good, and of enduring the evil and receiving the good forever.[77]

Walker is saying here that Christ's earthly life was a "probation," in which he had to prove himself, and so formed the model for our own probation in this life. This takes away the certainty and sufficiency of Christ's work, leaving his performance open to doubt and resting our salvation in our efforts to follow his example. This is surely the antithesis of the gospel message of salvation *apart from works*, and it robs the Christian of any assurance. Again appealing to the future tense of "I will be who I will be" as the name of YHWH, Walker asserts that Christ is God's son by a bestowal of the attributes of deity, a reward for work accomplished, rather than an intrinsic possession.

> Matthew and Luke tell us how he is first "Son of God" by begettal, according to the terms of God's covenant with "his father David:" I *will be* his Father, and he *shall be* my Son (2 Sam 7:14). Not, I *am* his Father and he *is* my Son. The "preexistence" in the case is not the "Son," but the Father and the Holy Spirit.[78]

> But "first that which is natural" (1 Cor 15:46). We must not make him first a co-equal and co-eternal "Son" with the Father after the manner of Trinitarian theology. He was "the Word made flesh." The pre-existence in this case was "the word," "the spirit of Christ," which was in the prophets. The "flesh" was the Son.[79]

Again we see the Christadelphian idea that the Son is not a divine preexistent person, but a manifestation of the Father in a body of flesh. It is unclear what Walker

---

77. Walker, *Theophany*, 192–93.

78. Ibid., 193.

79. Ibid., 196.

means by the two statements, first that the Father and Holy Spirit are the preexistent aspect, and then that the word which was in the prophets is the preexistent aspect. There is quite a bit of sleight of hand with the passages here quoted. Matthew certainly does speak of a long list of "begettals" from Abraham through David to Jesus, his human ancestry—no quarrel with that, but that is *not* the sense in which Jesus is Son of God. This begetting in the gospel genealogies is all about the natural way in which Jesus had a human ancestry and is the promised son of David and of Abraham. We have clearly shown that this is compatible with the trinitarian understanding of the authentically human nature of Christ. Neither is Luke saying that Jesus was begotten by God in the way this long line of men begat each other; "He was the son, *as was supposed*, of Joseph . . . the son of Adam, the son of God" (Luke 3:23, 38). Adam was the son of God in a completely different sense to which Jesus was.

In what sense was Jesus begotten by God? There are two Greek words which are translated "beget" or "begotten" in the KJV. The word which means to father a child in the normal sense is *gennaō*, and this is the word for all the "begats" in Matthew's genealogy (but does not appear in Luke). Elsewhere in the New Testament, *gennaō* means beget in either this natural sense (e.g., Stephen's narrative of the forefathers in Acts 7) or the allegorical (Paul begetting Christians through the gospel; 1 Cor 4:15; Phlm 1:10) except for two other applications.

One application is where Psalm 2:7 is quoted in three passages: Acts 13:33, Hebrews 1:5, and Hebrews 5:5. "I will tell of the decree: the LORD said to me, 'You are my Son; today I have begotten you.'" *Gennaō* here is in the perfect indicative active form, meaning a past action which is completed and has ongoing significance. When is the "today" when this "begetting" occurred? The Psalm gives no clear indication; it could be when the kings of the earth oppose the Son (Ps 2:1–3) or at the resurrection, which is the context of the Acts 13 quotation, it could be when God's king is installed in Zion (Ps 2:6) It could be future; "I will proclaim the decree" (Ps 2:7) or when the Son takes possession of the earth (Ps 2:10–12). The Psalm itself does not speak of the conception of the Son by the Holy Spirit as the point of begettal. The emphasis is on the exalted status of the Son in the New Testament contexts in which the passage is quoted. This is in contrast to Christadelphian arguments that the future fulfilment of all the Old Testament messianic prophecies "proves" that the Son did not yet exist. It "proves" nothing of the sort, but simply that the incarnation, ministry, death and resurrection of the Son were still future.

The other application of *gennaō* is in 1 John 5:1, 18, which speaks of believers in Christ being born of God, which is another way of speaking of our adoption. If *gennaō* means to "father" a child in respect to the conception of Jesus, then we must have been "fathered" in the same way, which is not what Scripture teaches.

So it is very tenuous to make a case of Jesus being the Son of God in the sense of God fathering a child the way the human ancestors of Jesus fathered their sons.[80]

---

80. Sometimes this is implied—unintentionally?—in Christadelphian writings. For example,

Instead, Luke simply tells us that "the Holy Spirit will come upon you, and the power of the Most High will overshadow you; therefore the child to be born will be called holy—the Son of God" (Luke 1:35). The biological "mechanics" or genetics of this wondrous event are none of our business, and we are not to presume that the conception of the Son of God, which trinitarians understand as the incarnation, the preexistent Word becoming flesh, is portrayed in terms of God "begetting" by the human method of conception, nor that this implies the beginning of existence of the Son. There is certainly a connection between the sonship of Jesus and the adoption of believers as sons of God; Romans 8:14–17 makes this clear, as do other passages. But these passages are not about proving that the Son of God had a starting point at his conception, before which he did not exist – that is simply not what they are talking about and it flies in the face of other passages which clearly testify to his preexistence.

The other word which the KJV translates as "begotten,"[81] but newer translations do not, is *monogenēs*, which we have discussed previously. In summary, it means not "begettal" but "one-of-a-kind" and is found in John 1:14, 18; 3:16, 18; Heb 11:17 and 1 John 4:9, always conveying the idea of God giving his *only* Son. The New Testament places much less emphasis on the virginal conception than do Christadelphians; in Scripture Jesus is presented as the Son of God by a diversity of arguments; divine declaration and commissioning (Mark 1:9–11; Acts 13:33) and by prior relationship with the Father as well as specific "signs" (throughout John's gospel). In Christadelphian writings, John's rich portrayal of Jesus as the Son sent from heaven by the Father is interpreted solely and in minimalistic fashion through the lens of the virgin birth, which John does not even directly discuss.

Walker argues that those who responded to the call of the Gospel and were baptized became those "in God the Father and in the Lord Jesus Christ" and hence "prospective units of a theophany hereafter to be revealed." Such called ones were to be witnesses empowered by the Holy Spirit: John 15:16; Luke 24:48–49; Acts 22:15. Walker argues a continuity between the witness of Israel (as it was meant to be; Isa 43:10–12) and that of the church. The same "Spirit of Christ" which was in the prophets was to be in the apostles (Acts 10:39–43; 1 Pet 1:11) and this is the sense of the indwelling of Christ and the Father (John 14:16–20), in other words, not through the indwelling of the Holy Spirit, but by God manifestation.[82]

The "manifestation of the sons of God" is seen as the culmination of God manifestation, which began with God manifesting himself in his representative messengers, especially the angel of his presence, and most fully in his Son Jesus Christ. Those who are in Christ will become a sort of "multitudinous Christ," (a popular term in

---

Morgan, *Understand the Bible*, 105–6: "God had never begotten a Son before and will never do so again . . . By fathering a Son who would live on earth . . ."

81. The KJV expression "first-begotten," in Heb 1:6 and Rev 1:5 is *prōtotokos*, firstborn, which we have seen refers to the rights of sonship, not necessarily birth order.

82. Walker, *Theophany*, 203–5.

some Christadelphian circles, but not found in Scripture), God manifested in *elohim*, mighty ones, through the resurrection, of which Christ is the first fruits. The verse from the KJV critical to this interpretation is

> For the earnest expectation of the creature waiteth for the manifestation of the sons of God (Rom 8:19, KJV).

Interestingly, the word for "manifestation" in this verse is actually not *phanerōsis*, but *apokalypsis*, unveiling. The context of the passage is the sharing of Christ's glory as the adopted sons of God, with the redemption of our bodies, brought about by the indwelling Spirit of him who raised Christ from the dead.

> The hope of the "manifestation of the sons of God" is founded upon the "manifestation" by resurrection from the dead of the Son of God . . . Christ is "the first-fruits" of a new order of "sons of God," antitypical of Adam "son of God" (Luke 3:38) and his "earthy" order. The kingdom of God in Christ is the objective, and "he must reign till he hath put all his enemies under his feet" (1 Cor 15:25). "Then cometh the end." The last enemy, death, is destroyed and God is all in all.[83]

Walker relates this to Ephesians 1 wherein Paul says God predestined us in love to be adopted as his sons through Jesus Christ, in whom we have redemption and forgiveness through his blood. The mystery of his will which he purposed in Christ is to be put into effect when the times have reached their fulfilment, to bring all things in heaven and on earth together under one head, Christ. The figure of Christ and his multitudinous bride, the church, is seen as another expression of God manifest in a redeemed multitude.[84] "When Christ who is your life is revealed, then you also will be revealed with him in glory" (Col 3:4; "revealed" in both instances is *phaneroō*).

Walker's understanding of the divine attributes of Christ is, in common with other Christadelphian writers, that they are derived, not intrinsic. He acknowledges the superiority of the Son over the angels as testified in Hebrews, but it is because he has *become* so much better than the angels because he has *obtained* a more excellent name by inheritance (Heb 1:4).[85] Likewise, this is his understanding of the divine ascriptions in Revelation. The one who was to come, is the Almighty (Rev 1:4) and this is the sense of the Old Testament designation, "Lord of hosts," translated in the LXX as *kurios ho pantokratōr*, the all-powerful or *Theos sabaoth*. The hosts are understood to be the multitude of the redeemed, in whom God will be manifested. Much is made in some Christadelphian literature of the meaning of "Lord of Hosts," YHWH *Tsabaoth*, or "Yahweh of armies" as prophetic-descriptive of God manifested in the multitude of his "mighty ones," the redeemed in Christ.

> When our Lord is at last manifested upon earth he will be the head of the "great multitude that no man can number," though their symbolic number is "144, 000"

---

83. Ibid., 213.

84. Ibid., 216–18.

85. Ibid., 221.

(Rev 7:9; 14:1). Those are the "hosts" of God, the "all in all," Alpha and Omega of the divine purpose upon earth.

Walker cites John Thomas' interpretation of Isaiah 41:4 ("I, the LORD, the first and with the last; I am he").

> The figure is found in the prophets, as Dr. Thomas has pointed out (Eureka, vol. 1, 112, etc.) "I the Lord the first, and with the last; I am he." Here "first" is singular (Christ the firstfruits) and "last" is plural ("afterwards they that are Christ's at his coming"). He is "the First to Zion" (Isa 41:27) . . . and when he comes again his multitudinous body will again be "the firstfruits unto God and to the Lamb" (Rev 14:4; 20:5–6).[86]

The seraphim/living creatures of Isaiah 6 and Ezekiel's prophecies are identified with the living creatures and elders of Revelation, the redeemed out of every nation, kings and priests, who will reign on the earth (Rev 5:9–10). These who are sealed, and clothed in white and who worship God and the Lamb are the (symbolic) 144,000 of the redeemed and the new Jerusalem, the bride of the Lamb.

In summary, Walker's book traces the revelation or manifestation of God throughout biblical history, foreshadowing and culminating in the resurrected multitude of the redeemed as the ultimate manifestation of God. In this overarching purpose, Jesus Christ is seen as the lynchpin, and the most perfect manifestation of YHWH, and the one through whom the multitude is redeemed and raised to become this "multitudinous Christ." In fulfilling this role, however, the Son's divinity is entirely derived.

Does "Yahweh" Mean "I am," or "I will be?" And Who or What Will He Be?

The Christadelphian understanding of God manifestation rests very much on their understanding of the meaning of YHWH, the name of God, and defers to John Thomas's insight into this interpretation.

> Dr Thomas has told us that *Yahweh* means "He who will be," and *Ehyeh asher ehyeh* "I will be who I will be." In *Eureka*, vol. i, page 98, we read: "The Deity said to Moses by his Elohim *Ehyeh asher ehyeh*, I WILL BE WHO I WILL BE; and he said, Thus shalt thou say unto the children of Israel, EHYEH hath sent me unto you . . . In the name and memorial thus revealed at the bush the Deity declared that *he would be a person or persons not then manifested*. He announced to Moses that He was the *Mighty Ones* who had appeared as "three men" to Abraham, and as "a host" to Jacob; but that at a future time He would manifest Himself in others, even in *persons* of the Adamic race. Hence in view of this new manifestation, and to keep it constantly in remembrance, He imposed upon Himself the name of EHYEH—"I will be" (page 99) . . . It (*Ehyeh*) does not mean, and never did,

---

86. Ibid., 227.

what it is meant to signify in the English version, i.e., "I am." The Deity did not give Himself this name, but on the contrary, said, "My name is I WILL BE."[87]

Before we discuss the definition of the Name, it should be pointed out that even granted it is in the future tense, Thomas has extrapolated significantly in suggesting that YHWH has defined who or what he "will be." The passage does not mention being manifested in persons, nor is the reference to being the God of Abraham necessarily confined to the incident with the "three men." In fact, God does not state or imply "who " or "what" he "will be," other than God.

There is great diversity of opinion and a multitude of scholarly works on the subject of the divine name YHWH, among Hebrew scholars of many persuasions, with no consensus.[88] Apart from anything else, this should constitute a warning as to the danger of basing a pillar of doctrine on something about which we cannot be certain. The original pronunciation is uncertain, but the weight of opinion and evidence suggests that the original pronunciation of YHWH was *Yahweh*. The earliest Hebrew Old Testament manuscripts lacked the vowels, but there are early Greek transliterations which read *Iabe* or *Iaoue*.[89] *Ehyeh* is the first person singular imperfect form of the verb "to be/become" and the Hebrew imperfect usually expresses the future, not the present. This renders Exodus 3:14 as "God said to Moses, 'I will be who I will be. This is what you are to say to the Israelites: "I will be" has sent me to you.'"[90] So in terms of the Hebrew grammar, John Thomas appears to be correct, at least according to many scholars. But it's quite a large leap to complete the sentence in such a way as to provide the foundation for the doctrine of God manifestation.

When the name of God occurs in the Hebrew Old Testament, the Tetragrammaton replaced by *Adonai* is invariably YHWH (present tense) not EHYEH (imperfect tense). Interestingly, the Septuagint translates God's declaration of his name as follows *ego eimi ho ōn*, using a present participle; "I am the being-one," in verse 14. In the Greek, *eimi* is the *present* indicative active of the verb to be; *ōn* is the nominative masculine singular of the *present* active participle of the verb to be; the being-one, or the one who is. Both are in the present tense. If the translators of the LXX had considered *ehyeh esher eyeh* to mean "I will be who I will be," presumably they would have used, unambiguously, the appropriate future tenses of the verb to be. This argues against the future meaning and any theological interpretation which rests upon it, provided that we accept the extant manuscripts of the Greek Old Testament as accurate and authoritative. Furthermore, in verse 15, the LORD is YHWH (present tense in Hebrew) and becomes *kyrios* (Lord) in Greek. So, we have an impasse.

87. Ibid., 10–11.

88. Freedman, "The Name of the God of Moses," 151.

89. For example in Clement of Alexandria c. AD 155–215 cited in Abba, "Divine Name Yahweh," 320.

90. Abba, "Divine Name Yahweh," 324.

In terms of the meaning and significance of the name, however, the situation is even less clear-cut. The Hebrew verb, unlike the Greek, does not convey a simple concept of being, or existing and this is where the multiplicity of interpretations comes in, John Thomas's being one among many opinions. I will select three as examples.

Raymond Abba argues that *ehyeh* never means pure existence but has the sense of happening or becoming, or being present and that it is essential to interpret it within the context of the passage. The divine name itself is demonstrably much older than the Exodus, and the revelation at the bush was not the revelation of a new name, but the disclosure of that name's significance. The context is the establishment of a new covenant relationship between God and Israel. God has heard their cry and is about to deliver them. He gives them the assurance "I will be (*ehyeh*) with you" in verse 12, and accompanies them on their journey in symbolic presence in the pillar of cloud and fire and in the ark. "It is this assurance of the presence of the Savior God with his covenant people which is embodied in the name Yahweh," concludes Abba; the name is to be understood as "I will be present."[91]

David Freedman discerns the original meaning of *ehyeh* as "I bring into being," and the form in which it appears in Exodus 3:14 uses the second verb as a predicate to emphasize the verbal action. So the meaning is "I create what I create." A similar construction is found in Exodus 33:19, also in association with the divine name, "I will be gracious to whom I will be gracious." The various name formulas in Exodus serve to highlight the qualities and attributes of the Creator God of the fathers, as revealed in the context of the Sinai covenant.[92]

Peter Enns argues that the actual name of God is not "I am who I am/I will be who I will be," but that expression is a prelude to the name. The name is "I am," *ehyeh*, a play on the verb to be, as also in verse 12 "I will be with you." In his opinion, verse 15 suggests that the import of the name is that it is the Lord God *of the fathers* that is important, which puts the emphasis on the covenant.[93]

These are just three scholarly views, well argued, and at least equally plausible with John Thomas's interpretation that "I will be" means "I will be (manifested in) mighty ones." The point to be made is that whilst many scholars have independently concluded that the Name is in the future tense, this by no means serves as proof in and of itself, of any one particular interpretation of the significance of that Name.

Evaluation of God Manifestation versus Incarnation

The strengths of the Christadelphian doctrine of God manifestation are its consistent telling of the story of God's self-revelation throughout salvation history and its emphasis on the centrality of the glory of God being manifested through his redeemed

91. Ibid., 324–26.
92. Freedman, "Name of the God of Moses," 152, 154–55.
93. Enns, *Exodus*, 102–3.

creation. It is true that God has revealed himself through angelic representation and spoken his word through the prophets and that his most complete revelation is in the person of his Son, Jesus Christ (Heb 1:1–2). It is also true that Christ is the firstfruits of a multitude of redeemed who will glorify God for eternity. In the sense that the man Christ Jesus, in whom the Word was made flesh, was foretold as the coming one and did not exist as Jesus Christ the man until his conception, there is a point in history at which God began to dwell among us. Nevertheless, to define the sonship of Christ entirely in terms of this conception is to ignore the rich evidence concerning his preexistence, his involvement in creation and his eternal relationship with the Father and Holy Spirit. There is a continuity of sonship which is not explained by Christ being merely a man in whom the Father was manifest. The Christadelphian doctrine actually blurs the distinction between Father and Son by making Christ the manifestation of the Father, not the incarnation of the Son, and trespasses into the arena of modalism.

God manifestation is an insufficient explanation for the attribution of divinity to Christ, not only following his exaltation but during his ministry on earth. It also fails to explain the teaching of Christ's humbling himself, being sent by the Father, and rejoining the Father in the glory they previously shared. Viewing Christ's lordship of all and his worthiness to be worshiped as gifts bestowed on him does not do justice to the principle that only God is worthy of worship, and will *not* share his glory with another, no matter how exalted one of his creations might be. God manifestation, as ingenious a unifying theme that it is, does not "prove" that the Son's divinity is derived, rather the Christadelphian portrayal *presupposes* this. It makes Jesus out to be merely a prototype super-human or super-angel. However, the role of angels as manifestations of God and bearers of his authoritative message is an inadequate explanation or model for the intrinsic authority of the Son of God who is demonstrably superior to the angels. As a central, all-encompassing metanarrative of salvation history, God manifestation falls short because it downplays the centrality of Christ's work on the cross, the hopelessly sinful state of humanity and the all-sufficiency of the atonement. To use our previous analogy, it places Christ alongside the angels, "below the line" that divides God from the rest of reality, in contrast to the clear, consistent and overwhelming testimony of Scripture.

The doctrine of the incarnation, as with the Christadelphian alternative, leaves a number of questions unanswered. However, the criterion for accepting the truth and validity of either explanation for the divinity and humanity of the person of Christ must lie with its overall consistency with the teachings of Scripture, not merely what seems reasonable from human experience. God has chosen to tell us very little of the "mechanics" of the conception and incarnation of the Son, and how this played out in Jesus' development from childhood to manhood. However, the incarnation of the Son does justice to the evidence for the preexistence of the Son with the Father, their eternal relationship and the Son's involvement in creation, which the Christadelphian construct does not. Ultimately, in the face of Jesus Christ we see all the fullness of the

Godhead in a sinless and perfect human being, the one who is, literally, God with us, and who is Lord of all, worthy of all praise and worship and who has reached down to his wayward creatures with love and undeserved favor.

Summary

- The doctrine of the incarnation is a difficult concept for Christadelphians and is often misunderstood and misrepresented.

- Jesus Christ, while being fully God and fully human, is nevertheless a united person, and although his human will potentially opposed his divine will, consistently the divine will prevailed.

- Throughout the history of the church, there have been erroneous ideas about the divine and human natures of Christ, overemphasizing one aspect at the expense of the other, blurring the distinctions between the two natures, or dividing him into two persons. The Chalcedonian definition of AD 451 was an attempt to define the boundaries of these doctrinal extremes.

- By taking on human nature, the Son accepted limitations to the exercise of his divinity, but did not put aside his divine nature.

- The doctrines of the incarnation and the unity of the two natures in Christ, while incompletely understood are not unreasonable and certainly not impossible. We must recognize the limitations of our own understanding of what God has chosen to reveal and acknowledge that both humanity and divinity are most fully revealed to us in Christ and it is inappropriate to limit God by our own finite experience and insight.

- Christadelphians believe that the Son's existence began at his conception, that the virginal conception defines his sonship, and that he did not preexist other than in the foreknowledge and intent of the Father.

- Christadelphians believe that the deity manifested in Christ is that of the Father, not of a separate divine person called the Son.

- Christadelphians understand the Son's divinity to be derived and bestowed, in contrast to the trinitarian view that the Son is intrinsically divine. Christadelphians understand the Son to have a single nature, which is human.

- The Christadelphian understanding of Jesus Christ is therefore not exactly the same as any other historical perspective; it has features in common with modalism and adoptionism, but is probably closest to Socinianism.

- Christadelphians reconcile and explain the divine and human aspects of Christ in terms of their doctrine of God manifestation. This is based on a specific interpretation of the future tense of the divine name YHWH and examples of God revealing himself historically in representatives such as angels, most fully in Jesus Christ and ultimately in the redeemed and resurrected multitude of "mighty ones;" those who are "in Christ." Christ, as the means by which God will thus manifest himself, has been exalted to a position of divine lordship.

- The doctrine of the incarnation of the Son and the two natures in the person of Christ is the best explanation for the scriptural evidence concerning the Son's eternal relationship with the Father, his lordship and his worthiness to be worshiped.

Further Reading

- Millard Erickson, *Christian Theology*, chapter 33, "The Unity of the Person of Christ."

- Alister E. McGrath, *Christian Theology: An introduction*, chapter 11, "The Doctrine of the Person of Christ" (an historical and contemporary survey of different views of the divine and human in Christ).

- Julian Clementson, "The Christadelphians and the Doctrine of the Trinity."

- C. C. Walker, *Theophany: A Study in God-Manifestation.*

7

The Holy Spirit

Misconception #12: That in calling the Holy Spirit a "person," trinitarians deny the scriptural emphasis on the Spirit as God's powerful activity in salvation and sanctification.

Corrective: The Holy Spirit's function in salvation history has primarily been as God's powerful activity in the lives of God's people.

Misconception #13: That the Holy Spirit is only personal in the sense of being an expression of the Father.

Corrective: The Spirit is spoken of as distinct from the Father, as divine and as having personal attributes.

ANY DISCUSSION OF GOD as triune must be predicated on an understanding of the deity and personhood of the Father, the Son and the Holy Spirit. We have to this point considered the deity of the Father and the Son and their relationship with each other. Before we draw together these ideas of "persons" within a Godhead who is One, and examine the Trinity *per se*, we need to consider the personhood and deity of the Holy Spirit.

It is essential to have a correct understanding of the Holy Spirit, because the Spirit is how God becomes personal to the believer, how God is active within our lives and resides in us. It is through the Holy Spirit that we experience God. It is through the Spirit that Christ indwells us, and it is the Spirit who testifies to our adoption as children of God.

> Do you not know that you are God's temple and that God's Spirit dwells in you? (1 Cor 3:16).

> You, however, are not in the flesh but in the Spirit, if in fact the Spirit of God dwells in you. Anyone who does not have the Spirit of Christ does not belong to him. But if Christ is in you, although the body is dead because of sin, the Spirit is life because of righteousness. If the Spirit of him who raised Jesus from the dead

dwells in you, he who raised Christ Jesus from the dead will also give life to your mortal bodies through his Spirit who dwells in you (Rom 8:9–11).

For all who are led by the Spirit of God are sons of God. For you did not receive the spirit of slavery to fall back into fear, but you have received the Spirit of adoption as sons, by whom we cry, "Abba! Father!" The Spirit himself bears witness with our spirit that we are children of God (Rom 8:14–16).

Who—or What—Is the Holy Spirit?

Articulating a doctrine of the Holy Spirit is difficult because "spirit" is a rather difficult and intangible concept. This has been compounded in the past by the terminology of the KJV, which translates *pneuma hagion* as "Holy Ghost." Another complicating factor is that in Greek, the word for spirit, *pneuma*, is neuter gender. This tells us nothing about personality, because the gender of a noun is a grammatical concept, and does not necessarily reflect the biological gender of the noun.[1] Interestingly though, masculine pronouns are sometimes used in the New Testament to refer to the Holy Spirit.

But the Helper, the Holy Spirit, whom the Father will send in my name, he [that one] will teach you all things and will bring to your remembrance all that I have said to you (John 14:26).

In this verse, the word for "Helper," *paraklētos*, is masculine, "the Holy Spirit" is neuter, "whom" is neuter and the untranslated "that one" is masculine, agreeing with "Helper." In John 15:26 and 16:13–14, masculine pronouns (underlined below) are used to describe the activities of the "Spirit of Truth." The context of the passage is the coming of the *paraklētos*.

- But when the Helper comes, <u>whom</u> I will send to you from the Father, the Spirit of truth, who proceeds from the Father, he ["<u>that one</u>"] will bear witness about me (John 15:26).

- When the Spirit of truth comes, he ["<u>that one</u>"] will guide you into all the truth, for he will not speak on his own authority ["<u>of himself</u>"], but whatever he hears he will speak, and he will declare to you the things that are to come. He ["<u>that one</u>"] will glorify me, for he will take what is mine and declare it to you (John 16:13–14).

The Christadelphian Understanding of the Spirit

The *Christadelphian Instructor*, first penned by Robert Roberts as a Sunday School catechism, is still used today in Christadelphian Sunday Schools and for preparing

---

1. Other examples include two words for "child," *teknon* and *paidion*, which are both neuter, and the word for virgin, *parthenos*, which is masculine in form but used with feminine articles, adjectives, etc. Interestingly, the Hebrew word for spirit is *ruach*, which is feminine!

adherents for baptism. Three of its questions and their answers provide a summary of Christadelphian teaching on the nature of the Spirit of God.[2]

> 16. In what way is God everywhere if He dwells in heaven?

> Answer: God is everywhere present by His spirit which proceeds from Him, and which fills all space.

> 17. What is the Spirit of God?

> Answer: It is His invisible power and energy breathed forth from His presence, and of like nature with His Glorious Person. By this, heaven and earth have been made and are preserved in being from moment to moment. In this we live and move and have our being in Him.

> 18. Is God separate and different from the Spirit of God?

> Answer: No. God and His Spirit cannot be separated. They are both one. The sun and the light that comes from the sun are both one. So God, and the Spirit that comes from God, are both one. God is the center and glorious substantial form of the Spirit that fills heaven and earth.

The more contemporary writer, Harry Tennant, explains it this way:

> God fills His creation. All of its activity is because of His wise and sustaining Spirit, the divine energy working out His gracious purpose. The Spirit is not a "separate" or "other" person. It is God's own radiant power, ever outflowing from Him, by which His "everywhereness" is achieved. The Spirit is personal in that it is of God himself: it is not personal in the sense of being some other person within the Godhead.[3]

Consistently throughout Christadelphian writings, the Holy Spirit is given the pronoun "it" and described as the power of God. Through this power, God inspired the writing of the Scriptures, worked miracles, raised Christ from the dead and anointed and empowered Jesus and the apostles to do the work of God and speak God's words. Christadelphians believe that the miraculous gifts of the Spirit, and the ability to pass these on to others, died out at the close of the apostolic age, replaced by the completed New Testament. In terms of the work of the Spirit in the life of believers today, this is seen as primarily worked out through the action of the inspired Scriptures in the mind of the believer.

> The result of an intelligent apprehension of what the word of God teaches and requires, is different from this ["revival meetings"]; this has its seat in the judgment, and lays hold of the entire mental man, creating new ideas and new affections, and, in general, evolving a "new man." In this work, the Spirit has no participation, except in the shape of *the written word*. This is the product of the Spirit—the ideas of the Spirit reduced to writing by the ancient men who were

2. Roberts, *The Christadelphian Instructor*.

3. Tennant, *The Christadelphians*, 115.

moved by it. It is, therefore, the instrumentality of the Spirit, historically wielded: the sword of the Spirit by a metaphor which contemplates the Spirit in prophets and apostles in ancient times, as the warrior. By this, men may be subdued to God—that is, enlightened, purified, and saved, if they receive the word into good and honest hearts, and "bring forth fruit, some thirty-fold, some sixty, and some a hundred." By this they may become "spiritually minded," which is "life and peace." The present days are barren days as regards the Spirit's direct operations.[4]

> Salvation comes from God . . . God has made compassionate and gracious provision in Christ. God's will was brought into action by His Spirit. None of this is known other than by the Word of God which is the message of the Spirit. The message of salvation is the power of God (Rom 1:16) which brings man into contact with the mind of God, the Spirit of God. An entirely new force enters into his life when he hears or willingly receives the Word of God.[5]

This impression of the Spirit's work today illustrates two characteristics of Christadelphian interpretation. There is a tendency to make something metaphorical (in this case the action of the Spirit) if the face-value interpretation is unacceptable. Secondly, there is a tendency to require an element of human effort in concert with the saving and sanctifying work of God. However, as Clementson has identified, contemporary Christadelphians, at least in some circles, are more open to allowing a more direct work of the Spirit in believers today.[6] This can be seen in various "unofficial" websites, discussion groups, and blogs rather than any "approved" publications coming out of the Christadelphian Office. One commentator has suggested:

> Christadelphians find any concept of the Holy Spirit working on the heart of the believer difficult because of their focus on being a rational faith based upon proof. They therefore tie any present day working of the Holy Spirit to the "Gifts of the Holy Spirit" and want signs. In this sense it has been noted that in a way the Christadelphians have a faith which rests upon the concept of a remote God. It has also been related to the period of time called "The Age of Enlightenment" and the "Denial of the Supernatural."[7]

Christadelphians reject the personhood of the Spirit, but they vary in the extent to which they are willing to attribute the personal attributes of God to his Spirit. They are very clear however, in rejecting the concept of any distinctiveness between the Spirit and the Father. *Doctrines to be Rejected*: number 6 is "That the Holy Spirit is a person distinct from the Father."[8]

Given that the Holy Spirit is seen by Christadelphians as an extension of God's presence and power and possibly (some writers imply) the outworking of his character, it is difficult to see how the Spirit could be "something" that could be passed on to

---

4. Roberts, *Christendom Astray*, 149–50.

5. Tennant, *The Christadelphians*, 121.

6. Clementson "Christadelphians and the Trinity," 162.

7. Woodall, "Christadelphian."

8. *Doctrines to be Rejected*, Ashton, *Studies in the Statement of Faith*, 141.

the Son in terms of his being granted the control or use of "it." How can "something" which they acknowledge as intrinsically part of God's (the Father's) identity be owned or controlled by anyone other than God? We will return to the relationship between Jesus and the Spirit to demonstrate that it is a strong argument for the trinitarian understanding of a relational Godhead.

The Spirit in the Old Testament

Both the Hebrew word *ruach* and the Greek word *pneuma*, translated spirit, are onomatopoeic words meaning essentially breath or wind—air in motion. Underlying this apparently simple concept is the idea of power, energy, activity and life. In the Old Testament, *ruach* is used to denote a wind or storm and an individual's life-breath or activating principle, as well as being associated with the activity of God.[9] Christadelphians are correct to associate the Old Testament use of Spirit with the power of God, but not in assuming that is the entire extent of the definition. Let's look at some Old Testament examples.

- And I have filled him [Bezalel] with the Spirit of God, with ability and intelligence, with knowledge and all craftsmanship (Exod 31:3).

- When he [Samson] came to Lehi, the Philistines came shouting to meet him. Then the Spirit of the LORD rushed upon him, and the ropes that were on his arms became as flax that has caught fire, and his bonds melted off his hands (Judg 15:14).

- And he [Saul] went there to Naioth in Ramah. And the Spirit of God came upon him also, and as he went he prophesied until he came to Naioth in Ramah (1 Sam 19:23).

- The Spirit of the LORD speaks by me [David]; his word is on my tongue (2 Sam 23:2).

- The Spirit of God has made me, and the breath of the Almighty gives me life (Job 33:4).

- When you send forth your Spirit, they are created, and you renew the face of the ground (Ps 104:30).

- And the Spirit of the LORD shall rest upon him, the Spirit of wisdom and understanding, the Spirit of counsel and might, the Spirit of knowledge and the fear of the LORD (Isa 11:2; a prophecy of Jesus).

- The Spirit lifted me [Ezekiel] up and took me away, and I went in bitterness in the heat of my spirit, the hand of the LORD being strong upon me (Ezek 3:14).

9. The discussion in this section is indebted to the exposition of Ferguson, *The Holy Spirit*, 16 and following.

- But as for me, I am filled with power, with the Spirit of the LORD, and with justice and might, to declare to Jacob his transgression, and to Israel his sin (Mic 3:8).

- And it shall come to pass afterwards, that I will pour out my Spirit on all flesh; your sons and your daughters shall prophesy, your old men shall dream dreams, and your young men shall see visions (Joel 2:28).

When the *ruach Yahweh* came "upon" people they exercised unusual powers; prophesying, working miracles, having ecstatic experiences. This is the energy, the force of God which exerts control over creation. But is this an impersonal expression of power, or does it denote a personal, active engagement of God with his creation?

God's Spirit has been engaged in all of his works from the beginning. Genesis 1:2 relates that "the earth was without form and void, and darkness was over the face of the deep. And the Spirit of God was hovering over the face of the waters."

The Spirit's creative work is borne out also in passages such as Job 33:4 and Psalm 104:30. The presence of the Spirit could be the referent in Genesis 1:26–27, "Let us make man in our image." The Spirit's activity appears to be extending God's presence into creation, ordering, completing and executing his plans, just as in the work of redemption in the New Testament (e.g. 1 Tim 3:16; 1 Pet 1:2). The Spirit is also portrayed as representing the face or presence of God in the Old Testament.

- Where shall I go from your Spirit? Or where shall I flee from your presence? (Ps 139:7).

- "And I will not hide my face any more from them, when I pour out my Spirit upon the house of Israel," declares the LORD God (Ezek 39:29).

The Spirit's distribution of gifts was also evident in the Old Testament. Examples include Joseph (Gen 41:38), Daniel (Dan 5:11–14), Moses (Num 11:17), Bezalel, and Oholiab (Exod 31:1–11). Such gifts were for the exercising of godly wisdom, governance, and creativity and in performing God's work. Such characteristics and abilities would be fully displayed in the Messiah (Isa 11:1–5; 61:1–3).

Even in the Old Testament we see evidence of the Spirit's *redemptive* work.

> I will recount the steadfast love of the LORD, the praises of the LORD, according to all that the LORD has granted us, and the great goodness to the house of Israel that he has granted them according to his compassion, according to the abundance of his steadfast love. For he said, "Surely they are my people, children who will not deal falsely." And he became their Savior. In all their affliction he was afflicted, and the angel of his presence saved them; in his love and in his pity he redeemed them; he lifted them up and carried them all the days of old. But they rebelled and grieved his Holy Spirit; therefore he turned to be their enemy, and himself fought against them. Then he remembered the days of old, of Moses and his people. Where is he who brought them up out of the sea with the shepherds of his flock? Where is he who put in the midst of them his Holy Spirit, who caused his glorious arm to go at the right hand of Moses, who divided the waters

before them to make for himself an everlasting name, who led them through the depths? Like a horse in the desert, they did not stumble. Like livestock that go down into the valley, the Spirit of the LORD gave them rest. So you led your people, to make for yourself a glorious name (Isa 63:7–14).

YHWH, the Savior-God, redeemed his people in love and mercy and gave them rest. These were activities of his Spirit, and it is his Spirit who was grieved at their rejection and rebellion. These works of the Spirit are powerful, but there is a personal aspect as well. The Spirit gave them rest, prefiguring the work of Jesus (Matt 11:28–30). It is God who saves and redeems, but it is God as Holy Spirit that they grieve in rejecting this. Paul takes up this very idea in Ephesians:

> And do not grieve the Holy Spirit of God, by whom you were sealed for the day of redemption (Eph 4:30).

The redemptive work of the Spirit is also evident in David's plea as he confesses his sin in Psalm 51:11–12 and asks God to not take his Holy Spirit from him, but restore to him "the joy of your salvation." The fruits of the Spirit, the moral and spiritual characteristics which result from the Spirit's work in believers are presented in Galatians 5:22–23, but these virtues were also displayed in Old Testament believers. If these characteristics are exclusively the Spirit's work as Paul asserts, then the Spirit must have been at work in the Old Testament believers who displayed love, joy, peace, patience, kindness, goodness, faithfulness, gentleness, and self-control. Perhaps this is why Jesus chastised Nicodemus for his failure to understand a basic principle about the Spirit—his regenerative activity, which should have been evident to a scholar of the Scriptures (John 3:5–10).

When the Spirit inspired the Old Testament prophets and writers, it was more than a mechanistic process. These men of God were inspired with God's very words, yet in such a way that their own personalities were not completely suppressed. The process was no mere dictation exercise. The diversity of literary forms and language and the marks of the personalities of the writers illustrate this.[10] David said, "the Spirit of the LORD speaks by me; his word is on my tongue" (2 Sam 23:2). Jeremiah recounts that "the LORD put out his hand and touched my mouth. And the LORD said to me, 'Behold, I have put my words in your mouth,'" (Jer 1:9). When Jeremiah tried to stop speaking God's words they were in his heart like a fire (Jer 20:9).

The activities of the Spirit in the Old Testament are therefore not limited to raw, impersonal outworkings of power, even though sometimes this is the emphasis. The Spirit's activity is personal. The Spirit of God instructs (Neh 9:20) admonishes (Neh 9:30) leads (Ps 143:10) and regenerates (Ezek 36:27). The Spirit of the Lord may be grieved (Isa 63:10) and angered (Mic 2:7). The Spirit of God is therefore not merely a synonym for the power of God; the Spirit's activity is both divine and personal in

---

10. One need only compare the straightforward, earthy Greek of Mark, and his frequent Semiticisms, with the educated Greek of Luke to see a clear example of this.

his relationship with creation and with God's covenant people. Further than this we cannot go within the Old Testament, because just as the Father is only fully revealed to us in and through Christ, so also the Spirit and his work. Peter speaks of the partial revelation of God's saving work prior to the advent of Christ.

> Concerning this salvation, the prophets who prophesied about the grace that was to be yours searched and inquired carefully, inquiring what person or time the Spirit of Christ in them was indicating when he predicted the sufferings of Christ and the subsequent glories. It was revealed to them that they were serving not themselves but you, in the things that have now been announced to you through those who preached the good news to you by the Holy Spirit sent from heaven, things into which angels long to look (1 Pet 1:10–12).

Just as the person and work of Christ was only partially revealed under the old dispensation, so also the work of the Spirit remained enigmatic.

> The Spirit had been active among God's people; but his activity was enigmatic, sporadic, theocratic, selective and in some respects external. The prophets longed for better days. Moses desired, but did not see, a fuller and universally widespread coming of the Spirit on God's people (Num 11:29). By contrast, in the anticipated new covenant, the Spirit would be poured out in a universal manner, dwelling in them personally and permanently (cf. Joel 2:28 onwards; Ezek 36:24–32).[11]

The Personal Deity of the Spirit in the New Testament

In the New Testament, the Holy Spirit is sometimes used interchangeably with "God." Peter, in rebuking Ananias in Acts 5, accuses him of lying to the Holy Spirit in verse 3, then in verse 4 of lying to God. In speaking of the Christian's body as a temple of the Holy Spirit, Paul also speaks of the body as God's temple (1 Cor 3:16–17 and 1 Cor 6:19–20, cf. Eph 2:22). The Holy Spirit is presented as possessing attributes or qualities of God.

- Omniscience (1 Cor 2:10–11; John 16:13)

- Power (Luke 1:35; Rom 15:19)

- Ability to convict and regenerate human hearts (John 3:5–8; 16:8–11 cf. Matt 19:26)

- Eternal not temporal (Heb 9:14 cf. Heb 1:10–12)

- Intrinsic holiness—the Spirit sanctifies (Rom 15:16) and is frequently designated "Holy"

We have already noted the interesting way in which the Spirit is grouped with the Father and the Son. This happens frequently in the New Testament and seems bizarre

11. Ferguson, *The Holy Spirit*, 30.

if the Father and the Son are persons and divine, but the Holy Spirit is an impersonal power. Here are a few of the most obvious examples:

- Disciples are to be baptized in *the name* (singular) of the Father and of the Son and of the Holy Spirit (Matt 28:19).

- Benedictions such as in 2 Corinthians 13:14; the grace of the Lord Jesus Christ, the love of God, and the fellowship of the Holy Spirit.

- Different gifts/service and working in believers come from the Spirit, Lord and God (1 Cor 12:4–6).

- Working together in the process of salvation: foreknowledge of God the Father, sanctifying work of the Spirit, sprinkling by Jesus' blood (1 Pet 1:2).

The Spirit is also presented as possessing attributes or performing functions of Christ; their ministries are parallel.

- Both the Spirit and Jesus are *paraklētos*; the Spirit is *another* (of the same kind; *allos*) *paraklētos* (Comforter or Helper): John 14:26; 15:26; 16:7—compare 1 John 2:1 and John 14:16.

- Mutual glorification: the Spirit glorifies the Son (John 16:14), the Son glorifies the Father (John 17:4), the Father glorifies the Son (John 8:54; 17:1, 5), the Father and Son glorify each other (John 13:31–32). The work of the Spirit seems to be connected with the glory of God (2 Cor 3:18; Phil 3:3; 1 Pet 4:14).

- The Spirit is also referred to as the Spirit of Christ (Rom 8:9; Phil 1:19; 1 Pet 1:11; Gal 4:6; 2 Cor 3:17).

- Both Jesus and the Spirit are sent by the Father and come from the Father, they both are truth, teachers, witnesses, both not recognized by the world. The coming of the Spirit is effectively the coming of Jesus (John 14:16–18—not to be confused with the *parousia* still future).

  > But when the Spirit of truth comes, he will guide you into all the truth, for he will not speak on his own authority, but whatever he hears he will speak, and he will declare to you the things that are to come (John 16:13).

The Holy Spirit is also presented as exhibiting personal attributes; acting in ways which would naturally be associated with a person, rather than an impersonal force.

- A course of action seemed good to the Holy Spirit and to us (Acts 15:28).

- The Holy Spirit said, "Set apart *for me* Barnabas and Saul for the work to which I have called them" (Acts 13:2).

- The Spirit determines which gifts to give and distributes them (1 Cor 12:4–6, 11; Acts 20:28).

- The Spirit can be grieved (Eph 4:30).

- The Spirit can be lied to (Acts 5:3–4) and blasphemed (Matt 12:31; Mark 3:29).

- The Spirit helps and intercedes in a personal involvement as we pray (Rom 8:26).

- The Spirit teaches (John 14:26; 1 Cor 2:13), convicts of sin (John 16:8), sanctifies (Rom 15:16), loves (Rom 15:30), indwells (John 14:17; 2 Tim 1:14), testifies (John 15:26; Acts 5:32; 20:23), hears (John 16:13), speaks (John 16:13; Acts 8:29; 11:12; 13:2; 21:11), forbids (Acts 16:6–7), justifies (1 Cor 6:11).

- The Spirit knows the deep things of God (1 Cor 2:10–11).

- The Spirit has fellowship (2 Cor 13:14).

The Spirit is spoken of as being sent by the Father (John 14:16, 26) and by the Son (John 15:26; 20:22). Jesus would baptize with the Holy Spirit (Matt 3:11; Mark 1:8; Luke 3:16).The Spirit is the agent of Christ as well as the Father; what the Spirit does in Christians Christ is said to do, just as elsewhere what the Spirit does is what God is said to do. There is a unity of activity and purpose here which transcends the Christadelphian understanding of the Spirit as an impersonal power of the Father, which Christ has been given rights to utilize. Nevertheless, the Spirit must be distinguishable from both the Father and the Son in order to be sent by either of them. It is overly simplistic to describe the Old Testament activity of the Spirit as the personal activity of the Father and the New Testament activity of the Spirit as the personal activity of Christ.[12] The Spirit relates us to both the Father and the Son, inspiring the cries of both "Abba, Father" (Rom 8:15) and "Jesus is Lord" (1 Cor 12:3).[13] The Spirit is also sent by both the Father and the Son. The Spirit makes us participants in the life of God, having that life enter ours to make us more like Jesus.

One Christadelphian response to the passages which present the Holy Spirit in such personal terms is to identify the Spirit as an angelic presence.[14] This idea has its roots in the angelic theophany (God manifestation) of the "angel of the Presence" which guided the Israelites in the wilderness (Exod 23:20–21). Returning to the passage in Isaiah 63:7–14 quoted at length above, one interpretation could be that the "angel of his presence" in verse 9 is the Holy Spirit who was "grieved." Angels, after all,

12. As does Nicholls, *Spirit of God*, 87.

13. Clementson, "Christadephians and the Trinity," 171.

14. This idea is presented in detail by Allfree, "The Holy Spirit," 110–88, who attributes all personifications of the Holy Spirit to the activity of the angel of the presence and considers this to explain away the Spirit's personal divinity. Allfree qualifies it with statements such as "Personification is a figure of speech that . . . may be being used in Jesus' words about the Comforter" (112), "There is merit to the suggestion that the specific promise of the Comforter related to an angelic presence . . ." (113), and "It is possible that when Jesus spoke to his disciples about the coming of the Comforter, he was promising them specific angelic help" (118). It is interesting that this is not a proposition made by Alfred Nicholls in *The Spirit of God*. The identification is a better fit in the opposite sense; sometimes Scripture uses the *malak YHWH* or angel (messenger) of the Lord to describe the workings of the personal Holy Spirit. See Malone, "Distinguishing the Angel of the Lord," 297–314.

are "ministering spirits sent out to serve" (Heb 1:14). The passage does not *require* this equation of the angel with the Holy Spirit and it would seem to be a bit of a stretch, but even if this is allowed because this particular angel is specifically said to bear God's name, it is a huge leap to make some/many/all (?) references to God's Spirit in the Old and/or New Testaments a reference to angels. Which of all the Spirit of the LORD passages refer to angels and which do not? Did angels cause Saul to prophesy or prompt the writing of Scripture? Did an angel cause the conception of the Lord Jesus Christ and descend on him at his baptism? Did angels descend on the apostles at Pentecost and enable them to speak in tongues? Does an angel decide how to distribute the gifts of the Holy Spirit? Are our bodies the temple of an angel? Does an angel sanctify us? An essential perspective to retain is that Jesus Christ is always presented as being superior to the angels (Heb 1) and that they serve him (Matt 4:11; 26:53; Luke 22:43).

Ultimately, God is the source of all comfort, as Paul expounds in the following passage. The underlined words are derivatives of the word *paraklētos*, used by Jesus to describe the coming Comforter/Advocate.

> Blessed be the God and Father of our Lord Jesus Christ, the Father of mercies and God of all <u>comfort</u>, who <u>comforts</u> us in all our affliction, so that we may be able to <u>comfort</u> those who are in any affliction, with the <u>comfort</u> with which we ourselves are <u>comforted</u> by God. For as we share abundantly in Christ's sufferings, so through Christ we share abundantly in <u>comfort</u> too. If we are afflicted, it is for your <u>comfort</u> and salvation; and if we are <u>comforted</u>, it is for your <u>comfort</u>, which you experience when you patiently endure the same sufferings that we suffer (2 Cor 1:3–6).

Because Christadelphians stress the impersonal aspect of "spirit"—the power aspect—and ignore the relational aspects, they tend to shy away from discussion of the work of the Spirit in the believer. Christadelphian writing on the Spirit tends to focus on the question of whether the miraculous empowerments of the Spirit in the biblical narrative are available to believers today. Because they (along with many mainstream Christians) believe that gifts of tongues, healing, prophecies, etc., are *not* in evidence today and also because they see the Spirit primarily as a force or power, they are obliged to deny much contemporary activity to the Spirit at all.

As we have seen, in Christadelphian thought, the teaching, convicting, sanctifying, and testifying aspects of the Spirit's work are transferred to the action of the Spirit-inspired Scriptures. Whilst not at all denigrating or detracting from the living and abiding word of God, quick and powerful as a two-edged sword, there is so much more to the Spirit's work than this. The very reception of God's word requires an action of the Spirit on the human heart. One can start to appreciate this wider perspective by attempting to substitute "Scripture" for Spirit in the array of verses cited above. Some aspects work, for example, "Scripture teaches" but most aspects don't; Scriptures do not "love," nor can they be "grieved." With this narrow approach, Christadelphians deny themselves the richness of the experience of the Spirit. Consider the following passages, and whether the Scriptures, a representative angel or an impersonal force could substitute for the Spirit in them.

- And hope does not put us to shame, because God's love has been poured into our hearts through the Holy Spirit, who has been given to us (Rom 5:5).

- You, however, are not in the flesh but in the Spirit, if in fact the Spirit of God dwells in you. Anyone who does not have the Spirit of Christ does not belong to him (Rom 8:9).

- If the Spirit of him who raised Jesus from the dead dwells in you, he who raised Christ Jesus from the dead will also give life to your mortal bodies through his Spirit who dwells in you (Rom 8:11).

- For all who are led by the Spirit of God are sons of God. For you did not receive the spirit of slavery to fall back into fear, but you have received the Spirit of adoption as sons, by whom we cry, "Abba! Father!" The Spirit himself bears witness with our spirit that we are children of God (Rom 8:14–16).

- Likewise the Spirit helps us in our weakness. For we do not know what to pray for as we ought, but the Spirit himself intercedes for us with groanings too deep for words. And he who searches hearts knows what is the mind of the Spirit, because the Spirit intercedes for the saints according to the will of God (Rom 8:26–27).

- May the God of hope fill you with all joy and peace in believing, so that by the power of the Holy Spirit you may abound in hope (Rom 15:13).

- Do you not know that you are God's temple and that God's Spirit dwells in you? (1 Cor 3:16).

- And it is God who establishes us with you in Christ, and has anointed us, and who has also put his seal on us and given us his Spirit in our hearts as a guarantee (2 Cor 1:21–22).

- And you show that you are a letter from Christ delivered by us, written not with ink but with the Spirit of the living God, not on tablets of stone but on tablets of human hearts (2 Cor 3:3).

- But I say, walk by the Spirit, and you will not gratify the desires of the flesh. For the desires of the flesh are against the Spirit, and the desires of the Spirit are against the flesh, for these are opposed to each other, to keep you from doing the things you want to do. But if you are led by the Spirit, you are not under the law . . . But the fruit of the Spirit is love, joy, peace, patience, kindness, goodness, faithfulness, gentleness, self-control; against such things there is no law. And those who belong to Christ Jesus have crucified the flesh with its passions and desires. If we live by the Spirit, let us also walk by the Spirit (Gal 5:16–25).

- For we are the circumcision, who worship by the Spirit of God and glory in

Christ Jesus and put no confidence in the flesh (Phil 3:3).

- But we ought always to give thanks to God for you, brothers beloved by the Lord, because God chose you as the firstfruits to be saved, through sanctification by the Spirit and belief in the truth (2 Thess 2:13).

- By the Holy Spirit who dwells within us, guard the good deposit entrusted to you (2 Tim 1:14).

- He saved us, not because of works done by us in righteousness, but according to his own mercy, by the washing of regeneration and renewal of the Holy Spirit (Titus 3:5).

- Whoever keeps his commands abides in God, and God in him. And by this we know that he abides in us, by the Spirit whom he has given us (1 John 3:24).

Surely, in considering these verses and many others like them, there can be no denial that the Spirit actively works within the believer in a very personal way, to regenerate, sanctify, convict and provide all manner of aid in the Christian life, just as we would expect from a divine Comforter and Advocate.[15]

Jesus and the Spirit

To begin to understand the Holy Spirit we need to understand his relationship to Jesus, because in Jesus is the Spirit most fully known.[16]

The *Paraclēte* as Witness

The word *paraklētos*, translated Helper, Comforter, or Advocate, appears only three times in the New Testament, all of these instances in Jesus' extended discourse on the coming of the Holy Spirit (John 14 to 16). Related words appear much more frequently, referring to those who mourn being comforted, awaiting the consolation of Israel, Barnabas the son of encouragement, exhortation, and so forth. The word *paraklētos* is a compound of the preposition *para*, meaning alongside, and the verb *kaleō*, call, so it literally translates as the one called alongside. In the Greek cultural context, a *paraklētos* was the Advocate for the defendant in a trial;[17] the one who could bear witness to the truth in support of the accused, in other words a character witness.

One of the significant themes of John's Gospel is the witness to Jesus; who he is and what he came to do. This is borne out by the purpose statement of the Gospel

---

15. A tremendously helpful and practical book on prayer by Tim Chester has a chapter on how the Spirit helps us as we pray: Chester, *You Can Pray*.

16. In the following two sections I have drawn heavily on the work of Ferguson, *The Holy Spirit*, 35–56.

17. BDAG, 766.

(John 20:30–31) and by his characteristic use of *sēmeion*, "sign," for the special works which point to Jesus' identity and mission. The apostles too were to be witnesses, by virtue of their being with Jesus from the beginning (John 15:26–27). So too, the Spirit was with Jesus from the beginning, his inseparable companion throughout his life and ministry.

In John 14, Jesus explains to his disciples that he must go away, to prepare a place for them in his Father's house (14:1–4). But Jesus will not abandon them in this process; "I will not leave you as orphans; I will come to you. Yet a little while and the world will see me no more, but you will see me" (14:18–19). Jesus is not speaking in *this* instance of his second coming, when "every eye will see him" and the coming of the Son of Man will be like lightning as he descends with his angels and the trumpet of God. Instead, he is speaking of the way in which he will be present with his disciples until the future day when they will again see him physically. Jesus will send them *another* Helper (the word is *allos*, another of the same) who will be with them forever; the Spirit of truth; he will live with them and be in them (14:16–17). Judas (not Iscariot) raises the question of why Jesus will only show himself to the disciples and not to the world (14:22) and Jesus expands on his previous statement, saying that for anyone who loves him and obeys his teaching, "my Father will love him and we will come to him and make our home with him" (14:23). The Counsellor, specifically identified as the Holy Spirit in verse 26, will be the means by which the Father and the Son dwell in and with believers. In verse 28, Jesus reiterates that he is coming back to them.

There follows the discourse in chapter 15 of the vine and the branches, where Jesus emphasizes the necessity of abiding in him—the vine—in order to bear fruit, and the necessity of loving each other. He goes on to speak of the world hating and persecuting his disciples, just as it hated and persecuted him. The whole context of this discourse is the situation of the disciples between the two physical comings of Jesus; what we experience now, when the age of the Spirit is inaugurated, but not yet fully consummated. It is in *this* context that Jesus states that the Spirit of truth, the Helper or Counsellor, will testify about him, as they the disciples must also testify (15:26–27). Interestingly, Jesus speaks of the Spirit being sent by the Father (14:16, 26) and by Jesus (15:26; 16:7). He explains that it is for the disciples' good that he is going away, because if he did not, the Helper would not come (16:7). When he comes, the Spirit of truth would guide the disciples into all the truth (16:13) because he will speak only what he has heard, and will bring glory to Jesus; he will take what is Christ's and make it known to the disciples (16:13–15). This is the essence of the Spirit's witness in the disciples, and through them, he will "convict the world concerning sin and righteousness and judgment" (16:8). John, in his first letter 5:6 declares, "The Spirit is the one who testifies, because the Spirit is the truth.

In Romans 8:9–10 we see the interchange of terms; "Spirit of God dwells in you," "have the Spirit of Christ" and "Christ is in you." These are three ways of describing the reality of the indwelling of the Spirit.

A major theme of the Acts of the Apostles is the witness of the Spirit through the disciples. Here are two examples:

- But you will receive power when the Holy Spirit has come upon you, and you will be my witnesses in Jerusalem and in all Judea and Samaria, and to the end of the earth (Acts 1:8).

- And when they had prayed, the place in which they were gathered together was shaken, and they were all filled with the Holy Spirit and continued to speak the word of God with boldness (Acts 4:31).

This was both an external witness to Jesus, convicting the world and speaking the truth about him, and an internal witness to the indwelling of God in the believer. The Spirit is the ultimate witness to Jesus, because he has been with Jesus "from the beginning."

The Spirit in the Life and Ministry of Jesus

The Spirit was intimately involved with the birth of Jesus.

> And the angel answered her [Mary], "The Holy Spirit will come upon you, and the power of the Most High will overshadow you; therefore the child to be born will be called holy—the Son of God" (Luke 1:35).

This is the language of the Old Testament; the Spirit "coming upon" someone and making a dramatic impact on his or her life. The word for overshadow is *episkazō*, which is also used in the Septuagint for the hovering of the cloud of God's glory during the exodus (Exod 40:35). God led the people through the wilderness by his Holy Spirit (Isa 63:9–11). This dwelling-glory, or *shekinah* glory seen in the cloud was in the temple of God. Ezekiel mourned the departure of this glory from the temple (Ezek 10:1–22) with the promise of the glory's return (Mal 3:1–5). Jesus Christ is that glory, the glory "we have seen," who came to his own but his own people did not receive him (John 1:11, 14). Luke uses *episkiazō* one more time in his gospel, when the cloud enveloped the disciples on the mount of transfiguration (Luke 9:34) in the context of Jesus' imminent exodus and in the presence of his glory. The work of the Spirit in the incarnation thus has echoes of the (new) creation and of the exodus. It was a completely new thing; born not of natural human relations (John 1:13), but a work of God.

Only such a work of God through his Spirit could accomplish the union of the human and the divine. Jesus was genuinely human; "in the likeness of sinful flesh" (Rom 8:3) the second Adam and yet he was "holy, innocent, unstained," sinless (Heb 7:26) and not personally under the condemnation of Adam, in order to be able to bring life, not condemnation (Rom 5:18–19; 1 Cor 15:47).

The Spirit worked in the life of Jesus to an extent never seen in any other person.

- And the Spirit of the LORD shall rest upon him, the Spirit of wisdom and under-standing, the Spirit of counsel and might, the Spirit of knowledge and the fear of the LORD (Isa 11:2).

- Behold my servant, whom I uphold, my chosen, in whom my soul delights; I have put my Spirit upon him; he will bring forth justice to the nations (Isa 42:1).

- The Spirit of the LORD God is upon me, because the LORD has anointed me to bring good news to the poor; he has sent me to bind up the broken hearted, to proclaim liberty to the captives, and the opening of the prison to those who are bound . . . (Isa 61:1).

Jesus in his divinity had an unparalleled relationship with the Father, and also in his human nature he grew in his knowledge of God by the Spirit. He spoke of things which he had seen with his Father, but also evidenced an intimate familiarity with Scripture (e.g. Matt 4:4, 7, 10; Luke 2:47; 4:17; John 7:15). Jesus was also anointed by the Spirit (Acts 10:38). We are not to understand this as the first encounter of Jesus with the Spirit, for it is clear that even whilst growing up Jesus evidenced traits which are associated with the Spirit, such as wisdom (Luke 2:40, 52). What then was the significance of the Spirit's descent at his baptism?

The apostles "received" the Holy Spirit at Pentecost, yet had experienced the Spirit's power previously—how else could they have ministered as they did (Matt 10:1, 8)? The outpouring at Pentecost was their commissioning, the inauguration of the new age as prophesied by Joel, enabling them to "do greater works" (John 14:12). However, Scripture speaks of subsequent episodes of being "filled" with the Spirit, even though they already "had" the Spirit (e.g. Acts 4:8, 31; 13:9, 52). Jesus was given the Spirit "without measure" (John 3:34) and was able to baptize with the Spirit (John 1:33–34). His own baptism marked his consecration and anointing for the work he was to commence. It was an empowerment, but also a setting apart.

He had attained the age of "about thirty years" (Luke 3:23) which probably re-flects a time of entry into service. Jesus was washed in water and anointed as High Priest, he took on the role of prophet, ready to speak God's words (cf. Deut 18:18; 2 Kgs 2:15) and the voice from heaven proclaimed him to be the anointed King (Ps 2:2, 7). So it is fitting that the Spirit descended in bodily form to visibly mark Jesus' anointing as Prophet, Priest, and King. It was a special, fresh and greater endowment of the Spirit who had been with him "from the beginning." The reality of Jesus' sonship, itself a work of the Spirit, was proclaimed. It is significant that following this com-missioning the Spirit drove Jesus out into the wilderness (Mark 1:12) for the specific purpose of facing temptations that questioned his commissioning for the work God had prepared.[18] This was a direct assault on the kingdom of this world, the "strong man" was bound, and in subsequently casting out demons "by the Spirit of God" the

---

18. The verb is *ekballō*, to cast out; also used for casting out demons and money changers!

kingdom was inaugurated (Matt 12:28–29, 32). Following this period of temptation, Jesus returned "in the power of the Spirit" and proclaimed his commissioning publicly (Luke 4:14, 18). The rest of the account of "all that Jesus began to do" (Acts 1:1), which continues in the second volume of Luke-Acts, is very much an account of the Spirit's activity in and through Jesus and subsequently in his apostles.

> For Jesus, then, the Spirit is a Spirit of Sonship and assurance, who will bear witness with his spirit that he is the Son of God and who will enable him, even in Gethsemane, to call God "Abba! Father!" (cf. Rom 8:15–16). The Spirit thus seals and confirms the bond of love and trust between the Father and the incarnate Son.[19]

The work of the Spirit in the earthly ministry and life of Jesus was by no means limited to expressions of power. He was the most perfect expression of what it means to be walking in the Spirit and displaying the fruits of the Spirit; love, joy, peace, patience, kindness, goodness, faithfulness, gentleness, and self control. Like Christ, those who belong to Christ walk in and live by the Spirit and not according to the sinful nature (Gal 5:16–26).

The Spirit also ministered during Jesus' death and resurrection.

> How much more will the blood of Christ, who through the eternal Spirit offered himself without blemish to God, purify our conscience from dead works to serve the living God (Heb 9:14).

Just as Father, Son, and Holy Spirit were united and active in the incarnation (Luke 1:35) and Jesus' anointing (Luke 3:22) so also in his resurrection. The resurrection is attributed to "God," by which is primarily implied the Father (Acts 2:24; 3:26; 4:10; 5:30; 10:40; 13:30, 37; Rom 10:9; 1 Cor 6:14; 15:15; 2 Cor 4:14; Eph 1:19–20; Col 2:12; 1 Thess 1:10; Heb 13:20; 1 Pet 1:21). Most explicitly, in Galatians 1:1 Paul describes himself as "an apostle—not from men nor through man, but through Jesus Christ and God the Father, who raised him from the dead."

The resurrection is also seen as an action of the Son (John 2:19–21, cf. Matt 27:63; John 10:17–18) and of the Holy Spirit (Rom 1:4, with 1 Tim 3:16; 1 Pet 3:18). Romans 1:4 is particularly interesting because it highlights the role of the Spirit in declaring (witnessing to) the sonship of Jesus in the resurrection, just as at his baptism and in his incarnation.

As a result of his resurrection and glorification, Jesus, the "last Adam," became "a life-giving spirit" (1 Cor 15:45). Jesus came into such complete possession of the Spirit that he is one with the Spirit in effectual ministry; Christ in turn is the source of our resurrection life. Both Spirit and Son are *parakletos*. To have the Spirit is to have Christ, to be indwelt by him.

- You, however, are not in the flesh but in the Spirit, if in fact the Spirit of God dwells in you. Anyone who does not have the Spirit of Christ does not belong to

19. Ferguson, *The Holy Spirit*, 47.

him. But if Christ is in you, although the body is dead because of sin, the Spirit is life because of righteousness. If the Spirit of him who raised Jesus from the dead dwells in you, he who raised Christ Jesus from the dead will also give life to your mortal bodies through his Spirit who dwells in you (Rom 8:9–11).

- Now the Lord is the Spirit, and where the Spirit of the Lord is, there is freedom. And we all, with unveiled face, beholding the glory of the Lord, are being transformed into the same image from one degree of glory to another. For this comes from the Lord who is the Spirit (2 Cor 3:17–18).

The Lord here is Christ, as is evident from the context. This is one of several passages that speak of the Spirit as the Spirit of Christ (eg., Phil 1:19; 1 Pet 1:11). Jesus, like the Father, sends the Spirit (Mark 1:8; John 15:26; 16:7–8; 20:22; Acts 2:33; 1 John 3:24). But what does it mean to say "the Lord is the Spirit"? This does not blur the distinction between the Son and the Spirit, even though they are one in their ministry. The Greek of verse 17 is unambiguous:

ho de kurios to pneuma estin

(but) the lord the spirit is

However, verse 18 can be read several ways, depending on how the genitive case is applied to "spirit" and "lord." The genitive is the case which governs the preposition *apo*, "from," but as in English it can be used to indicate possession or source.

kathaper apo kuriou pneumatos

just as from lord [genitive] spirit [genitive]

Hence the possibilities are: "from [the] spirit of the Lord," "from [the] Lord [who is the] spirit" or "from [the] lord of [the] Spirit. Jesus now so completely possesses the Spirit that he is "Lord of the Spirit" or even he "is the Spirit." This is why Jesus can speak of the coming of the Spirit as his coming to us. The Spirit working within us causes us to be conformed to Christ, bearing his fruits and "being transformed into the same image from one degree of glory to another."[20]

The Spirit and the Believer

The Spirit's central roles are to reveal Christ to us, to bring us to him and unite us with him and with each other as the body of Christ.

> On the last day of the feast, the great day, Jesus stood up and cried out, "If anyone thirsts, let him come to me and drink. Whoever believes in me, as the Scripture has said, 'Out of his heart will flow rivers of living water.'" Now this he said about

20. Ibid., 55–56.

the Spirit, whom those who believed in him were to receive, for as yet the Spirit had not been given, because Jesus was not yet glorified (John 7:37–39).

As we have seen, the coming of the Spirit would only occur following Jesus' departure; Jesus spoke of this in the immediately preceding verses. This idea is further developed in John 14 to 16, where the Spirit is spoken of as another Helper, Comforter, or Advocate, and the means whereby Jesus would dwell with them. This would be a rich bounty, like the upwelling of water, to eternal life, and would only occur in its fullness with the completion of Jesus' work.

> And I will ask the Father, and he will give you another Helper, to be with you forever, even the Spirit of truth, whom the world cannot receive, because it neither sees him nor knows him. You know him, for he dwells with you and will be in you. I will not leave you as orphans; I will come to you. Yet a little while and the world will see me no more, but you will see me. Because I live, you also will live. In that day you will know that I am in my Father, and you in me, and I in you (John 14:16–20).

The Spirit is to be experienced by believers; believers know him as the world cannot know him, and he is the means by which Christ indwells us and we belong to him (Rom 8:9; 2 Tim 1:14; 1 John 3:24). This is not to suggest that the coming of the Spirit in any way replaces the physical resurrection of Jesus, nor his literal second coming. The consequence of Jesus' resurrection is new life mediated by the Spirit, experienced now in part and to be experienced in its fullness at his physical return, when our natural bodies will be transformed into spiritual bodies (Rom 8:11).

The Spirit empowers the believer's witness to Christ (John 15:26–27; Acts 1:8; 1 John 5:6–9). The Spirit is the means by which we apprehend the love of God (Rom 5:5). The Spirit brings joy (1 Thess 1:6). The mind controlled by the Spirit is life and peace and is able to please God (Rom 8:5–9) and to bear the fruits of the Spirit (Gal 5:16, 22–23). Those who are led by the Spirit of God are sons of God; we have received the Spirit of sonship by whom we are entitled and enabled to call God our Father, as co-heirs with Christ (Rom 8:14–17; Gal 4:6). The Spirit in our hearts is a deposit, a seal of God's ownership of us, guaranteeing what is to come (2 Cor 1:21–22; 5:5; Gal 5:5; Eph 1:13–14) The Spirit helps us in prayer and intercedes—which is the role of an Advocate (Rom 8:26–27; Jude 1:20). The Holy Spirit renews and sanctifies believers (Rom 15:16; 2 Thess 2:13; Titus 3:5–7; 1 Pet 1:2) and reveals to us the deep things of God (1 Cor 2:9–12).

> The natural person does not accept the things of the Spirit of God, for they are folly to him, and he is not able to understand them because they are spiritually discerned (1 Cor 2:14).

The indwelling of the Spirit is the means by which God indwells (tabernacles in) us; whereby our bodies become his temple and members of Christ's body (1 Cor 3:16; 6:14, 19; Eph 2:22). The Spirit gives us the ability to discern and appreciate the things of God; only by the Spirit can we truly call Jesus "Lord" (1 Cor 12:3). The Spirit distributes gifts of Christian ministry and service, for the edification of the body, as he sees fit (1 Cor 12:7–11—and notice who it is that distributes these gifts). We worship (Phil 3:3) and have fellowship by the Spirit of God (Phil 2:1).

The work of the Spirit in the believer is real, it is a present experience, it is personal, effectual, and powerful and is nothing less than the seal of our promised inheritance in Christ. Far from being merely an impersonal force or power, or means to an end limited to the apostolic era, the Holy Spirit indwells believers and equips us for service to God. God forbid that we should grieve him, deny him or resist him.

Summary

- A correct understanding of the Holy Spirit is essential, because the Spirit is how we experience God, how he indwells us and applies salvation to us.

- Christadelphians believe that the Holy Spirit is God's power, in a similar sense to light radiating from the sun, but is not a person, and that the Spirit works in believers today only through the written Word.

- In the Old Testament the Spirit is associated with God's power, as evidenced in creation and the effects of the Spirit coming upon people with supernatural results. There are traces and foretastes of the Spirit's redemptive work in the Old Testament, and the Spirit inspired the writing of the Scriptures.

- In the New Testament, the Spirit is used interchangeably with "God" and is presented as possessing divine attributes. The Spirit is often grouped with the Father and the Son in name and in work.

- The Spirit is also presented as having attributes and performing functions of Christ; their ministries are parallel.

- The Holy Spirit has definite personal attributes.

- The Holy Spirit is sent by and from both the Father and the Son and relates the believer to both Father and Son.

- By denying the personality and deity and present experience of the Spirit in the life of believers, Christadelphians deny themselves the richness of the experience of the Spirit.

- The Holy Spirit is most fully known in and through Jesus Christ. The Spirit is described as *paraklētos*, another Helper, Advocate, or Counsellor, who would be given as a result of Jesus' finished work.

- The Spirit witnesses to Christ and is the means of the indwelling of God/Christ in the believer. He is the Spirit of adoption.

- The Spirit accomplished the union of human and divine in the incarnate Word, anointed Jesus for his work as Prophet, Priest, and King, empowered him in his life and ministry and in his death and resurrection. Jesus received the Spirit without measure.

- The Spirit works in believers today to reveal Christ to us, unite us with him and with each other as the body of Christ; he gives gifts to edify the body, he witnesses to Christ and enables us to bear fruit pleasing to God. He is a deposit, a seal guaranteeing the fullness of the life we now experience in part. He renews and sanctifies believers and allows us to discern the deep things of God. In short, the Holy Spirit applies Christ's saving work to believers.

Further Reading

- J. I. Packer, "Holy Spirit." A succinct summary of the person and work of the Holy Spirit, tightly packed with scriptural evidence.

- Sinclair B. Ferguson, *The Holy Spirit.*

- Millard Erickson, *Christian Theology*, chapters 39 and 40.

- D. A. Carson, *Showing the Spirit: A Theological Exposition of 1 Corinthians 12–14.* An excellent and scripturally balanced treatise on the gifts of the Spirit, which is beyond the scope of this present book.

8

Three in One?

Misconception #14: That because the word "Trinity" is not found in Scripture, it cannot be a scriptural doctrine.

Corrective: The doctrine of the Trinity encapsulates the scripturally demonstrable facts about the Godhead.

Misconception #15: That because the Trinity is hard to understand, it cannot be a scriptural doctrine.

Corrective: The authority of Scripture is greater than human reason, and we should not expect to completely understand God.

THIS CHAPTER BRINGS TOGETHER the threads of the previous chapters. Having shown from Scripture that Jesus and the Holy Spirit are divine—that they are each in some way God, then in conjunction with the unity of the Godhead and the humanity of Christ, we must come face to face with the theological dilemma that has exercised the people of God for two millennia. The concept of the Trinity is the way to make sense of the apparent paradoxes that result from our considerations so far.

Fundamental Principles

In previous chapters we have presented the scriptural basis for understanding that:

- There is one God, who is the only divine being and is separate from the universe which he created.

- The Father, Son, and Holy Spirit are each personal and divine and can be rightly called "God."

Summary of the Scriptural Perspective

The Unity of God (One ousia)

- "God is one" is a foundational Old Testament principle and is the basis of God's unique and exclusive claim over Israel. Therefore, YHWH alone is to be worshiped (Deut 6:4–5/Matt 22:37–40; Deut 32:39; 1 Kgs 8:60; Isa 43:11–13; 44:6; 45:5; Ezek 39:25; Rom 3:30; Jas 2:19).

- God is separate from his creation and no creature can be worshiped as God; God alone is intrinsically holy and eternal (Isa 40:25, 28; Rev 4:11; Rom 1:25; Isa 6:3–5; John 12:41; Rev 1:8).

- The unity of God encompasses the lordship of Jesus, his role as creator and his worthiness to be worshiped (1 Cor 8:5–6; Col 1:16; Matt 28:17; Heb 1:6; 7:26; Rev 22:13).

Three Persons Spoken of as God

1. The Father is God

   (Deut 32:6; John 8:54; John 20:17; Matt 23:9; 1 Cor 8:6; Eph 4:6; Rev 1:6; Rom 1:7; 15:6; Gal 1:1)

2. The Son is God

   - The Son was active in creation and is above all created things (Col 1:15–17; 1 Cor 8:6; Heb 1:3, 8, 10; John 1:1–2, 14).

   - The name of God is ascribed to Jesus, as well as key titles of God such as LORD (Exod 3:14; Isa 41:4; 43:25; 44:6; 45:19; 46:4; 48:12; 52:6/John 6:20; 8:24, 28, 58; 13:19; Rev 1:8/Rev 22:13; Acts 2:36; Rom 10:9; 1 Cor 16:22; 2 Cor 4:5; Isa 45:22–23/Phil 2:6–11; Ps 32:2/Rom 4:8; Joel 2:32/Acts 2:16, 21, 36; Rom 10:13; Deut 10:17; Ps 136:1–3; 1 Tim 6:15/Rev 17:14; 19:13–16; Rom 14:9; Ps 68:4, 17–18/Eph 4:8; Mal 3:1; Isa 40:3, 9/Matt 1:22–23; Luke 1:43; 2:11; John 20:28; Rom 9:5; Heb 1:8; Phil 2:6).

   - The saving work of God is accomplished by Jesus (Exod 15:2; Ps 68:20; Isa 43:3/Luke 2:11; 1 Cor 6:11; Rom 5:1, 11; Rom 6:23; 1 Thess 5:9; Ezek 34:1–16/John 10; Heb 13:20; 1 Pet 2:25; 5:4; Rev 7:17).

   - The Day of YHWH is the Day of the Lord Jesus (Isa 13:6–9; Ezek 30:3; Joel 1:15; 2:31; 3:14; Amos 5:18–20; Zech 14:1; Mal 4:5/1 Thess 5:2; 1 Cor 1:8; 5:5; 2 Cor 1:14; 2 Thess 2:2).

   - God's judgments are accomplished by Jesus (Ps 50:6; 96:13; Isa 33:22; Joel 3:2,

12; Jer 11:20; 17:10/Isa 11:1–4; Rom 2:16; 14:10; 2 Cor 5:10; Rev 2:23; John 5:17, 22).

- The Son is worthy of worship, a prerogative of God alone (Rev 5:12–13; 19:10; Heb 1:6; Matt 2:2, 11; Matt 14:33; 28:9; Luke 24:52; John 9:38).

- The Son forgives, a prerogative of God alone (Ps 103:1–3; Isa 43:25/Mark 2:5–12; Luke 7:47–50; Acts 10:43).

3. The Holy Spirit is God

- The Spirit acts as God in creation and redemption and is spoken of inter-changeably with "God" (Gen 1:2; Job 33:4; Ps 104:30; Ps 139:7; Ezek 39:29; Isa 63:7–14/Eph 4:30; 2 Sam 23:2; Acts 5:3–4; 1 Cor 3:16–17; 6:19–20; Eph 2:22).

- The Spirit possesses attributes of God (Luke 1:35; John 3:5–8; 16:7–11,13; Rom 15:19; Rom 15:16; 1 Cor 2:10–11; Heb 2:4; 9:14).

- The Spirit is described in personal terms (John 14:26; 15:26; 16:13–14 (mas-culine pronouns); Gen 6:3; Neh 9:20; Ps 143:10; Isa 63:10; Ezek 36:27; Mic 2:7; Matt 12:31; John 14:26; 15:26; 16:8, 13; Acts 8:29; 11:12; 13:2; 16:6–7; 20:28; 21:11; Rom 8:26; 15:16; 30; 1 Cor 2:10–13; 6:11; 12:4–6; 2 Cor 13:14; Eph 4:30; 2 Tim 1:14).

- The Spirit is grouped with the Father and Son (Matt 28:19; 2 Cor 13:14; 1 Pet 1:2).

- The Spirit possesses attributes of, and performs functions of Christ (John 14:16, 26; 15:26; 16:7, 13–14; Rom 8:9; Phil 1:19; 1 Pet 1:11; Gal 4:6; 2 Cor 3:17).

On face value, these statements appear mutually contradictory and so they have been misconstrued by non-trinitarians such as Christadelphians. The misconstruc-tion arises because a superficial appraisal of these statements could lead one to errone-ously think that God is one *in exactly the same sense* in which he is three. Clearly, this would be a contradiction, and an impossibility. As Paul Fiddes puts it, the doctrine of the Trinity is not an exercise in mathematics, it is not a numerical puzzle designed to test faith or baffle the human mind, stating the paradox that God is one being and three beings at the same time, or one person and three persons.[1]

To reconcile these truths as summarized above, which have abundant scriptural support, we need to understand the sense in which God is one, and the sense in which he is three. To do this necessitates some additional vocabulary, and an understanding of what certain terms meant to the original articulators of the doctrine, and what they don't mean.

---

1. Fiddes, *Participating in God*, 4–5.

Watch Your Language

Before we get down to this, a slight digression is in order. One of the criticisms which Christadelphians level at trinitarians concerns the use of such "non-scriptural" terms as "trinity," "incarnation" and "three persons in one essence." To an extent, such criticism may be valid, but only insofar as the terms are ill-defined or incorrectly understood and explained. Julian Clementson makes this point; "Much popular language used to explain the Trinity simply makes no sense to Christadelphians and, in the author's experience, is obscure to many evangelicals as well."[2]

But fair is fair. Trinitarians are not the only ones to make use of non-scriptural terms to elucidate doctrines, as a couple of examples from Christadelphian works will illustrate. Robert Roberts said of Jesus, "He is now the corporealisation of life-spirit as it exists in the Deity."[3] and John Thomas spoke of "the Eternal Christ-power, veiled in and manifested through the flesh."[4] Nor are trinitarians the only ones to use analogies which by reason of their age may now appear somewhat inappropriate: consider Robert Roberts' appeal to the cutting-edge science of his day to explain the Spirit of God.

> Now, it is a fact that in our day, there has been discovered a subtle, unanalysable, incomprehensible principle, which, though inscrutable in its essence, is found to be at the basis of all the phenomena of nature—itself eluding the test of chemistry or the deductions of philosophy. Scientists have called it ELECTRICITY . . . Could a better name be devised than what the Scriptures have given it—SPIRIT? It is one of the highest proofs of the truth of Jewish revelation, that its disclosure of the Deity in His relation to the universe coincides with the facts brought to light by the researches of the human intellect in the field of nature.[5]

So if at this point Christadelphians cry "Foul!" because I have quoted this somewhat embarrassing and very outdated comment from their pioneer, let's all be reminded to use the same desired, gracious latitude when coming to terms with the two thousand-year-old thought world and vocabulary of the early Greek and Latin Christian theologians, as they grappled with an analogy to explain nothing less than what it means to be God.

In Search of a Model of God

We are not to make images of God or reduce him to analogies from nature. However, it is helpful to have some concept of God which reconciles the unity and relational diversity of the Godhead.

2. Clementson, "Christadelphians and the Trinity," 157.

3. Roberts, *Christendom Astray*, 160.

4. John Thomas, cited in Nicholls, *Remember the Days of Old*, 41.

5. Roberts, *Christendom Astray*, 143–44.

Some Inadequate Models

Many models have been advanced to explain or describe how three distinct persons, the Father, Son, and Holy Spirit, can each be God and yet there be only one divinity, one Godhead. An inadequate or wrong model will fail to encompass both aspects which Scripture teaches:

- There is one God, who is the only divine being and separate from the universe which he created.

- The Father, Son, and Holy Spirit are each personal and divine and can be rightly called "God."

If the distinctiveness of the three, Father, Son, and Holy Spirit is denied, we have the various forms of *modalism*. Modalism teaches that one God was manifest as different persons at different phases of salvation history. Some unhelpful analogies sometimes used to describe the Trinity, such as water existing as ice, liquid, and vapor actually model modalism. But this denies the distinctive roles of each person, and their relationships with one another; the Father sent the Son, the Son submitted to the Father, the Son and Father send the Holy Spirit, the Holy Spirit leads us to Christ, they glorify each other, etc. As we have seen, the Christadelphian doctrine of God manifestation comes close to modalism, and also loses the distinctiveness of the Holy Spirit, making him an impersonal emanation from the Father (rather like electricity, actually).

If the full deity of the Son and Holy Spirit are denied, making the Father the only true God, then the richness of biblical teaching on the divinity of the Son and Holy Spirit must be ignored. We will fail to honor the Son as we do the Father, and fail to ascribe him due worship. This was the error of Arianism, Subordinationism, and the various forms of Unitarianism. Christadelphians, as we have seen, deny the full and underived deity of the Son and Holy Spirit. Jehovah's Witnesses subscribe to a modern version of Arianism.

The full deity of Father, Son, and Holy Spirit could also be accommodated by denying there is one God; this would be tritheism, which Christadelphians have falsely accused trinitarians of upholding. Tritheism has not been a common error and is certainly not what mainstream Christians understand by the doctrine of the Trinity.[6]

Gerald Bray, who has written extensively on the history of trinitarian theology, makes a distinction between monotheism, the doctrine of one Godhead, and unitarianism, which limits this one Godhead to one person.

> Of course Christians agree with Jews and Muslims that there is only one God, but much to the latter's bewilderment, they insist that this one God is also a Trinity of persons. To make matters more complicated, Christians do not believe that

---

6. Thomas Gaston is to be commended for his accurate, albeit unsympathetic, definition of the Trinity in his introduction to *One God the Father*, 11–12. He, at least, has done his homework.

the Trinity is formed by cutting God up into three pieces, or by regarding him from three different angles—ideas which, however unacceptable they may be in themselves, would at least preserve a semblance of basic monotheism. Christians insist that each of the persons is fully God in his own right, while remaining at the same time distinct from the others. To Jews or Muslims it might appear that Christians affirm everything they believe about God, and then go on to add two extra persons, whose existence seems to contradict an otherwise common affirmation of monotheism . . .

The revelation of the Trinity, as opposed to the implied unitarianism of Judaism, can be explained only by the transformation of perspective brought about by Jesus. The Trinity belongs to the inner life of God, and can be known only by those who share in that life. As long as we look at God on the outside, we shall never see beyond his unity; for, as the Cappadocian Fathers and Augustine realized, the external works of the Trinity are undivided. This means that an outside observer will never detect the inner reality of God, and will never enter the communion with him which is promised to us in Christ.[7]

Bray goes on to explain that the early Christians "felt compelled to abandon the unitarian assumptions of their inherited Judaism, without rejecting its fundamental monotheism," as we saw in our consideration of how Paul incorporates Christ into the *Shema*. Jesus was not just a theophany of the Father, but a person in intimate relationship with him. To know who Jesus is, to know the triune God, is "to pass from the old dispensation to the new." As we shall see in the next chapter, the story of the struggles of the early church to formulate a conceptual framework which would allow them to express their belief that Father, Son, and Holy Spirit are all equally God, without sacrificing Old Testament monotheism,[8] is the story of the elucidation and exploration of the doctrine of the Trinity.

Consider the following diagram,[9] where each side of the triangle represents one of three aspects of the correct understanding of the Godhead. (Please note that this is *not* a "model" of the triune God!) The orthodox or mainstream trinitarian view is represented by the circle, which touches equally on all three sides and holds to each of these three truths. Each point of the triangle marks an error which comes about when the truth on the opposite side is denied, even though the other two "sides" are accepted.

---

7. Bray, *Doctrine of God*, 115, 119.

8. For a full treatment of Jesus and monotheism, see Bauckham, *Jesus and the God of Israel*.

9. This diagram is reproduced from Nicole, "The Meaning of the Trinity," 4. With permission.

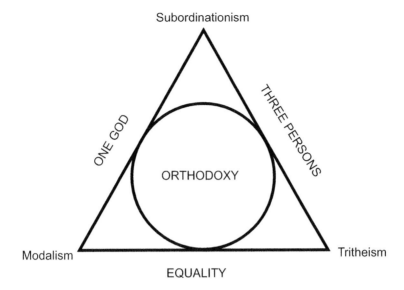

Subordinationism

ONE GOD

THREE PERSONS

ORTHODOXY

Modalism

Tritheism

EQUALITY

From the vantage point of one error, orthodoxy may come to resemble one of the other two errors. Extremes beget extremes, and if there is an imbalance in one aspect of doctrine, those who disagree are likely to be condemned as having an "opposite" heretical view. Because Christadelphians stress the oneness of God to the exclusion of recognizing the divinity of Christ and the Holy Spirit, they hover between a sort of subordinationist and modalistic view of God, and accuse trinitarians of tritheism.

> It is important to recognize that the doctrine of the Trinity is a mystery. It is not, however, an absurdity, as some people have viewed it. Specifically, it is not assert-ed that God is one in the same respect in which he is three. What is propounded is that there is unity of essence, that this one essence is shared alike by each of the three persons, and that the three are conjoined in a total harmony of will and being, which far surpasses the unity observed between distinct individuals in humanity . . . Probably it is wise to recognize that certain aspects of the Trinity may be reflected in a limited way in the created world, but that nothing reflects it in its entirety, precisely because it is the prerogative of God alone to be triune, and he shares with nothing else this particular distinctive.[10]

It is important not to start with our own experience and define God from there, for that would be to make him in our image. We must start with the scriptural truths that have been carefully unpacked so far, and search for a way of understanding the Godhead that does justice to each, all the while recognizing that we will not ultimately be able to fully understand God. We will explore the concept of "essence" and "per-sons" a little later, but for now it's important to accept that just because every human being we have ever met is one person with a single essence, that this does not preclude God from having three persons within his essence. So let's further explore what *cannot*

10. Nicole, "The Meaning of the Trinity," 4, 6.

be meant by three persons in one essence, before grappling with how the doctrine has been understood historically and is understood today.

Firstly, God's being or essence is not divided into three equal parts, such that we have to add them up before we get "God." With the Father, the Son, or the Holy Spirit considered individually, we do not have a partial God.

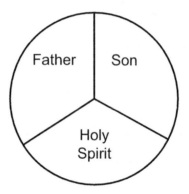

Secondly, the three persons are not simply different ways of looking at the one God, depending on the context or the viewer's perspective. Nor are the persons merely distinctions or additional attributes added on to the essential being of God, like software applications.

So, what sort of model can represent the three-in-one God? We need a representation of a unified essence, with Father, Son, and Spirit comprising that essence, in relationship with each other yet distinct from everything outside that essence. Because they are relational and they are active, we need a dynamic image. Such a model hardly does justice to the complexity that is God, and it is little wonder that we are prohibited from portraying God in any sort of image that carries a likeness of a created thing.

Essence and Person

Trinitarian vocabulary was forged in the controversies of the first few centuries as a way of expressing the orthodox understanding of the Godhead. A middle ground was sought between the error of tritheism (three Gods) on the one hand and that of modalism (Father, Son, and Holy Spirit as merely modes or expressions of one God) on the other. The fourth-century Greek theologians known as the Cappadocian fathers; Basil the Great, Gregory of Nyssa and Gregory of Nazianzus, expressed succinctly what became the classic formulation of the Trinity.

The Greek term they used to describe the essence or substance of God, his nature or divine being was *ousia*. *Ousia* is something that exists, that has substance.[11] The Latin equivalent depends on the writer, which inevitably caused some confusion.

11. BDAG, 740.

Substantia (substance) and *essentia* (essence) have both been used. God has one *ousia*, one substance or essence and this is the sense in which he is one God. No being other than God has this divine *ousia*. The Creed of the Council of Constantinople, AD 381, declared the Son to be of the same substance—*homoousia*—as the Father, as against *homoiousia*, of similar substance to the Father. Father, Son, and Holy Spirit share the divine *ousia* and in unity they constitute God, the one and only Divinity.

The sense in which God is three must be a different sense to that in which he is one. The three-ness of God, the distinctiveness of the Father, Son, and Holy Spirit, has been expressed in terms of "personhood." The original Greek word employed by the Cappadocians was *hypostasis*, which means the essential or basic structure of an entity or being. This word has a fairly broad etymological range, and its Latin equivalent could be taken to be *substantia*, but also *persona*, again depending on the writer. Following the Council of Chalcedon in 451 the ambiguity was resolved in favor of *persona*. A *persona* was originally a mask worn in theatre to portray a character, but over time it came to mean more what we understand as an individual person, complete with their intrinsic traits and properties. Thus it came to be viewed as an appropriate term to describe the distinctive personalities or modes of being within the Godhead. Its theological meaning is quite specific. Today, the word "person" is possibly less helpful, as it carries strongly individualistic connotations, which tends to overemphasize in the modern mind the three-ness of God over against his unity.[12] As McGrath explains.

> When we talk about God as one person, we mean one person in the modern sense of the word, and when we talk about God as three persons, we mean three persons in the ancient sense of the word . . . Confusing these two senses of the word "person" inevitably leads to the idea that God is actually a committee.[13]

To use trinitarian language then, God is one *ousia* in three *hypostaseis* or *personae*. Each of the individual *hypostaseis*, Father, Son, and Holy Spirit is the *ousia* of God distinguished by the properties and characteristics peculiar to him. The early theologians differed somewhat in their approach to understanding the Trinity. The Greek thinkers in the East tended to stress the distinctiveness of the *hypostaseis*, the persons, and saw their unity as grounded in relationships of "begettal" and "procession." The Western thinkers, writing in Latin, tended to start with the unity of God and explore their relationships. Obviously, an imbalance in either view would misrepresent the truth.

---

12. We must show both respect and caution when dealing with vocabulary. Words uncommonly translate exactly (i.e., with precisely the same semantic range) from one language to another (for example from Greek to Latin in the same era) or from one time to another (consider the English of the KJV or RV compared with that of today). With early theological vocabulary we face the combined effect of both. We must be careful not to misrepresent a doctrine by attacking or redefining its vocabulary.

13. Alister McGrath, cited in Sherlock, *God on the Inside*, 118.

The Athanasian Creed emphasizes the unity of the Godhead whilst acknowledging the three persons who comprise God.[14]

> Neither confounding the Persons (*hypostaseis*) nor dividing the substance (*ousia*) . . . So the Father is God, the Son is God and the Holy Spirit is God and yet they are not three Gods but one God.

The three *hypostaseis* of the Godhead, Father, Son, and Holy Spirit, share the same will, nature and essence (*ousia*) yet each has special attributes, activities and roles and a specific relationship to each of the others. The Cappadocians expressed these relationships as follows:

- The Father generates the Son, the Son is eternally generated from the Father, hence there is an eternal Father–Son relationship (Matt 11:27; John 3:17; 5:17–18; 6:46; 8:42; 17:5, 24).

- The Spirit proceeds from the Father. To this was later added that the Spirit also proceeds from the Son (John 14:16, 26; 15:26).

These distinctions did not come about when Jesus was conceived, they belong to the eternal nature of God. They embrace, but transcend, how we perceive God functionally and how he acts in relation to salvation history. In speaking of the eternal nature of God, theologians refer to the "immanent Trinity," which describes who God is in himself, eternally three *hypostaseis* in one *ousia*. This is God outside the limitations of created time and space. In terms of how God interacts with his creation, specifically in the processes of creation and salvation, theologians speak of the "economic Trinity." The word "economic" in its fundamental meaning has nothing to do with numbers, money or housekeeping, but comes from the Greek word *oikonomia*, meaning the way in which one's affairs are ordered. The economic Trinity is a way of describing how the Father, Son, and Holy Spirit worked in creation and work in salvation history; it is God's "self-disclosure."

The way we experience God, through creation and through his saving work, (the economic Trinity), must not conflict with or be fundamentally different from his essential and eternal nature; the immanent Trinity. It is not the activities of the three within salvation history that ultimately distinguish them, but their relationships, for all these actions of creation and redemption are the work of the unified Godhead, the one God. The God who is known to us through his works corresponds to the way God actually is; his revelation of himself corresponds to his essential nature. To experience God's saving action is to experience God's life.

---

14. The Athanasian Creed was actually not written by Athanasius (AD 297–373). It was probably composed around the mid-fifth century and may be found in full at https://www.ccel.org/creeds/athanasian.creed.html.

God is Love: The Relational Trinity

These ideas of the immanent and economic understandings of God are important in light of the statement that God is love (1 John 4:8, 16). If, prior to creation, God the Father was the sole person in existence; one person, one substance, not the triune God we have been describing—in what sense was God "love"? Love is a relational term. John is not saying "Love is God" or, "love is divine, " his grammar is unambiguous. God is, in his character and essence, *love*. For God to be love presupposes relationship, one (or more) who loves and one (or more) who is loved. Love has no existence apart from the relationship between lover and beloved. Throughout eternity, Father, Son, and Holy Spirit have been in a relationship of love. This relationship was self-sufficient and in no way lacking. God did not *need* to create, out of boredom or loneliness! God does not need anything apart from himself (Acts 17:25). Trinitarian love describes God's inner life, through eternity, apart from any reference to his creation.

- The Father loves the Son and has given all things into his hand (John 3:35).

- For the Father loves the Son and shows him all that he himself is doing (John 5:20).

- "Father, I desire that they also, whom you have given me, may be with me where I am, to see my glory that you have given me because you loved me before the foundation of the world" (John 17:24).

This love which has characterized God through eternity is now directed toward God's creation and supported by the jealousy proper to an exclusive and loving relationship, which is why God's people are sometimes described in terms of a bride or children of God. The proper response to the love of God is to imitate it, in loving relationship with God and with each other. In so doing, we share in the life of God. As you read these passages, take special note of the relationships of love between the Father, Son, and Holy Spirit and believers.

- For God so loved the world, that he gave his only Son, that whoever believes in him should not perish but have eternal life (John 3:16).

- And he said to him, "You shall love the Lord your God with all your heart and with all your soul and with all your mind. This is the great and first commandment. And a second is like it: You shall love your neighbor as yourself" (Matt 22:37–39).

- A new commandment I give to you, that you love one another: just as I have loved you, you also are to love one another. By this all people will know that you are my disciples, if you have love for one another (John 13:34–35).

- I in them and you in me, that they may become perfectly one, so that the world may know that you sent me and loved them even as you loved me (John 17:23).

- And hope does not put us to shame, because God's love has been poured into our hearts through the Holy Spirit who has been given to us (Rom 5:5).

- I appeal you, brothers, by our Lord Jesus Christ and by the love of the Spirit, to strive together with me in your prayers to God on my behalf (Rom 15:30).

- That according to the riches of his glory he may grant you to be strengthened with power through his Spirit in your inner being, so that Christ may dwell in your hearts through faith—that you, being rooted and grounded in love, may have strength to comprehend with all the saints what is the breadth and length and height and depth, and to know the love of Christ that surpasses knowledge, that you may be filled with all the fullness of God (Eph 3:16–19).

- Therefore be imitators of God, as beloved children. And walk in love, as Christ loved us and gave himself up for us, a fragrant offering and sacrifice to God (Eph 5:1–2).

- So if there is any encouragement in Christ, any comfort from love, any participation in the Spirit, any affection and sympathy, complete my joy by being of the same mind, having the same love, being in full accord and of one mind (Phil 2:1–2).

Probably the most complete discussion of the love of God is found in the first letter of John. Notice what he says about God being love, love originates with God, and his love for us must bear fruit in reciprocal love.

> Beloved, let us love one another, for love is from God, and whoever loves has been born of God and knows God. Anyone who does not love does not know God, because God is love. In this the love of God was made manifest among us, that God sent his only Son into the world, so that we might live through him. In this is love, not that we have loved God but that he loved us and sent his Son to be the propitiation for our sins.
>
> Beloved, if God so loved us, we also ought to love one another. No one has ever seen God; if we love one another, God abides in us and his love is perfected in us. By this we know that we abide in him and he in us, because he has given us of his Spirit. And we have seen and testify that the Father has sent his Son to be the Savior of the world.
>
> Whoever confesses that Jesus is the Son of God, God abides in him, and he in God. So we have come to know and to believe the love that God has for us. God is love, and whoever abides in love abides in God, and God abides in him. By this is love perfected with us, so that we may have confidence for the day of judgment, because as he is so also are we in this world.
>
> There is no fear in love, but perfect love casts out fear. For fear has to do with punishment, and whoever fears has not been perfected in love. We love because he first loved us. If anyone says, "I love God," and hates his brother, he is a liar; for he who does not love his brother whom he has seen cannot love God whom he has not seen. And this commandment we have from him: whoever loves God must also love his brother (1 John 4:7–21).

Throughout eternity the divine life has been characterized by the reciprocal love between Father, Son, and Holy Spirit, this love that is now poured out into our hearts by the Spirit. Love unites the Godhead, and love unites the community of believers to God, because God first loved us. To deny the eternal trinitarian relationship, therefore, is to make God *dependent upon his creation* for the expression of the fundamental attribute of his character; love. Stanley Grenz expresses these concepts well:

> Viewed theologically, therefore, John's statement, "God is love," refers first of all to the intra-trinitarian relationship within the eternal God. God is love within himself: The Father loves the Son; the Son reciprocates that love; and the love between the Father and the Son is the Holy Spirit. In short, through all eternity God is the social Trinity, the community of love.
>
> In that God is love apart from the creation of the world, love characterizes God. Love is the eternal essence of the one God. But this means that trinitarian love is not merely one attribute of God among many. Rather, love is the fundamental "attribute" of God. "God is love" is the foundational ontological statement we can declare concerning the divine essence. God is foundationally the mutuality of the love relationship between Father and Son, and this personal love is the Holy Spirit.
>
> Because throughout eternity and apart from the world the one God is love, the God who is love cannot but respond to the world in accordance to his own eternal essence, which is love. Thus, this essential characteristic of God likewise describes the way God interacts with his world. "Love," therefore, is not only the description of the eternal God in himself, it is likewise the fundamental characteristic of God in relationship with creation. With profound theological insight, therefore, John bursts forth, "For God so loved the world that he gave . . ." (John 3:16).[15]

Perichoresis and Appropriation: Dynamic Relationships within the Godhead

When we try to use simple diagrams or analogies to help us visualize the concept of three persons in one essence, we are limited because such representations are finite and static. Any pictorial or conceptual representation of God must, by nature, fall far short of the marvelous and complex reality that is God. An idea hinted at in the early centuries of Christian thought, which came into general use in the sixth century, is a more dynamic model. This model is described by the Greek term *perichōrēsis*,[16] which can be translated as "mutual indwelling" or "interpenetration" and describes the way the three persons relate to each other. The concept is that Father, Son, and Spirit are distinct, yet each shares intimately in the life of the others (John 17:21–23). In other words, the Trinity is a community of being, or as we discussed above, a community of mutual love. This community is not a collection of individual members of a class of beings called "deity," but the three persons in their mutual relationship as the one and only God.

15. Grenz, *Theology*, 72.

16. from *peri-*, a preposition meaning (depending on case) around, approximately or concerning and *choreuō*, dance. The idea is of a chorus of dancers dancing around each other in harmony.

Baptism into this threefold name (Matt 28:19) is the outward sign of adoption into the family of God, "that they may be one, even as we are one" (John 17:11).

Perichōrēsis, although not itself a biblical word, can be thought of as a useful descriptive term which embraces these scriptural concepts which we have already explored:

- The Father and the Son share goals and values (Heb 10:7; Matt 26:39; Phil 2:9–11).

- The Father and the Son are "in one another" (John 14:20; John 1:18).

- The Son has shared the Father's glory from the foundation of the world (John 16:28; 17:5).

- The incarnate Son was conceived through the Spirit (Matt 1:18, 20; Luke 1:35) and the Spirit descended on him at his baptism (Matt 3:16) and anointed him for his ministry (Luke 4:18–19).

- Jesus did his mighty works by the power of the Spirit (Matt 12:18–28).

- The Spirit glorifies Jesus (John 16:13–14).

- The Spirit indwells believers, but also the Son is in us (Rom 8:9–11; John 14:17; Gal 2:20; Col 1:27).

Recently, theologians such as Jurgen Moltmann and Stanley Grenz have drawn on the ancient doctrine of perichoresis to develop a "social" picture of the Trinity. The Greek fathers taught that Father, Son, and Spirit were ontologically identical, that is, one in substance (*ousia*) or essence, each fully and mutually filled by one another. However, the modern revival of perichoresis may be in danger of representing the Godhead as three diverse beings coming together as a family.[17] Again we see the tension between three-ness and one-ness that the early church fathers strove to describe in a balanced way. It gets tricky when God's *essence* (*ousia*) is *defined* as an inter-relationship of three persons, in other words, that this relationship *constitutes* Deity. As Holmes observes, "for Moltmann's Trinity, despite all the rhetoric of unity, it is difficult not to conclude that everything metaphysically important does not remain three and separate."[18] In this respect, Bauckham's thesis has merit, that speaking of Father, Son, and Spirit in terms of sharing the unique identity of the one God may be more helpful than the traditional vocabulary of "person" and "substance." He argues that it was Jewish, not Hellenistic philosophical categories that allowed attribution of divinity to Jesus from the earliest time. Simple Platonist definitions of divine "substance" and "nature" may have represented Jesus incorrectly as a semi-divine being,

---

17. For a brief critique of Moltmann's perichoresis and further reading on the subject, see Holmes, *Quest for the Trinity*, 16–24.

18. Holmes, *Quest for the Trinity*, 22.

whereas Nicene theology was able to resist this and reappropriate this vocabulary into the context of the New Testament's inclusion of Jesus into the unique divine identity.[19]

A related doctrine to perichoresis is that of "appropriation:" the works of the Trinity are a unity, with each of the three involved in every outward action of the Godhead. God is not defined by his creation; he is Father, Son, and Spirit in relationship whether the created order exists or not, but he *chooses* to draw us into his life. Although the Father is distinctively the originator of creation and redemption, he did not act independently of the Son and Spirit (Gen 1:1–2; John 1:3, 10; Col 1:16; Heb 1:2). It was the distinctive work of the Son to become incarnate, bear our sins and secure redemption for fallen humankind, but all three were again involved (John 3:16; Acts 2:23; Heb 9:14; Gen 22:8). Sanctification may be seen as the distinctive work of the Spirit, yet not in isolation (John 17:17–19; Rom 15:16; 1 Cor 6:11; 1 Thess 5:23; 2 Thess 2:13; 1 Pet 1:2). As we shall see in the final chapter, because Father, Son, and Spirit work together in salvation, it is wholly a unified work of God from first to last and this gives the Christian absolute assurance.

> Taken together, the doctrines of *perichoresis* and appropriation allow us to think of the Godhead as a "community of being," in which all is shared, united and mutually exchanged. . . Father, Son and Spirit are not three isolated and diverging compartments of a Godhead, like three subsidiary components of an international corporation. Rather, they are differentiations within the Godhead, which become evident within the economy of salvation and the human experience of redemption and grace. The doctrine of the Trinity affirms that, beneath the surface of the complexities of the history of salvation and our experience of God lies one God, and one God only.[20]

Since God exists as persons in relationship, so we too, being made in the image of God are invited into communion—community—with him and with each other. The children of God are distinctive yet united; being Jew, Greek, male, female, slave or free no longer defines us for we are "all one in Christ Jesus" (Gal 3:28).

Summary

- The Trinity is the concept of God that reconciles the essentials of his being.

  - There is one God, who is the only divine being and separate from the universe which he created.

  - The Father, Son, and Holy Spirit are each personal and divine and can be rightly called "God."

  - God is one in a different sense to that in which he is three.

---

19. Bauckham, *Jesus and the God of Israel*, 7, 58.

20. McGrath, *Christian Theology*, 252–253.

- Some inadequate models of the Godhead include:

  - *Modalism*, which seeks to uphold the unity of God, but denies the distinctiveness of the persons.

  - *Arianism*, which also sought to uphold the unity of God, but relegated the Son and Spirit to lesser, created beings with derived divinity.

  - *Tritheism*, an uncommonly expressed model in which the three persons are distinct Gods, which denies the unity of the Godhead.

- The three persons are not each one-third of God, nor are they accessories or additional attributes of the essential being of God.

- Theologians speak of God being one in essence or substance (*ousia*) but this divine nature is expressed in three distinct persons (*hypostasis, persona*).

- The distinctions between the persons belong to the essential and eternal nature of God (the immanent Trinity) which is consistent with but not limited to how God has revealed himself in salvation history (the economic Trinity).

- God is love; he has existed eternally in loving relationship as Father, Son, and Holy Spirit. This love has been poured out on created, redeemed humanity, who now share in the love of God and respond by loving God and others.

- The three persons can be perceived as relating to each other through mutual indwelling (*perichōrēsis*) as one divine unity, in dynamic interrelationship. Their distinctiveness is apparent in the roles they play in salvation history, yet even in this they work together (appropriation).

Further Reading

- Millard Erickson, *Christian Theology*, chapter 14, "God's Three-in-Oneness: The Trinity."

- Wayne Grudem, *Systematic Theology*, chapter 14, "God in Three Persons: The Trinity."

- Stanley J. Grenz, *Theology for the Community of God*, chapter 2, "The Triune God."

- Charles Sherlock, *God on the Inside: Trinitarian Spirituality*. Not merely an academic or intellectual dissertation on the triune God, but a practical and thought-provoking study of the application of the doctrine to knowing and living in and for the God we worship.

9

A History of Trinitarian Thought

Misconception #16: That the Trinity is a fourth-century fabrication of an apostate church.

Corrective: Although the full doctrine of the Trinity was not articulated comprehensively until the fifth century, the theology which underlies it can be clearly demonstrated from the earliest writings of the church, independently of the path taken by the Roman church toward papal apostasy.

THIS IS AN IMPORTANT chapter, not because we rely on theologians' ideas above scriptural truth, or set the authority of "The church" above the Word of God—quite the contrary. I am not going to use extrabiblical theological writings to attempt to "prove" that God is triune. I don't have to—the Bible provides evidence enough, as has been demonstrated. The chapter is important because the doctrine of the Trinity has also been attacked from a *historical* standpoint. Christadelphians and other non-trinitarians assert that the Trinity is not scriptural, but a later fabrication of the apostate church as it moved further and further away from pure apostolic doctrine. In particular, Christadelphians often disparage the creeds of the church, with a vigor that belies a fundamental misunderstanding of what the creeds really mean, and the purposes for which they were written. "The Trinity," asserts one representative, contemporary Christadelphian writer, "is the key, hallmark doctrine of the Apostasy."[1] And from an earlier era:

> "These Synods or Councils, of which no vestige appears before the middle of this [second] century, changed nearly the whole form of the church . . . gradually they made higher pretensions, maintaining that power was given them by Christ himself, to decide upon rules of faith and conduct for the members of his church . . ." Decide upon rules of faith and conduct! In the face of such claims and such testimony to the departure from the early faith, what credence can be placed in their doctrines?[2]

1. B. N. Luke, intro to White, *The Trinity*, vi.

2. White, *The Trinity*, citing a work by a "Dr Mosheim." White quotes extensively and selectively from secondary sources without providing context or author credentials. White's attack is against the Roman Church, yet he seems not to realize that the trinitarian and christological controversies were largely associated with Greek theologians. White even cites Tertullian to support his thesis, even

This thinking is not original; it has its roots in the anti-trinitarianism of Michael Servetus and Faustus Socinus in the later Reformation era and which was developed by the Enlightenment-inspired Unitarianism of the eighteenth century. Exalting human reason above biblical revelation as the ultimate authority, the Rationalists rejected trinitarianism as incoherent and the miraculous as irrational.[3]

Unfortunately, Christadelphian writings often lack critical scholarship, drawing on secondary sources and quoting "experts" with little or no comment on context or their credentials. Because the movement has generally eschewed formal theological education, their understanding of Christian history often comes across as piecemeal, selective and inaccurate. Sometimes anti-trinitarian writers are quoted without acknowledgement that they are overtly Unitarian, and that there is not so much common ground with Christadelphians as might be supposed. Doctrines, creeds, heresies, and the theological positions of the main protagonists appear to be misunderstood and are consequently misrepresented.

Some Christadelphian authors and speakers appeal to passages in the latter New Testament Scriptures which speak of "grievous wolves entering the flock," the antichrist, and imminent heresies and apply them specifically to the third- and fourth-century christological controversies, when in fact the scriptural and historical context is more properly directed against the second-century heresies of Docetism and Gnosticism and the pressure of imperial religion. Christadelphian writings often appeal to the relatively late expression of the complete doctrine of the Trinity, and the disputes between say, orthodoxy and Arianism, as if there was general resistance to the concept of the deity of Christ amongst mainstream Christians that was overridden by Constantine or by the papacy. It will shortly be demonstrated that the deity of Christ was believed from New Testament times and that the foundational principles of trinitarian doctrine (God is one, the Father, Son, and Holy Spirit are divine) were believed and taught by the early church.

Two broad schools of theological thought and writing are recognized in the early centuries; that of the Latin-speaking West and the Greek-speaking East.[4] In the West we have writers such as Tertullian and Irenaeus, in the East Origen, Cyril, and Clement of Alexandria and the Cappadocians. Generally, the Greek theologians were intellectual explorers, drilling down into doctrines in detail, rarely content with a superficial gloss and often speculative in taking the consequences of a belief as far as possible down a given pathway. It was the Greek wing of the church that was most obsessed with defining the nature of the Godhead and reconciling the divine and human in

---

though Tertullian coined the term *Trinitas*. White's work is peppered with historical factual errors.

3. For a discussion of the development of biblical and rationalist anti-trinitarianism and its common elements, see Holmes, *Quest for the Trinity*, 170–81. Several chapters tracing the concurrence of Christadelphian thought with the Unitarian movement may be found in Gaston, *One God the Father*.

4. Nevertheless, the Eastern and Western theologians can be shown to agree in the fundamentals of trinitarian theology, as has been demonstrated by Holmes, *Quest for the Trinity*, 144–46.

Christ and it was the Greeks who generated the early creedal formulations. The Western church, on the other hand, was cautious and traditional and much more likely to accept a doctrine on its (scriptural) face value and be content with saying, "that's the way it is," without further intellectual thrashing about. In fact, the relatively cool-headed influence of Leo bishop of Rome helped reconcile the escalating theological tensions between the Greeks during the fifth-century christological controversies. It was, however, the Western wing of the church which later became politically obsessed with apostolic succession, the primacy of the bishop of Rome and the authority of the popes. Christadelphians have a tendency to blur these distinctions and relegate all trinitarian discussions to the apostasy of papal Rome, often lumping Constantine's motives together with that of the Roman bishop's ascendancy.

The Second- and Third-Century Churches

The deity of Christ and, to a lesser extent, the Spirit, figures clearly in the earliest extant writings of the church following the close of the New Testament period. The developed doctrine of the fourth and fifth centuries was not something entirely novel.

> Certainly the technical terminology and conceptuality necessary to give a tight account of how it is possible to speak of one God existing in three hypostases is only developed in the fourth century, but we should see this not so much as the development of a new confession, as the discovery of the necessary theology to give firm intellectual grounding to an idea that is so deeply engraved in Christian devotion and confession as to be inescapable. The early Christians worshiped the Trinity from the first; the tale of the development of Trinitarian theology is an account of how they came to find a satisfying way of speaking of the One they worshiped.[5]

The Apostolic Fathers

These writings are the earliest surviving writings from the post-apostolic period, AD 70 to 135, within the lifetimes of many of the original twelve apostles. They are a very diverse collection of works, written for a range of purposes and they generally just witness to the traditional apostolic faith rather than seeking to interpret it. Two doctrines were clearly taken for granted; the preexistence of the Son and his role in creation as well as in redemption. There is no sense of ditheism or tritheism, but neither do they wrestle with monotheism, as if their beliefs about Christ contradicted it. They do use triadic formulae with some regularity along the pattern of Matthew 28:19 and elsewhere in the New Testament and they do assume the deity of Christ.

---

5. Holmes, *Quest for the Trinity*, 57–58.

The Letters of Clement of Rome

The letter from the church of Rome to the church of Corinth is, strictly speaking, anonymous, but well-attested tradition identifies it as the work of a presbyter of Rome, Clement. It was almost certainly written about AD 95 to 97, in the last year of Domitian or the first year of Nerva's imperial reign. The persecution under Domitian is doubtless what Clement refers to in his opening as "the sudden and repeated misfortunes which have happened to us" (1:1).

> For as God lives, and as the Lord Jesus Christ lives, and the Holy Spirit, who are the faith and the hope of the elect, so surely will the one who with humility and constant gentleness . . . be enrolled and included among the number of those who are saved through Jesus Christ . . . (*1 Clem.* 58.2).

The much shorter 2 Clement is not a letter but a sermon by an anonymous presbyter, probably written around AD 100.

> If Christ, the Lord who saved us, became flesh, even though he was originally spirit, and in that state called us, so also we will receive our reward in this flesh (*2 Clem.* 9:5).

The Letters of Ignatius, Bishop of Antioch

Ignatius was martyred during the reign of Trajan (AD 98 to 117) and wrote seven known letters to the churches of Smyrna, Ephesus, Magnesia, Philadelphia, Trallia, and Rome and to his friend Polycarp, whilst en route to Rome to be executed. Ignatius was preoccupied by three major concerns in these letters; the struggle against false teachers within the church, the unity and structure of the churches and, understandably, his own impending death. The false teachers fell into two camps, consistent with what we know of heresies in the church at this time; the Judaizers whose teaching diminished the divinity of Christ and the Docetists, who denied the reality of Jesus' humanity. Ignatius opposes the false teachers by emphasizing *both* the divinity and authentic humanity of Christ, and by stressing the importance of the office of the overseer-bishop (*episkopos*) as an answer to schism within the church.[6] Here are a few extracts.

- Ignatius, who is also called Theophorus, to the church at Ephesus in Asia, blessed with greatness through the fullness of God the Father, predestined before the ages for lasting and unchangeable glory forever, united and elect through genuine suffering by the will of the Father and of Jesus Christ our God . . . (Ign. *Eph.*, introduction).

- Being as you are imitators of God, once you took on new life through the blood

6. Holmes, *The Apostolic Fathers*, 129–31.

of God you completed perfectly the task so natural to you (Ign. *Eph.* 1:1).

- There is only one physician, who is both flesh and spirit, born and unborn, God in man, true life in death, both from Mary and from God, first subject to suffering and then beyond it, Jesus Christ our Lord (Ign. *Eph.* 7:2).

- For our God, Jesus the Christ, was conceived by Mary according to God's plan, both from the seed of David and of the Holy Spirit (Ign. *Eph.* 18:2).

- Consequently all magic and every kind of spell were dissolved, the ignorance so characteristic of wickedness vanished, and the ancient kingdom was abolished, when God appeared in human form to bring the newness of eternal life, and what had been prepared by God began to take effect (Ign. *Eph.* 19:3).

- . . . having been entrusted with the service of Jesus Christ, who before the ages was with the Father and appeared at the end of time (Ign. *Magn.* 6:1).

- Therefore as the Lord did nothing without the Father, either by himself or through the apostles, for he was united with him . . . Let all of you run together as to one temple of God, as to one altar. To one Jesus Christ, who came forth from one Father and remained with the One and returned to the One (Ign. *Magn.* 7:1, 2).

- . . . in faith and love, in the Son and the Father and in the Spirit . . . Be subject to the bishop and to one another, as Jesus Christ in the flesh was to the Father . . . (Ign. *Magn.* 13:1, 2).

- . . . in accordance with faith in and love for Jesus Christ our God . . . heartiest greetings blamelessly in Jesus Christ our God (Ign. *Rom.* intro).

- For our God Jesus Christ is more visible now that he is in the Father (Ign. *Rom.* 3:3).

- Allow me to be an imitator of the suffering of my God (Ign. *Rom.* 6:3).

- I glorify Jesus Christ, the God who made you so wise . . . (Ign. *Smyrn.* 1:1).

The Martyrdom of Polycarp

Polycarp, the aged bishop of Smyrna, was burnt to death around AD 160 for failing to recant his Christianity and worship the emperor. This letter gives an eyewitness account of his martyrdom. Polycarp had been a disciple of the Apostle John. These final words of prayer are attributed to him just before his pyre was lit.

> I praise you, I bless you, I glorify you, through the eternal and heavenly High Priest, Jesus Christ, your beloved Son, through whom to you with him and the Holy Spirit be glory both now and for ages to come (*Mart. Pol.* 14:3).

The Epistle of Barnabas

This is an anonymous essay written sometime between the destruction of the Jerusalem temple in AD 70 and the rebuilding of the city by the emperor Hadrian after the AD 132 to 135 revolt. The essay explores the relationship between Christians and the Old Covenant, which was very much a hot topic at this time when Christianity was facing antagonism from the Jews. Barnabas is very clear about the preexistence of Christ.

> And furthermore, my brothers: if the Lord submitted to suffer for our souls, even though he is Lord of the whole world, to whom God said at the foundation of the world, "Let us make man according to our image and likeness," how is it, then, that he submitted to suffer at the hand of men? Learn! (*Barn.* 5:5).

The Epistle to Diognetus

Diognetus is an apologetic tract which addresses specific enquiries regarding the Christian faith. It is an anonymous work of unknown date, but probably late second to early third century.

> On the contrary, the omnipotent Creator of all, the invisible God himself, established among men the truth and the holy, incomprehensible word from heaven and fixed it firmly in their hearts, not, as one might imagine, by sending to men some subordinate, or angel or ruler or one of those who manage earthly matters, or one of those entrusted with the administration of things in heaven, but the Designer and Creator of the universe himself, by whom he created the heavens, by whom he enclosed the sea within its proper bounds, whose mysteries all the elements faithfully observe . . . by whom all things have been ordered and determined and placed in subjection . . . this one he sent to them!
> . . . He sent him in gentleness and meekness, as a king might send his son who is a king, he sent him as God; he sent him as a man to men . . . (*Diogn.* 7:2–4).

> So then, having already planned everything in his mind together with his Child, he permitted us during the former time to be carried away by undisciplined impulses as we desired . . . (*Diogn.* 9:1).

> This is why he sent the Word, namely, that he might appear to the world; though dishonored by the chosen people, he was preached by apostles and believed in by Gentiles. This is he who was from the beginning, who appeared as new yet proved to be old . . . This is the Eternal One, who today is accounted a Son . . . (*Diogn.* 11:3–5)

The conclusion to be drawn from these citations, some of which are integral to the writers' arguments and some of which are "passing comments" in the texts, is that the deity and preexistence of Christ was something with which the second-century church was very comfortable. It was assumed, it was taken for granted, it was accepted as scriptural. It might be argued that these are isolated extracts—were there not complete theological dissertations or statements of the faith available from this time to back up the assertion that second-century Christians believed that Christ is God? If there were, there are none extant, and for a very good reason.

This era immediately followed the apostolic era and many of the writers and teachers, such as Polycarp, had been direct disciples of the original twelve, or at least had heard them preach. The earliest writings may even have been written at the same time as the later New Testament writings. There was little disagreement as to what the central truths of Christianity were, except with respect to countering the major heresies of the day: Judaizing, Docetism, and Gnosticism, plus the pressure to conform to the imperial religion. It was also a time when the church, still not recognized as a legitimate religion, experienced episodes of persecution—so they were understandably preoccupied.

Thus, in the second and third centuries, persecuted Christians were largely occupied with polemics and apologetics, defending the faith against Greco-Roman pagan religions and the incorrect accusations levelled at Christians and their beliefs. The deity of Christ was accepted, but not really grappled with. It was simply a given. The big confessional issue was the proclamation that "Jesus is Lord." The Christian who proclaimed the lordship of Jesus not only affirmed that he was YHWH, but that Caesar was *not* Lord. One thing is clear when reading the Apostolic Fathers, however, and that is how steeped most of their writings were in scriptural quotations and paraphrases.

J. N. D. Kelly, the recognized authority on early Christian doctrines, gives the following summary of the patristic period:

> Being still at the formative stage, the theology of the early centuries exhibits the extremes of immaturity and sophistication. There is an extraordinary contrast, for example, between the versions of the Church's teaching given by the second-century Apostolic Fathers and by an accomplished fifth-century theologian like Cyril of Alexandria. Further, conditions were favorable to the coexistence of a wide variety of opinions even on issues of prime importance . . . The explanation is not that the early Church was indifferent to the distinction between orthodoxy and heresy. Rather it is that, while from the beginning the broad outline of revealed truth was respected as a sacrosanct inheritance from the apostles, its theological explication was to a large extent left unfettered. Only gradually, and even then in regard to comparatively few doctrines which became subjects of debate, did the tendency to insist upon precise definition and rigid uniformity assert itself.[7]

In other words, the wrestling with doctrine arose, not from a departure from Scripture, but from a deeper engagement with it.

---

7. Kelly, *Early Christian Doctrines*, 3–4.

The Apostolic Fathers were definitively monotheistic, in contrast to the polytheistic pagan world around them. Their tradition of God as Almighty Creator was firmly rooted in the Old and New Testament scriptures. But as with the New Testament, their writings were peppered with an acceptance that somehow the Son of God, the Lord Jesus Christ, shared in the divinity of the one God.

The second through fourth centuries were the heyday of Gnosticism, a heterogeneous collection of beliefs which influenced not only Christianity but Judaism and pagan religions as well. A common foundation of the various versions of Gnosticism was the Greek dualism of "matter is evil, spirit is good," which led to the conclusion that the supreme Deity could not have sullied his hands by creating matter. Creation in Gnostic mythology was assigned to a lesser, corrupt, demiurge (demigod) which in the Judeo-Christian versions of Gnosticism was equated with YHWH, the volatile god of the Old Testament. Second- and third-century polemicists such as Irenaeus vehemently opposed this and asserted that the supreme God, the Father of the Lord Jesus, was also the Creator. The same Greek spirit–matter dualism was responsible for the heresy of Docetism, which rejected the idea that the Savior could have been truly human. We see in the writings of the church at this time clear arguments for the true humanity of Christ, in opposition to this.

The doctrine of one God, the Father and Creator was the undisputed premise of the early Christian faith and was defended against polytheism, Gnosticism and other dualistic philosophies. The theological problem which began to emerge was how to integrate this with the clear teachings of the New Testament concerning the divinity and preexistence of Christ, in whom God had made himself fully known, and the pouring out of the Holy Spirit upon the church. Although it would be late in the fourth century before a satisfactory "model" was found to reconcile and integrate these concepts, tentative theories were advanced in the first couple of Christian centuries.

Triadic formulae and confessions, particularly in connection with baptism, occur regularly. The *Didache*, a late first-century/early second-century manual for Christian life and church practice, also commands baptism "in the name of the Father and of the Son and of the Holy Spirit."[8]

The Second-Century Apologists and Polemicists

A major preoccupation of second-century writers from within the persecuted church was to defend the faith against criticism. Christians were accused of being "atheists," because they denied the Greco-Roman pantheon, of being at best antisocial and at worst treasonous for avoiding "normal" social interactions and religious rituals associated with pagan worship. They were also accused of a collection of absurd practices such as eating children and ritual sexual immorality. The Apologists were those

---

8. *The Didache*, 7.1–7.3, reproduced in Holmes, *The Apostolic Fathers*, 259.

writers such as Justin Martyr (AD 100 to 165) and his contemporary Theophilus of Antioch (died c. 180), whose works primarily explained and defended Christian belief and practice to outsiders.

The Apologists were ardently monotheistic, as opposed to the polytheistic religions of their world. As a result, theirs were the first extant writings to try to reconcile monotheism with the divine attributes of Christ. They tended to do this by presenting the preexistent Christ as the Father's thought or mind, manifested in creation and revelation. The obvious model on which to rely was the imagery of the divine *Logos* or Word of late Judaism (e.g., the writings of Philo) and of Stoicism. This idea was common in the first- and second-century Greco-Roman thought world and the Apostle John had already, under inspiration, appropriated and redefined this idea in his gospel to present the incarnation of the preexistent Son. Justin taught that the preexistent *Logos* was distinct from the Father and was his agent in creating the universe and revealing truth to humankind. The *Logos* is God's offspring, not a created being, and is not separated from the Father any more than the spoken word is separate from the thought that engendered it, or the sun's light is separate from the sun.[9]

Athenagoras of Athens (c. AD 133 to 190) identified the Word of God, by whom the universe was created and is governed, as the Son of God. He explains that the Son of God is not like the mythological sons of the Greek gods, but "the Father's Word in idea and in actualization." "The Son being in the Father and the Father in the Son by the unity and power of divine spirit, the Son of God is the Father's intelligence and Word." Whilst the Son is derived from the Father, he was not created.[10]

Although the Apologists employed triadic formulae, they were much more vague and inconsistent about the status and role of the Spirit compared with that of the Son. Their emphasis with respect to the Spirit's work was on the inspiration of Scripture. Justin wrote of veneration of the Father, Son and the "prophetic spirit," Athenagoras described the Spirit as "an effluence of God" similar to a sunbeam from the sun, and described Christians as "men who acknowledge God the Father, God the Son and the Holy Spirit, and declare both their power in union and their distinction in order." Theophilus identified the Spirit with Wisdom and spoke of a "triad" in the Godhead: God, his Word, and his Wisdom.[11]

The Polemicists were second- and third-century writers whose primary focus was internal; the refutation of heresies rather than the defense of the faith to outsiders. The best known polemicist was Irenaeus of Lyons (c. AD 130 to 202) the vigorous defender of the faith against Gnosticism. He rejected the Gnostic distancing of God from his creation and the necessity of semi-divine intermediaries, placing the Son and Spirit on the divine side of the line. He gave a summary of instruction for catechumens (candidates for baptism) which included belief in:

9. Kelly, *Early Christian Doctrines*, 95–98.

10. Athenagoras, "Supplication," cited in Kelly, *Early Christian Doctrines*, 99–100.

11. Kelly, *Early Christian Doctrines*, 101–3.

- God the Father, not made, not material, invisible, one God the creator of all things

- The Word of God, Son of God, Christ Jesus our Lord . . . through whom all things were made, who also at the end of the age, to complete and gather up all things, was made man among men, visible and tangible . . .

- The Holy Spirit, through whom the prophets prophesied, and the fathers learned the things of God, and the righteous were led into the way of righteousness, who at the end of the age was poured out in a new way . . . [12]

Irenaeus wrote of God from two perspectives, his intrinsic being and how he manifests himself in the "economy" of his self-disclosure. Intrinsically, God is the Father of all things, he is one God, yet contains in himself from eternity his Word and his Wisdom. In his self-revelation he manifests as the Son and the Spirit, who are his "hands." Hence in his essence and nature and being God is one, but "according to the economy of our redemption," three. This is actually very close to the orthodox concept of the Trinity, three persons in one essence. Irenaeus gave much fuller and more consistent treatment of the Spirit than did the Apologists.

> Without the Spirit it is impossible to behold the Word of God . . . since the knowledge of the Father is the Son, and the knowledge of the Son of God can only be obtained through the Spirit, and according to the Father's good pleasure the Son ministers and dispenses the Spirit to whomsoever the Father wills, and as he wills . . .
>
> The Father is God, and the Son is God, for whatever is begotten of God is God. The Spirit of the Father . . . purifies a man and raises him to the life of God. [13]

Irenaeus had the most fully developed proto-trinitarian concept of God for the age, although he stopped short of the full personhood of the three because of his monotheistic focus in defense against Gnosticism. Because he was concerned with denying Gnostic concepts of mediators he identified the Son/Word and Spirit/Wisdom as identical with God. Nevertheless he made real distinctions between the Father, Son, and Spirit, all of whom he regarded as divine and preexistent, and part of God's intrinsic being from eternity, yet only fully manifested in the "economy" of salvation. [14]

It has been alleged that the corpus of extant second-century Christian writings is theologically skewed, in that "the works that have been preserved are preserved because they resemble later orthodoxy closely enough to pass muster. The works of non-trinitarians were not preserved and we are reliant on brief references as witness to their existence." [15] This may or may not be the case, and it constitutes an argument from

---

12. Irenaeus, "Demonstration," 6, cited in Kelly, *Early Christian Doctrines*, 89.

13. Cited in Kelly, *Early Christian Doctrines*, 107.

14. Kelly, *Early Christian Doctrines*, 104–8; Holmes, *Quest for the Trinity*, 62–67.

15. Gaston, "After the Apostles," 133. Nevertheless, there are plenty of Gnostic and other apocryphal works extant to make this a moot point.

silence. Conversely, the rising influence of Gnosticism within the Christian community and the persecution of Christians may also have produced a tendency to selectively destroy documents which exalted Jesus as Lord—who can tell? Regardless of who was burning what, these proto-trinitarian works did not, and will not, simply go away.

The Third Century

Prior to the third century, the pressing needs to defend the faith against polytheism and to refute the errors of Gnosticism had kept the emphasis in Christian writings on the unity of God. As we have seen, the second-century writers believed in the divinity and preexistence of the Son and Holy Spirit and were aware of the distinctions within the Godhead, but these had been poorly enunciated. So we arrive at the third century with a concept of a triad within the Godhead, inseparably one in being and yet revealed in the economy of creation and redemption.

In the Western church, some were uncomfortable with emphasis on the triadic aspect, fearing that it clashed with monotheism. The reaction gave rise to the various forms of modalism or monarchialism. A monarch is a single ruler, and so they envisaged a single God, the Father, who manifested in certain circumstances as Son or as Holy Spirit. On the other hand, in the East, theologians were attempting to do justice to the distinctions between the three within the Godhead, without sacrificing monotheism and this would give rise to the concept of three persons with one essence.

Hippolytus of Rome (170 to 235) and Tertullian of Carthage (160 to 225) were two Western theologians writing in the early third century. They were both monotheists (although the monarchialists labelled them polytheists) and were adamantly anti-Gnostic. They both saw a plurality in the Godhead from eternity; the former viewing the Spirit as God's Wisdom, the latter equating Wisdom with the Word. Hippolytus said, "Though alone, he [God] was multiple, for he was not without his Word and his Wisdom, his power and his counsel."[16] Tertullian expressed it this way:

> Before all things God was alone, being his own universe, location, everything. He was alone, however, in the sense that there was nothing external to himself. But even then he was not really alone, for he had with him that Reason which he possessed within himself . . .[17]

Tertullian described the Son and Spirit as persons (*personae*) from the Roman legal concept of a party to a legal action, in this case, the covenant God entered with his people. The Son is a person "second in addition to the Father" with the Spirit the deputy or representative of the Son, issuing from the Father by way of the Son, "third from the Father and the Son, just as the fruit derived from the shoot is third from the root, and as the channel drawn off from the river is third from the spring, and as the

---

16. Ibid., 111.

17. Tertullian, "Against Praxeas," cited in Kelly, *Early Christian Doctrines*, 111.

light point in the beam is third from the sun." Tertullian employed for the first time the word *trinitas,*—Trinity, to describe the Godhead.

> We believe in one only God, yet subject to this dispensation [Latin *dispensatio*], which is our word for economy [Greek *oikonomia*], that the one only God has also a Son, his Word, who has issued out of himself . . . which Son then sent, according to his promise, the Holy Spirit, the Paraclete, out of the Father . . . the mystery of the economy, which distributes the unity into trinity, setting forth Father, Son and Spirit as three.

Tertullian was at pains to argue that the three persons were manifestations of a single indivisible power, like a government with several agencies, and that the distinction between the three was a distribution, not a separation and that the three are one in substance/divine nature/essence (*substantia*).[18] Tertullian invented the vocabulary which would later be used in the orthodox doctrine of the Trinity, true, but he had not invented a new doctrine. He stated clearly what must be confessed to do justice to the early church's understanding of Scripture and its devotional practice.

Meanwhile in the East, some serious thinking was also occurring within the Alexandrian catechetical school, and the prime thinkers were Clement (c. 150 to 215) and Origen (c. 185 to 254). Clement's view of the Godhead can be summarized as follows:

- God is transcendent and incomprehensible, embracing all reality, and God is unity.

- The Father can be known only through the Son, his Word, who is his mind or rationality, his image, inseparable from him.

- The Son is one with the Father and eternally generated.

- The Spirit is the light issuing from the Word, the power of the Word, and attracts men to God.

> One is the Father of the universe and one also the Word of the universe; the Holy Spirit, again, is one and everywhere the same.[19]

Origen diverged from the ideas we have discussed so far in some key respects, and it is important to recognize that Origen's teachings are not accepted as the orthodox understanding of the Trinity. Origen was heavily influenced by Platonist thought. Nevertheless, in some respects his ideas are insightful and show a further development of thought which came to have an important influence on later trinitarian discussions.

Origen regarded the Father as God alone in the strict sense (*autotheos*) and as alone ingenerate. The Father brought into existence a world of souls or spiritual beings, eternal with himself (and here we see the basis of his idea of immortal preexistent

18. Ibid., 112–14. Also discussed in Holmes, *Quest for the Trinity*, 71.

19. Clement of Alexandria, various writings, cited and summarized in Kelly, *Early Christian Doctrines*, 127.

souls of humans). To mediate between his absolute unity and their multiplicity, he generated his Son to be the revelation of himself. The Father begets the Son by an eternal act, so that there was never a time when the Son did not exist; the Son is therefore God, even though his divinity is derived from the Father. (The starting point for Arianism can be seen here in the idea of a derived divinity or *deuteros theos*, second God, although Arius differed in teaching that there was a time when the Son "was not," contra Origen.) Third, there is the Holy Spirit "the most honorable of all the beings brought into existence through the Word, the chief in rank of all the beings originated by the Father through Christ." Origin asserted that the Father, Son, and Holy Spirit are three persons (*hypostaseis*), distinct from all eternity and not just manifested in the "economy" as they were for Hippolytus and Tertullian.

Origen's concept of union between the Father and Son is one of love, will and action, and although he speaks of the Son and Spirit as derived from the Father, "the fountainhead of deity" his emphasis is on the distinctiveness of the three.

> But the Son and the Spirit are also in their degrees divine, possessing, although derivatively, all the characteristics of deity; distinct from the world of creatures, they cooperate with the Father and mediate the divine life flowing from him.[20]

Origen also had a subordinationist view of the divine Triad. The Father alone is *autotheos*; the Son is a secondary god, his goodness and truth a reflection of the Father's and in activity he is the Father's agent. This hierarchical approach was a direct product of his Platonistic influence. As a result, Origen's teachings heavily influenced later subordinationists and his emphasis on the distinctiveness of the three persons was also used in refutation of monarchianism. Even though Origen seemed to struggle to find the right vocabulary to express the relationships between them, he was committed to the unity of the Godhead and to the distinction between Father, Son, and Holy Spirit.

So it is evident that in the third century, the concepts of the Godhead were diverging, partly as a result of different thought processes and exacerbated by language disparities between East and West. The West was already tending to emphasize unity above diversity, monotheism above distinctions between the persons, whereas the East was tending to accentuate the distinctiveness of the persons at the expense of a clear articulation of the unity of the Godhead. This inevitably led to misunderstandings and accusations of heresy; the East accused the West of modalistic tendencies and the West accused the East of tritheism. This was compounded by the common translation of *hypostasis* as *substantia*, which led some Latin speakers to conclude that the Greeks were teaching three separate substances in the Godhead. These strands of thought and competing emphases were to come to a head in the subsequent century.

Despite these differences and the gradual and progressive awakening of the church with respect to grappling with the "nuts and bolts" of reconciling the unity of God with the divinity of Father, Son, and Holy Spirit, it can be seen that the doctrine

---

20. Origen, various works, cited and summarized in Kelly, *Early Christian Doctrines*, 128–31.

of the Trinity did not just pop up from nowhere in the fourth-century church councils. The foundational beliefs were present consistently from the very end of the New Testament period.

The Fourth and Fifth Centuries: From Nicea to Chalcedon

The orthodox doctrine of the Trinity was hammered out in response to conflict. The seedbed of conflict was already laid, as we have seen, with different emphases arising out of the principles of the oneness and three-ness of the Godhead. The catalyst which forced the church to come to a consensus, which resulted in the doctrine as we now comprehend it, was the teaching of Arius of Alexandria.

By the early decades of the fourth century, the Western church was continuing to highlight the unity of the Deity and was content to leave the distinctions within the Godhead as mysteries to be accepted. In the East, the influence of Origen continued to be dominant. On the broader church scene a tremendous change took place. In AD 313, after two centuries of persecution, the dominant policy of imperial Rome toward Christians did a complete about-face. The new emperor Constantine aligned himself with Christianity.

It has been a subject of ongoing debate as to whether Constantine himself actually became a Christian. On the one hand, he professed a faith in Christ, and following a vision he received prior to a critical battle which effectively brought him to the throne, he adopted the Chi-Rho symbol of Christianity as his own; "in this sign, conquer." He instituted sweeping reforms which stopped short of making Christianity the state religion (that came later) but certainly he overtly favored it. He produced a syncretistic imperial religion, outwardly the same as the pagan version in its pomp and ceremony, its festivals and hierarchical structures, its blending of church and state, yet substituting Christian concepts and terminology. Constantine himself was not baptized until on his death bed, he retained the title Pontifex Maxiumus (pagan high priest), he continued to take part in pagan rituals and he exercised, or at least attempted to exercise, an authority over the church.

Constantine's overriding concern was for church unity, because that made for unity within the empire and political stability. Because serious doctrinal disputes threatened that unity, he determined they had to be resolved, and threw the power and financial assistance of the throne behind the church councils to this end. It is wrong, however, to attribute to him personally the decisive theological input which led to the formulation of the orthodox doctrine of the Trinity, or the definition of the canon of Scripture, or the other critical decisions which took place around this time.

The Arian Controversy

The crux of this debate was the status of the Word in relation to the Godhead; was he fully divine or was he a creature of the Father who is only designated divine as a courtesy? Although there are important differences between Christadelphianism and Arianism (the modern adherents to which are the Jehovah's Witnesses), there are also some similarities, and Christadelphians, although not affirming the preexistence of the Son as Arius did, would agree with him that the Son of God is essentially a creature.

Arius, a presbyter of the church in Alexandria, affirmed "one God, who is alone ingenerate (self-existent), alone eternal, alone without beginning, alone true, alone possessing immortality, alone wise, alone good, alone sovereign, alone judge of all, etc." The being (*ousia*) of God is unique, transcendent and indivisible and cannot be shared or communicated, hence whatever or whoever else exists must have come into existence by an act of creation out of nothing. For Arius, this God was the Father alone.

The Son, Arius reasoned, must be a creature whom the Father formed out of nothing, begetting only in the sense of "making." He is nevertheless a perfect creature. As a creature, the Son must have had a beginning, which was "before the times and the ages," because he is the creator, so he was born outside time. This premise gave rise to the Arian slogan, "There was when he was not." The Son had no intrinsic direct communication with the Father and was distinct from the Father's essential Word and Wisdom, although he participates in them. He is, like all other creatures, "alien from and utterly dissimilar to the Father's essence and individual being" and can neither see nor know the Father perfectly accurately. The Son, as a creature, and unlike the Father, must be liable to change and have the potential to sin.[21]

In what sense, then, could the Arians call the Son "God" or "Son of God?" The answer was that they are effectively courtesy titles, that he is God in name only. The scriptural passages advanced in support of their position were the same ones used by Christadelphians and Jehovah's Witnesses today. It might be helpful at this point to summarize the comparisons between orthodoxy, Arianism and Christadelphianism.

Orthodox	Arianism	Christadelphians
God is one in essence; all three persons are eternal and uncreated	God is one, the Father; he alone is uncreated and eternal	God is one, the Father; he alone is uncreated and eternal

21. Teachings of Arius, as cited and summarized in Kelly, *Early Christian Doctrines*, 226–30.

Orthodox	Arianism	Christadelphians
The Son shares the Father's nature and is intrinsically divine	The Son is a created being who is not intrinsically divine; he was created out of nothing	The Son is a created human being who is not intrinsically divine; he was conceived by the Holy Spirit
The Son is eternal; like the Father he has no beginning	The Son had a beginning, before the creation of time	The Son had a beginning, at his conception in Mary's womb
The Son was the agent of creation	The Son was the agent of creation	The Son was not involved in creation; he did not yet exist
The Son has full and intimate knowledge of the Father	The Son has no intrinsic knowledge of the Father	The Son grew in knowledge of God with the help of the Holy Spirit
The Son can intrinsically be called God, equally with the Father	The Son may be called God as an honorary title	The Father bestowed on the Son the name and honor due to "God" at his exaltation
The Son in his divine nature does not change or sin, however in his human nature he was weak and liable to change and could have sinned	The Son was changeable and could have sinned; but by his own effort and the grace of the Father he did not	The Son was changeable and could have sinned, but by his own effort and reliance on the Father and Holy Spirit he did not.
The Son is equal in status and dignity to the Father, although differing in role (economy)	The Son is inferior to the Father in status and dignity as well as role	The Son is inferior to the Father in status and dignity as well as role, although he has been exalted

Arius was opposed by a number of other theologians, including his own bishop, Alexander. However, he was a persuasive preacher and master of propaganda, engaging the public through use of popular songs and slogans. The Greek church was threatened with a major division and so Constantine convened and sponsored an ecumenical council which met at Nicea in June of AD 325. Its dual purpose was to organize the church in its new position within the empire and to resolve the Arian crisis. About 300 bishops, mostly from the Eastern churches, were present. It was a remarkable gathering; only a few years ago many of these same bishops had been tortured and imprisoned by the state, which now sponsored their gathering! The decision making at the Council itself was only open to the bishops, but in attendance was a young theologian and deacon named Athanasius, who eventually became a bishop himself, but more importantly has become known as the champion of the orthodox position against Arianism. Athanasius' arguments were that Arianism was basically a reversion to polytheism by undermining the complete unity of the Godhead, that it went against baptism in the threefold name and the worthiness of Jesus to be worshiped and most importantly, that it undermined redemption. Only if the Savior and Mediator was himself divine, argued Athanasius, could humans be reconciled to God. We will explore the implications of the theology of the Godhead for that of the atonement in the final chapter.

The Council opposed Arianism and condemned Arius, attesting to the divinity and immutability of the Son. Because both sides could put forward individual scriptural passages and construct arguments which supported their own position and opposed the other (consider the breadth of passages we have covered in this book, for comparison), there was some difficulty in making a succinct statement, using Bible quotations alone, that could unmistakably express the positive position and reject the negative. Hence it was decided to formulate a creed that summarized the orthodox position. The critical decision was to use the word *homoousios*—of the *same* substance—to describe the Son's relation to the Father's being or essence, rather than *homoiousios*—of *similar* substance. What a difference a single iota makes!

It is in the whole context of the theological controversy, the centuries of background theology that underpinned it, and the objectives of the Council that the Nicene Creed must be understood. When Christadelphians attack this creed and accentuate the apparent theological leap between it and its predecessor, the Apostles' Creed (with which they have little disagreement) they do so without engaging with this context. Instead, they focus on the extra-scriptural terms without respect for the tremendous body of scriptural evidence and theological discussion that supports them. Rather than the Nicene Creed being the manifesto of an apostate church, it can be readily shown that the Apostles' Creed and the Nicene Creed are both documents for their times and address the burning theological issues and controversies of their respective ages. The same is true for any of the creeds and confessions of the church and is equally true for the Christadelphians' own *Statement of the Faith* (which is not devoid of anachronisms, either).

The Apostles' Creed was probably formulated in Rome around AD 150 as a baptismal confession and is quite simple. It is concerned with countering the heresies of the day: Gnosticism and Docetism and, to an extent, Judaizing influences.

I believe in God the Father Almighty; maker of heaven and earth.	Counters the Gnostic idea of the inferior creator demi-god, a lesser being than the supreme God
And in Jesus Christ his only Son our Lord; who was conceived by the Holy Spirit	Upholds the lordship of Jesus against Jewish rejection and contra the lordship of Caesar; upholds his divine origin and incarnation
born of the virgin Mary; suffered under Pontius Pilate, was crucified, dead and buried	Upholds the real humanity of Jesus as against Docetism
the third day he rose from the dead;	As against Gnostic dualism that saw the soul's destiny as escape from entrapment in matter
he ascended into heaven; and sitteth at the right hand of God the Father Almighty; from thence he shall come to judge the quick and the dead.	Links Jesus to the OT Messianic promises and upholds his exaltation and Lordship and role as judge
I believe in the Holy Spirit; the holy catholic church; the communion of saints; the forgiveness of sins;	Brief and to the point, relatively non-controversial ("catholic" here means universal)
the resurrection of the body and the life everlasting. Amen.	As against Gnostic dualism

In terms of expressing the nature of unity and diversity within the Godhead and in particular the status of the Son, the Apostles Creed did not go far enough, hence a new creed was required, without discarding the older one. The Apostles Creed forms the common basis of faith for evangelical and other Western churches today. Whilst also based on a triadic formula, the Nicene Creed has a different context and objective. It is not a "de-volution," but a different theological tool.

The original form is the creed of Nicea, AD 325. As we shall see, it was ratified in a modified form by the Council of Constantinople in 381 to become the Niceno-Constantinopolitan creed and accepted in its present form at the Council of Chalcedon in 451. A further addendum, the controversial *filioque*, was added in 589. Here is the original form as written down by Eusebius of Caesarea, the fourth-century church historian.[22]

> We believe in one God, the Father Almighty, Maker of all things visible and invisible, And in one Lord Jesus Christ, the Son of God, the only-begotten of the Father, that is, from the substance of the Father, God of God, light of light, true God of true God, begotten not made; of one substance [*homoousios*] with the Father; through whom all things were made, both in heaven and on earth, who for us men and for our salvation, descended and became incarnate, becoming human, suffered and rose again on the third day, ascended to the heavens, and will come to judge the living and the dead. And in the Holy Spirit.

An addendum anathematized Arianism:

> But those who say that there was when he was not, and that before being begotten he was not, or that he came from that which is not, or that the Son of God is of a different substance [*hypostasis*] or essence [*ousia*] or that he is created, or mutable, these the catholic [i.e., universal] church anathematizes.

The objective here is clearly on explaining the orthodox position as against Arianism, which is why there is no detail on the Holy Spirit. The later form ratified at Chalcedon reintroduces some of the details of the Apostles' Creed, making it a broader statement of orthodox faith. This later creed also puts forward the deity of the Holy Spirit, concerning which considerable further discussion had taken place in the interim. This was largely the work of the Cappadocian theologians, Basil, Gregory, and Gregory.

> We believe in one God, the Father, Ruler of all, Maker of heaven and earth, of all things visible and invisible,
> And in one Lord Jesus Christ, the only-begotten Son of God, begotten from the Father before all ages, light from light, true God from true God, begotten not made; of one substance [*homoousios*] with the Father; by whom all things were made; Who for us men and for our salvation, came down from heaven and was incarnate by the Holy Ghost and the Virgin Mary, and became man and was crucified for us under Pontius Pilate and suffered and was buried, and rose again on the third day according to the Scriptures; and ascended into heaven, and sitteth on the right hand of the Father, and will come again with glory to judge the quick and the dead; Whose kingdom shall have no end.
> And in the Holy Spirit, the Lord and giver of life, Who procedeth from the Father _and the Son_,[23] Who with the Father and Son together is worshiped and glorified; Who spake through the prophets;
> In one holy Catholic and Apostolic Church

22. Eusebius of Caesarea, "Epistle to the Caesareans," as quoted in Gonzalez, *Story of Christianity*, 165.

23. The underlined phrase is the *filioque*, which later caused division between the Eastern and Western churches, because the former did not accept that the Spirit proceeds from the Son as well as the Father.

Despite the almost unanimous endorsement of the creed by the bishops at Nicea, the controversy did not end. In fact, by a combination of politics and propaganda, Arianism gained ascendancy in the Eastern church for some time. The early missionaries to the barbarians outside the Roman Empire were Arians, so the Goths and other tribes became Arian Christians. Athanasius took up the task of championing orthodoxy and was exiled several times for his convictions. Eventually however, orthodoxy won the day and became established as official doctrine of the Eastern and Western churches, and was ratified at the Council of Constantinople in 381 with the publication of the Niceno-Constantinopolitan creed above.

The Doctrine of the Trinity

The Arian controversy and the Council of Nicea were preoccupied with the deity of the Son. The original Nicene Creed simply affirmed belief in the Holy Spirit without elaboration. During the period between Nicea and Constantinople there was increasing interest in, and discussion about, the status of the Spirit in relation to the Godhead. The theological movers and shakers in this discussion were the Cappadocians, Basil the Great, Gregory of Nazianzus, and Gregory of Nyssa; and in the West, Augustine of Hippo (AD 354 to 430).

Arius regarded the Spirit in the same way he regarded the Son—as of different essence from the Father. Eusebius of Caesarea, an Origen sympathist, considered the Spirit to be a hypostasis, but third in rank from the Father and Son, who had come into existence through the Son. Nevertheless, because he is included with the Father and Son in scriptural triadic formulae, he must be above other beings. In contrast, Cyril of Jerusalem wrote in the late 340s that in union with the Spirit, the Son participates in the Father's Godhead and the Spirit is "a being divine and ineffable."[24]

Around 360, Athanasius began to expound a theology of the Spirit. He taught that the Spirit is fully divine, consubstantial (of the same substance, *homoousios*) with the Father and the Son. According to Scripture, the Spirit has nothing in common with creatures and is one with the Godhead. He belongs in essence to the Son as to the Father, he is the Spirit of the Son and bestowed by the Son. He joined with the Son in creation and he sanctifies and enlightens and makes us partakers of God. If he were a creature, he could not do these things. The Godhead, therefore, exists eternally as a triad of persons, sharing one identical and indivisible essence and they accomplish the Father's work together.[25]

The Cappadocians took this up and in 380 Gregory of Nazianzus gave an account of the widely varying opinions of the day concerning the Spirit, from being a force, to being a creature, to being God. Basil the Great highlighted the testimony of Scripture to the greatness and dignity of the Spirit, to be accorded the same honor and worship

24. Kelly, *Early Christian Doctrines*, 255–56.
25. Ibid., 257–58.

as the Father and Son and to the immensity of the Spirit's power. He also affirmed the Spirit's intimate association with the Father and Son, especially in the work of sanctification, but stopped short of calling him God or affirming his consubstantiality. Gregory of Nyssa argued that the Spirit's activity and nature were the same as that of the Father and Son, and Gregory of Nazianzus affirmed that he is consubstantial, since he is God. This was countered by the Arians with the proposition that this implied that the Father had two Sons.

Gregory of Nyssa provided what became the definitive understanding of the Eastern church, that the Spirit is out of God and is of Christ; he proceeds *from* the Father *through* the Son. The Western interpretation, which was to provide the source of conflict centered around the *filioque* phrase, is that the Spirit proceeds *from* the Father and *from* the Son.[26] Gregory's concerns were to simultaneously defend three principles: God as unity, simple and undivided; the distinction between Creator and creation which precludes any degrees of divinity and the evidence that Father, Son, and Holy Spirit are each real and distinguishable and each properly named God. What was being sought by Gregory in the East and Augustine in the West was not the definitive statement of what constitutes the divine essence, because that is beyond human comprehension. Rather, they sought a coherent way of expressing revealed truths in appropriate language. The underlying issue was (and for Christadelphians still is) whether the Father alone is the monarchial God, in which case the Son must be "below the line" and hence of infinitely inferior rank, or whether the monarchy is the shared glory, "above the line," of Father, Son, and Holy Spirit.[27]

The result was the fully developed doctrine of the Trinity, as expressed in the Creed of Constantinople in 381:

> We believe in one God, the Father, Ruler of all, Maker of heaven and earth, of all things visible and invisible,
> And in one Lord Jesus Christ, the only-begotten Son of God, begotten from the Father before all ages, light from light, true God from true God, begotten not made; of one substance with the Father; by whom all things were made . . .
> And in the Holy Spirit, the Lord and giver of life, Who proceedeth from the Father [later adds *and the Son*] Who with the Father and Son together is worshiped and glorified; Who spake through the prophets . . .

The formula which expresses the understanding of the Godhead and recognizes the unity of God in conjunction with the divinity of Father, Son, and Spirit is one *ousia* in three *hypostases*. Basil expressed it this way:

> Everything that the Father is, is seen in the Son, and everything that the Son is belongs to the Father. The Son in his entirety abides in the Father, and in return possesses the Father in entirety in himself. Thus the hypostasis of the Son is, so to

---

26. Ibid., 259–63.

27. This point is very well explained, along with a more detailed explanation of the Cappadocians' contribution, by Holmes, *Quest for the Trinity*, 106–10.

speak, the form and presentation by which the Father is known, and the Father's hypostasis is recognized in the form of the Son.[28]

Gregory of Nazianzus wrote that "The three have one nature, viz., God, the ground of unity being the Father, out of Whom and towards Whom the subsequent persons are reckoned." The analogy is that of the universal term "human" and the particular characteristics of an individual person who shares the nature common to humankind. The commonality in the Godhead is the divine nature, and the distinctive characteristics are paternity, sonship and sanctifying power, according to Basil.[29]

In the Western church, Augustine was the one to give final expression to the doctrine, in his work *De Trinitate* (AD 419). In keeping with the Western theological worldview, he began with the immutability of the divine nature or essence. This essence exists in trinity, with whatever is affirmed of God being affirmed equally of the three persons. One and the same substance constitutes each of them, therefore "no single person of the three is less than the Trinity itself." Augustine's emphasis was on the oneness of the divine nature, so Father, Son, and Spirit are not three separate individuals the way three human beings are representative of *Homo sapiens*, but they indwell or coinhere with one another. This is very much the flavor of the Athanasian creed. The three persons operate as one principle, inseparably. Nevertheless, each possesses the divine nature in a particular manner, and executes appropriate specific roles in the external operation of the Godhead. Thus Augustine laid the groundwork for the later defined doctrines of perichoresis and appropriation discussed in our previous chapter. The Father is distinguished as Father because he begets the Son, the Son is distinguished as Son because he is begotten. The Spirit is distinguished because he is bestowed by them as their common gift. Thus the three are distinct and real relations, although he found the word *persona* somewhat inadequate. Augustine's distinctive view of the Spirit was as the bond of love which unites Father and Son; he is the Spirit of both Father and Son, and proceeds from both. Augustine saw triadic patterns in creation, which he believed were patterns or analogies of the triune nature of God, such as the mind, its self-knowledge and its self-love, but he was careful not to carry these too far and recognized their limitations.[30] When all is said and done, however, Augustine's theology is very much in line with the conclusions reached by Nicene orthodoxy.[31]

---

28. Cited in Kelly, *Early Christian Doctrines*, 264. These statements will be recognized as paraphrases of well-known scriptures.

29. Ibid., 265.

30. Augustine, *De Trinitate*, cited and discussed in Kelly, *Early Christian Doctrines*, 272–78.

31. The arguments to support this assertion are presented by Holmes, *Quest for the Trinity*, 129–39, 144–46.

The Christological Controversies of the Fourth and Fifth Centuries

The Niceno-Constantiopolitan Creed affirmed both the full deity and the real humanity of Christ, against Arianism on the one hand and Gnosticism and Docetism on the other, but at this stage the theologians had not really got their heads around how deity and humanity were united in Jesus Christ. The christological controversies were initially a predominantly Eastern church issue; the West, content with Tertullian's definitions, contributed later. By the fourth century there were two dominant schools of Greek Christian thought, those of Alexandria and Antioch. Whilst the two teachings had different emphases, the controversies were as much attributable to philosophical differences, misunderstanding and misrepresentation, as to specific teachings.

Alexandria, nurtured by the Platonists Clement and Origen, promoted an allegorical style of Scripture interpretation, based on assumed multiple layers of meaning in the text; the literal, the moral and the spiritual. The difficulties faced by Alexandrine theology related to the place of the human soul in Jesus, disregarding it or making it redundant.[32] The Alexandrines conceptualized God as a "personal nature," the Word, who united with inert flesh without actually changing. Christ had only one nature, the divine Word.[33] This is also called the "Word-flesh" doctrine. The divinity and humanity of Jesus were held together by a "transfer of properties" (*communicatio idiomatum*) from the divine Word to the human Jesus, enabling expression of divine miraculous powers in human flesh. Jesus' sufferings, thirst, growth in wisdom, and professed ignorance of the time of the *parousia* were therefore problematic. The best explanation the Alexandrines proposed was that the Word "feigned" weakness and ignorance.

The Antiochenes, in contrast, were Christian Aristotelians, favouring grammatico-historical scriptural exegesis (what we would call the "plain meaning" of the text). Antioch stressed the humanity of the Christ of the gospels. The extreme viewpoint, "Nestorianism," understated the divinity of Christ and made him subservient to the Father. Antiochenes believed that Christ had a true human soul and identity and that after the incarnation the two natures, human and divine, although joined in one Person, were still evident. This has been described as the "Word-man" theology; the Word became a whole, complete human being, body and soul, without discarding His divinity. The Antiochenes denied both the Word's replacing the human soul, and the *communicatio idiomatum*. It was Jesus' human soul and flesh that developed, showed weakness, experienced temptation, suffered and died.[34] Their difficulty was defining *how* the two natures were joined and laid them open to the charge of splitting the person of Christ into two.

Alexandrine ideas were taken to their logical extreme by Apollinarius of Laodicea. Apollinarius believed that separation of the divine and human in Christ would

---

32. Bray, *Creeds, Councils and Christ*, 150.

33. Kelly, *Early Christian Doctrines*, 281.

34. Bray, *Creeds, Councils and Christ*, 152.

negate salvation, because a fallible human Christ could not redeem mankind.[35] Hence he spoke of Jesus in terms of "flesh-bearing God," "God born of a woman," and having "divine flesh" which could be worshiped. He denied that Christ had human free will because that would make the Word changeable and able to sin; instead, the Word took the place of a human mind in Christ, eliminating "contradictory wills and intelligences." Apollinarius was condemned at the second ecumenical council in Constantinople in 381. Christadelphians, at least in some writings, appear to confuse mainstream trinitarian doctrine with Apollinarianism.

The Cappadocian fathers upheld Antiochene "two natures" Christology and the necessity of Christ's human intelligent soul. Gregory of Nazianzus pronounced, "What has not been assumed cannot be restored; it is what is united with God that is saved."[36] Gregory of Nyssa saw Jesus as the "God-receiving man,"[37] whose human will was distinct from and occasionally contrary to the prevailing divine will. Christ's human experiences belonged to his humanity, the impassible Godhead remaining unaffected.

Eustathius of Antioch expounded the dual-nature, "Word-man" Christology, but had trouble explaining *how* they were united, describing the Word dwelling in the "God-bearing man" as in a temple.[38] Theodore of Mopsuestia denied that the Word was the soul of Christ, arguing "He took not on a body but a complete man."[39] Theodore viewed Christ's humanity as complete and independent, undergoing growth in knowledge and being tempted. He speaks of Jesus as "the man assumed" and of the union as "indwelling" or clothing.[40] Unfortunately he distanced the Word (assumer) from the man (the assumed), using the term "conjunction" rather than "union."

In 428 Nestorius of Constantinople, an Antiochene, rejected *Theotokos* (God-bearer) as a title for the Virgin Mary, arguing that she bore the vehicle of divinity but did not bear "God." Christ had two natures, distinct and unaltered in the union and the impassable Word could not have changed or suffered.[41] What followed was rather disgraceful; the major players anathematized each other and tended to misrepresent each other's positions and the debate got hotter and nastier. Soteriologically, the Alexandrines insisted that only a perfect savior, the divine Word, could be effective.[42] The Antiochenes stressed that only those aspects of humanity borne by Christ could be saved. Alexandrines accused Antiochenes of adoptionism and of dividing the person

35. Kelly, *Early Christian Doctrines*, 290–91.

36. Gregory of Nazianzus, Epistle 101,7, quoted in Kelly, *Early Christian Doctrines*, 297.

37. Kelly, *Early Christian Doctrines*, 298–99.

38. Ibid., 283–84.

39. Theodore of Mopsuestia, *Catechetical Homilies 5, 19*, quoted in Kelly, *Early Christian Doctrines*, 304.

40. Kelly, *Early Christian Doctrines*, 304–5.

41. Ibid., 312.

42. Boersma, "The Chalcedonian Definition," 47–63.

of Christ into two. Conversely, Antiochenes denounced the Alexandrines as teaching "confusion" of the two natures and of denying the reality of Christ's human nature. The Alexandrine response was, "He who divides the natures posits two Sons; he does not believe the Scripture which says, 'The Word was made flesh.'"[43]

They couldn't see that they were each contending for the same principles, but with different emphases. Unfortunately, sometimes this same spirit of misrepresentation and a desire for victory in debate discolors discussions both within and between mainstream Christian groups and Christadelphian groups, so we should all be careful not to cast the first stone.

> So intent was each upon securing for itself the victory, that it would not stop to enquire whether its opponents did not after all believe what they said they believed.[44]

The *Symbol of Union* was a subsequent compromise, defining Christ as "consubstantial with the Father in respect of His divinity and at the same time consubstantial with us in respect of His manhood. For a union of two natures has been accomplished . . ."[45]

The next crisis came in 448 over the doctrines of Eutyches, who taught a confused, extreme, almost docetic, form of Alexandrianism. He maintained that Christ's humanity was totally absorbed by his divinity and only had the appearance of humanity.[46] He was condemned at a synod in Constantinople. In 449 Leo, bishop of Rome, dispatched his famous *Tome* to Emperor Flavian, upholding traditional Western theology and opposing the one nature doctrine. Leo's *Tome* was significant in marking the entry of conventional Western theology into the Eastern christological dispute, reconciling the views of both schools.[47] Leo argued for the foundation of redemption as the *being* of Christ, not his work.[48] The Chalcedon settlement at the fourth council in 451 reaffirmed the creed of Nicea/Constantinople and condemned both Nestorianism and Eutychianism.

The Chalcedonian *Definition of Faith* is an important document to understand. It is not primarily a first-principles dissertation on who Jesus *is* (although it is appropriate and useful to read it this way) so much as a definition of the boundaries beyond which lies what Jesus is *not*. It demonstrates that the two theologies were fundamentally equivalent and complementary, despite their different emphases, which were at times carried to extremes by their proponents. The definition helps to safeguard

---

43. Cyril of Alexandria, *Dial. cum. Nestor, PG lxxvi.252C*, quoted in Sellers, *Two Ancient Christologies*, 207.

44. Sellers, *Two Ancient Christologies*, 203.

45. "Symbol of Union," quoted in Kelly, *Early Christian Doctrines*, 328.

46. Kelly, *Early Christian Doctrines*, 332.

47. Ibid., 337.

48. Boersma, "The Chalcedonian Definition," 47–63.

against overemphasizing Jesus' divinity to the exclusion of his real humanity, and safe-guards his divinity against an overemphasis on his humanity.

> We, then, following the holy Fathers, all with one consent, teach people to con-fess one and the same Son, our Lord Jesus Christ, the same perfect in Godhead and also perfect in manhood; truly God and truly man, of a reasonable [ratio-nal] soul and body; consubstantial with the Father according to the Godhead, and consubstantial with us according to the Manhood; in all things like unto us, without sin; begotten before all ages of the Father according to the God-head, and in these latter days, for us and for our salvation, born of the Virgin Mary, the Mother of God,[49] according to the Manhood; one and the same Christ, Son, Lord, only begotten, to be acknowledged in two natures, inconfusedly, un-changeably, indivisibly, inseparably; the distinction of natures being by no means taken away by the union, but rather the property of each nature being preserved, and concurring in one Person and one Subsistence, not parted or divided into two persons, but one and the same Son, and only begotten God, the Word, the Lord Jesus Christ; as the prophets from the beginning have declared concerning Him, and the Lord Jesus Christ Himself has taught us, and the Creed of the holy Fathers has handed down to us.[50]

If the nature of the Godhead—the sense in which God is one and the sense in which he is three—the relationships between Father, Son, and Holy Spirit and the way Jesus Christ combines both divinity and humanity were being described from scratch today, beginning with and reconciling the whole weight of scriptural teaching, perhaps the end result would use different words and phrases. Even at the time, a lot of misunderstandings arose simply from translating Greek words like *hypostasis* and *ousia* into Latin. It is true that the terms used are extra-biblical, and that they necessarily come with the baggage and presuppositions of the Greco-Roman thought world in which they were developed, but the same would be true today. Whatever analogies were chosen, whatever vocabulary, whatever mental pictures were formed, it would be colored by the way we think and act, in our case as twenty-first-century English speakers. Just as the seventeenth-century language of the King James Ver-sion is difficult for modern readers, and can lead to some erroneous interpretations if taken literally using modern meanings of the words,[51] so too the ancient creeds, on the surface, can appear obscure and theologically off-track. But if we take the time to unpack them in the context in which they were written, and to understand which

---

49. I can feel the collective cringe at this expression! In the context of the Definition it needs to be understood not as advocating the worship or veneration of Mary, but a statement as to who was born of her; not just a man but the incarnate Son. In other words, the incarnation occurred in Mary's womb, not before or after.

50. The Chalcedonian Definition of 451 can be found in various texts and websites. This English translation is taken from http://en.wikipedia.org/wiki/Chalcedonian_Definition.

51. Lest I cause offense to the many Christadelphians who still regard the KJV as the definitive and most reliable translation, I qualify this by referring to examples such as "study to show yourselves worthy," "The law was a schoolmaster to bring us to Christ," "the greatest of these is charity," "Holy Ghost," God's "unspeakable gift," etc.

scriptural truths they were designed to uphold and which heresies to refute, they are still extremely valuable statements of faith today.

The Reformation and the Anabaptist Movement

Within Augustine's lifetime, Rome fell to the barbarians and the Western Roman empire came to an end. The bishops of Rome, or "popes," effectively took the place of emperors, ruling over a "Christendom" that in doctrine and practice certainly diverged from the early apostolic and post-apostolic faith. Justification by grace through faith became corrupted into a church-dispensed grace-by-works system, through the priestly administered sacraments. The popes eventually claimed formally what they had long argued for; ultimate authority in matters of doctrine and practice on the basis of "apostolic succession." Meanwhile in the East, the emperors acted as "popes;" holding sway politically and often doctrinally over the church, with the Patriarch of Constantinople often in a subsidiary role. Christadelphians and mainstream Protestants rightly point to the corrupt teachings and practices of medieval Christendom, but what I hope has been established so far in this chapter is that the doctrine of the Trinity was not a product of this apostasy. The divinity of Christ and the Holy Spirit, and the triune nature of the Godhead owe their origin to scriptural teaching and can be demonstrated to have been believed consistently from New Testament times. Even though the enunciation of the detail of these doctrines took place over time, there were good reasons for this, and the orthodox or mainstream understanding of the Trinity was established well before Roman Catholicism held sway over Europe.

The Reformers and the Trinity

In the wake of the Renaissance there was a rediscovery of the ancient languages and philosophies and a new worldview that, in God's providence, provided the fertile soil for Reformation. Men like Wycliffe and Tyndale, Hus, Luther, and Calvin pioneered the translation of Scripture into the native tongues of their people, and with this came a reanalysis of doctrine from the Scriptures themselves. The hundred and thirty years of the Reformation period were world-shaking. Between 1517 when Martin Luther nailed his Ninety-Five Theses to the door of the Wittenberg Castle Church and ignited the spark, and 1647 when the Puritans finished framing the great Reformed theological Westminster Confession, Europe was transformed from medieval Roman Catholic Christendom to a collection of independent nation states, each with its own flavor of Christianity. The Protestants dispensed with many teachings and practices that had been introduced or corrupted by the medieval Roman Catholic church.

The Reformation in Germany, which produced the Lutheran church, and the Reformation in Switzerland which produced the Zwinglian church in Zurich and the Calvinist church in Geneva, gave birth to daughter churches throughout Europe, including Britain. Yet each of these versions of Protestantism had a number of theological and sociopolitical marks in common. Theologically, the Protestant churches subscribed to the five great *solas*, which distinguished them from Roman Catholicism:

- *Sola fide*—Salvation through faith alone

- *Sola gratia* —Salvation by grace alone

- *Sola scriptura* —Scripture alone as the authority for doctrine and practice

- *Sola Christo* —Salvation in Christ alone

- *Sola deo gloria*—To the glory of God alone

The magnitude of the turn-around in thinking here should not be underestimated. Gone was the idea that the pope's authority or the traditions of the church superseded that of Scripture. Gone was the idea of salvation through sacramentalism, dependent upon the ministrations of a priestly class. Gone was the veneration of intermediaries—Mary and the saints, to list just the more obvious changes.

If ever there was an opportunity to rediscover scriptural truths and boldly discard what didn't stack up against this ultimate measuring line, this was it. The Bible went under the microscope, so to speak, for the first time in centuries as the definitive arbiter of doctrine and practice. If ever there was an opportunity to demonstrate that any doctrine was an emperor without clothes, it was during the Reformation period. Yet the doctrine of the Trinity withstood this scrutiny and emerged unscathed and fully endorsed, because the Reformers recognized its scriptural basis and upheld it. The early Protestants didn't agree on everything; the sacraments of baptism and the Lord's supper were particularly contentious because of their implications for what it meant to be a member of the body of Christ. But one of the fundamental doctrines held in common was the Trinity. All the mainline Reformers were committed to the historical doctrine of the Trinity because they believed it to be scriptural and therefore they did not initially write much about it.

Nevertheless, it wasn't as if the Reformers simply rubber-stamped the Trinity and moved on; in time they were involved in dissertations and even controversies.[52] Calvin, for example, saw the Trinity as a whole as Creator, Redeemer and Sanctifier, each contributing to all of the works of God. In *each* of these works of God,

> . . . to the Father is attributed the beginning of activity, and the fountain and wellspring of all things; to the Son, wisdom, counsel and the ordered disposition of all things; but to the Spirit is assigned the power and efficacy of that activity.[53]

---

52. Bray, *Doctrine of God*, 197–98, 202–3 describes a fresh perspective on the nature of the triune God as "fundamentally different from anything which had gone before, or which has appeared since." Bray argues that the Reformers saw the essence of God as of secondary importance, emphasising the coequality of the Persons and rejecting the conventional "division of labour" within the Godhead which characterised the Father as Creator, the Son as Redeemer, and the Holy Spirit as Sanctifier.

53. Calvin, *Institutes*, I.13.18, 142–43.

The statement of faith of the Lutheran church was the *Augsburg Confession*,[54] principally authored by Martin Luther's successor Philip Melanchthon and delivered in 1530.

> Article I—Of God. The churches, with common consent among us, do teach that the decree of the Nicene Synod concerning the unity of the divine essence and of the three persons is true, and without doubt to be believed: to wit, that there is one divine essence which is called and is God, eternal, without body, indivisible (without part), of infinite power, wisdom, goodness, the Creator and Preserver of all things, visible and invisible; and that yet there are three persons of the same essence and power, who also are co-eternal, the Father, the Son, and the Holy Ghost. And they use the name of person in that signification in which the ecclesiastical writers (the fathers) have used it in this cause, to signify, not a part or quality in another, but that which properly subsists.
>
> Article III—Of the Son of God. Also they teach that the Word, that is, the Son of God, took unto him man's nature in the womb of the blessed Virgin Mary, so that there are two natures, the divine and the human, inseparably joined together in unity of person; one Christ, true God and true man: who was born of the Virgin Mary, truly suffered, was crucified, dead, and buried, that he might reconcile the Father unto us, and might be a sacrifice, not only for original guilt, but also for all actual sins of men.

John Calvin, the great Swiss reformer, upheld the doctrine of the Trinity in his *Institutes of the Christian Religion*, the final version of which was published in 1560. Chapter XIII of Book I is entitled, "In Scripture, from the Creation onward, we are taught one essence of God, which contains three Persons." Calvin was not one to mince his words when condemning the apostasy of the Roman Catholic church (in fact, he makes Christadelphian pioneer Robert Roberts look very restrained!), but he is in no doubt that the doctrine of the Trinity is biblical. He engages with the original Greek and Latin words and the controversies surrounding them.

> Now, although the heretics rail at the word "person," or certain squeamish men cry out against admitting a term fashioned by the human mind, they cannot shake our conviction that three are spoken of, each of which is entirely God, yet that there is not more than one God . . . but what prevents us from explaining in clearer words those matters in Scripture which perplex and hinder our understanding, yet which conscientiously and faithfully serve the truth of Scripture itself, and are made use of sparingly and modestly and on due occasion? . . . However, the novelty of words of this sort (if such it must be called) becomes especially useful when the truth is to be asserted against false accusers, who evade it by their shifts . . .[55]

Calvin goes on to explain, as we have done, how the terminology came to be used to counter such doctrines as Arianism and modalism. He then goes on to expound in detail the theological terms, the deity of the Word, the divinity of Christ in the Old

---

54. The full text of the confession can be found online at the Christian Classic Ethereal Library http://www.ccel.org/ccel/schaff/creeds3.iii.ii.html and elsewhere.

55. Calvin, *Institutes*, I.XIII.3, 4, 123–24.

and New Testaments, the deity of the Spirit, the distinctions of the three persons and their relationships, and the unity of the Godhead, with abundant scriptural references.

We can't leave Calvin, however, without considering his objection to the teachings of Michael Servetus[56] (c. 1511 to 1553) and his subsequent condemnation of this man. Servetus was a Spanish physician and theologian whose unorthodox teachings (not just in regard to the Trinity, by the way) led to his condemnation as a heretic by both Roman Catholics and Protestants. Servetus first published his ideas on the Trinity in 1531; the Word is eternal and a mode of God's self-expression and the Spirit is God's motion or power within the hearts of men. The Son is the union of the eternal Word with the man Jesus. Both Catholics and Protestants objected to a number of his teachings, which also concerned prophecy, astrology and the nature of the church-state relationship.

Servetus objected to the Nicene Creed, which he believed was tainted by Constantine's involvement and the apostasy of the imperial Roman church, although he valued the work of the ante-Nicene fathers. Servetus was condemned to death by the Catholic Inquisition, but escaped to Geneva, where he was tried for heresy. Calvin opposed his teachings at trial, but preferred a commutated sentence, although Servetus was subsequently burned at the stake. This decision was, regrettably, par for the course in the sixteenth century when burning was the standard response to heresy by both Catholics and Protestants. Calvin was, and has since, been severely criticized for his involvement.

Whilst our twenty-first-century worldview finds little in common with this sixteenth-century response to theological disagreement, it is important to differentiate what was disputed, from how it was (mis)handled. The truth of a doctrine stands or falls on its scriptural basis, not on the status or actions of its proponents or opponents and right doctrine is important. Three considerations would seem to apply in evaluating Geneva's treatment of Servetus. Firstly, fiery judgment is God's prerogative, not ours (2 Thess 1:7–8; Rev 20:10). Secondly, for the church to administer punishment in this way confuses the roles of church and state (Rom 13:1–5) an issue with which the churches of the Reformation period were desperately struggling. Finally, Scripture tells us how to deal with false teachers (2 John 7–11).

Calvin's system of church government is known as presbyterian, from the Greek *presbuteros*, meaning "elder," but his theology is known as "reformed." Reformed theology is today embraced by a number of non-Lutheran Protestant churches, including Presbyterians, Dutch Reformed Church and Particular Baptists. Reformed theology is based on the starting point of the absolute sovereignty of God, and influenced many of the great Protestant confessions. The Reformed faith encompasses the trinitarian understanding of the Godhead.

56. http://www.britannica.com/EBchecked/topic/535958/Michael-Servetus; Gonzalez, *The Story of Christianity*, 67. Calvin's response to Servetus may be found in part in *Institutes*, I.XIII.22.

The later Reformation period saw the Protestantization of England and Scotland. Whilst the English reformation arose *politically* because of the machinations of Henry VIII, *theologically* it was founded on the same fundamental scriptural principles as the Continental Reformation, and was heavily influenced by Calvinist Reformed theology. The English Reformation oscillated under the Tudors between thinly veiled Catholicism under Henry, to radical Protestantism under Edward, back to Roman Catholicism under Mary and finally the so-called "middle way" of moderate Protestantism under Elizabeth. The final form of the Thirty Nine Articles[57] of the Church of England was constructed under Elizabeth and endorses the Nicene and Apostles' Creeds as being "proved by most certain warrants of Holy Scripture."

> Article I. Of Faith in the Holy Trinity. There is but one living and true God, everlasting, without body, parts or passions; of infinite power, wisdom, and goodness; the Maker, and Preserver of all things both visible and invisible. And in unity of this Godhead there be three Persons, of one substance, power, and eternity: the Father, the Son, and the Holy Spirit.
>
> Article II. Of the Word or Son of God, which was made very man. The Son, which is the Word of the Father, begotten from everlasting of the Father, the very and eternal God, and of one substance with the Father, took Man's nature in the womb of the blessed Virgin, of her substance: so that two whole and perfect Natures, that is to say, the Godhead and Manhood, were joined together in one Person, never to be divided, whereof is one Christ, very God, and very Man; who truly suffered, was crucified, dead and buried, to reconcile his Father to us, and to be a sacrifice, not only for original guilt, but also for actual sins of men.

In these two articles can be seen the essentials of the early theological controversies and their resolution, three persons in one substance and the full and real deity and humanity united in Christ.

During Elizabeth's reign and the reigns of her successors the Stuart dynasty, there were varying degrees of antipathy towards Roman Catholicism but also a fairly constant objection to the more extreme forms of Protestantism, particularly the presbyterian and congregationalist systems of church government, represented by the diverse group known as the Puritans. The Puritans sought to take the reformation of the church further than the Church of England had progressed and this met with resistance, primarily on political grounds. The Puritans were also concerned with integrity and piety in Christian life and worship and viewed the preaching and reception of the word of God as the central focus of public worship and private devotion. During the mid 1600s they gained some ascendancy and in 1646 a gathering of theologians called the Westminster Assembly produced the *Westminster Confession of Faith*, which describes the accepted doctrinal basis for Reformed churches today. The

---

57. The Thirty-Nine Articles can be readily found in texts and on the internet, for example: https://www.churchofengland.org/prayer-worship/worship/book-of-common-prayer/articles-of-religion.aspx.

Confession's rootedness in the affirmation of the sovereignty of God is the hallmark of the Reformed faith.

Chapter 2 of the *Confession*[58] affirms the doctrine of the Trinity.

> There is but one only, living, and true God, who is infinite in being and perfection, a most pure spirit, invisible, without body, parts, or passions; immutable, immense, eternal, incomprehensible, almighty, most wise, most holy, most free, most absolute; working all things according to the counsel of his own immutable and most righteous will, for his own glory . . . God hath all life, glory, goodness, blessedness, in and of himself; and is alone in and unto himself all-sufficient, not standing in need of any creatures which he hath made, nor deriving any glory from them, but only manifesting his own glory in, by, unto, and upon them. He is the alone fountain of all being, of whom, through whom, and to whom are all things; and hath most sovereign dominion over them . . .
>
> In the unity of the Godhead there be three persons, of one substance, power, and eternity; God the Father, God the Son, and God the Holy Ghost: the Father is of none, neither begotten, nor proceeding; the Son is eternally begotten of the Father; the Holy Ghost eternally proceeding from the Father and the Son.

The Westminster theologians clearly accepted the Niceno-Constantinopolitan creed and the *filioque* phrase which was part of the theological tradition of the Western church. The minutes of the debates in the Assembly have been preserved, which gives insight into what the participants thought as they formulated these doctrinal expressions. There is no record of any discord concerning the eternal relations of the three persons or the acceptance of the orthodox trinitarian settlement. The same doctrinal positions are clearly stated in the *Larger Catechism*, which was also a product of the Assembly. Elsewhere in the *Confession*, the trinitarian basis is explicit or implicit, with respect to the activities of God in revelation, election, creation and salvation.[59]

Were the Anabaptists Non-Trinitarians?

Misconception #17: That the Anabaptists were non-trinitarians.

Corrective: Whilst some branches of the later Anabaptist movement became Unitarian, the majority of early Anabaptists upheld the doctrine of the Trinity.

Many Christadelphians consider the Anabaptists as their forebears. The seminal work which promoted this idea was Alan Eyre's *The Protesters*, published in 1975. It must be acknowledged that this is one of the most scholarly works produced by a Christadelphian author, and contains the evidence of much careful historical research. Nevertheless, his thesis that there has been a consistent doctrinal consensus leapfrogging

---

58. The *Westminster Confession* is found in many texts and can be readily downloaded from the internet. For example, http://www.pcaac.org/resources/wcf/.

59. A comprehensive discussion of trinitarian theology within the *Westminster Confession* can be found in Letham, *The Westminster Assembly*, 164–73.

from group to group since the sixteenth century that now finds its culmination in the Christadelphian faith, "the torch carried through the centuries," is tenuous. A number of the persons and groups he discusses in the intervening period were Unitarian. The other concern with this work is the implication, whether intended or not, that the Anabaptists rather uniformly held to all or most of the central tenets of the Christadelphian faith, their common objective and achievement being to "preserve or revive the original Christianity of apostolic times."[60] Eyre may not say it himself in so many words, but the implication is there and that is certainly the understanding of many Christadelphians.

> It is necessary first of all to discover what it was that these people [i.e., the Anabaptists] considered important to conserve or revive. Among the religious tenets and ethical principles of early Christianity—before Greek philosophical concepts gradually overlaid and superseded Jewish, especially Old Testament, modes of thought—none of particular importance for this study will now be mentioned briefly . . .

Eyre goes on to list the authority of the Scriptures, believers' baptism, the future reign of Christ on earth, the mortality of the soul, refutation of hell, repudiation of the Trinity, the ethic of love, the nature of the church and the Lord's supper. He does qualify what might be assumed from this list, that each became a key issue "at some time in the centuries and in the countries covered by this work." The preface to the book, however, contains statements which might encourage what has come to be a more general assumption within the Christadelphian community that the Anabaptists were "just like us."

> . . . those devout believers in God of former centuries, whose aim and attitude were the same [as us] . . . It is a matter of great encouragement to us, whose religious views are regarded as unorthodox by our contemporaries, to find that in a number of cases where major doctrines are concerned, these early believers had come to the same conclusions as ourselves. And how should it be otherwise, for we have sought to do what they did—go back to the Scriptures alone in our search for truth.[61]

It's quite remarkable that this author doesn't recognize that the Reformation as a whole was characterized by a return to *sola Scriptura*. There is no doubt that the Anabaptist convictions regarding baptism and the nature of the church were essentially the same as those of modern day Christadelphians and those mainstream Christian groups who practice believers' baptism and view the church as a gathered community of such believers—but were they anti-trinitarian as well?

The Anabaptist movement originated in Switzerland in the sixteenth century, from within the Swiss Reformation, and needs to be understood in that context. They were one wing of the so-called Radical Reformation, which also included the

---

60. Eyre, *Protesters*, 11, 177.

61. FTP, presumably Fred Pearce, in Eyre, *Protesters*, preface.

Spiritualists and the Evangelical Rationalists. The European Protestant movement as manifested in the state churches of the emerging nations is known as the magisterial reformation, because the churches were state-based and nationalistic in flavor. If one was born in Calvin's Geneva, or Zwingli's Zurich, one was automatically a member of that state church and was baptized as an infant into that church covenant community. It is important to realize that this did not equate to or replace the individual's profession of faith upon attaining an age of responsibility, but it did make the child a member of the covenant community. The various magisterial reformers understood baptism somewhat differently, with Calvin most clearly articulating the idea of the covenant relationship, akin to circumcision in the Israelite community.[62] Nevertheless, what the magisterial reformers had in common was the idea of church membership equating with nationalistic loyalty. There was a pragmatism in this, whether one agrees with the theology or not; only as a state church could a Protestant movement withstand the political and military pressures imposed by the Papacy through the Catholic states which surrounded and threatened the fledgling churches. The Protestant churches relied in these early days on the support of the princes of the cantons and provinces and this meant having a reciprocal loyalty. It was seen as a matter of life and death—rightly or wrongly.

Against this background, we have the Radical Reformation. The Spiritualists held that the influence of the Holy Spirit was the ultimate source of divine authority, the Evangelical Rationalists held it to be human reason, and gave rise to the Unitarian movement, while the Anabaptists stuck with the authority of Scripture.[63] All three held that being a Christian was not a matter of being first a member of a community by birth, but a matter of making an individual decision for Christ. The church then was a gathered community of such disparate believers, with no particular political or national affinity. Seen in this light, it might be appreciated why the Anabaptists were persecuted by the magisterial reformers. The dispute was not entirely about whether adults or infants should be baptized, and certainly not much about the *mode* of baptism, but about *what constituted the church*. The Anabaptists were considered to pose a threat to the stability of society and the very survival of the Protestant states. Between and within the various groups of Radical Reformers was a great diversity of beliefs. Some Anabaptists such as Louis Haetzer and Adam Pastor were anti-trinitarian,[64] but most of the early ones were not, particularly the sixteenth-century Anabaptists discussed in Eyre's *The Protesters*.

So it is incorrect to view the Anabaptists as a group of proto-Christadelphians, uniform and revolutionary in a wide spectrum of beliefs. In fact, the Anabaptists were not really a single movement at all. Their theology was quite diverse and some held

---

62. Calvin, *Institutes*, IV.XVI.3–6.

63. Williams, *Spiritual and Anabaptist Writers*, 20–22.

64. Ibid., 20.

extreme views such as Unitarianism. What the various Anabaptist groups held in common,[65] over against the state Protestant churches, was:

- The church is a voluntary fellowship of believers, not a state institution into which one is born.

- Baptism is made upon confession of faith and marks one's separation from the world and commitment to Christian discipleship.

- Separation from the world and non-resistance.

- A soteriological emphasis on regeneration and newness of life rather than justification, underpinned by an acceptance of the freedom of the will.

- Reliance on the Holy Spirit's empowerment.

If we want to learn about early Lutheran theology, it's pretty easy; we can look at the writings of Martin Luther, his successor Phillip Melanchthon, and the early Lutheran confessions and catechisms. Similarly, if we want to know about Calvinism, we can read Calvin's *Institutes* and some of his other writings. In contrast, the Anabaptists did not produce any one theologian who commanded unanimous support. They tended to die young, and they didn't publish detailed theological treatises. They tended to steer away from creeds, and even confessions of faith, preferring to rest on the authority of Scripture alone. Those confessions which are extant are of individuals or small groups and not necessarily representative of the broader movement. Nevertheless, collectively there is a reasonable amount of material which can be studied to form an appreciation of the breadth of Anabaptist theology.

The Anabaptists were certainly regarded as heretics by their contemporaries, but not because of their doctrine of God. They accepted the Apostle's creed, the Trinity, incarnation, atoning work of Christ, and authority of the Scriptures just as the magisterial reformers did and contemporary mainstream Christians do (except for the later Unitarian spin-offs of the movement). The Anabaptists wrote very little about these topics, almost certainly because they had no disagreement with other Protestants. The Brethren subscribed to the historic creeds of the church and evidently considered themselves to be in the mainstream of Christian faith. Conrad Grebel, Balthasar Hubmaier, and Pilgram Marpeck, for example, all refer to trinitarian concepts and/or the creeds.[66]

> I believe also in Jesus Christ, thine only begotten Son, our Lord, that he for my sake has expiated before thee for this fall . . . I hope and trust him wholly that he will not let his saving and comforting name Jesus (for I believe he is Christ, true God and man) be lost on me, a miserable sinner, but that he will redeem me from all my sins.
>
> I believe also in the Holy Spirit, who proceedeth from the Father and the Son, and yet with them is the only and true God, who sanctifieth all things, and

65. Loewen, "Anabaptist Theology," 18–19.

66. Estep, *The Anabaptist Story*, 131–32.

without him is nothing holy, in whom I set all my trust that he will teach me all truth, increase my faith and kindle the fire of love in my heart by his holy inspiration . . . For that I pray thee from the heart, my God, my Lord, my Comforter.[67]

Here, Christian reader, you see clearly these three separate and distinct substances: soul, spirit and body, in every man, made and united after the image of the Holy Trinity.[68]

We believe that there is one God and one divine Essence, but in the same divine Essence three independent (separate) Persons, the Father, the Son and the Holy Spirit; that all three are one God and that each Person possesses in Himself, undivided, the fullness of the divine essence, which is also common to all three. It is our Christian faith that there are not three Gods, but only one God in three Persons and that each Holy Person in the Godhead, the Son as well as the Father, and the Holy Spirit as well as the Son, is God in essence, of like power, might, honor, glory and splendor.[69]

God, we believe and confess with the Scriptures to be the eternal, incomprehensible Father with His eternal, incomprehensible Son, and with His eternal, incomprehensible Holy Spirit . . . we also believe and confess the eternal, begetting heavenly Father and the eternally begotten Son, Christ Jesus.[70]

Whilst Eyre is certainly right in deploring the brutal and un-Christian manner in which the Catholic and Protestant churches alike treated the "radical reformers," their quiet, godly submission in the face of their powerful opponents' unconscionable behavior is nevertheless not the arbiter of doctrinal integrity. It is no more conclusive for Christadelphians to attempt to support their doctrines or bolster their confidence in their unique appreciation of "the Truth" by appealing to the Anabaptists, than it would be for mainstream Christians to attempt to "prove" the Trinity based on the work of the church fathers who were brutally persecuted by the Romans. Christadelphians need to be cautious as to which of the Anabaptists and their successors they cite as their theological predecessors, as a number of them are also claimed by the Unitarians as their founding fathers.

From the sixteenth through the eighteenth century the rise of "biblical" anti-trinitarianism can be traced. Servetus was an isolated example of an anti-trinitarian and his view of God, which was significantly different from both mainstream and Christadelphian positions, attracted few followers. In contrast, Faustus Socinus left a more influential legacy and Socinian teachings are the closest to primordial Christadelphianism that can be identified. John Biddle (1615 to 1652) has been called the "father of English Unitarianism." He taught an adoptionist view of the human person

---

67. Balthasar Hubmaier, "The Twelve Articles of Christian Belief," articles 2 and 8, cited in Estep, *The Anabaptist Story*, 135.

68. Balthasar Hubmaier, "On Free Will," in Williams, *Spiritual and Anabaptist Writers*, 117.

69. Pilgram Marpeck, cited in Estep, *Anabaptist Story*, 136.

70. Menno Simons, "A Solemn Confession of the Triune, Eternal, and True God, Father, Son and Holy Ghost," cited in Estep, *Anabaptist Story*, 137–38.

Jesus Christ. His arguments against the orthodox understanding of the Trinity are based on a redefinition of the terminology used by the fathers, which he then attacks. Effectively, he changes the meaning of their words, then refutes them. This is hardly playing fair, and shows the danger of attacking the vocabulary used rather than the underlying concepts.

The eighteenth century saw the philosophers of the Enlightenment or "Age of Reason" enter the fray. This period's worldview was dominated by a rejection of scriptural and ecclesiastical authority in subservience to human reason. Voltaire and others decried the doctrine of the Trinity and other scriptural teachings as being irrational, because they could not be derived "from reason." This provided the platform for later liberal theologizing which questioned the authority, divine origin and historical reliability of Scripture and discarded elements of the miraculous, the influence of which persists today.

> Rational anti-Trinitarianism begins with, and rapidly simply assumes, the claim that the received Trinitarian doctrine is incoherent; it further claims that there is a natural theology that teaches monotheism; and that this natural theology is what is important in matters of belief . . . it turns largely on the acceptance of a redefinition of terms: if "person" (in particular, but also "essence," "substance," etc.) is assumed to mean something radically different from what the Fathers meant by hypostasis, then the Trinitarian arguments of the Fathers will appear incoherent . . . but does not constitute a logical demonstration that classical Trinitarianism is false [71]

Unfortunately Christadelphians, in the grand tradition of rationalism dominant in the nineteenth century, are prone to such misinterpretations and redefinitions of terms, thus moving the goal posts whenever the Trinity is discussed. The first and final appeal must be to Scripture, as the Anabaptists would certainly concur.

The respected prayer of the nineteenth-century Christadelphian pioneer John Thomas, in which he vowed to find out "the truth of the matter" with respect to biblical teaching, does not of itself prove that he *found* that truth. Doubtless thousands of earnest and genuine truth seekers through the ages have prayed essentially that same prayer for insight into truth, with somewhat different results from John Thomas in most cases. Whether they—or he—are right or wrong is ultimately not a question of sincerity, behavior, manner of life, numerical support or who else may be in agreement.

The Christadelphian claim that the truth of the Bible can be discovered by independent, rational analysis without the need for church authority or additional input from the Holy Spirit has ironically resulted in a dogmatism within the movement whereby any "independent thought" that does not actually arrive at the same conclusions as the *Statement of the Faith*, in contrast to the *Doctrines to be Rejected*, is itself rejected.

---

71. Holmes, *Quest for the Trinity*, 180.

The interpretation of the Bible is integral to Christadelphian claims because the position they have adopted comes from one central claim by John Thomas. That is that everyone else had failed to correctly understand the Bible on its central teachings and that salvation was dependent upon that being correctly done. He claimed this occurred because of the lack of independence of thought and searching of the Scripture and claimed God never reveals himself in another way, such as helping through the Holy Spirit . . .

The big claim is that the Christadelphians do not read their interpretations into Scripture, unlike the majority of churches which do. They will point out that John Thomas never claimed any special knowledge or guidance from God (he was antagonistic to such beliefs), but instead promoted the way to saving truth as being the independent examination of scripture. His initial claims were that creeds and church authority were suppressive and antagonistic to that. Today the community holds a dual position of promoting the independent examination of Scripture whilst dogmatically opposing all who never reach the same conclusions, and maintaining that position through a creedal system.[72]

The Christadelphian position, markedly different in so many respects from mainstream Christian theology, rests on an assumption that they must have a superior intellectual grasp of the Bible in its entirety and its detail, which is defended by a "verse-against-verse" hermeneutic. Conversion becomes an intellectual exercise and dissent a cause for withdrawal of "fellowship." The very diversity of beliefs of those upon whose shoulders Christadelphians claim to stand, and those Christians through the ages who have wrestled with Scripture to elucidate its meaning, testifies to the shaky ground on which their exclusive claim to "the Truth" stands.

Summary

- The deity of Christ, and to a lesser extent the Spirit, figures clearly in the earliest extant writings of the church, the Apostolic Fathers, showing a continuity of belief from New Testament times.

- Second-century church writings mainly reflect the agendas of defense of the faith to outsiders and refutation of the heresies of the day (Gnosticism, Docetism, Judaizing) and the pressure to conform to the imperial cult. Nevertheless, the foundations of trinitarian thought were present.

- In the third and fourth centuries, Greek (Eastern) and Latin (Western) theological emphases developed, examining the concepts of three-ness and oneness in the Godhead from different perspectives. The different languages and thought-worlds sometimes led to misunderstandings, reinforcing the need to clearly articulate doctrine.

72. *Christadelphian Research*, http://www.christadelphianresearch.com/foundationalclaims.htm. Some interesting discussion on the Christadelphian hermeneutic and approach to the Bible through "independent" thought, and their perspective on John Thomas' "rediscovery of authentic Christianity," may be found on this website.

- The Arian controversy in the early fourth century provided the impetus to clarify the church's understanding of the divinity of the Son and his relationship to the Father. The Nicene Creed was written to explain the orthodox understanding as against Arianism.

- The Cappadocian fathers explored and explained the doctrine of the deity of the Spirit and the concept of three persons in one substance as accounting for the scriptural testimony about God. The result of these further reflections was the Niceno-Constantinopolitan creed.

- The christological controversies of the fourth and fifth centuries concerned the church's understanding of how divinity and humanity were combined in Christ, and reflected the different perspectives of the Antiochene and Alexandrine schools. The final consensus was expressed in the Chalcedonian definition.

- The sixteenth-century Protestant reformation was characterized by an appeal to Scripture as the basis for doctrine and practice, and whilst many Roman Catholic doctrines were repudiated on this basis, the Trinity was accepted as being scriptural and predating the Roman apostasy. The Trinity features in each of the Protestant creeds and confessions.

- Christadelphians claim the Anabaptists as their theological and ecclesiastical forerunners, and tend to imply that the Anabaptists were non-trinitarians, however this was not generally the case. An offshoot of the radical reformation became the Unitarian movement, which has influenced Christadelphian teaching.

Further Reading

- J. N. D. Kelly, *Early Christian Doctrines*. A very thorough, scholarly treatise with extensive quotes from primary sources. A serious read; not for the fainthearted!

- Donald K. McKim, *Theological Turning Points: Major Issues in Christian Thought*. A very readable discussion of the development of Christian doctrinal understanding through the history of the church.

- Alan Eyre, *The Protesters*.

- William R. Estep, *The Anabaptist Story*.

- Gerald Bray, *Creeds, Councils and Christ*. This is a detailed but readable book which addresses the question, "Did the Early Christians Misrepresent Jesus?" Bray is a leading authority on the history of trinitarian thought and engages with the thinking of the philosophers, apologists, polemicists, and theologians that contributed to the developing Christian understanding of the Godhead. A serious read, but well worth the effort.

- Stephen R. Holmes *The Quest for the Trinity: The Doctrine of God in Scripture, History and Modernity*. This is another serious read, but also worth the effort.

10

Atonement and Salvation

THE GREAT MESSAGE OF the Christian gospel is that the God of the universe has not abandoned his creation, but has intervened personally and intimately to secure our salvation. The all-sufficient God, who is One and who is also in a real sense a Community, has effected our adoption so that his children may be one with him (John 17:20–23). The implications of our understanding of the Godhead are profound; it is not merely an intellectual exercise. The right apprehension of the truth about God, affects, informs, and empowers our lives.

> And this is eternal life, that they know you the only true God, and Jesus Christ whom you have sent (John 17:3).

John tells us that God so loved the world that he gave his one and only Son, that whoever believes him should not perish but have this eternal life; this life of God which is intrinsically his and which he, in his love, imparts to us (John 1:4; 3:16). Our response is worship, and true worshipers must worship in spirit and in truth (John 4:23). Ultimately, we will join with all creation to bow at the Name, the name of Jesus, to the glory of God the Father (Phil 2:10–11).

Misconception #18: That Christ died merely as a representative of humanity, not a substitute.

Corrective: The subsitutionary aspect of the atonement is central and integral to the understanding of Christ as God our Savior.

Misconception #19: That justification by faith still requires a life of obedience and that we cannot have complete assurance of salvation prior to judgment.

Corrective: Justification by faith precludes any works-based contribution to salvation on our part; salvation is wholly of God and therein lies the Christian's assurance. Good works are to be the grateful Christian's response to salvation.

In this final chapter we will explore some of the implications of the understanding of the triune nature of God, and his most profound and tangible expression as the incarnate Word. In particular we will see that:

- The work of Father, Son, and Holy Spirit is continuous and unified in creation, through salvation history and to the final consummation.

- Father, Son, and Holy Spirit work together to effect salvation.

- The saving work of Jesus is rooted in his divinity and his humanity.

- An understanding of this salvation gives the Christian absolute assurance.

The Unified Work of God

One of the foundational principles of the Christian understanding of the Godhead is that Father, Son, and Holy Spirit work together in *all* aspects of God's interaction with his creation. This was true of creation, and it is true throughout salvation history and the wondrous work wrought on the cross. Because the work of salvation is entirely of God (not of us) it is *absolutely dependable*.

Christadelphians seem to waver on this point of assurance. Because they view Jesus Christ as merely human, his being sinless is problematic, unless a special divine input is acknowledged. This comes from God being his Father, although as we have seen, the exact nature of this influence is difficult to pin down. They deny any form of coercion or inevitability in Christ being able to live a sinless life and complete his saving work, which seems to imply there was at least a chance that Christ would fail.[1] That hardly seems reassuring, nor consistent with the water-tight promises in the Old Testament that God would provide a Savior and that his work would succeed (Gen 3:15; Isa 53:11; 59:16; Heb 6:17–19). On the one hand, amazement is expressed that a mere human could do this,[2] yet on the other, a divine influence sufficient to overcome sin at every phase of his life must be acknowledged.[3]

Why is this any more difficult a concept than Christ having both fully human and fully divine natures? One cannot have it both ways, Christ being exactly like us, and yet not quite like us; the promises of a sovereign God guaranteed, and yet subject to a degree of uncertainty because Christ in his humanity might not have quite pulled it off.

---

1. Morgan, *Understand the Bible*, 109, 111.

2. Benson, "Monotheism and the Atonement," 267, admits "Understanding the humanity of Christ inspires wonder at the greatness of his victory. That one like us, subject to the same temptations and trials of life, should *never* sin is awe-inspiring."

3. Robert Roberts allows, "How then . . . was he, with sinful flesh, to be sinless? God's relation to the matter is the answer. God did it. The weak flesh could not do it." And, "Surely he was made superior to man in some respects: Unquestionably. He was not a mere man—not a mere Jew—not mere flesh. He was the flesh of Abraham in a special form" (Roberts, *The Blood of Christ*, 19, 21). Also, "His perfect obedience (possible only because he was God's only begotten Son)" affirms Michael Ashton, *Studies in the Statement of Faith*, 42.

We must agree with Christadelphian Richard Benson that "How we understand the relationship between Father and Son influences how we understand God's plan of salvation."[4] But beyond this we part company, for in having an inadequate understanding of the person of Christ, Christadelphians have an inadequate understanding of the atonement, and as a consequence, an admitted lack of personal assurance of salvation.

Salvation As a Recovery and Completion of Creation

The Bible in one respect is a lopsided book; it takes two chapters to describe creation, half a chapter to describe mankind's rebellion, and the remainder of its sixty-six books tell what God did about that. Even before the end of chapter 3 of Genesis we have the beginning of the unfolding of God's solution, the *inevitable* defeat of the serpent's seed by the seed of the woman (Gen 3:15). But God's solution didn't begin even here; in his total foreknowledge and plan the solution preceded the problem. In the eternal counsels of the Godhead the path was mapped out for the Lamb "slain from the creation of the world" (Rev 13:8).

In an earlier chapter we saw that Father, Son, and Holy Spirit were each involved in creation. With profound simplicity the opening words of Genesis state, "In the beginning God created the heavens and the earth . . ." We saw also that the Spirit of God was hovering over the waters and that numerous passages testify to the agency of the Spirit in creation (eg., Job 33:4; Ps 104:30). The Son was also active in creation, and with the Father in the beginning (John 1:1–3; Col 1:16; Heb 1:10). When sin entered the world and fractured the relationship between God and his creation, the results extended beyond the immediate effects on the sinners themselves. The created order itself became subject to the effects of corruption.

> For the creation waits with eager longing for the revealing of the sons of God. For the creation was subjected to futility, not willingly, but because of him who subjected it, in hope that the creation itself will be set free from its bondage to corruption and obtain the freedom of the glory of the children of God. For we know that the whole creation has been groaning together in the pains of childbirth until now (Rom 8:19–22).

What Christ achieved on the cross was not only the redemption of humankind but of all creation. In the consummation of all things, there will be a renewal of heavens and earth; the One seated on the throne will make everything new (Rev 21:1, 5). The effects of this renewal will touch every aspect of life on earth (Isa 11:6–9; 35:1–10; Rev 22:1–5). Christ is the firstborn, the titled heir over all creation and those in Christ are a new creation (2 Cor 5:17). In order to save and renew his creation and make it into the God-glorifying entity it was intended to be, God himself intervened within that very creation.

4. Benson, "Monotheism and the Atonement," 257.

> He is the image of the invisible God, the firstborn of *all creation*. For by him *all things* were created, in heaven and on earth, visible and invisible, whether thrones or dominions or rulers or authorities—*all things* were created through him and for him. And he is before *all things*, and in him *all things* hold together. And he is the head of the body, the church. He is the beginning, the firstborn from the dead, that in *everything* he might be preeminent. For in him *all* the fullness of God was pleased to dwell, and through him to reconcile to himself *all things*, whether on earth or in heaven, making peace by the blood of his cross (Col 1:15–20).

God entered the world in the person of his Son, the image of God, the very fullness of God dwelling in flesh, Creator and created, "God with us," in order to reconcile all things in heaven and earth to himself. On one level, this is astounding, almost unbelievable, that the High and Holy One did not look upon the sinfulness of mankind and the tragedy that had befallen his creation and simply press "delete."

"You who are of purer eyes than to see evil and cannot look at wrong," observed Habakkuk (1:13) and the Psalmist says "For you are not a God who delights in wickedness; evil may not dwell with you" (Ps 5:4). Instead, he pressed "save;" God so loved the world, that "while we were still sinners, Christ died for us" (Rom 5:8). We can rightly marvel that God should treat his undeserving creation this way, and yet on another level, we should expect no less from him. God created man in his image, to glorify him, and all creation is made for the glory of God. This purpose of God will not be thwarted, for all the earth *will* be filled with the glory of the Lord (Num 14:21). Even now, God receives glory from his creation, and from his work upon earth and he will not yield this glory to another (Ps 8:1–9; 29:1–11; Isa 48:11). God's name is also glorified in his saving acts, as he shows mercy and forgiveness to his undeserving creatures (Ps 79:9, 97:6; Rom 9:22–23).

Athanasius (c. AD 296 to 373) wrote at length about how fitting it was that the Creator redeemed his creation by entering into it.

> You must understand why it is that the Word of the Father, so great and so high, has been made manifest in bodily form . . . He has been manifested in a human body for this reason only, out of the love and goodness of His Father, for the salvation of us men . . . The first fact that you must grasp is this: the renewal of creation has been wrought by the self-same Word who made it in the beginning. There is thus no inconsistency between creation and salvation for the One Father has employed the same Agent for both works, effecting the salvation of the world through the same Word who made it in the beginning . . .
>
> What, then, was God to do? What else could He possibly do, being God, but renew His Image in mankind, so that through it men might once more come to know Him? And how could this be done save by the coming of the very Image Himself, our savior Jesus Christ?[5]

The Apostle Paul expresses it this way in 2 Corinthians 5:19, "In Christ God was reconciling the world to himself, not counting their trespasses against them, and

5. Athanasius, *On the Incarnation*, 2, 12.

entrusting to us the message of reconciliation." Another possible way of rendering this verse is "that God was in Christ, reconciling the world unto himself" (KJV). Either way, the reconciliation between God and mankind took place at God's own initiative, in the person of his Son.

The Centrality of Christ

In the work of creation and in the renewal and redemption of that creation, Christ is central. All things were created by him and for him (Col 1:16) and he is the agent and heir of God's work (1 Cor 8:6; Heb 1:2). The writer to the Hebrews expounds the absolute superiority of the Son, superior to the angels and to the types in the law, worthy of worship and addressed as God and Lord. John, in the context of the discussion of all that the Son has authority to do, relates the words of Jesus, instructing "that all may honor the Son, just as they honor the Father. Whoever does not honor the Son does not honor the Father who sent him" (John 5:23).

Paul, writing to the Ephesians, presents Christ as the conduit for "every spiritual blessing." God chose us *in him* and predestined us to adoption *though him. Through him* we have grace and redemption; *in him* we were chosen. The mystery of God's will, which he purposed *in Christ*, is to bring all things in heaven and on earth together under one head, even Christ (Eph 1:3–12). To glorify Christ is to glorify God (Phil 2:9–11; John 8:54; 11:4; 13:31–32; 14:13; 17:1; Rom 16:27; 2 Cor 4:4; and compare Phil 4:20; 1 Pet 4:11; 2 Pet 3:18; Rev 4:11; 5:13).

If Christ were not God, we would have much contradiction here. The Father glorifying the Son, the Son glorifying the Father, the Holy Spirit bringing glory to both; Christ addressed as Lord and God, the centrality of Christ in every aspect of God's plan, the worthiness of Christ to be worshiped; how could that possibly sit with a God who *will not share his glory with another*, who proclaims that *he alone* is God? It brings us around to the inescapable hypothesis that there is one God, and yet the Father, Son, and Holy Spirit are each divine, with all the attributes of divinity, part of the divine Identity. Yes, God is one, there is no other being in the universe who can be called "God"; this God-ness, or "substance"—divinity for want of a better word, is what the Father, Son, and Spirit have in common. And yet in the great unfolding drama of creation, redemption and renewal of creation we see three distinct but related roles, or *personae*. God's actions with and within his creation reflect the working together of the three persons in relationship. As previously discussed, theologians speak of this in terms of the "economic Trinity" (the way God works in creation) reflecting the "immanent Trinity" (the way God is in his very being).

In our poor human reflection of relationships we struggle with the concept of an eternal, loving, and mutually glorifying relationship within the Godhead. In human terms, if a father, demanding reparation for the loss of his honor, were to require his son to bear the consequences, to carry the penalty for that, it would seem unjust and as some feminist critiques have recently expressed it, a form of "child abuse." But nothing could be further from the truth. Rather than an overbearing father forcing or coercing his son, we see a mutuality, an eternal relationship of love and reciprocal glorification, which generated an eternal plan to create and to redeem. The Son was sent by the Father, yes, but he went freely; God himself provided the Lamb, God himself entered creation to redeem it and God himself is glorified. The consequences of undervaluing Christ, then, are grievous.

The Work of Atonement

The Bible provides a number of metaphors and descriptors for the atoning work of Christ, what it was that he actually accomplished on the cross and how it effected our salvation. Some of these pictures are Old Testament types: the cutting of the covenant, redemption from slavery, the Levitical sacrifices, the scapegoat, the Day of Atonement, and the Passover. Others are expounded more fully in the New Testament; ransom, reconciliation, propitiation and justification. Two very helpful works on the subject of the Atonement are Leon Morris's *The Atonement* and John Stott's *The Cross of Christ.*[6] Both make the point that no single metaphor, analogy, or model comprehensively describes the atoning work of Christ, but taken together, a comprehensive picture can be formed.

Christ, Our Substitute

There are two aspects to Christ's saving work. Firstly, he led a perfect life of obedience to the requirements of God's laws, a sinless life; this is something we are totally incapable of doing. Even Adam, who was created in a "very good" state, failed miserably. Christ as the second Adam achieved what Adam—and we—could not, and hence by his obedience many are made righteous.

- For as by the one man's disobedience the many were made sinners, so by the one man's obedience the many will be made righteous (Rom 5:19).

- For as in Adam all die, so also in Christ shall all be made alive (1 Cor 15:22).

Secondly, Christ took on himself *our sins* and bore the penalty for them. He is the fulfilment of the types of the animal sacrifices under the law, as well as the scapegoat.

6. Morris, *The Atonement, Its Meaning and Significance* (1983) is a more recent revision and expansion of material from his highly regarded work, *The Apostolic Preaching of the Cross*. Chapter 7 of John Stott, *The Cross of Christ* (1986), is especially relevant to the present discussion.

He suffered and died for our sins, he bore the punishment, the chastisement, the penalty that was due us. This is seen clearly in the suffering servant prophecy of Isaiah:

> Surely he has borne our griefs and carried our sorrows . . . he was wounded for our transgressions; he was crushed for our iniquities; upon him was the chastisement that brought us peace, and with his stripes we are healed . . . the LORD has laid on him the iniquity of us all . . . stricken for the transgression of my people . . . when his soul makes an offering for guilt . . . the righteous one, my servant, (will) make many to be accounted righteous, and he shall bear their iniquities . . . he bore the sin of many, and makes intercession for the transgressors (Isa 53:4–12).

> He himself bore our sins in his body on the tree, so that we might die to sin and live to righteousness. By his wounds you have been healed (1 Pet 2:24).

The substitutionary nature of Christ's sin bearing is fully evident here. Unfortunately, Robert Roberts finds that "the idea that Christ has borne our punishment and paid our debts, and that his righteousness is placed to our credit, and that the only thing we have to do is to believe it, is demoralizing."[7] Christadelphians deny the substitutionary aspect of the atonement and see Christ merely as a representative of sinful humanity, his death an example of what sinful humanity deserves and his sinlessness an example to be emulated.[8] Although there are certainly aspects of Christ's atoning work in which he stands as the representative of humanity, as did Adam before him, representation alone does not go far enough. He *bore* our very sins, our iniquities were laid *on him* and he was pierced, crushed, punished and stricken *for us*.

In Genesis 22, a foundational Old Testament atonement passage, Isaac, a type of Christ, goes willingly beside his father to the place of sacrifice and is assured by Abraham that God himself will provide the lamb for the burnt offering. With profound insight the narrator continues; "So they went both of them together" (verse 8). In Abraham's eyes, Isaac was as good as dead, although he evidently trusted that somehow God would restore him (Heb 11:17–19). God calls Isaac "your son, your only son"—the Septuagint renders this "your beloved son"—and reiterates that on the very mountain which was to become the mount of crucifixion, "The Lord will Provide" (Gen 22:8–14). John the Baptist identified Jesus as "the Lamb of God, who takes away the sin of the world" (John 1:29). His Jewish audience would have been familiar with the sin offering and the offerings on the day of Atonement, but these were not necessarily lambs; they could be bulls or goats and they weren't provided (directly) by God, but brought by the person offering the sacrifice, or by the whole assembly of Israel. Yet here John speaks of the Lamb of God—God's provision for the sin of the world and

---

7. Roberts, *The Blood of Christ*, 23. Although this is a very old work, it has been consistently republished and is still seen as the definitive Christadelphian statement on the atonement.

8. Thomas, "Forgiveness of Sins," 42–45; Benson, "Monotheism and the Atonement," 45, 264, 265, 268. See also Roberts, *The Christadelphian Instructor*: "Concerning the Death of Christ" and "Concerning the Way of Salvation," available on line at http://www.thechristadelphians.org/btcd/BTCD/htm/ci/index.htm.

he is surely referring to Genesis 22 rather than Leviticus. The strong inference in this passage is that of Father and Son working together to effect the sacrifice; it was the Lord's provision and it was willingly undertaken.

Whilst Father, Son, and Spirit each played a role in the atonement, it is proper to think of atonement as the specific work of the Son. With the departure of the Son, his death, resurrection and ascension, the overt work of the Spirit began (John 14:16–18, 26; 15:26; 16:7–8, 13–15; Acts 1:4–5). There is other evidence of the cooperation and involvement of each member of the Godhead in the Son's atoning work. The Father sent and gave the Son (Matt 21:37; John 3:16–17; John 10:36; Rom 8:3, 32; Gal 4:4; 1 John 4:10, 14) and we should not underestimate the costliness of this. God's beloved Son, loved from eternity and perfect in obedience, given over to ungrateful and unworthy humanity to do with as they wished. God _so_ loved the world that he did this! The Holy Spirit was also present and involved in the atonement, supporting the Lord Jesus. Jesus was commissioned for his work by anointing with the Spirit and the Spirit drove him into the wilderness for the purpose of temptation, the overcoming of which was essential to his atoning work.

> How much more will the blood of Christ, who through the eternal Spirit offered himself without blemish to God, purify our conscience from dead works to serve the living God (Heb 9:14).

The Son was no ignorant or unwilling victim, coerced against his will; this is not the meaning of substitutionary atonement, despite what its critics imply.

- Then I said, "Behold, I have come to do your will, O God, as it is written of me in the scroll of the book" (Heb 10:7).

- Was it not necessary that the Christ should suffer these things and enter his glory? (Luke 24:26; The Greek grammatical construction anticipates an affirmative answer; yes, it was necessary).

- So Jesus said to Peter, "Put your sword into its sheath; shall I not drink the cup that the Father has given me?" (John 18:11).

- He was oppressed, and he was afflicted, yet he opened not his mouth; like a lamb that is led to the slaughter, and as a sheep that before its shearers is silent, so he opened not his mouth (Isa 53:7).

- For this reason the Father loves me, because I lay down my life that I may take it up again. No one takes it from me, but I lay it down of my own accord. I have authority to lay it down, and I have authority to take it up again. This charge I have received from my Father (John 10:17–18).

- For to this you have been called, because Christ also suffered for you, leaving you an example, so that you might follow in his steps. He committed no sin, neither was deceit found in his mouth. When he was reviled, he did not revile in return;

when he suffered, he did not threaten, but continued entrusting himself to him who judges justly (1 Pet 2:21–23).

If Jesus is not God, then substitutionary atonement becomes a parody of justice; "You deserve punishment, but I'll inflict it on someone else." But because Jesus *is* God, the atonement is not only God's initiative, but wholly his work; the Lord required and the Lord provided. As John Stott expresses it,

> All four images [of the atonement] emphasize that the saving initiative was taken by God in his love. It is he who has propitiated his own wrath, redeemed us from our miserable bondage, declared us righteous in his sight and reconciled us to himself . . . Substitution is not a "theory of the atonement." Nor is it even an additional image to take its place as an option alongside the others. It is rather the essence of each image and the heart of the atonement itself.[9]

The element of substitution in the atonement cannot be ignored; it is central to the various ways in which it is portrayed in Scripture. God the Father himself put our sins on Christ, and in doing so imputed our sins to him, just as Adam's sin had been imputed to us. In so bearing the sin of the world Christ took it away, far more effectively than the scapegoat ever did. Note the clear substitution element in the following verses.

- For our sake he made him to be sin who knew no sin, so that in him we might become the righteousness of God (2 Cor 5:21).

- Christ redeemed us from the curse of the law by becoming a curse for us—for it is written, "Cursed is everyone who is hanged on a tree" (Gal 3:13).

- So Christ having been offered once to bear the sins of many, will appear a second time, not to deal with sin but to save those who are eagerly waiting for him (Heb 9:28).

- All we like sheep have gone astray; we have turned—every one—to his own way; and the LORD has laid on him the iniquity of us all (Isa 53:6).

- He himself bore our sins in his body on the tree, that we might die to sin and live to righteousness. By his wounds you have been healed (1 Pet 2:24).

Propitiation and Reconciliation: The Effect of Christ's Work on God

The atoning work of Christ is not something that only affected sinners; first and foremost it affected God himself. This is not just because it was God who suffered in the person of Christ, and in the Father's giving his beloved Son, but because it brought about a profound change in God's relationship with his creation. Scripture

9. Stott, *Cross of Christ*, 235–36.

uses specific words to describe the effect of Christ's sin-bearing on God: *propitiation* and *reconciliation*.

The words propitiate and propitiation are not found in all English translations; sometimes they are rendered "expiation" or "atoning sacrifice." In the original Greek, they have to do with the appeasement of wrath;[10] *hilasmos* (propitiation) (1 John 2:2; 4:10) *hilastērion* (propitiating) (Rom 3:25) *hilaskomai* (to propitiate) (Heb 2:17; Luke 18:13). The ESV, KJV, and NAS use the English words based on "propitiate" to translate this word group.

- [Christ Jesus] whom God put forward as a propitiation by his blood, to be received by faith. This was to show God's righteousness, because in his divine forbearance he had passed over former sins (Rom 3:25).

- Therefore he had to be made like his brothers in every respect, so that he might become a merciful and faithful high priest in the service of God, to make propitiation for the sins of the people (Heb 2:17).

- He is the propitiation for our sins, and not for ours only but also for the sins of the whole world (1 John 2:2).

- In this is love, not that we have loved God but that he loved us and sent his Son to be the propitiation for our sins (1 John 4:10).

There are many verses which speak of the wrath of God directed at sin and sinners (for example, Jer 7:20; Ezek 7:8–9; John 3:36; Rom 1:18) and whilst we must not think of God's anger in the way we think of most human anger (as irrational, inconsistent, selfish rage), it is nevertheless an intrinsic part of the character of a holy and loving God to hate and to be wrathful toward the sin that mars his creation. God is love, and therefore he shows wrath toward sin and jealousy for his relationships. God is slow to anger and delights to show mercy (Mic 7:18; Ps 85:2–3; Exod 34:6) and the ultimate and final expression of this is in his propitiating our sins once and for all through the sacrifice of Christ. To reject this sacrifice means God's wrath remains on that person (John 3:36) because the wrath of God rests on unredeemed mankind (Rom 1:18; Eph 5:6).

What can mere humans do to appease the wrath of a holy God in his unremitting antagonism to sin? The answer is, contra to the attempts of pagans to placate the capricious wrath of their deities, *absolutely nothing*. There is no work, no intrinsic righteousness, no ransom that we can offer God; we deserve nothing but judgment and condemnation.

> But God shows his love for us in that while we were still sinners, Christ died for us (Rom 5:8).

---

10. Not all theologians have agreed with this interpretation, but the subject is effectively and convincingly addressed by Morris in *The Atonement*, 151–76.

God himself took the initiative; "not that we have loved God but that he loved us and sent his Son to be the propitiation for our sins" (1 John 4:10). God's love is the *cause*, not the *result* of the atonement, and this was so from eternity. In the words of John Stott,

> It is God himself who in holy wrath needs to be propitiated, God himself in holy love who undertook to do the propitiating and God himself in the person of his Son died for the propitiation of our sins. Thus God took his own loving initiative to appease his own righteous anger by bearing it in his own self in his own Son when he took our place and died for us. There is no crudity here to evoke our ridicule, only the profundity of holy love to evoke our worship.[11]

Only the sinless Son of God was qualified to bear our sins in our place and impart to us the gift of righteous standing before God. It wasn't that God needed a reason to love us, he always loved us (John 3:16; 1 John 4:10; Rom 5:6) but he needed a means of reconciliation. The relationship between God and humankind was broken and this required reconciliation. Reconciliation is the restoration of a broken relationship, in this case our relationship with God. The holy God could not look upon sin or sustain the intimate relationship he had with Adam and Eve once they fractured it by sinning. The Bible often uses the expression "peace with God" to describe this reconciliation which has restored the relationship. The related concept is that of adoption into God's family, a new and better relationship. Reconciliation is, once again, God's initiative and it was achieved through Christ.

> Since, therefore, we have now been justified by his blood, much more shall we be saved by him from the wrath of God. For if while we were enemies we were reconciled to God by the death of his Son, much more, now that we are reconciled, shall we be saved by his life. More than that, we also rejoice in God through our Lord Jesus Christ, through whom we have now received reconciliation (Rom 5:9–11).

Earlier in this passage, Paul spoke of reconciliation in this way:

> Therefore, since we have been justified by faith, we have peace with God through our Lord Jesus Christ. Through him we have also obtained access by faith into this grace in which we stand, and we rejoice in the hope of the glory of God (Rom 5:1–2).

Restoration of our relationship with God brings access to the Father through Jesus Christ by the Spirit. Once again we see the unified work of the Godhead. The Spirit is in this sense called the Spirit of adoption because he mediates this relationship established in the atoning work of Christ.

- For through him [Christ] we both have access in one Spirit to the Father (Eph 2:18).

- For you did not receive the spirit of slavery to fall back into fear, but you have

11. Stott, *Cross of Christ*, 175.

received the Spirit of adoption as sons, by whom we cry, "Abba! Father!" The Spirit himself bears witness with our spirit that we are children of God, and if children, then heirs—heirs of God and fellow heirs with Christ, provided we suffer with him in order that we may also be glorified with him (Rom 8:15–17).

- All this is from God, who through Christ reconciled us to himself and gave us the ministry of reconciliation: that is, in Christ God was reconciling the world to himself, not counting their trespasses against them, and entrusting to us the message of reconciliation (2 Cor 5:18–19).

This newly restored relationship gives us the status of children of God, fellow heirs with Christ and boldness to approach the Father through Christ.

- Let us then with confidence draw near to the throne of grace, that we may receive mercy and find grace to help in time of need (Heb 4:16).

- Therefore, brothers, since we have confidence to enter the holy places by the blood of Jesus, by the new and living way that he opened for us . . . let us draw near with a true heart in full assurance of faith (Heb 10:19–22).

- And because you are sons, God has sent the Spirit of his Son into our hearts, crying, "Abba! Father!" So you are no longer a slave, but a son, and if a son, then an heir through God (Gal 4:6–7).

There are two further aspects to the atoning work of Christ which describe its effect on us: *justification* and *redemption*.

Justification and Redemption: Effects of Christ's Work on Us

In the processes of justification and redemption we see two further images, and once again the initiative was taken by God and the work is all his. Romans 8:33–34 poses the rhetorical question, "Who shall bring any charge against God's elect? It is God who justifies. Who is to condemn?" The answer is, no one! In Luke 1:68, Zechariah joyfully proclaims, "Blessed be the Lord, the God of Israel, for he has visited and redeemed his people."

"Justification" is a term with strong legal connotations. It refers to the verdict of a judge in a law court and is the opposite of condemnation. "It is God who justifies—who is to condemn?" Justification and condemnation are juxtaposed as opposites.

Likewise in Romans 5:18: "Therefore, as one trespass led to condemnation for all men, so one act of righteousness leads to justification and life for all men."

Justification is the process by which God bestows on us a righteous standing in his eyes, imputing to us the righteousness of Jesus Christ. This can never be of our own doing, for our own righteousness is as a polluted garment (Isa 64:6; KJV has "filthy rags") and no one is truly righteous, that is, in right standing before God, in and of themselves (Romans 3:9–12). Righteousness is apprehended through faith in Jesus Christ and unequivocally comes from God.

> And be found in him, not having a righteousness of my own that comes from the law, but that which comes through faith in Christ, the righteousness from God that depends on faith (Phil 3:9).

> For in it [the gospel] the righteousness of God is revealed from faith for faith, as it is written: "The righteous shall live by faith" (Rom 1:17).

The words "Justification," "justify," and those related to them actually carry the same meaning as "righteous," "righteousness" and related words. They are all derivatives of the Greek root word *dikai*, as a scan through any concordance or Bible software program will readily reveal.[12]

dikaios—right, righteous, just

dikaioō—to make right, just; to render a favorable verdict, vindicate, to do justice

dikaiosynē—rightness, justice, fairness, righteousness, uprightness

Therefore it is evident that the declaration of righteousness is a "not guilty" verdict which is given to those who have faith in Christ.[13] Christ's own righteousness has been imputed to them and they stand uncondemned in God's sight. This remarkable act is a paradox, for the holy God has justified *the wicked*. Those who should be under his wrath and stand condemned have been declared to be in right standing with him.[14] This is possible because of the cleansing of our sin through the blood of Christ; the act of redemption and propitiation. This is wholly the work of God, in Christ, and we can do nothing to obtain it, except hold out our empty hands in faith.

> For what does the Scripture say? "Abraham believed God, and it was counted to him as righteousness." Now to the one who works, his wages are not counted as a gift but as his due. And to the one who does not work but believes in him who justifies the ungodly, his faith is counted as righteousness, just as David also speaks of the blessing of the one to whom God counts righteousness apart

12. Comprehensive definitions for the word group may be found in BDAG and show clearly the legal emphasis of these words.

13. Roberts, *The Blood of Christ*, 15, clearly does not understand the meaning of the *dikaios* word group when he dismisses the legal connotations of justification and claims that "The whole sacrificial institution and our endorsement of it in baptism is comparable to a form of apology presented by the Majesty of Heaven as the condition of our receiving His mercy."

14. As Luther helpfully put it, *Simul iustus et peccator*: "simultaneously justified and yet sinners."

from works: "Blessed are those whose lawless deeds are forgiven, and whose sins are covered; blessed is the man against whom the Lord will not count his sin" (Rom 4:3–8).

Without the propitiating sacrifice of Christ, God could not justify the wicked (declare righteous the unrighteous) without compromising his holiness. God's love and mercy toward humankind drove him to find a way of reconciliation, yet to simply dismiss or ignore sin would be unthinkable for a holy God. So, his own arm wrought salvation; by bearing our sin and the punishment for it, the Son propitiated the Father's wrath, enabling God to be both just *and* the one who justifies.

> But now the righteousness of God has been manifested apart from the law, although the Law and the Prophets bear witness to it—the righteousness of God through faith in Jesus Christ for all who believe. For there is no distinction: for all have sinned and fall short of the glory of God, and are justified by his grace as a gift, through the redemption that is in Christ Jesus, whom God put forward as a propitiation by his blood, to be received by faith. This was to show God's righteousness, because in his divine forbearance he had passed over former sins. It was to show his righteousness at the present time, so that he might be just and the justifier of the one who has faith in Jesus. Then what becomes of our boasting? It is excluded. By what kind of law? By a law of works? No, but by the law of faith. For we hold that one is justified by faith apart from works of the law (Rom 3:21–28).

Justification must not be confused with *sanctification*, which we will discuss shortly, and which is primarily the work of the Holy Spirit. When Roman Catholics speak of justification what they are really describing is a process of sanctification, becoming more like Christ, which is gradual and takes place throughout this life, only to be completed when we are glorified. Biblical justification, in contrast, is an instantaneous and complete declaration of righteousness bestowed on the sinner who comes to Christ in faith. It is our assurance of acceptance on the day of judgment for there is *now* no condemnation for those in Christ Jesus, in whom the righteous requirements of the law have been fully met by the condemnation of sin in the sacrifice of Christ (Rom 8:1–4).

As a consequence of the atonement made by Christ, sinners are redeemed, bought back from slavery to sin. The Greek words for "ransom" and "redeem" (*lutron, lutrōsis, apolutrōsis*) relate unequivocally to purchase out of slavery. Other words used relate to purchase. This image connotes the costliness of our salvation, for the price paid was no less than the blood of the Son of God.

- Pay careful attention to yourselves and to all the flock, of which the Holy Spirit has made you overseers, to care for the church of God, which he obtained[15] with his own blood (Acts 20:28).

- For you were bought[16] at a price. So glorify God in your body (1 Cor 6:20).

15. The Greek verb is *peripoieomai*, to preserve, acquire or obtain.
16. The Greek word is *agorazō*, to buy.

- Knowing that you were ransomed[17] from the futile ways inherited from your forefathers, not with perishable things such as silver or gold, but with the precious blood of Christ, like that of a lamb without blemish or spot (1 Pet 1:18–19).

- And they sang a new song, saying, "Worthy are you to take the scroll and to open its seals, for you were slain, and by your blood you ransomed[18] people for God from every tribe and language and people and nation" (Rev 5:9).

The image of redemption was used to describe God's deliverance of his people from Egypt, a costly expenditure of divine power. The Law of Moses prescribed the payment of ransoms for the redemption of slaves, animals and property. Jesus stated clearly that his life was to be a ransom (*lutron*) for many (Mark 10:45). Consequently, his sacrifice has freed us from sin and death (Rom 5:18).[19] In the Greek world, a slave could be set free by payment of a sum at the shrine of a god, effectively purchasing them for that deity, never to be enslaved again. The expression used was payment "for freedom," and this familiar term was used by Paul to speak of the liberation achieved by Christ (Gal 5:1).

The New Testament emphasis is on the *price* paid for our redemption; but the analogy is not to be pushed to the point of considering *to whom* the price was paid. One historical view of the atonement, known ambiguously as the "ransom theory," speculated that Christ paid a ransom price to Satan, who held sinners captive. Christadelphians sometimes seem to confuse this theory with the scriptural doctrine of the atonement discussed above. We have seen that humans are captive to sin, not to Satan, and that God himself is the one who required propitiation and payment. The transaction is one conducted in the eternal counsel and purposes of God and as has been repeatedly stressed, is all of him (2 Cor 5:21; Isa 53:6, 10).

As a result of our purchase by the precious blood of Christ, we are no longer our own, to act as we please. In 1 Corinthians 6:19–20 Paul explains that the purchased believer is indwelt by the Holy Spirit, received from God. Because we were bought at a great price, we are to honor God with our bodies. Created by God, one day to be resurrected to glory by God, purchased by God and indwelt by God, as Stott puts it, we belong to God "three times over, by creation, redemption and indwelling." We are, in the words of Paul, crucified with Christ, dead to sin and alive to God in Christ Jesus, and sin has no more dominion over us (Rom 6:11; Gal 2:20).

17. The Greek verb is *lutroomai*, to redeem.

18. The Greek is *agorazō*, to buy.

19. In contrast, Roberts, *The Blood of Christ*, 23, is adamant that "no debt of ours has been paid or can be paid . . . what the death of Christ has done has been to declare God's righteousness" and "this passing by of our sins is the act of his forbearance." In other words, Christ has not paid the price for our sins, there is no "redemption" and God will merely overlook our sin if we admit he is righteous.

Regeneration and Sanctification: More Effects of Christ's Work on Us

We have seen that justification is received by faith and that it is a gift of God, a gracious act of which we are totally undeserving. Along with this declaration of right standing before God comes a real change in the believer, an ability to apprehend spiritual things and to partake of spiritual life. This is regeneration, or as the Bible sometimes describes it, the new birth. As with all processes involved in the salvation of sinners, it is wholly a work of God; Father, Son, and Holy Spirit.

- But to all who did receive him, who believed in his name, he gave the right to become children of God, who were born, not of blood nor of the will of the flesh nor of the will of man, but of God (John 1:12–13).

- Jesus answered him, "Truly, truly, I say to you, unless one is born again he cannot see the kingdom of God." Nicodemus said to him, "How can a man be born when he is old? Can he enter a second time into his mother's womb and be born?" Jesus answered, "Truly, truly, I say to you, unless one is born of water and the Spirit, he cannot enter the kingdom of God. That which is born of the flesh is flesh, and that which is born of the Spirit is spirit. Do not marvel that I said to you, 'You must be born again'" (John 3:3–7).

- Of his own will he brought us forth, by the word of truth, that we should be a kind of firstfruits of his creatures (Jas 1:18).

- Blessed be the God and Father of our Lord Jesus Christ! According to his great mercy, he has caused us to be born again to a living hope through the resurrection of Jesus Christ from the dead (1 Pet 1:3).

- But God, being rich in mercy, because of the great love with which he loved us, even when we were dead in our trespasses, made us alive together with Christ— by grace you have been saved (Eph 2:4–5).

- And you, who were dead in your trespasses and the uncircumcision of your flesh, God made alive together with him, having forgiven all our trespasses (Col 2:13).

- Since you have been born again, not of perishable seed but of imperishable, through the living and enduring word of God (1 Pet 1:23).

Christadelphians struggle with an active work of the Holy Spirit in the life of the believer, apart from the effect of reading the Bible on our minds. Hence they also struggle with the concept of being "born again," and avoid much reference to it. Typically, they equate the new birth with the act of baptism, which is seen as the actual point of receiving forgiveness and becoming Christ's.[20] Whilst not denigrating the importance

20. "A believing, repentant person receives forgiveness of sins by being baptized . . . The incorruptible seed of the Word of God . . . brings forth the new man through baptism by bringing the believer into Christ . . . Our former fleshly birth . . . is superseded by this new spiritual birth by which

of baptism, it is interesting that the scriptural verses which speak of new birth do not specifically mention baptism. Jesus tells Nicodemus that the new birth is a work of the Spirit, not of flesh/water like a natural birth, and marvels that he, a teacher of Israel, doesn't understand this.[21]

The Father and the Holy Spirit are especially responsible for regeneration, although this work would not be possible without the work of Christ, for it is through him and with him that we are made alive. This quality of life, *eternal* life is ours now in a real sense, even though the fullness of its realization is yet to come. In the following verses, the verbs marked * are in the present tense.

- Whoever believes in the Son has* eternal life; whoever does not obey the Son shall not see life, but God's wrath remains on him (John 3:36).

- I give* them eternal life, and they will never perish, and no one will snatch them out of my hand (John 10:28).

- I write these things to you who believe in the name of the Son of God that you may know that you have* eternal life (1 John 5:13).

The work of God in the sacrifice of Christ occurred on the cross in one complete and final act; "It is finished!" (John 19:30). There is <u>nothing</u> that needs to be added to it to make it effective; to suggest otherwise is to downgrade the work of God, to suggest it was lacking in effectiveness. In application to the individual sinner, however, this work can be said to be ongoing and this application commences at the beginning of the individual Christian life; God calls us, regenerates, justifies and adopts us. The sinner believes and repents, trusting in Christ. Repentance is essential, and to suggest that the substitutionary atonement circumvents the need for conviction and repentance on the part of the one accepting Christ is a gross misrepresentation (Matt 4:17; Luke 5:32; Acts 2:38; 17:30; 20:21; Rom 2:4; 2 Cor 7:10; Heb 6:1; 2 Pet 3:9; Rev 2:5).

This, of course, is only the beginning of the Christian life or "walk," and it is by no means the end of God's work in us. Progressively God works in us in a process called *sanctification*, the process of becoming holy. Sanctification is a cooperative effort between the Sanctifier and the sanctified, a development that continues until death and is incomplete in this life. It is the course of growth in holiness and involves ongoing repentance.

---

we become sons of God" (Tennant, *The Christadelphians*, 208–9). Marshall, *The New Life*, 18–21 in what is basically a handbook of things one should and shouldn't do as a disciple of Christ, also equates "being born again" with the act of baptism.

21. Neither, it seems, do Christadelphian writers. One whole book dedicated to the work of the Spirit doesn't discuss being born again or born of the Spirit, nor mention the Nicodemus discourse, except to say, "Thus is accomplished the work of the Holy Spirit in the minds and hearts of believers; not by a miraculous or independently direct influence, but by the searching, cleansing and sanctifying power of His Word to beget sons and daughters in His own spiritual image with their willing cooperation" (Pearce, *God's Spirit*, 49).

The Greek root word for holiness or sanctification is *hagios*, meaning to be set apart or dedicated to God. God is holy; he is Other than his creation, set apart by reason of his purity and goodness. The Old Testament laws of worship were designed to illustrate the separateness of God, and the need to approach him in the right way, on his terms. From these laws and institutions we learn that there are gradations of holiness. Because of the association with the separateness of God, God's people are called to be holy, to be separate from the evil and contaminating effects of sin. The word "saint" simply means one who is sanctified, made holy, or separated out. The New Testament word for saint is *hagios*, holy/separate one.

Sanctification begins with regeneration, when we are made clean and new creatures in God's sight. It marks a break—a *separation*—with the old life under sin's dominion (Rom 6:11, 14, 18).

> And such were some of you. But you were washed, you were sanctified, you were justified in the name of the Lord Jesus Christ and by the Spirit of our God (1 Cor 6:11).

As part of our calling to be separate (sanctified, holy), we are obligated to respond to Christ's sanctifying work in us by living lives of holiness and endeavoring to grow spiritually.

- I am speaking in human terms, because of your natural limitations. For just as you once presented your members as slaves to impurity and to lawlessness leading to more lawlessness, so now present your members as slaves to righteousness leading to sanctification . . . But now that you have been set free from sin and have become slaves of God, the fruit you get leads to sanctification and its end, eternal life (Rom 6:19, 22).

- And have put on the new self, which is being renewed in knowledge after the image of its creator (Col 3:10).

- Strive for peace with everyone, and for the holiness without which no one will see the Lord (Heb 12:14).

- To the church of God that is in Corinth, to those sanctified in Christ Jesus, called to be saints [holy ones], together with all those who in every place call on the name of our Lord Jesus Christ, both their Lord and ours (1 Cor 1:2).

- Since we have these promises, beloved, let us cleanse ourselves from every defilement of body and spirit, bringing holiness to completion in the fear of God (2 Cor 7:1).

- And to put on the new self, created after the likeness of God in true righteousness and holiness (Eph 4:24).

- And it is my prayer that your love may abound more and more, with knowledge and all discernment, so that you may approve what is excellent, and so be pure and blameless for the day of Christ, filled with the fruit of righteousness that comes through Jesus Christ, to the glory and praise of God (Phil 1:9–11).

One way the New Testament writers express this growth in holiness is that the Christian becomes more like Christ.

- And we all, with unveiled face, beholding the glory of the Lord, are being transformed into the same image from one degree of glory to another. For this comes from the Lord who is the Spirit (2 Cor 3:18).

- My little children, for whom I am again in the anguish of childbirth until Christ is formed in you! (Gal 4:19).

- For we are his workmanship, created in Christ Jesus for good works, which God prepared beforehand, that we should walk in them (Eph 2:10).

- Until we all attain to the unity of the faith and of the knowledge of the Son of God, to mature manhood, to the measure of the stature of the fullness of Christ (Eph 4:13).

- To them God chose to make known how great among the Gentiles are the riches of the glory of this mystery, which is Christ in you, the hope of glory. Him we proclaim, warning everyone and teaching everyone with all wisdom, that we may present everyone mature in Christ (Col 1:27–28).

This is not something we can do in our own strength; it requires real help from God through his indwelling Spirit.[22] As with all aspects of God's dealings with us, sanctification is a unified work of the Godhead, although it is appropriate to speak of it as predominantly a work of the Holy Spirit.

- Are you so foolish? After begun the Spirit, are you now being perfected by the flesh? (Gal 3:3).

- For it is God who works in you, both to will and to work for his good pleasure (Phil 2:13).

- And because of him [God] you are in Christ Jesus, who became to us wisdom from God, righteousness and sanctification and redemption (1 Cor 1:30).

- Now may the God of peace himself sanctify you completely, and may your whole spirit and soul and body be kept blameless at the coming of our Lord Jesus Christ (1 Thess 5:23).

---

22. This is a problem for Christadelphians, most of whom see the only ongoing work of the Spirit as the influence of God's word on the believer's mind. For them, the Christian life is a striving to be found worthy through works. One of their *Doctrines to be Rejected* (no. 24) is "That the Gospel alone will save, without the obedience of Christ's commandments." Robert Roberts states that "He only is righteous who doeth righteousness . . . we have to 'work out our salvation' by a 'patient continuance in well-doing,' and that he only that endureth to the end shall be saved" (Roberts, *The Blood of Christ*, 23).

- But we ought always to give thanks to God for you, brothers beloved by the Lord, because God chose you as the firstfruits to be saved, through sanctification by the Spirit and belief in the truth (2 Thess 2:13).

- But I say, walk by the Spirit, and you will not gratify the desires of the flesh. For the desires of the flesh are against the Spirit, and the desires of the Spirit are against the flesh, for these are opposed to each other, to keep you from doing the things you want to do. But if you are led by the Spirit, you are not under the law . . . But the fruit of the Spirit is love, joy, peace, patience, kindness, goodness, faithfulness, gentleness, self-control; against such things there is no law. And those who belong to Christ Jesus have crucified the flesh with its passions and desires. If we live by the Spirit, let us also walk by the Spirit (Gal 5:16–25).

- [Elect] according to the foreknowledge of God the Father, in the sanctification of the Spirit, for obedience to Jesus Christ and for sprinkling with his blood: May grace and peace be multiplied to you (1 Pet 1:2).

- Whoever keeps his commands abides in God, and God in him. And by this we know that he abides in us, by the Spirit whom he has given us (1 John 3:24).

In chapter 7 we looked in some detail at the work of the Spirit and saw the evidence for his divinity and personhood. The Spirit is the other Counsellor/Helper, who sanctifies, strengthens and empowers us to grow in godliness and Christ-likeness. This is not an impersonal effect of an impersonal power, but a quickening, a life-giving and personal influence in our lives.

Now—and Not Yet

Christian theologians often speak of the "now and the not yet" when it comes to the kingdom age, salvation and new life. The technical terms are *inaugurated* and *realized eschatology*. Eschatology[23] is the consideration of the "Last Things," which Christadelphians think of (rightly) in terms of the return of Christ and the consummation of the kingdom of God. Our salvation, and its associated conditions of justification, adoption and sanctification, like the kingdom of God itself, are in one sense a present reality and in another sense still to come. The first coming of Jesus inaugurated the kingdom (or more correctly, the reign) of God (Matt 12:28; Luke 4:21; 17:20–21) and his death and resurrection ushered in a new age. He made possible our redemption, reconciliation, justification and sanctification. These things are both present (yet incomplete) and still to come in their fullness, to be completely realized at Christ's second coming. This is a huge subject in itself, but because it seems to be alien to Christadelphian thinking, and a source of confusion when discussing matters of salvation and assurance, it's worth spending a little time exploring the topic.

23. From the Greek word *eschatos*, meaning "last."

The time between the resurrection of Jesus and his return is an overlapping of two ages; the old age with its rebellion against God, its sin and death still continues but its days are—literally—numbered. The powers of the new age have irrupted into the old. That's what Jesus meant when he said he saw Satan fall; the "strong man" had been bound and now it was time to plunder his house! (Luke 10:18; Matt 12:28–29). Notwithstanding, the kingdom or reign of God in its fullness is still to come (Matt 6:10). Those who are now in Christ effectively live in that kingdom, in that they live under the reign of God, which is the most literal rendering of the expression *hē basileia tou Theou.* In Christ, we taste the blessings of that kingdom and the powers of the age to come (Heb 6:4–5). This is because Christ's work on the cross is finished, it is complete, there is nothing to add. In John 19:30, when Jesus cried from the cross, "It is finished!" it was a cry of triumph. The word is *tetelestai,* to finish or fulfil, and the perfect indicative passive form means the accomplishment is complete, with ongoing effect. He has done everything needful for the salvation of his people and the preparation of the kingdom. Here are some verses that speak of salvation and kingdom life as a *present* reality.

- For by grace you have been saved through faith. And this not your own doing; it is the gift of God (Eph 2:8; "have been saved" is in the perfect tense, designating an action completed in the past with ongoing effect).

- Who saved us and called us to a holy calling, not because of our works but because of his own purpose and grace, which he gave us in Christ Jesus before the ages began (2 Tim 1:9).

- He saved us, not because of works done by us in righteousness, but according to his own mercy, by the washing of regeneration and renewal of the Holy Spirit (Titus 3:5).

- Therefore, since we have been justified by faith, we have peace with God through our Lord Jesus Christ (Rom 5:1).

- And such were some of you. But you were washed, you were sanctified, you were justified in the name of the Lord Jesus Christ and by the Spirit of our God (1 Cor 6:11).

Here are some verses that speak of salvation as an *ongoing*, present process:

- . . . Praising God and having favor of all the people. And the Lord added to their number day by day those who were being saved* (*present participle; ongoing; Acts 2:47).

- For the word of the cross is folly to those who are perishing, but to us who are being saved* it is the power of God (*present tense, continuous; 1 Cor 1:18).

- . . . And are justified* by his grace as a gift, through the redemption that is in Christ Jesus. (*present participle; continuous; Rom 3:24).

And finally, some verses which speak of salvation as a *future* experience.

- And you will be hated by all for my name's sake. But the one who endures to the end will be saved (Matt 10:22).

- Since, therefore, we have now been justified by his blood, how much more shall we be saved by him from the wrath of God (Rom 5:9; note that *justification* is a present state).

- Since God is one—who will justify the circumcised by faith and the uncircumcised through faith (Rom 3:30).

Here is a very interesting verse, which puts the "timeline" into perspective. The verbs here are all in a simple past tense, the aorist.

> And those whom he predestined he also called, and those whom he called he also justified, and those whom he justified he also glorified (Rom 8:30).

Because of God's predestination and absolute foreknowledge—his sovereign election—those whom he called and justified are *guaranteed* to be glorified. It's as if it has already happened! We reflect God's glory in only the tiniest way now, but God will complete the work begun in his people and secure their salvation for eternity.

This concept of inauguration means that our salvation is in hand, a certainty from God's viewpoint, even though it is ongoing and, *from our time-bound perspective,* incomplete. This is a troublesome concept for Christadelphians. They tend to overplay the "not yet" aspects of the kingdom and salvation to the detriment of their personal assurance. This is a topic to which we will return.

To summarize this section, the atoning work of Christ is something complex and wonderful, and it requires a number of images or metaphors to describe. Central and foundational to each of these word-pictures, types, and analogies however is the principle that salvation is all of God. It was his initiative and it is his work, a unified work of Father, Son, and Holy Spirit. Each Person plays different roles in different aspects of the process, but it is the work of the one God, from beginning to end. The consequences of this are that salvation is *assured* for those who genuinely embrace it, not because they are intrinsically worth saving, or have done something worth rewarding, but because God offers it freely to those who come to him in penitence with the empty hands of faith. Because it is *all God's work* there is nothing we can add to it, no works, no righteousness of our own. Instead, we can trust in God's own righteousness, and this is the solid rock on which we confidently stand.

Before we move on to examine the assurance we have in Christ, it is important to reinforce the necessity of both the divinity and humanity of Christ in this process of salvation. A denial of either robs the atonement of its credibility and its power.

The Savior Had to Be Human, the Savior Had to Be God

> If Christ was only man, then he is entirely irrelevant to any thought about God;
> if He is only God, then He is entirely irrelevant to any experience of human life.[24]

We may not agree entirely with Dorothy Sayers' rather confrontational statement, but it certainly provokes thought as to how the atonement could possibly work if Jesus were not both God and man. We have already discussed extensively the scriptural evidence for both the divinity and humanity of the Lord Jesus Christ. It just remains to put this into the perspective of the atonement. The mainstay of the Christadelphian argument for their concept of the atonement is the humanity of Christ.[25] But as we have seen, proving the humanity of Christ does not disprove the Trinity; quite the opposite, for the trinitarian concept of Christ and his atoning work fully embraces his genuine humanity, as we saw in chapter 2.

If Jesus was not fully and truly human, he could not have effected our atonement. There is abundant scriptural evidence for this. Jesus had to be the second Adam, to live a blameless life, a truly righteous life, which Adam failed to do. The first Adam brought condemnation, the guilty verdict, to all humanity (who are spoken of as "in Adam") whereas the second Adam brought justification, the "not-guilty" verdict to all who are "in Christ." Notice how Jesus is repeatedly referred to as *a man* in this passage.

> But the free gift is not like the trespass. For if many died through one man's trespass, much more have the grace of God and the free gift by the grace of that one man Jesus Christ abounded for many. And the free gift is not like the result of that one man's sin. For the judgment following one trespass brought condemnation, but the free gift following many trespasses brought justification. For if, because of one man's trespass, death reigned through that one man, much more will those who receive the abundance of grace and the free gift of righteousness reign in life through the one man Jesus Christ. Therefore, as one trespass led to condemnation for all men, so one act of righteousness leads to justification and life for all men. For as by the one man's disobedience the many were made sinners, so by the one man's obedience the many will be made righteous (Rom 5:15–19).

Jesus had to be tempted just as we are, and overcome sin in the very same flesh it which it usually reigned. This also qualifies him to be our Advocate and mediator (Rom 6:10; 8:2–4; Heb 2:14–18; 4:15–16).

We have seen that substitution lies at the heart of the efficacy of atonement. "Christ our Passover" (1 Cor 5:7), the Lamb of God (John 1:29), has been sacrificed for us. He bore our sins, he was made sin for us. Nevertheless, for Christ to be a sacrifice in this way he needed to also be representative of humanity; it's just that representation is not the *whole* story. The shedding of the blood of bulls and goats

---

24. Sayers, "Creed or Chaos?," 31.

25. This is the essential argument of, for example, Benson, "Monotheism and the Atonement," 258–62.

merely prefigured the shedding of the blood of the perfect man. Without the shedding of blood there can be no remission of sins (Heb 9:22) and the blood of bulls and goats was just not sufficient because it was limited to an outward, ritual cleansing, not a cleansing of the heart (Heb 9:13–14; 10:1–5).

It was necessary, then, for Christ to be a flesh and blood human being, for his literal blood to be shed. What cost, and yet what power! Justification, redemption, propitiation, reconciliation, access to God, sanctification—all by the blood of Jesus.

- Since, therefore, we have now been *justified* by his *blood*, how much more shall we be saved by him from the wrath of God (Rom 5:9).

- In him we have *redemption* through his *blood*, the forgiveness of our trespasses, according to the riches of his grace (Eph 1:7).

- And through him to *reconcile* to himself all things, whether on earth or in heaven, by making peace by the *blood* of his cross (Col 1:20).

- Therefore, brothers, since we have confidence to enter the holy places by the *blood* of Jesus (access to God) (Heb 10:19).

- He entered once for all into the holy places, not by means of the blood of goats and calves but by means of his own *blood*, thus securing an eternal *redemption* (Heb 9:12).

- So Jesus also suffered outside the gate in order to *sanctify* the people through his own *blood* (Heb 13:12).

Historically, the church has affirmed the necessity of Christ's humanity. Gregory of Nazianzius articulated the truth that what was not assumed (taken on) by the incarnation was not saved, so underlining the need for Christ to be fully human in body and in soul. It was to uphold this truth that the Apostles' Creed stated concerning the Lord Jesus Christ, "who, for us men and for our salvation, came down from heaven, and was incarnate by the Holy Spirit of the Virgin Mary, and was made man . . ."

But if we were to stop at this point we would have no atonement. If humanity was all that was required, effectively any human being empowered by God so as to not sin would have sufficed as the atoning sacrifice, the propitiation, the substitute sin-bearer. Or would they? Up to this point, Christadelphians would be, I dare say, in full agreement with mainstream Christianity. Christ was sinless as a result of the influence of his paternity (in an unspecified way) sustained by the aid of the Holy Spirit throughout his life, and in his character and authority was the manifestation of the Father. This was the only aspect, they claim, in which he differed from other men.

> How could sin be condemned in Christ who was sinless? And how could the righteousness of God be declared in the blood-shedding of a righteous man?
>
> Answer: Because being born of Adam's condemned race, and partaking of their condemned nature, Christ was made subject, equally with them, to the

consequences of Adam's transgression. Therefore his public execution was a public exhibition of what was due to a man from God. It pleased God to require this before inviting men to reconciliation through the man in whom this vindication should take place.[26]

But is this really good enough? Does this do justice to the complex imagery of the atonement, its richness, its depth? It is obvious that no *mere* human could overcome sin and lead a perfectly righteous life by their own power. There is not a great deal of clarity in Christadelphian writings as to how Jesus maintained his sinlessness throughout his life and it has been cause for disagreement and division in the group over the years. As a rule, discussion of the matter is limited to affirmations that he was sinless and the importance of this. If any mention is made of how this would be possible for a human being, it is generally explained as being Jesus' own effort.

> Jesus was tested by sin. Human nature urged him to do the wrong things. Jesus resisted. He did not sin. He was sinless . . . These temptations were real. They would have had no point if Jesus had been unable to sin. The Bible shows us he had to fight to overcome them. It was a struggle, but Jesus was victorious.[27]

Robert Roberts goes about as far as any writer, saying "The combination of condemned human nature with personal sinlessness was effected through divine power begetting a son from Mary's substance. A 'Lamb of God' was thus produced, guileless from his paternity, and yet inheriting the human sin-nature of his mother."[28]

So we are left with a quandary. Without doubt, *no* human could be sinless without significant divine enabling. Everything we know from Scripture about human nature and the fruitlessness of human effort precludes this. The influence of the Holy Spirit must have been absolute in order to override sin's natural domination. The faithful of old had the presence of the Spirit to varying degrees, yet they all sinned; David is a case in point (Ps 51:11). For the man Christ Jesus to have *never* sinned, the Spirit, or in some other way the influence of God, must have *absolutely* dominated his human nature, which seems to contradict the clear assertions of Scripture that Jesus in his humanity was tempted in every way like us; he would cease to be truly representative. There has to be a way of understanding the combination of true humanity with a divine influence strong enough to keep him holy, harmless and undefiled without circumventing the reality of temptation. The concept of two natures in Christ allows this.

Jesus' sinlessness in the face of temptation is not an example of how hard we must try—because it's not about the ability of humans to try and to have hope of success. Jesus' temptations serve as an example in the sense that they show us how recourse to Scripture and a single-minded focus on God's goals are the *framework* for right thinking in the face of temptation, but they are not an example for people to try to conquer

---

26. Roberts, *Christadelphian Instructor*, article 55.

27. Roberts, *Bible, Lord Jesus and You*, 54.

28. Roberts, *Christendom Astray*, 169.

sin in their own strength. To quote from a rather excellent sermon[29] I once heard on the subject of Jesus' temptations, they don't teach us that we need an example to follow to overcome temptation, they teach us that we need a Savior, because we can't do it.

But as soon as we allow enough divine input into Jesus to allow him as a human being to remain sinless, we have to admit that he was more than human, that there was significant and overriding divine influence at work. Of course Christ had to be human, but it is a mistake to think that the success of the atonement required him to be *only* human. If Christ was not God, substituting for us, if he was merely a representative man (albeit imbued with divine traits) salvation would come down to works, to human effort, something to be emulated and achieved. It would take the initiative from God and be a human accomplishment. This flies in the face of all we have read about atonement and salvation being wholly of God, from first to last. Non-trinitarians face a contradiction, a paradox: the more divine influence that has to be added to our picture of Christ in order for him to overcome sin, the further he moves from being solely human. The less divinity we attribute to him, the greater the impossibility of him overcoming sin by his own efforts.

> The Adoptionist Christology began with the human achievement of Jesus and brought God in at the end, so that it was a case of "first man, then God" or a man becoming God, instead of "first God, then man" or God becoming man. It was, of course, perfectly right to regard the life lived by Jesus as a human achievement. To deny that or to obscure or minimize it would be to fall into the opposite type of error . . . All goodness in human life is wrought by God. That is the other side, and somehow that side comes first, without destroying the human. And therefore the goodness of Jesus can ultimately be described only as the human side of a divine reality, which, so to say, was divine before it was human.[30]

The atonement is a work of God, from beginning to end, which is why it is efficacious; there was no (mere) "man," able to do it, so his own arm brought salvation (Isa 59:16) and God himself provided the Lamb. God reconciled us to himself in Christ (2 Cor 5:18–19) and purchased us with his own blood (Acts 20:28). Christ gives eternal life (John 10:28) and with the Father and Holy Spirit, sanctifies (1 Cor 1:2; 1 Thess 5:23; 2 Thess 2:13).

Another problem with the Christadelphian perspective is that it is a major oversimplification. It is essentially based on God saying, "Here's what I think of sin, sinful nature deserves crucifixion. Accept that, identify with it, and that's the basis of forgiveness and reconciliation."[31] Where is the rich scriptural tapestry that speaks of a judicial declaration of righteousness, the substitutionary foundation of the sacrificial system which prefigured the perfect sacrifice, the payment of a costly ransom, the literal bear-

---

29. David Walker, Willows Presbyterian Church, Townsville, c. 2010.

30. This helpful perspective comes from Baillie, *God was in Christ*, 130. Baillie points out that the doctrine of God becoming man is distinctly Christian, whereas the idea of exalting a man to become God came from the Greek tradition.

31. Roberts, *The Blood of Christ*, 14.

ing of our sins and propitiating the wrath of God? Scripture is clear, repeatedly, that Jesus Christ *bore our sins*. He didn't just represent them, he bore them, carried them, nailed them to his cross and died for them. Read again Isaiah 53 to see that the sinless Son of God took upon himself the sins of humanity and bore them, and bore the punishment for them so that with his stripes we are healed. This is no metaphor or "figure of speech."[32] The antitype of the scapegoat, Jesus *took away* the sins of the world. No wonder that the anticipation of this caused him to plead that if it were possible this cup might be removed. How could a single human being bear in himself the sins of the world and the punishment for them? How could any finite creature? Salvation is of God, through and through, from the initiative within God's eternal counsels, through the incarnation, to the redemptive event itself and, ultimately at the consummation of all things. God himself was the Just One, requiring propitiation and also the Justifier (Rom 3:25–26). The Savior had to be Christ, the LORD (Luke 2:11).

Did Christ Benefit from His Own Death?

To mainstream Christians this seems to be a strange question, yet it is another foundational aspect of the Christadelphian understanding of the atonement. They reject the substitutionary aspect of Christ's death on the basis that his human nature was under condemnation (although he himself did not sin) and had to be redeemed. The argument goes like this:

> The popular view is that Christ's blood was shed that we might go free, on the principle on which a man about to be beheaded has been supposed to go free if some one comes and takes his place . . . the substitute is beheaded, and the other goes free: so Christ's blood is shed, and we go free from our condemnation. Now this cannot be the right view, for this remarkable reason, that Christ himself is exhibited to us as coming under the beneficial operation of his own death.[33]

Roberts supports this assertion from Hebrews 13:20, which says that God brought Jesus from the dead through the blood of the everlasting covenant, and Hebrews 9:12 that states that Jesus entered the Most Holy Place by means of his own blood, "thus securing an eternal redemption." That redemption, Roberts argues, must include Christ himself, although that seems a rather tenuous inference from one verse, given all the other references to the redemption of humanity and the sinlessness of Christ. Additional verses cited[34] in support of Christ's self-redemption are Romans 6:9, "death no longer has dominion over him," implying that it once did and he had to submit to death and be raised in order to escape the thing he was submitting to. This is paired with Hebrews 5:7, speaking of Jesus' prayers "to him who was able to save him from death." In response,

32. The Christadelphian explanation of the "bearing our sins" passages is that they are figurative, speaking of Christ having our fleshly nature, e.g., Roberts, *The Blood of Christ*, 12.

33. Roberts, *The Blood of Christ*, 5.

34. Benson, "Monotheism and the Atonement," 261–62.

it should be noted that the context of this verse is "in the days of his flesh," and that his suffering was for the purpose of learning obedience. Jesus willingly submitted to death, to its "dominion" in order to destroy "him who had the power of death;" at no stage did Jesus lose control (John 10:18; 19:10–11; Acts 2:24). It is also argued that Jesus, although sinless, was not *perfected* "until the potential for sin was removed from him,"[35] by dying on the cross and being raised. The verses cited are from Hebrews, interestingly, given its theme of the superiority and sufficiency of Christ:

- For it was fitting that he, for whom and by whom all things exist, in bringing many sons to glory, should make the founder of their salvation perfect through suffering (Heb 2:10).

- And being made perfect, he became the source of eternal salvation to all who obey him (Heb 5:9).

- For the law appoints men in their weakness as high priests, but the word of the oath, which came later than the law, appoints a Son who has been made perfect forever (Heb 7:28).

The implication drawn from these verses is that Jesus was imperfect until he had suffered, died and risen again. The words "make perfect" in each of these are the verb *teleioō*, which means to complete, bring to an end, finish, accomplish, fulfil or make perfect. The cognate noun is *telos*, meaning the end point or completion.[36] It is the same word as in 1 Corinthians 13:10 "when the perfect comes," which is taken to mean "the complete." When Jesus died on the cross, his last words were a cry of triumph, *Tetelestai*, "It is finished!" When Jesus suffered in our place, died and rose again and was exalted to "the highest place," his work was finished; he was perfected. All was fulfilled, all was completed.

The Christadelphian idea is that because Jesus was fully human, he was subject to temptation, sin, and death, death being the inevitable consequence of possessing fallen human nature—even though Jesus personally did not sin. The only way to escape from this imperfection was to live a sinless life and willingly submit to death, and thereby "condemn sin in the flesh" (Rom 8:3), the flesh in which sin normally reigns. This is how Christ is seen to be our representative (not our substitute): The Christadelphian view is not that the Son had to be made human in order to die, but that the Son had to die because he was human (sinless or not).

> His victory can ultimately be ours. He is freed from sin, and no longer under death's dominion. For Christ's sake, and because of his sinless life, we can become related to his victory, and not to Adam's failure.[37]

35. Norris, *The Person of the Lord Jesus Christ*, 37.

36. BDAG, 996, 998.

37. Ashton, *Studies in the Statement of Faith*, 44.

Christadelphians do not use the term "original sin,"[38] but confess that Adam broke the law by which the continuance of his life was contingent upon obedience, hence he was sentenced to death, "a sentence which defiled and became a physical law of his being, and was transmitted to all his posterity." Jesus Christ "though wearing (humanity's) condemned nature, was to obtain a title to resurrection by perfect obedience, and, by dying, abrogate the law of condemnation for himself and all who should believe and obey him." As a consequence they reject what they call "clean flesh," or the idea that there is "no sin in the flesh,"[39] as if sin was an intrinsic property of flesh ("sin-in-the-flesh," not "sin—which is in the flesh").

> Sin could not have been condemned in the body of Jesus, if it had not existed there. His body was as unclean as the bodies of those for whom he died; for he was born of a woman, and "not one" can bring a clean body out of a defiled body; for "that", says Jesus himself, "which is born of the flesh is flesh".[40]

This statement seems to fly in the face of Hebrews 7:26 which describes Christ (in all his humanity) as "holy, innocent, unstained, separated from sinners." Ultimately, the Christadelphian position is a circular argument: *Christ is not God, he is only human. Therefore he is our representative, not our substitute, and he himself needed redemption from his fleshly nature which intrinsically IS sin. Because he was in this situation, he cannot be God.* But by demonstrating either the true divinity of Christ *and/or* by showing that his atoning work went far beyond mere representation and setting an example, the Christadelphian perception of the atonement is revealed to be inadequate.

Furthermore, if the whole argument of Hebrews 7 through 10 is considered, rather than plucking individual verses out of context, it can be seen that the priesthood and sacrifice of Jesus is in every way superior to that of the Mosaic rituals, which were merely a shadow of the heavenly realities.[41] They do not limit or define him; he surpasses and fulfils them. The Levitical high priest had limited access to God's presence in the Most Holy Place, had to offer sacrifice first for himself and then for the nation, and entered with blood that was not his own. Jesus was offered once for all, was worthy to enter the Most Holy Place (heaven) through a single offering of his

---

38. The trouble is, "original sin," or the manner in which the sin of Adam affects all human beings, has been interpreted differently through history and is therefore a rather ambiguous term. Augustine taught that sin was biologically inherited. Anselm believed all persons were germinally present in Adam and hence all sinned "in Adam." Luther and Calvin understood it as the internal necessity to sin rooted in the perversity of human nature, and Calvin saw an imputation of Adam's sin to mankind, similar to the imputation of Christ's righteousness to the believer. Still other perspectives have been described. Colwell, "Sin," 641–43.

39. *Statement of Faith* articles IV, V and VIII and *Doctrines to be Rejected*, no. 27.

40. Thomas, *Elpis Israel*, 137.

41. One of the hermeneutical problems that Christadelphians have is a tendency to interpret the New Testament in terms of the Old, rather than the Old in terms of the New. It may seem like a subtle difference, but the consequences can be significant. Jesus is not to be defined by the limitations of the Levitical priesthood; it is but a poor shadow of a greater reality.

own blood and obtained redemption for all. There is no sense here that Jesus needed to make atonement for himself, nor that his offering was in any way "imperfect."

- *For our sake* he made him to be sin who knew no sin, so that in him we might become the righteousness of God (2 Cor 5:21).

- He committed no sin, neither was deceit found in his mouth . . . He himself bore *our sins* in his body on the tree, that we might die to sin and live to righteousness. By his wounds you have been healed (1 Pet 2:22–24).

Jesus had to be "made sin," for he knew no sin; sin was not intrinsically part of him; it was *our* sins he bore in his body. He achieved victory over sin in the very flesh in which sin normally reigns.

Jesus was and is holy (Luke 1:35; Mark 1:24; John 6:69; Acts 2:27, 3:14, 4:27, 30; Heb 7:26; Rev 3:7). Sharing our nature did not intrinsically defile him or require him to redeem himself. It is sin that defiles and requires a sinner to be redeemed (Isa 59:2; Mark 7:20 –23; Jas 1:15); Jesus had no sin.

Representative or Substitute? What Did the Death of Christ Achieve for Christadelphians?

Christadelphians reject the major ways in which the atonement has been understood—specifically they reject penal substitutionary atonement along with other historical viewpoints, such as the ransom, moral influence and example theories.[42] Unfortunately, in their rejection they tend to dismiss all explanations and theories out of hand with little attempt at a fair engagement with them and what little explanations are offered generally betray a lack of understanding.[43] Oftentimes the evangelical perspective on penal substitutionary atonement is confused with aspects of the other theories, such as the "ransom to Satan" idea.

Despite the absolute centrality of the cross in the apostolic preaching and gospel narratives of the New Testament,[44] the atonement usually occupies relatively little space in Christadelphian treatises. For example, Robert Roberts discusses "the cru-

---

42. Evangelical Christians hold to the penal substitutionary basis of the atonement. Other perspectives have been put forward in the history of Christian thought and are not mainstream thinking today. Irenaeus proposed that the death of Christ was a ransom paid to the devil, and the Christus Victor model portrays Christ as overcoming the devil in a heavenly battle. Anselm of Canterbury emphasized that Jesus rendered satisfaction to God for sin. Peter Abelard presented the death of Christ primarily as an example of love. These views are explained in McGrath, *Christian Theology*.

43. For example, "Popular teaching brings it down to a level with the sacrifices of idolatrous superstition, by which wrathful deities are supposed to be placated by the blood of a substitutionary victim" (Roberts, *The Blood of Christ*, 1).

44. The Gospels have been popularly described as crucifixion narratives with extended prologues because of the disproportionate amount of space and detail assigned to the last few days of Jesus' earthly life.

cifixion" in less than seven pages of his 456 page work, *Christendom Astray*. Even Harry Tennant devotes a mere ten pages to the topic, out of 282 in *The Christadelphians: What They Believe and Preach*. Essentially, Roberts explains the atonement as the satisfaction of the law; human nature deserved death and so Christ, having human nature, died. He was a representative, but not a substitutionary, sacrifice. As our representative, he enables us to go through what he went through and in so doing declared the righteousness of God. Because he was sinless, death could not hold him and so God raised him. If we align ourselves with Christ, we share in his resurrection. The process of this alignment is baptism.

Harry Tennant, with uncharacteristic misdirection, dismisses the propitiatory aspect of the atonement by asserting that the motivating force of redemption was love, but this is to misunderstand that the wrath of God against sin, rather than contradicting his love, is a necessary and consequent aspect of his love for his creation, and ignores the weight of evidence for Christ's sacrifice as a propitiation.[45] He also dismisses the perspective of the atonement as a ransom and attributes an automaticity to substitutionary atonement that he asserts would totally remove the necessity to seek forgiveness. This, unfortunately, misrepresents the scriptural basis and the church's understanding of this doctrine.[46] Robert Roberts again:

> Christ suffering as the representative of his people, is one with them, and they are one with him. In what he went through they went through. Hence, Paul says believers were crucified with Christ, and baptized into his death. This death he declares to have been "the declaration of the righteousness of God," which God required as the basis of the work of reconciliation and forgiveness (Rom. 3:24–26) . . . But Christ, having suffered the natural penalty of disobedience in human nature, having been raised from the dead to live for evermore, he is "the Savior of all such as come to him". . . Life is deposited in him for our acceptance, on condition of allying ourselves to him, yea, on condition of our entry into him, and becoming part of him . . . Divine wisdom, which is foolishness with men, has provided a means whereby we get the benefit of the result achieved in Christ. Baptism in water is the ceremony by which believing men and women are united to Christ, and constituted heirs of the life everlasting which he possesses in his own right.[47]

This explanation struggles to do justice to what the Bible presents as the central, defining moment in salvation history. Roberts' emphasis, like that of other Christadelphian authors, is not on what *God* has done in Christ, but what *we* must do. A later chapter sets out the necessity of belief and baptism, but mainstream Christian readers will find themselves in surprisingly unfamiliar territory here. For rather than faith

---

45. Tennant, *The Christadelphians*, 70. Interestingly, Article XII of the *Statement of Faith* uses the term propitiation, without definition, and hymn 238 in the *Christadelphian Hymn Book* speaks of the wrath of the Eternal being turned away. However, other writers explain propitiation simply as an "atoning sacrifice."

46. Tennant, *The Christadelphians*, 71.

47. Roberts, *Christendom Astray*, 169–70.

being seen as an acknowledgement of the sinner's complete helplessness and unworthiness before God: "nothing in my hand I bring, simply to thy cross I cling"; it is presented paradoxically as a meritorious work. Examples are cited of faithful men and women such as Abraham "who believed God and it was counted as righteousness," in the sense of something one has to *do*. "The first thing a man has to do, then, in order to gain salvation, is to believe the gospel."[48] On face value, this statement seems entirely scriptural. The catch is this: belief must be entirely in line with the Christadelphian understanding of the gospel with its heavy emphasis on the kingdom of God as the consummation of the kingdom of Israel, rather than the gospel as "the power of God for salvation to everyone who believes" (Rom 1:16). The name of Jesus Christ is something which is to be apprehended by another work, the physical act of baptism.

> We must therefore understand "the things concerning the kingdom of God AND the name of Jesus Christ," before we can understand and believe the gospel which is the power of God unto salvation. The one without the other is of no efficacy. To be ignorant of "the things concerning the kingdom of God," is to be ignorant of the gospel . . . One of the fundamental conditions of salvation is belief of certain definite matters of teaching . . . What more fitting than that such a knowledge, and such a faith, should be required as a condition of fitness for an eternal existence of service based thereupon?[49]

The problem with Roberts' approach is not that he thinks correct doctrine is important, it is that this belief is presented as something required by human effort and in conformity with the very detailed and specific doctrinal understanding of the enlightened few. And woe betide the sinner who embraces wrong doctrine! This has led to the practice in Christadelphia of the rigorous examination of candidates for baptism to ensure their conformity with the Christadelphian understanding of "the Truth," together with a rejection of doctrines disallowed by this body. The present author well remembers her own interrogation, and that of a dear friend, whose sincere faith and desire to embrace Christ was initially thwarted when she failed to provide the precise doctrinal specifications at her baptismal "interview." "I'm not clever enough," she said, in abject discouragement.

Furthermore, baptism,[50] rather than conversion, is seen as the defining point at which one becomes eligible for salvation, and the point at which sins are forgiven. Even then salvation is *not secured*, but depends upon continued obedience.

> Upon believing the gospel, a man must be immersed in water for a union with the name of Christ, that his sins may be forgiven, that he may be placed in a position to work out his own salvation with fear and trembling, by patient

48. Ibid., 400.

49. Ibid., 402–3.

50. This is not to diminish the importance of baptism, which is specifically commanded by Christ and an extremely important sign of the covenant we enter in becoming Christ's (Acts 2:37–38). Baptism is a large topic in itself and there isn't space to discuss it fully in the present work. Nevertheless, the NT perspective is not that the act of baptism is *itself* the point of conversion.

continuance in well-doing . . . The obedience of the commandments of Christ is essential to the salvation of those who believe the Gospel. While faith (made effectual in baptism) turns a sinner into a saint, obedience only will secure a saint's acceptance at the judgment seat of Christ. A disobedient saint will be rejected more decisively than even an unjustified sinner.[51]

This perspective is utterly wrong, and leads to fear, persisting guilt and a lack of assurance as to whether one can ever be good enough to be granted eternal life at the final judgment. In contrast, let the Scriptures speak for themselves:

- But to all who did receive him, who believed in his name, he gave the right to become children of God (John 1:12).

- All that the Father gives me will come to me, and whoever comes to me I will never cast out. For I have come down from heaven, not to do my own will but the will of him who sent me. And this is the will of him who sent me, that I should lose nothing of all that he has given me, but raise it up on the last day. For this is the will of my Father, that everyone who looks on the Son and believes in him should have eternal life, and I will raise him up on the last day (John 6:37–40).

- Because, if you confess with your mouth that Jesus is Lord and believe in your heart that God raised him from the dead, you will be saved. For with the heart one believes and is justified, and with the mouth one confesses and is saved. For the Scripture says, "Everyone who believes in him will not be put to shame." For there is no distinction between Jew and Greek; for the same Lord is Lord of all, bestowing his riches on all who call on him. For "everyone who calls on the name of the Lord will be saved" (Rom 10:9–13).

Christadelphians do not emphasize the grace of God, nor the efficacy of Christ's sacrifice. They talk a lot about faith (a prescribed set of beliefs to which one's thinking must conform) but very little about the *grace* that saves through faith. Because they view Christ as a man whose divinity is derived, and not as God incarnate, he is seen merely as a representative of fallen humans who was aided by the Spirit to remain sinless. The perspective therefore shifts from the all-encompassing and undeserved grace of the Father and the completed work of Christ, to the effort of the sinner in believing a set of doctrines and his or her subsequent conforming obedience. Even baptism is not a sign of the covenant already established, the outward sign of grace already received, but a work by which forgiveness of sins and adoption into the body of Christ are obtained. It is not a *response* of the redeemed, "an appeal to God for a good conscience" (1 Pet 3:21), but the *means* of salvation. For a body that fervently attacks anything reminiscent of Roman Catholic doctrine, they are remarkably close to sacramentalism here. Rather than good works and obedience being the *response* of

---

51. Roberts, *Christendom Astray*, 451.

the redeemed sinner to God's inexpressible gift, they are the *means* of securing and maintaining his favor.

As a consequence of their devaluing the person of Christ, Christadelphians devalue his work. By denying Christ's divinity, Christadelphians cannot accept a substitutionary atonement. Because his work is seen as only representative, not substitutionary, it is incomplete and conditional; it requires the believer to conform to what Christ represents. It is adding to Christ's work, declaring it to be insufficient without human effort. This leads to a real problem for individual Christadelphians; assurance of salvation.

Ask almost any Christadelphian, young or old in the faith, whether they *know* they are saved, or whether they are certain of being "in the kingdom" when Christ returns, and you will almost never get a confident answer in the affirmative. I've posed this question on many occasions and the response is typically one of doubt and uncertainty, because the one questioned doubts that they are "worthy." This is not admirable humility, it is doubt, and it is guilt. It is a denial of the power and willingness of God to save, as if somehow my sins are greater than Christ's work on the cross. Paradoxically, it is also a twisted version of pride, as if I were to say to Christ, "Sorry, but I can't take you on your word that your grace is sufficient, that your sacrifice was efficacious; I need to contribute something too. I need to pay my way."

The judgment seat of Christ figures very large on the horizon for Christadelphians. In one sense this is quite appropriate. We are told we must all appear before it, the books will be opened and the secrets of our hearts will be judged. We will give account of our idle words and our works will be tried by fire to see what they are made of (Matt 12:36; Rom 14:10; 2 Cor 5:10; 1 Cor 3:11–15). Notice that Paul says the fire will judge the quality of the man's *work*, whether it is something worthwhile built on the foundation of Christ; if it is, he will be rewarded, but if it is not, those works will be destroyed but *he himself will be saved*. But Christadelphians see their eternal destiny, their very salvation, as hanging in the balance on judgment day.

> Thus, those who are alive when the Lord comes, and those who emerge from the grave at that period, will be on a footing of perfect equality. They will all be gathered together into one Great Presence, for the one great dread purpose of inquisition. Not until they hear the spoken words of the King will they know how it is to fare with them. All depends upon the "account" [which we have to give of ourselves]. This can only be accurately estimated by the Judge.[52]

Because of the emphasis on perseverance in good works as an essential prerequisite for salvation, Christadelphians are prone to doubting their assurance of salvation. Because of the emphasis on works, rather than grace, they perceive a necessity to "work out their own salvation" and to "study to show themselves worthy," to cite two popular passages that have been greatly misapplied. On face value, concern with one's personal worthiness appears to be admirably humble. But this is to completely miss

52. Ibid., 126.

the point of grace. *None of us is worthy!* No one is righteous, not even one, says Paul (Rom 3:10) and it is certainly impossible to achieve righteousness by any effort on our part! To assume so, to assume that we must prove ourselves worthy, despite all that Christ has done, in fact speaks of arrogance, not humility, and is the antithesis of the gospel. Let's hear what else Paul has to say.

> For by works of the law no human being will be justified in his sight, since through the law comes knowledge of sin. But now the righteousness of God has been manifested apart from the law, although the Law and the Prophets bear witness to it — the righteousness of God through faith in Jesus Christ for all who believe. For there is no distinction: for all have sinned and fall short of the glory of God, and are justified by his grace as a gift, through the redemption that is in Christ Jesus, whom God put forward as a propitiation by his blood, to be received by faith. This was to show God's righteousness, because in his divine forbearance he had passed over former sins. It was to show his righteousness at the present time, so that he might be just and the justifier of the one who has faith in Jesus. Then what becomes of our boasting? It is excluded. By what kind of law? By a law of works? No, but by the law of faith. For we hold that one is justified by faith apart from works of the law (Rom 3:20–28).

> Yet we know that a person is not justified by works of the law but through faith in Jesus Christ, so we also have believed in Christ Jesus, in order to be justified by faith in Christ and not by works of the law, because by works of the law no one will be justified (Gal 2:16).

> For by grace you have been saved through faith. And this is not your own doing; it is the gift of God, not a result of works, so that no one may boast. For we are his workmanship, created in Christ Jesus for good works, which God prepared beforehand, that we should walk in them (Eph 2:8–10).

> Not that we are sufficient in ourselves to claim any thing as coming from us, but our sufficiency is from God . . . for the letter kills, but the Spirit gives life (2 Cor 3:5–6).

Paul's argument is that humans cannot achieve righteousness by their own efforts, so God provided a righteousness that comes from him, apart from law. It comes through faith in Jesus to all who believe: free justification by his grace. No works, no boasting, and conversely, every reason to be confident on the day of judgment because it's all about what *Christ* has done, *not what we have done.* The result?

- There is therefore now *no condemnation* for those who are in Christ Jesus (Rom 8:1).

- For all the promises of God find their Yes in him. That is why it is through him that we utter our Amen to God for his glory. And it is God who establishes us with you in Christ, and has anointed us, and who has also put his seal on us and given us his Spirit in our hearts as a guarantee (2 Cor 1:20–22).

- I give them eternal life, and they will never perish, and no one will snatch them out of my hand. My Father, who has given them to me, is greater than all, and no one is able to snatch them out of the Father's hand (John 10:28–29).

- In whom [Christ Jesus] we have boldness and access with confidence through our faith in him (Eph 3:12).

- And I am sure of this, that he who began a good work in you will bring it to completion at the day of Jesus Christ (Phil 1:6).

- I write these things to you who believe in the name of the Son of God that you may know that you have eternal life (1 John 5:13).

- See what kind of love the Father has given to us, that we should be called children of God; and so we are. The reason why the world does not know us is that it did not know him. Beloved, we are God's children now, and what we will be has not yet appeared; but we know that when he appears we shall be like him, because we shall see him as he is (1 John 3:1–2).

- And those whom he predestined he also called, and those whom he called, he also justified, those whom he justified, he also glorified (Rom 8:30).

To suggest that there is any doubt of a Christian's acceptance by God is to doubt the efficacy of Christ's work, to suggest that our weakness is somehow stronger than his strength, that his purposes can be thwarted. In contrast, as we read through the New Testament epistles, there is a great confidence, an assurance that what God has promised he will deliver. Those who are Christ's can be confident of his love and that he will finish the work begun in them. There is no room for doubt. The reason is, it is *God* upon whom we rely, not on ourselves but on the finished work of Christ. Those who belong to Christ have eternal life. They have the Spirit as a guarantee of God's commitment to them. They have been justified—pronounced "not guilty" and in God's eyes it is as if they are already glorified.

This confidence in our salvation does not abrogate the need for repentance, nor our responsibility to live as Christ would have us live. A godly life is our *response* to the grace bestowed, enabled by the indwelling of God's Spirit and subject to the merciful provision of ongoing forgiveness when we fail (1 John 2:1–2). It is not arrogance, it is not permissiveness, it is a simple faith in God's ability to grant what he has promised. Such assurance of salvation belongs rightfully with its Author. If we *did* have to add something to Christ's work—if it was up to us to prove ourselves "worthy" then, agreed, it would be impossible to have assurance. Unfortunately, by denying the all-sufficiency of Christ's propitiating, reconciling, justifying, redemptive, substitutionary work of atonement this is the position in which Christadelphians find themselves. Would that they might reconsider the Person of Christ and the power of his death and resurrection, who has achieved all that is necessary, and be able to say with the conviction of the Apostle Paul:

What then shall we say to these things? If God is for us, who can be against us? He who did not spare his own Son but gave him up for us all, how will he not also with him graciously give us all things? Who shall bring any charge against God's elect? It is God who justifies. Who is to condemn? Christ Jesus is the one who died—more than that, who was raised—who is at the right hand of God, who indeed is interceding for us. Who shall separate us from the love of Christ? Shall tribulation, or distress, or persecution, or famine, or nakedness, or danger, or sword? As it is written, "For your sake we are being killed all the day long; we are regarded as sheep to be slaughtered." No, in all these things we are more than conquerors through him who loved us. For I am sure that neither death nor life, nor angels nor rulers, nor things present nor things to come, nor powers, nor height nor depth, nor anything else in all creation, will be able to separate us from the love of God in Christ Jesus our Lord (Rom 8:31–39).

Amen!

Summary

- Just as Father, Son, and Holy Spirit worked together in creation, so they have worked and continue to work to secure our salvation and the redemption of creation.

- The Son of God, Jesus Christ, is central to the work of the Godhead in renewal and redemption of creation, through his atoning work, which he willingly undertook.

- Christ acted as both representative (the second Adam) and substitute in redeeming fallen humanity; substitution is at the heart of the various biblical images of the atonement.

- Christ's sacrifice propitiated the wrath of God against sinful humanity, thus permitting reconciliation with a righteous and holy God. Only the sinless Son of God could fulfil this task and provide access to God and adoption as his children.

- Christ's sacrifice brought justification—a "not guilty" verdict—for those in him, in a costly act of redemption from slavery to sin; God is therefore both just and justifier.

- God effects a real change in the believer, a regeneration or new birth, primarily through the work of the Holy Spirit, who indwells the believer. From this point the process of sanctification begins, which will be completed at our resurrection and glorification. This is a process of becoming more like Christ.

- Salvation is in a real sense a present condition, since those in Christ have been justified and redeemed, yet it will not be fully realized until the consummation of God's kingdom upon Christ's return. We can think of this in terms of an overlapping of ages, or the idea of "now, but not yet."

- In order to fulfil all these aspects of the atonement, the Savior needed to be fully human but also fully God. Salvation is all of God and owes nothing to human effort.

- The Christadelphian concept of the atonement is inadequate in that it denies the substitutionary aspect and robs it of the full spectrum of efficacy attributed in Scripture. This is because it is based on an inadequate view of Christ, denying his divinity. The result is a works-based concept of salvation and a demonstrable lack of assurance.

Further Reading

- John Stott, *The Cross of Christ*, particularly chapter 7, "The Salvation of Sinners."

- Leon Morris, *The Atonement, Its Meaning and Significance.*

- Wayne Grudem, *Systematic Theology*, particularly chapters 26 ("The Person of Christ"), 27 ("The Atonement"), and 38 ("Sanctification").

- Charles Sherlock, *God on the Inside: Trinitarian Spirituality.*

Bibliography

Abba, Raymond. "The Divine Name Yahweh." *Journal of Biblical Literature* 80 (1961) 320–28.

Abel, Ron. *Wrested Scriptures*. Birmingham, UK: Christadelphian, 2011.

Adey, John. "One God: The Shema in Old and New Testaments." In *One God, the Father*, edited by Thomas Gaston, 26–39. East Boldon, UK:Willow, 2013.

Aland, Barbara, et al., eds. *The Greek New Testament*. 4th ed. New York: United Bible Societies, 2001.

Allfree, Mark. "The Holy Spirit." In *One God, the Father*, edited by Thomas Gaston, 107–19. East Boldon, UK: Willow, 2013.

Ashton, Michael, ed. *Studies in the Statement of Faith*. Birmingham, UK: Christadelphian, 1991.

Athanasian Creed. http://www.ccel.org/creeds/athanasian.creed.html.

Athanasius. *On the Incarnation of the Word*. Christian Classics Ethereal Library http://www.ccel.org/ccel/athanasius/incarnation.html.

Augsburg, Diet of. *The Augsburg Confession*. http://www.ccel.org/ccel/schaff/creeds3.iii.ii.html.

Augustine. *De Trinitate*. 2nd ed. Translated by Edmund Hill. New York: New City, 2012.

———. "Questiones in Heptateuchum." http://www.augustinius.it/latino/questioni_ettayeuco/index2.htm.

Baillie, D. M. *God Was in Christ: An Essay on Incarnation and Atonement*. London: Faber & Faber, 1958.

Bauckham, Richard. *Jesus and the God of Israel*. Grand Rapids: Eerdmans, 2008.

Beale, G. K. *The Book of Revelation: The New International Greek Text Commentary*. Grand Rapids: Eerdmans, 1999.

Beilby, James K., and Paul R. Eddy, eds. *Divine Foreknowledge: Four Views*. Downers Grove, IL: InterVarsity, 2001.

Benson, Richard. "Monotheism and the Atonement." In *One God, the Father*, edited by Thomas Gaston, 257–70. East Boldon, UK:Willow, 2013.

Benson, Tony, ed. *Which Translation?* Norwich, UK: Testimony, 2000.

Bilezikian, Gilbert. "Hermeneutical Bungee-Jumping: Subordination in the Godhead." *Journal of the Evangelical Theological Society* 40/1 (1997) 57–68.

Bird, Michael F. *A Bird's-Eye View of Paul*. Nottingham, UK: InterVarsity, 2008.

Black, M. "The Christological Use of the Old Testament in the New Testament." *New Testament Studies* 18 (1971–72) 1–14.

Blomberg, Craig L. *Jesus and the Gospels : An Introduction and Survey.* 2nd ed. Nottingham, UK: Apollos, 2009.

Boersma, H. "The Chalcedonian Definition: Its Soteriological Implications." *Westminster Theological Journal* 54 (1992) 47–63.

Bowman, Robert M., Jr., and J. Ed Komoszewski. *Putting Jesus in His Place: The Case for the Deity of Christ.* Grand Rapids: Kregel, 2007.

Bray, Gerald. *Creeds, Councils and Christ.* Fearn, Ross-shire, UK: Christian Focus, 1997.

———. *The Doctrine of God.* Downers Grove, IL: InterVarsity, 1993.

Brenton, Lancelot C. L. *The Septuagint with Apocrypha: Greek and English.* Peabody, MA: Hendrickson, 2003.

Breward, I. "Unitarianism." In *New Dictionary of Theology*, edited by Sinclair B. Ferguson and David F. Wright, 700–701. Leicester: InterVarsity, 1988.

Calvin, John. *Institutes of the Christian Religion.* 2 vols. Translated by Ford Lewis Battles. London: Westminster John Knox, 2006.

Carr, Reg, ed. *The Testimony Handbook of Bible Principles.* King's Lynn, UK: Testimony, 2010.

Carson, D. A. *The Gospel According to John.* Grand Rapids: Eerdmans, 1991.

———. *Showing the Spirit: A Theological Exposition of 1 Corinthians 12–14.* Grand Rapids: Baker, 1987.

Chester, Tim. *You Can Pray.* Nottingham, UK: InterVarsity, 2014.

Christadelphian Hymn Book. Birmingham, UK: Christadelphian, 2002.

Christadelphian Statement of the Faith. http://www.christadelphia.org/basf.htm.

Christophe, T. Alan. *Jesus is Lord.* Hertfordshire: Evangelical, 1982.

Clementson, Julian. "The Christadelphians and the Doctrine of the Trinity." *Evangelical Quarterly* 75/2 (2003) 157–76.

Coleman, Ron. "Jesus, Son of Man, Son of God, parts 1–4." *Endeavour* 72, 74, 75, 76 (1987).

Colwell, J. E. "Sin." In *New Dictionary of Theology*, edited by Sinclair B. Ferguson and David F. Wright, 641–43. Leicester: InterVarsity, 1988.

Danker, Frederick, ed. *Bauer's A Greek-English Lexicon of the New Testament and other Early Christian Literature* (BDAG). 3rd ed. Chicago: University of Chicago Press, 2000.

Dunn, James D. G. *The Theology of Paul the Apostle.* Grand Rapids: Eerdmans, 1998.

E. J. N. *Jesus the Son of God.* Pamphlet series. Birmingham, UK: Christadelphian, n.d.

Enns, Peter. *Exodus: The NIV Application Commentary.* Grand Rapids: Zondervan, 2000.

Erickson, Millard. *Christian Theology.* 3rd ed. Grand Rapids: Baker, 2013.

Estep, William R. *The Anabaptist Story.* Grand Rapids: Eerdmans, 1963.

Eyre, Alan. *The Protesters.* Birmingham, UK: Christadelphian, 1975.

Fairbairn, Patrick. *The Typology of Scripture.* Vol. 1. Hertfordshire: Evangelical, 1975.

Fee, Gordon D. *The First Epistle to the Corinthians.* New International Commentary on the New Testament. Grand Rapids: Eerdmans, 1987.

Ferguson, Sinclair B. *The Holy Spirit.* Downers Grove, IL: InterVarsity, 1996.

Ferguson, Sinclair B., and David F. Wright, eds. *New Dictionary of Theology.* Leicester: InterVarsity, 1988.

Fiddes, Paul S. *Participating in God.* London: Darton, Longman & Todd, 2000.

Freedman, D. N. "The Name of the God of Moses." *Journal of Biblical Literature* 79 (1960) 151–56.

Gaston, Thomas E. "After the Apostles." In *One God, the Father*, edited by Thomas E. Gaston, 121–36. East Boldon, UK: Willow, 2013.

———, ed. *One God, the Father.* East Boldon, UK: Willow, 2013.

Gonzalez, Justo L. *The Story of Christianity*. 2 vols. San Francisco: HarperCollins, 1984.

Gorman, Michael J. *Reading Paul*. Sheffield, UK: Paternoster, 2008.

Green, Stephen. "God Manifestation." In *The Testimony Handbook of Bible Principles*, edited by Reg Carr, 53–56. King's Lynn, UK: Testimony, 2010.

Grenz, Stanley J. *Theology for the Community of God*. Grand Rapids: Eerdmans, 1994.

Grudem, Wayne. *Systematic Theology: An Introduction to Biblical Doctrine*. Leicester: InterVarsity, 1994.

Heavyside, Peter. "Jesus in the Synoptic Gospels." In *One God, the Father*, edited by Thomas E. Gaston, 56–74. East Boldon, UK: Willow, 2013.

Holmes, Michael W., ed. *The Apostolic Fathers: Greek Texts and English Translations*. Grand Rapids: Baker, 1999.

Holmes, Stephen R. *The Quest for the Trinity: The Doctrine of God in Scripture, History and Modernity*. Downers Grove, IL: InterVarsity, 2012.

Howard, George. "The Tetragram and the New Testament." *Journal of Biblical Literature* 96/1 (1977) 63–83.

Hurtado, Larry W. *Lord Jesus Christ: Devotion to Jesus in Earliest Christianity*. Grand Rapids: Eerdmans, 2003.

———. *One God, One Lord: Early Christian Devotion and Ancient Jewish Monotheism*. Edinburgh: T. & T. Clark, 1998.

Hyndman, Rob J. "Biblical Monotheism Today." In *One God, the Father*, edited by Thomas E. Gaston, 225–40. East Boldon, UK: Willow, 2013.

———, ed. *The Way of Life: An Introductory Study Guide to Bible Teaching*. Beechworth, Aus.: Bethel, 2002.

International Council on Biblical Inerrancy. *Chicago Statement on Biblical Inerrancy*. 1978.

Jewett, Robert. *Romans: A Commentary*. Minneapolis: Fortress, 2007.

Kelly, J. N. D. *Early Christian Doctrines*. 5th ed. London: Continuum, 1977.

Kohlenberger, John R., III. *The Interlinear NIV Hebrew-English Old Testament*. Grand Rapids: Zondervan, 1987.

Kovach, Stephen D., and Peter R. Schemm Jr. "A Defense of the Doctrine of the Eternal Subordination of the Son." *Journal of the Evangelical Theological Society* 42/3, (1999) 461–76.

Ladd, George Eldon. *A Theology of the New Testament*. Grand Rapids: Eerdmans, 1993.

Letham, Robert. *The Westminster Assembly: Reading Its Theology in Historical Context*. Phillipsburg, NJ: P&R, 2009.

Lewis, C. S. *Mere Christianity*. London: Fount, 1977.

Loewen, H. J. "Anabaptist Theology." In *New Dictionary of Theology*, edited by Sinclair B. Ferguson and David F. Wright, 18–20. Leicester: InterVarsity, 1988.

Malone, Andrew S. "Distinguishing the Angel of the Lord." *Bulletin for Biblical Research* 21/3 (2001) 297–314.

Marshall, John. *The New Life*. Birmingham, UK: Christadelphian, 1971.

Mathews, Kenneth A. *The New American Commentary, Genesis 1–11:26*. Nashville: Broadman & Holman, 1996.

McGrath, Alister E. *Christian Theology: An Introduction*. 4th ed. Oxford: Blackwell, 2007.

McKim, Donald K. *Theological Turning Points: Major Issues in Christian Thought*. Louisville: Westminster John Knox, 1988.

Michener, James A. *The Source*. New York: Random House, 1965.

Morgan, Tecwyn. *Understand the Bible: Work It Out for Yourself.* Birmingham, UK: Christadelphian Bible Mission, 2006.

Morris, Leon. *The Atonement: Its Meaning and Significance.* Downers Grove, IL: InterVarsity, 1983.

Mounce, W. D. *Basics of Biblical Greek.* Grand Rapids: Zondervan, 1993.

Nicholls, Alfred. *The Name That Is Above Every Name.* Birmingham, UK: Christadelphian, 1983.

———. *Remember the Days of Old.* Editorial articles from *The Christadelphian*, 1977. Republished in book form. Birmingham, UK: Christadelphian, 1978.

———. *The Spirit of God.* Birmingham, UK: Christadelphian, 1976.

Nicole, Roger. "The Meaning of the Trinity." In *One God in Trinity*, edited by Peter Toon, 1–10. Westchester, IL: Cornerstone, 1980.

Norris, Alfred. *The Person of the Lord Jesus Christ.* Birmingham, UK: Christadelphian, 1985.

Packer, J. I. "Holy Spirit." In *New Dictionary of Theology*, edited by Sinclair B. Ferguson, 316–19. Leicester: InterVarsity, 1998.

Pearce, Fred. *God's Spirit in Work and Word.* Birmingham, UK: Christadelphian, 1989.

———. *Jesus: God the Son or Son of God?* Birmingham, UK: Christadelphian, n.d.

———. *Who are the Christadelphians?* Birmingham, UK: Christadelphian, n.d.

Perry, Andrew. "Jewish Monotheism in the First Century." In *One God, the Father*, edited by Thomas E. Gaston, 40–55. East Boldon, UK: Willow, 2013.

Peterson, David. *Engaging with God: A Biblical Theology of Worship.* Downers Grove, IL: InterVarsity, 1992.

Pinnock, Clark, et al. *The Openness of God.* Downers Grove, IL: InterVarsity, 1994.

Prior, David. *The Message of 1 Corinthians.* Nottingham: InterVarsity, 1985.

Purkis, Richard, et al. *Which Translation?* Norwich, UK: Testimony, 2000.

Rennie, I. S. "Evangelical Theology." In *New Dictionary of Theology*, edited by Sinclair B. Ferguson and David F. Wright, 239–40. Leicester: InterVarsity, 1988.

Riddell, Michael. *Threshold of the Future.* London: SPCK, 1998.

Roberts, John S. *The Bible, The Lord Jesus and You.* Birmingham, UK: Christadelphian, n.d.

Roberts, Robert. *The Blood of Christ.* 1895. Repr., Birmingham, UK: Christadelphian, 2006.

———. *The Christadelphian Instructor.* 1891. Repr., West Beach, Aus.: Logos, 1985.

———. *Christendom Astray from the Bible.* 1884. Repr., West Beach, Aus.: Logos, 1984.

———. *The Ways of Providence.* 1881. Repr., Birmingham, UK: Christadelphian, 1980.

Rosel, Martin, "Reading and Translation of the Divine Name in the Masoretic Tradition and the Greek Pentateuch." *Journal for the Study of the Old Testament* 31/4 (2007) 411–28.

Sayers, Dorothy L. "Creed or Chaos?" *Modern Reformation* 20/4 (July–August 2011) 29–32.

Schreiner, Thomas R. *Paul: Apostle of God's Glory in Christ: A Pauline Theology.* Downers Grove, IL: InterVarsity, 2001.

Sellers, R. V. *Two Ancient Christologies.* London: SPCK, 1954.

Sherlock, Charles. "Human Wholeness—A Biblical Perspective." *Interchange* 37 (1987) 41–60.

———. *God on the Inside: Trinitarian Spirituality.* Canberra: Acorn, 1991.

Smith, Leonard. "Truth in a Heresy? Socinianism." *Expository Times* 112/7 (2001) 221–24.

Snobelen, Stephen D. "Antitrinitarian Textual Criticism in Early Modern Europe." In *One God, the Father*, edited by Thomas E. Gaston, 180–202. East Boldon, UK: Willow, 2013.

Socinus, Faustus. *Racovian Catechism.* 1605. http://webuus.com/timeline/Socinus.html.

Steinman, A. E. "Cherubim." In *Dictionary of the Old Testament: Pentateuch*, edited by T. Desmond Alexander and David W. Baker, 112–13. Downers Grove, IL: InterVarsity, 2003.

Stott, John. *The Cross of Christ*. Leicester: InterVarsity, 1986.

Szczucki, Lech. "Socinianism." In *Oxford Encyclopedia of the Reformation*, edited by Hans J. Hildebrand, 4:83–87. Oxford: Oxford University Press, 1996.

Tennant, Harry. *The Christadelphians: What they Believe and Teach*. Birmingham, UK: Christadelphian, 1998.

Thiselton, Anthony C. *The First Epistle to the Corinthians*. The New International Greek Testament Commentary. Grand Rapids: Eerdmans, 2000.

Thomas, Jeremy. "Forgiveness of Sins." In *The Testimony Handbook of Bible Principles*, edited by Reg Carr, 42–45. King's Lynn, UK: Testimony, 2010.

Thomas, John. *Elpis Israel: An Exposition of the Kingdom of God*. 1849. Repr., 15th ed. Birmingham, UK: Christadelphian, 2000.

Thorpe, John. "Jesus and Paul: A Summary of Pauline Christology." In *One God, the Father*, edited by Thomas E. Gaston, 92–106. East Boldon, UK: Willow, 2013.

Walker, C. C. *Theophany: A Study in God-Manifestation*. 1929. Repr., Birmingham, UK: Christadelphian, 1967.

Warfield, Benjamin B. *Biblical Doctrines*. Edinburgh: Banner of Truth, 1988.

———. "The Human Development of Jesus." In *Selected Shorter Writings of Benjamin B Warfield*, edited by J. E. Meeter, 1:158–166. Nutley, NJ: Presbyterian and Reformed, 1970.

Wenham, Gordon J. *Word Biblical Commentary, Genesis 1–15*. Nashville: Thomas Nelson, 1987.

Wenham, J. W. *The Elements of New Testament Greek*. Cambridge: Cambridge University Press, 1991.

White, Percy E. *The Doctrine of the Trinity Analytically Examined and Refuted*. 1913. Repr., Torrens Park, Aus.: Christadelphian Scripture Study Service, 1996.

Williams, George H., ed. *Spiritual and Anabaptist Writers*. Library of Christian Classics 25. London: SCM, 1957.

Witherington, Ben, III. *The Many Faces of the Christ: The Christologies of the New Testament and Beyond*. New York: Crossroad, 1998.

Woodall, Tim, ed. "The Christadelphian Process of Salvation." http://www.christadelphianresearch.com/processofsalvation.htm.

Wright, Christopher J. H. *The Mission of God*. Downers Grove, IL: InterVarsity, 2006.

Wyns, Paul. "Jesus in John's Writings." In *One God, the Father*, edited by Thomas E. Gaston, 75–91. East Boldon, UK: Willow, 2013.

Index of Subjects

Index of Scripture

1 Corinthians

Revelation (continued)

Printed in Great Britain
by Amazon

22293481R00176